A H A B

Major Literary Characters

CHELSEA HOUSE PUBLISHERS

Major Literary Characters

DAVID COPPERFIELD
Charles Dickens, *David Copperfield*

ROBINSON CRUSOE
Daniel Defoe, *Robinson Crusoe*

DON JUAN
Molière, *Don Juan*
Lord Byron, *Don Juan*

HUCK FINN
Mark Twain, *The Adventures of
Tom Sawyer, Adventures of
Huckleberry Finn*

CLARISSA HARLOWE
Samuel Richardson, *Clarissa*

HEATHCLIFF
Emily Brontë, *Wuthering Heights*

ANNA KARENINA
Leo Tolstoy, *Anna Karenina*

MR. PICKWICK
Charles Dickens, *The Pickwick Papers*

HESTER PRYNNE
Nathaniel Hawthorne, *The Scarlet Letter*

BECKY SHARP
William Makepeace Thackeray, *Vanity Fair*

LAMBERT STRETHER
Henry James, *The Ambassadors*

EUSTACIA VYE
Thomas Hardy, *The Return of the Native*

TWENTIETH CENTURY

ÁNTONIA
Willa Cather, *My Ántonia*

BRETT ASHLEY
Ernest Hemingway, *The Sun Also Rises*

HANS CASTORP
Thomas Mann, *The Magic Mountain*

HOLDEN CAULFIELD
J. D. Salinger, *The Catcher in the Rye*

CADDY COMPSON
William Faulkner, *The Sound and the Fury*

JANIE CRAWFORD
Zora Neale Hurston, *Their Eyes Were
Watching God*

CLARISSA DALLOWAY
Virginia Woolf, *Mrs. Dalloway*

DILSEY
William Faulkner, *The Sound and the Fury*

GATSBY
F. Scott Fitzgerald, *The Great Gatsby*

HERZOG
Saul Bellow, *Herzog*

JOAN OF ARC
William Shakespeare, *Henry VI*
George Bernard Shaw, *Saint Joan*

LOLITA
Vladimir Nabokov, *Lolita*

WILLY LOMAN
Arthur Miller, *Death of a Salesman*

MARLOW
Joseph Conrad, *Lord Jim, Heart of
Darkness, Youth, Chance*

PORTNOY
Philip Roth, *Portnoy's Complaint*

BIGGER THOMAS
Richard Wright, *Native Son*

CHELSEA HOUSE PUBLISHERS

Major Literary Characters

AHAB

Edited and with an introduction by
HAROLD BLOOM

CHELSEA HOUSE PUBLISHERS
New York ◊ Philadelphia

Jacket illustration: Painting of Ahab by Rockwell Kent from *Moby-Dick* (New York: Random House, 1930). Courtesy of the Rockwell Kent Legacies, New York Public Library, Astor, Lenox & Tilden Foundations. *Inset:* Title page from the first American edition of *Moby-Dick.* Courtesy of the Beinecke Rare Book and Manuscript Library, Yale University.

Chelsea House Publishers

Editor-in-Chief Remmel T. Nunn
Managing Editor Karyn Gullen Browne
Picture Editor Adrian G. Allen
Art Director Maria Epes
Manufacturing Manager Gerald Levine

Major Literary Characters

Senior Editor S. T. Joshi
Copy Chief Richard Fumosa
Designer Maria Epes

Staff for AHAB

Picture Researcher Wendy P. Wills
Assistant Art Director Noreen Romano
Production Manager Joseph Romano
Production Coordinator Marie Claire Cebrian

©1991 by Chelsea House Publishers, a division
of Main Line Book Co.

Introduction © 1991 by Harold Bloom

Printed and bound in the United States of America

First Printing

1 3 5 7 9 8 6 4 2

Library of Congress Cataloging-in-Publication Data

Ahab / edited and with an introduction by Harold Bloom.
p. cm.—(Major literary characters)
Includes bibliographical references and index.
ISBN 0-7910-0933-5.—ISBN 0-7910-0988-2 (pbk.)
1. Melville, Herman, 1819–1891. Moby Dick. 2. Melville, Herman,
1819–1891—Characters—Captain Ahab. 3. Ahab, Captain
(Fictitious character) I. Bloom, Harold. II. Series.
PS2384.M62A37 1991
813'.3—dc20
90-40960
CIP

CONTENTS

THE ANALYSIS OF CHARACTER

Harold Bloom

"Character," according to our dictionaries, still has as a primary meaning a graphic symbol, such as a letter of the alphabet. This meaning reflects the word's apparent origin in the ancient Greek *charactēr*, a sharp stylus. *Charactēr* also meant the mark of the stylus' incisions. Recent fashions in literary criticism have reduced "character" in literature to a matter of marks upon a page. But our word "character" also has a very different meaning, matching that of the ancient Greek *ēthos*, "habitual way of life." Shall we say then that literary character is an imitation of human character, or is it just a grouping of marks? The issue is between a critic like Dr. Samuel Johnson, for whom words were as much like people as like things, and a critic like the late Roland Barthes, who told us that "the fact can only exist linguistically, as a term of discourse." Who is closer to our experience of reading literature, Johnson or Barthes? What difference does it make, if we side with one critic rather than the other?

Barthes is famous, like Foucault and other recent French theorists, for having added to Nietzsche's proclamation of the death of God a subsidiary demise, that of the literary author. If there are no authors, then there are no fictional personages, presumably because literature does not refer to a world outside language. Words indeed necessarily refer to other words in the first place, but the impact of words ultimately is drawn from a universe of fact. Stories, poems, and plays are recognizable as such because they are human utterances within traditions of utterances, and traditions, by achieving authority, become a kind of fact, or at least the sense of a fact. Our sense that literary characters, within the context of a fictive cosmos, indeed are fictional personages is also a kind of fact. The meaning and value of every character in a successful work of literary representation depend upon our ideas of persons in the factual reality of our lives.

Literary character is always an invention, and inventions generally are indebted to prior inventions. Shakespeare is the inventor of literary character as we know it; he reformed the universal human expectations for the verbal imitation of personality, and the reformation appears now to be permanent and uncannily inevitable. Remarkable as the Bible and Homer are at representing personages, their characters are relatively unchanging. They age within their stories, but their habitual modes of being do not develop. Jacob and Achilles unfold before us, but without metamorphoses. Lear and Macbeth, Hamlet and Othello severely modify themselves not only by their actions, but by their utterances, and most of all through *overhearing themselves*, whether they speak to themselves or to others. Pondering what they themselves have said, they will to change, and actually do change, sometimes extravagantly yet always persuasively. Or else they suffer change, without willing it, but in reaction not so much to their language as to their relation to that language.

I do not think it useful to say that Shakespeare successfully imitated elements in our characters. Rather, it could be argued that he compelled aspects of character to appear that previously were concealed, or not available to representation. This is not to say that Shakespeare is God, but to remind us that language is not God either. The mimesis of character in Shakespeare's dramas now seems to us normative, and indeed became the accepted mode almost immediately, as Ben Jonson shrewdly and somewhat grudgingly implied. And yet, Shakespearean representation has surprisingly little in common with the imitation of reality in Jonson or in Christopher Marlowe. The origins of Shakespeare's originality in the portrayal of men and women are to be found in the *Canterbury Tales* of Geoffrey Chaucer, insofar as they can be located anywhere before Shakespeare himself. Chaucer's savage and superb Pardoner overhears his own tale-telling, as well as his mocking rehearsal of his own spiel, and through this overhearing he is emboldened to forget himself, and enthusiastically urges all his fellow-pilgrims to come forward to be fleeced by him. His self-awareness, and apocalyptically rancid sense of spiritual fall, are preludes to the even grander abysses of the perverted will in Iago and in Edmund. What might be called the character trait of a negative charisma may be Chaucer's invention, but came to its perfection in Shakespearean mimesis.

The analysis of character is as much Shakespeare's invention as the representation of character is, since Iago and Edmund are adepts at analyzing both themselves and their victims. Hamlet, whose overwhelming charisma has many negative components, is certainly the most comprehensive of all literary characters, and so necessarily prophesies the labyrinthine complexities of the will in Iago and Edmund. Charisma, according to Max Weber, its first codifier, is primarily a natural endowment, and implies a primordial and idiosyncratic power over nature, and so finally over death. Hamlet's uncanniness is at its most suggestive in the scene of his long dying, where the audience, through the mediation of Horatio, itself is compelled to meditate upon suicide, if only because outliving the prince of Denmark scarcely seems an option.

Shakespearean representation has usurped not only our sense of literary character, but our sense of ourselves as characters, with Hamlet playing the part of the largest of these usurpations. Insofar as we have an idea of human disinterestedness, we tend to derive it from the Hamlet of Act V, whose quietism has about it a ghostly authority. Oscar Wilde, in his profound and profoundly witty dialogue, "The Decay of Lying," expressed a permanent insight when he insisted that art shaped every era, far more than any age formed art. Life imitates art, we imitate Shakespeare, because without Shakespeare we would perish for lack of images. Wilde's grandest audacity demystifies Shakespearean mimesis with a Shakespearean vivaciousness: "This unfortunate aphorism about art holding the mirror up to Nature is deliberately said by Hamlet in order to convince the bystanders of his absolute insanity in all art-matters." Of *Hamlet*'s influence upon the ages Wilde remarked that: "The world has grown sad because a puppet was once melancholy." "Puppet" is Wilde's own deconstruction, a brilliant reminder that Shakespeare's artistry of illusion has so mastered reality as to have changed reality, evidently forever.

The analysis of character, as a critical pursuit, seems to me as much a Shakespearean invention as literary character was, since much of what we know about how to analyze character necessarily follows Shakespearean procedures. His hero-villains, from Richard III through Iago, Edmund, and Macbeth, are shrewd and endless questers into their own self-motivations. If we could bear to see Hamlet, in his unwearied negations, as another hero-villain, then we would judge him the supreme analyst of the darker recalcitrances in the selfhood. Freud followed the pre-Socratic Empedocles, in arguing that character is fate, a frightening doctrine that maintains the fear that there are no accidents, that overdetermination rules us all of our lives. Hamlet assumes the same, yet adds to this argument the terrible passivity he manifests in Act V. Throughout Shakespeare's tragedies, the most interesting personages seem doom-eager, reminding us again that a Shakespearean reading of Freud would be more illuminating than a Freudian exegesis of Shakespeare. We learn more when we discover Hamlet in the Freudian Death Drive, than when we read *Beyond the Pleasure Principle* into *Hamlet*.

In Shakespearean comedy, character achieves its true literary apotheosis, which is the representation of the inner freedom that can be created by great wit alone. Rosalind and Falstaff, perhaps alone among Shakespeare's personages, match Hamlet in wit, though hardly in the metaphysics of consciousness. Whether in the comic or the modern mode, Shakespeare has set the standard of measurement in the balance between character and passion.

In Shakespeare the self is more dramatized than theatricalized, which is why a Shakespearean reading of Freud works out so well. Character-formation after the passing of the Oedipal stage takes the place of fetishistic fragmentings of the self. Critics who now call literary character into question, and who proclaim also the death of the author, invariably also regard all notions, literary and human, of a stable character as being mere reductions of deeper pre-Oedipal desires. It becomes

clear that the fortunes of literary character rise and fall with the prestige of normative conceptions of the ego. Shakespeare's Iago, who wars against being, may be
the first deconstructionist of the self, with his proclamation of "I am not what I am."
This constitutes the necessary prologue to any view that would regard a fixed ego
as a virtual abnormality. But deconstructions of the self are no more modern than
Modernism is. Like literary modernism, the decentered ego came out of the
Hellenistic culture of ancient Alexandria. The Gnostic heretics believed that the
psyche, like the body, was a fallen entity, mechanically fashioned by the Demiurge
or false creator. They held however that each of us possessed also a spark or
pneuma, which was a fragment of the original Abyss or true, alien God. The soul
or psyche within every one of us was thus at war with the self or pneuma, and only
that sparklike self could be saved.

Shakespeare, following after Chaucer in this respect, was the first and remains
still the greatest master of representing character both as a stable soul and a
wavering self. There is a substance that endures in Shakespeare's figures, and there
is also a quicksilver rendition of the unsettling sparks. Racine and Tolstoy, Balzac and
Dickens, follow in Shakespeare's wake by giving us some sense of pre-Oedipal
sparks or drives, and considerably more sense of post-Oedipal character and
personality, stabilizations or sublimations of the fetish-seeking drives. Critics like Leo
Bersani and René Girard argue eloquently against our taking this mimesis as the only
proper work of literature. I would suggest that strong fictions of the self, from the
Bible through Samuel Beckett, necessarily participate in both modes, the sublima-
tion of desire, and the persistence of a primordial desire. The mystery of Hamlet
or of Lear is intimately invested in the tangled mixture of the two modes of
representation.

Psychic mobility is proposed by Bersani as the ideal to which deconstructions
of the literary self may yet guide us. The ideal has its pathos, but the realities of
literary representation seem to me very different, perhaps destructively so. When
a novelist like D. H. Lawrence sought to reduce his characters to Eros and the
Death Drive, he still had to persuade us of his authority at mimesis by lavishing upon
the figures of *The Rainbow* and *Women in Love* all of the vivid stigmata of
normative personality. Birkin and Ursula may represent antithetical and uncanny
drives, but they develop and change as characters pondering their own pronounce-
ments and reactions to self and others. The cost of a non-Shakespearean representation is enormous. Pynchon, in *The Crying of Lot 49* and *Gravity's Rainbow*,
evades the burden of the normative by resorting to something like Christopher
Marlowe's art of caricature in *The Jew of Malta*. Marlowe's Barabas is a marvelous
rhetorician, yet he is a cartoon alongside the troublingly equivocal Shylock. Pynchon's personages are deliberate cartoons also, as flat as comic strips. Marlowe's
achievement, and Pynchon's, are beyond dispute, yet they are like the prelude and
the postlude to Shakespearean reality. They do not wish to engage with our hunger
for the empirical world and so they enter the problematic cosmos of literary
fantasy.

No writer, not even Shakespeare or Proust, alters the available stock that we agree to call reality, but Shakespeare, more than any other, does show us how much of reality we could encounter if only we retained adequate desire. The strong literary representation of character is already an analysis of character, and is part of the healing work of a literary culture, which implicitly seeks to cure violence through a normative mimesis of ego, *as if it were stable,* whether in actuality it is or is not. I do not believe that this is a social quest taken on by literary culture, but rather that we confront here the aesthetic essence of what makes a culture *literary,* rather than metaphysical or ethical or religious. A culture becomes literary when its conceptual modes have failed it, which means when religion, philosophy, and science have begun to lose their authority. If they cannot heal violence, then literature attempts to do so, which may be only a turning inside out of the critical arguments of Girard and Bersani.

I conclude by offering a particular instance or special case as a paradigm for the healing enterprise that is at once the representation and the analysis of literary character. Let us call it the aesthetics of being outraged, or rather of successfully representing the state of being outraged. W. C. Fields was one modern master of such representation, and Nathanael West was another, as was Faulkner before him. Here also the greatest master remains Shakespeare, whose Macbeth, himself a bloody outrage, yet retains our imaginative sympathy precisely because he grows increasingly outraged as he experiences the equivocation of the fiend that lies like truth. The double-natured promises and the prophecies of the weird sisters finally induce in Macbeth an apocalyptic version of the stage actor's anxiety at missing cues, the horror of a phantasmagoric stage fright of missing one's time, of always reacting too late. Macbeth, a veritable monster of solipsistic inwardness but no intellectual, counters his dilemma by fresh murders, that prolong him in time yet provoke him only to a perpetually freshened sense of being outraged, as all his expectations become still worse confounded. We are moved by Macbeth, however estrangedly, because his terrible inwardness is a paradigm for our own solipsism, but also because none of us can resist a strong and successful representation of the human in a state of being outraged.

The ultimate outrage is the necessity of dying, an outrage concealed in a multitude of masks, including the tyrannical ambitions of Macbeth. I suspect that our outrage at being outraged is the most difficult of all our affects for us to represent to ourselves, which is why we are so inclined to imaginative sympathy for a character who strongly conveys that affect to us. The Shrike of West's *Miss Lonelyhearts* or Faulkner's Joe Christmas of *Light in August* are crucial modern instances, but such figures can be located in many other works, since the ability to represent this extreme emotion is one of the tests that strong writers are driven to set for themselves.

However a reader seeks to reduce literary character to a question of marks on a page, she will come at last to the impasse constituted by the thought of death, her death, and before that to all the stations of being outraged that memorialize her own drive towards death. In reading, she quests for evidences that are strong representations, whether of her desire or her despair. Such questings constitute the necessary basis for the analysis of literary character, an enterprise that always will survive every vagary of critical fashion.

EDITOR'S NOTE

This volume gathers together a representative selection of the best criticism that has been devoted to Ahab, captain of the *Pequod* in Herman Melville's *Moby-Dick*. I am grateful to Richard Fumosa for his assistance in editing this book.

My introduction centers upon Ahab as a Gnostic quester, and so as the principal incarnation of the American Religion in a major literary character.

Because the reviews of *Moby-Dick* were so inadequate, the section of critical extracts begins with only one of the early responses, by Evert A. Duyckinck. The late Lewis Mumford represents the Melville revival of the 1920s, as does D. H. Lawrence, and is followed here by R. P. Blackmur as critical representative of the 1930s. From the poet W. H. Auden onwards, critical response to Ahab becomes a flood. Some of the more remarkable extracts in this section include crucial insights by Marius Bewley, James Baird, Ann Douglas, and Wai-Chee Dimock.

Full-scale critical essays begin here with F. O. Matthiessen's celebration of Ahab's tragic grandeur in *American Renaissance* (1941), and continue with Maurice Friedman's more circumspect view of Ahab's tragedy as being Promethean. A vision of Ahab as one trapped in a cosmic entropism is provided by Robert Zoellner, while Bainard Cowan reads Ahab as double, with touches both of Christ and of Prometheus. Michael Paul Rogin interprets Ahab in terms of the American politics of the election of 1848, finding particular parallels in the monomanias of John C. Calhoun and Ahab.

Ahab's Gnosticism, exalted in my introduction, is viewed very differently by William B. Dillingham, who argues that Melville intended Ahab to show the ruinous effects of the Gnostic heresy. We return to politics with Larry J. Reynolds, who associates Ahab with Napoleon (as mediated by Emerson) rather than with Calhoun. A personal element is emphasized by Neal L. Tolchin, who finds in Ishmael's equivocal responses to Ahab something of Melville's work of mourning for his own father.

Edward J. Ahearn gives a Marxist interpretation of Ahab as one who both rebels against the commercial system and yet presides over a destructive ritual dedicated to the financial drive. This book concludes with Leo Bersani's brilliant polemic, in which Ahab is seen as a cultural and historical orphan, and *Moby-Dick* as a vast orphanage of a book.

INTRODUCTION

When I was a boy, and first read *Moby-Dick*, my sympathy for Captain Ahab's heroic quest was overwhelming, despite my uneasy sense that his name had very dark Biblical overtones. Half-a-century later, endlessly rereading Melville's grand log of the *Pequod*'s voyage, I still cannot yield to the critical chorus that would qualify my awed admiration for this greatest of American fictive hero-villains. Ahab cannot match his strongest precursors, Macbeth and Milton's Satan, but I prefer him to Byron's Manfred and Cain, or even to Shelley's Prometheus. And though he destroys his crew (except for Ishmael) as well as himself, I scarcely can bear to regard Ahab as culpable. More Job's wife than Job, Ahab chooses to curse God and die. Job would not have struck the sun, had it insulted him, but we believe Ahab's defiant assertion, even as we believe his fierce vows of apotheosis-through-revenge in regard to Moby Dick. Ahab's reply to the voice of God in the whirlwind is to insist that he *will* draw out Leviathan with a hook.

Moby Dick, whatever else he represents, certainly is a latter-day incarnation of Job's Leviathan, another King over the Children of Pride. As such, the White Whale is a crucial part of the demiurgical Creation, against which Ahab, like an ancient Gnostic, rebels. That Creation, viewed as the work of the normative Christian God, is judged as ordained and even benign (ultimately) by only two figures in the book—Father Mapple and Starbuck. But Starbuck is evidently the only Christian aboard the *Pequod*. Fedallah and his men are Parsees and so Manichaeans, while the fierce crew are pagans of many varieties. Stubb and Flask are remote from any religion, while Ishmael is something like a Spinoza-inspired pantheist. Ahab, as I have learned to understand him, is the archetypal American Gnostic, and so is one of the fictive founders of what should be called the American Religion, post-Christian yet somehow still Protestant. Ahab is an Emersonian gone even wilder, a transmuter of Self-Reliance into the final quest for metaphysical vengeance upon the normative God of the Jews and the Christians.

In the great Chapter 36, "The Quarter-Deck," Ahab's Gnostic venture receives its first full statement in the Captain's fervent reply to his First Mate Starbuck's accurate charge of blasphemy:

> "All visible objects, man, are but as pasteboard masks. But in each event—in the living act, the undoubted deed—there, some unknown but still reasoning thing puts forth the mouldings of its features from behind the unreasoning mask. If man will strike, strike through the mask! How can the prisoner reach outside except by thrusting through the wall? To me, the white whale is that wall, shoved near to me. Sometimes I think there's naught beyond. But 'tis enough. He tasks me; he heaps me; I see in him outrageous strength, with an inscrutable malice sinewing it. That inscrutable thing is chiefly what I hate; and be the white whale agent, or be the white whale principal, I will wreak that hate upon him. Talk not to me of blasphemy, man; I'd strike the sun if it insulted me. . . ."

To strike through the mask is to break through what the ancient Gnostics called the Kenoma, the cosmological emptiness into which we have been thrown by the Creation-Fall. The *kenoma* is a prison, the wall of which is Moby Dick himself. Ahab admits that nihilism is a temptation, and also that he does not know whether Moby Dick is the Demiurge or false god himself, or merely a servant of the god of nature or the fallen world. Either way the Gnostic challenge is enough. The Creation-Fall represents a malicious strength, to which the Gnostic quester responds with pride and defiance. Ahab has been injured and insulted by Moby Dick, or by the White Whale's normative creator. To strike at Moby Dick indeed is to strike the sun, because the sun, like the White Whale, indubitably represents Ignorance, and Ahab asserts a higher Knowledge as his ultimate moral sanction. It is inevitable that Ahab has allied himself with Fedallah, a Parsee or Manichaean, because Fedallah represents one of the principal Gnostic survivals.

Ahab's complex approach to the Parsee (or ancient Persian) religion is the center of Chapter 119, "The Candles," where Moby Dick's pursuer addresses the corpusants:

> "Oh! thou clear spirit of clear fire, whom on these seas I as Persian once did worship, till in the sacramental act so burned by thee, that to this hour I bear the scar; I now know thee, thou clear spirit, and I now know that thy right worship is defiance. To neither love nor reverence wilt thou be kind; and e'en for hate thou canst but kill; and all are killed. No fearless fool now fronts thee. I own thy speechless, placeless power; but to the last gasp to my earthquake life will dispute its unconditional, unintegral mastery in me. . . . Come in thy lowest form of love, and I will kneel and kiss thee; but at thy highest, come as mere supernal power; and though thou launchest navies of full-freighted worlds, there's that in here that still remains indifferent. Oh, thou clear spirit, of thy fire thou madest me, and like a true child of fire, I breathe it back to thee."

If the right worship of fire is to defy fire, then Ahab's defiance of the Leviathan that maimed him may be a kind of worship also. Ahab's deepest affect is his primal ambivalence towards all of the spiritual world. The clear fire of Ahab is at one with the fathering force invested in the Zoroastrian fire. That force is an impersonal power; Ahab confronts it as the American personality, free of the Creation, because what is best and oldest in him goes back before the Creation. Hence his further address to the fire:

> "There burn the flames! Oh, thou magnanimous! now I do glory in my genealogy. But thou art but my fiery father; my sweet mother, I know not. Oh, cruel! what hast thou done with her? There lies my puzzle; but thine is greater. Thou knowest not how came ye, hence callest thyself unbegotten; certainly knowest not thy beginning, hence callest thyself unbegun. I know that of me, which thou knowest not of thyself, oh, thou omnipotent. There is some unsuffusing thing beyond thee, thou clear spirit, to whom all thy eternity is but time, all thy creativeness mechanical. Through thee, thy flaming self, my scorched eyes do dimly see it. Oh, thou foundling fire, thou hermit immemorial, thou too hast thy incommunicable riddle, thy unparticipated grief. Here again with haughty agony, I read my sire. Leap! leap up, and lick the sky! I leap with thee; I burn with thee; would fain be welded with thee; defyingly I worship thee!"

Ahab, true knower, is the Gnostic adept who acknowledges the fathering force, yet proclaims its ignorance of the mother, the primal Abyss that preceded the Creation-Fall. The "unsuffusing thing," the beyond, cannot be named by Ahab, but at least he knows what he does not know, whereas the fire is ignorant of everything but itself. If Ahab is villain as well as hero, then his villainy is closer to that of Edmund in *King Lear* than that of Iago in *Othello,* and far closer to Milton's Satan than to Macbeth. The whiteness of the whale is an affront to Ahab because it is emblematic of the sanctioned tyranny of nature over man, even though man is better and older than nature. Even Ishmael, who as narrator is not altogether of Ahab's party, gives us a meditative sense of the malevolence involved in that whiteness:

> Though in many of its aspects this visible world was formed in love, the invisible spheres were formed in fright.

This is Ishmael's conclusion, but Ahab's justification. The American Religion is the faith of Ahab, and it is not another variant upon Protestant Christianity. Christ, and God the Father, are not parts of Ahab's vision. To conclude that Ahab ought to be condemned as culpable would be to stand with Starbuck holding the musket in Chapter 123, at the point of murdering Ahab. No reader wishes Starbuck to fire at the old man, and Starbuck cannot, despite Ahab's fatal pride. "I misdoubt me that I disobey my God in obeying him!" Starbuck says to himself later, and we have to agree with the sanest man upon the *Pequod.* A Christian morality would countenance Starbuck's rebellion, and the proper role for Starbuck would be like that of Abdiel in Milton's *Paradise Lost*. But the American Religion demands its sacrifices, and the *Pequod*'s crew (except for Ishmael) die for the sake of Ahab's quest. Why, as reader's, do we feel the rightness of that sacrifice, the heroism of that quest?

The Christian consciousness is represented most wonderfully in *Moby-Dick* not by Starbuck but by Father Mapple, whose eloquent sermon achieves an apotheosis when it proclaims that: "top-gallant delight is to him, who acknowledges no law or lord, but the Lord his God, and is only a patriot to heaven." Ahab is only a patriot to his own self, which he identifies ultimately with the Abyss, and so with an alienated Godhood that preceded the normative God. The reply to Father Mapple's sermon is made in Ahab's death-speech, with its Gnostic and antithetical celebration of catastrophe: " 'Oh, lonely death on lonely life! Oh, now I feel my topmost greatness lies in my topmost grief.' " Both Mapple and Ahab stare up at the topmost of their ships, but where the Protestant sees delight, Ahab sees grief and loneliness. Yet clearly Ahab's topmost is higher, and he attains a greatness that Mapple would ascribe only to God.

Ahab's quest is supremely American because its God is identical with the inner self, and not with the outer God who presides over Heaven. Father Mapple is godly, but Ahab is himself godlike, a true charismatic. The deliberate overtones of Shakespeare's King Lear in Ahab's character work so as to help remove Ahab from a Christian context, for *Lear* is no more Christian a work than is *Moby-Dick*. King Lear begins as a pagan believer, but ends, as W. R. Elton demonstrates, wholly skeptical of his earlier faith. Captain Ahab dies as a Gnostic should, still defying the sanctified monster who is ordained to destroy him. But there is a difference; the royal Lear is broken, despite his greatness, while Ahab goes down unconquered, fighting to the end. Nature wins a tragic victory over both Lear and Ahab, but Ahab is unchanged by his defeat, which he cannot grant is a defeat. The American self, a spark or breath older than the soul, survives its catastrophe, and the *Pequod*'s captain dies the grandest of American fictive deaths. Faulkner's protagonists repeat the patterns of Ahab's death, as it is the exemplary death of the American Religion, in a complex way a kind of atonement for our national pride in the self.

Camille Paglia, in her *Sexual Personae*, sees Ahab as an outlaw male hero destroyed by female nature, but she intimates also that there is something ambiguous in Ahab's relation to nature. Ahab refuses to identify the ocean with the beyond, with the primal fullness that preceded Creation. As captain, Ahab stands against the ocean, and incarnates the primal fullness in his own mysterious inwardness, in his constantly growing inner self. His most revealing moment may come in Chapter 99, where he contemplates the doubloon he has set as prize for whoever first sights Moby Dick. Upon the doubloon, Ahab reads the evidences of the self:

> "There's something ever egotistical in mountain-tops and towers, and all other grand and lofty things; look here,— three peaks as proud as Lucifer. The firm tower, that is Ahab; the volcano, that is Ahab; the courageous, the

undaunted, and victorious fowl, that, too, is Ahab; all are Ahab; and this round gold is but the image of the rounder globe, which, like a magician's glass, to each and every man in turn but mirrors back his own mysterious self."

Tower, volcano, and crowing cock: all are Gnostic emblems here, set against nature or the way things are. Ahab, as authentic American, demands victory, rather than the great defeat of another Golgotha. I am echoing Emerson, but so does Ahab, throughout his quest. Self-reliance in Ahab may become a religion of madness, and it leads to immolation, for the self and for others, but it does not lead to defeat. Moby Dick prevails, but the white whale is not God, nor even God's surrogate. What the ancient Gnostics called the Demiurge either is Moby Dick, or more likely has made the whale as his surrogate. You cannot destroy the Demiurge or his Leviathan. But you can deny the God of this world and his underling any triumph over your innermost self.

—H. B.

CRITICAL EXTRACTS

EVERT A. DUYCKINCK

There are evidently two if not three books in *Moby-Dick* rolled into one. Book No. I. we could describe as a thorough exhaustive account admirably given of the great Sperm Whale. The information is minute, brilliantly illustrated, as it should be—the whale himself so generously illuminating the midnight page on which his memoirs are written—has its level passages, its humorous touches, its quaint suggestion, its incident usually picturesque and occasionally sublime. All this is given in the most delightful manner in "The Whale." Book No. 2 is the romance of Captain Ahab, Queequeg, Tashtego, Pip & Co., who are more or less spiritual personages talking and acting differently from the general business run of the conversation on the decks of whalers. They are for the most part very serious people, and seem to be concerned a great deal about the problem of the universe. They are striking characters withal, of the romantic spiritual cast of the German drama; realities of some kinds at bottom, but veiled in all sorts of poetical incidents and expressions. As a bit of German melodrama, with Captain Ahab for the Faust of the quarter-deck, and Queequeg with the crew for Walpurgis night revellers in the forecastle, it has its strong points, though here the limits as to space and treatment of the stage would improve it. Moby Dick in this view becomes a sort of fishy moralist, a leviathan metaphysician, a folio Ductor Dubitantium, in fact, in the fresh water illustration of Mrs. Malaprop, "an allegory on the banks of the Nile." After pursuing him in this melancholic company over a few hundred squares of latitude and longitude, we begin to have some faint idea of the association of whaling and lamentation, and why blubber is popularly synonymous with tears.

The intense Captain Ahab is too long drawn out; something more of *him* might, we think, be left to the reader's imagination. The value of this kind of writing can only be through the personal consciousness of the reader, what he brings to the book; and all this is sufficiently evoked by a dramatic trait or suggestion. If we had as much of Hamlet or Macbeth as Mr. Melville gives us of Ahab, we should be tired

7

even of their sublime company. Yet Captain Ahab is a striking conception, firmly planted on the wild deck of the *Pequod*—a dark disturbed soul arraying itself with every ingenuity of material resources for a conflict at once natural and supernatural in his eye, with the most dangerous extant physical monster of the earth, embodying, in strongly drawn lines of mental association, the vaster moral evil of the world. The pursuit of the White Whale thus interweaves with the literal perils of the fishery—a problem of fate and destiny—to the tragic solution of which Ahab hurries on, amidst the wild stage scenery of the ocean. To this end the motley crew, the air, the sky, the sea, its inhabitants are idealized throughout. It is a noble and praiseworthy conception; and though our sympathies may not always accord with the train of thought, we would caution the reader against a light or hasty condemnation of this part of the work.

—EVERT A. DUYCKINCK, "Melville's *Moby-Dick; or, The Whale,"*
Literary World, November 22, 1851, pp. 403–4

D. H. LAWRENCE

You are some time before you are allowed to see the captain, Ahab: the mysterious Quaker. Oh, it is a God-fearing Quaker ship.

Ahab, the captain. The captain of the soul.

I am the master of my fate.
I am the captain of my soul!

Ahab!
"Oh, captain, my captain, our fearful trip is done."
The gaunt Ahab, Quaker, mysterious person, only shows himself after some days at sea. There's a secret about him? What?

Oh, he's a portentous person. He stumps about on an ivory stump, made from sea-ivory. Moby Dick, the great white whale, tore off Ahab's leg at the knee, when Ahab was attacking him.

Quite right, too. Should have torn off both his legs, and a bit more besides.

But Ahab doesn't think so. Ahab is now a monomaniac. Moby Dick is his monomania. Moby Dick must DIE, or Ahab can's live any longer. Ahab is atheist by this.

All right.

—D. H. LAWRENCE, "Herman Melville's *Moby Dick," Studies in Classic
American Literature* (New York: Thomas Seltzer, 1923), pp. 220–21

LEWIS MUMFORD

⟨. . .⟩ *Moby-Dick,* admirable as it is as a narrative of maritime adventure, is far more than that: it is, fundamentally, a parable on the mystery of evil and the accidental malice of the universe. The white whale stands for the brute energies of existence, blind, fatal, overpowering, while Ahab is the spirit of man, small and feeble, but purposive, that pits its puniness against this might, and its purpose against the blank senselessness of power. The evil arises with the good: the white whale grows up among the milder whales which are caught and cut up and used: one hunts for the one—for a happy marriage, livelihood, offspring, social companionship and cheer—and suddenly heaving its white bulk out of the calm sea, one comes upon the other: illness, accident, treachery, jealousy, vengefulness, dull frustration. The South Sea savage did not know of the white whale: at least, like death, it played but a casual part in his consciousness. It is different with the European: his life is a torment of white whales: the Jobs, the Aeschyluses, the Dantes, the Shakespeares, pursue him and grapple with him, as Ahab pursues his antagonist.

All our lesser literature, all our tales of Avalon or Heaven or ultimate re-demption, or, in a later day, the Future, is an evasion of the white whale: it is a quest of that boyish beginning which we call a happy ending. But the old Norse myth told that Asgard itself would be consumed at last, and the very gods would be de-stroyed: the white whale is the symbol of that persistent force of destruction, that meaningless force, which now figures as the outpouring of a volcano or the atmo-spheric disruption of a tornado or again as the mere aimless dissipation of unused energy into an unavailable void—that spectacle which so disheartened the learned Henry Adams. The whole tale of the West, in mind and action, in the philosophy and art of the Greeks, in the organization and technique of the Romans, in the precise skills and unceasing spiritual quests of the modern man, is a tale of this effort to combat the whale—to ward off his blows, to counteract his aimless thrusts, to create a purpose that will offset the empty malice of Moby Dick. Without such a purpose, without the belief in such a purpose, life is neither bearable nor significant: unless one is polarized by these central human energies and aims, one tends to become absorbed in Moby Dick himself, and, becoming a part of his being, can only maim, slay, butcher, like the shark or the white whale or Alexander or Napoleon. If there is no God, exclaims Dostoyevsky's hero, then we may commit murder: and in the sense that God represents the totality of human purpose and meaning the conclusion is inevitable.

It is useless to derive man's purposes from those of the external universe; he is a figure in the web of life. Except for such kindness and loyalty as the creatures man has domesticated show, there is, as far as one can now see, no concern except in man himself over the ceaseless motions and accidents that take place in nature. Love and chance, said Charles Peirce, rule the universe: but the love is man's love, and although in the very concept of chance, as both Peirce and Captain Ahab declare, there is some rough notion of fair play, of fifty-fifty, of an even break, that is small immediate consolation for the creature that may lose not the game, but his life, by an unlucky throw of the dice. Ahab has more humanity than the gods he defies: indeed, he has more power, because he is conscious of the power he wields, and applies it deliberately, whereas Moby Dick's power only seems deliberate because it cuts across the directed aims of Ahab himself. And in one sense, Ahab achieves victory: he vanquishes in himself that which would retreat from Moby Dick and acquiesce in his insensate energies and his brutal sway. His end is tragic: evil engulfs him. But in battling against evil, with power instead of love, Ahab himself, in A.E.'s phrase, becomes the image of the thing he hates: he has lost his humanity in the very act of vindicating it. By physical defiance, by physical combat, Ahab cannot rout and capture Moby Dick: the odds are against him; and if his defiance is noble, his methods are ill chosen. Growth, cultivation, order, art—these are the proper means by which man displaces accident and subdues the vacant external powers in the universe: the way of growth is not to become more powerful but to become more human. Here is a hard lesson to learn: it is easier to wage war than to conquer in oneself the tendency to be partial, vindictive, and unjust: it is easier to demolish one's enemy than to pit oneself against him in an intellectual combat which will disclose one's weaknesses and provincialities. And that evil Ahab seeks to strike is the sum of one's enemies. He does not bow down to it and accept it: therein lies his heroism and virtue: but he fights it with its own weapons and therein lies his madness. All the things that Ahab despises when he is about to attack the whale, the love and loyalty of Pip, the memory of his wife and child, the sextant of science, the inner sense of calm, which makes all external struggle futile, are the very things that would redeem him and make him victorious.

Man's ultimate defence against the Universe, against evil and accident and malice, is not by any fictitious resolution of these things into an Absolute which justifies them and utilizes them for its own ends: this is specious comfort, and Voltaire's answer to Leibniz in *Candide* seems to me a final one. Man's defence lies within himself, not within the narrow, isolated ego, which may be overwhelmed, but in that self which we share with our fellows and which assures us that, whatever happens to our own carcasses and hides, good men will remain, to carry on the work, to foster and protect the things we have recognized as excellent. To make that self more solid, one must advance positive science, produce formative ideas, and embody ideal forms in which all men may, to a greater or less degree, participate: in short, one must create a realm which is independent of the hostile forces in the universe—and cannot be lightly shaken by their onslaught. Melville's method, that of writing *Moby-Dick,* was correct: as correct as Ahab's method, taken literally, that of fighting Moby Dick, was fallacious. In *Moby-Dick,* Melville conquered the white whale in his own consciousness: instead of blankness there was significance, instead of aimless energy there was purpose, and instead of random living there was Life. The universe *is* inscrutable, unfathomable, malicious, so—like the white whale and his element. Art in the broad sense of all humanizing effort is man's answer to this condition: for it is the means by which he circumvents or postpones his doom, and bravely meets his tragic destiny. Not tame and gentle bliss, but disaster, heroically encountered, is man's true happy ending.

—LEWIS MUMFORD, *"Moby-Dick," Herman Melville* (New York: Literary Guild of America, 1929), pp. 184–87

R. P. BLACKMUR

As it happens, Melville's is not a putative smallness but a putative immensity, and he puts it with such eloquence that the mere statement produces a lasting tone in the general atmosphere. He was without knowing it in the habit of succumbing to the greatest insincerity of all, the intoxicating insincerity of cadence and rhythm and apt image, or, to put it on another plane, the insincerity of surrendering to the force of a single insight, which sometimes amounts to a kind of self-violation. Who can measure for example the effect of the preparatory statements about Ahab upon our actual reception of him when he appears? For instance, in chapter XVI there is a paragraph about the greatness of some whaling men rising from a combination of Quaker blood and the perils of the sea. "Nor will it at all detract from him, dramatically regarded, if either by birth or other circumstances, he have what seems a half wilful, overruling morbidness at the bottom of his nature. For all men tragically great are made so through a certain morbidness. Be sure of this, O young ambition, all mortal greatness is but disease." . . . This is but one of the many preparatory, almost minatory statements that Melville made about Ahab. Many directly named him; many more, like this one, were purely indirect and putative in character. Ahab is not mentioned, but the reader who remembers the passage will know that it was he who was meant all the same; and if the reader does remember it may well occur to him that Melville meant his sentences about greatness and disease to spread throughout the novel. They were planted of a purpose, whether by instinct or intention, to prefigure in the general atmosphere the specific nature of the burden Ahab wore.

The interesting thing is that Melville preferred to make his statement, in which one version of the whole theme of the book is expressed, not only baldly in isolation, but out of place and rootlessly; which is how the reader will ultimately remember it. It worked, indeed; but it worked outside the story. A dramatist would have been compelled to find the sentiment of these sentences in a situation, an action, and they could have been used only as the situation called for them and the action carried them along; and a novelist when he can should follow the example of the dramatist. Melville, as we have said, preferred the nondramatic mode. To put it sharply, he did not write of characters in action; he employed the shells of stock characters, heightened or resounding only by the eloquence of the author's voice, to witness, illustrate, decorate, and often as it happened to impede and stultify an idea in motion. This is, if you like, the mode of allegory—the highest form of the putative imagination, in which things are *said* but need not be *shown* to be other than they seem, and thus hardly require to *be* much of anything. But successful allegory—*La Vita Nuova* and *Pilgrim's Progress*—requires the preliminary possession of a complete and stable body of belief appropriate to the theme in hand. Melville was not so equipped; neither was Hawthorne; neither was anyone in nineteenth-century America or since. That is why Melville's allegorical devices and patterns had to act *as if* they were agents in a novel; and that is why we are compelled to judge Melville at his most allegorical yet formally as a novelist.

Perhaps the point needs laboring. Many critics—many students of Melville—have done a good deal to make an allegorical interpretation of *Moby-Dick*, and I am sure they are right and accurate in the form of what they say. Melville certainly had allegorical intentions. My argument—again it is technical—is that the elaboration of these intentions was among the causes that prevented him from the achievement of enacting composition and the creation of viable characters. He mistook allegory in *Moby-Dick* as a sufficient enlivening agent for the form of the novel. Actually it was a chief defective element which, due to the peculiarly confused, inconsistent and incomplete state of belief he was in, he could not possibly have used to good advantage. In the craft of writing, in any form of expression, artificial allegory, like willed mysticism (of which Melville showed a trace), is a direct and easy mode only in that it puts so much in by intention as to leave nearly everything out in execution. Bad allegory, even to the allegorist, comes very soon to seem not worth doing; which is why charades and political parties break down. Melville's allegory in *Moby-Dick* broke down again and again and with each resumption got more and more verbal, and more and more at the mercy of the encroaching event it was meant to transcend. It was an element in the putative mode in which, lofty as it was, Melville himself could not long deeply believe.

We have so far been concerned mostly with what Melville did not do as a practitioner in the novel and with certain possible causes which, technically, prevented him from doing what he wanted to do. Let us now examine particular instances of what he did do under the two heads first mentioned: dramatic form with its inspiriting conventions, and the treatment of language itself as medium. If anything so far said has made its point it will be in the degree that it certifies and illuminates what follows—in the degree, that is, that it makes it seem natural and just and necessary to find so much fault in a genius so great.

The dramatic form of a novel is what holds it together, makes it move, gives it a center and establishes a direction; and it includes the agency of perception, the consciousness set up in the book upon which, or through which, the story is registered. Dramatic form cannot in practice be wholly isolated from other formal elements; form is the way things go together in their medium—and the medium itself, here language, may properly be considered the major element of form; but we may think of different ways in which things go together in a given work, and strangely, the labor of abstraction and violation will seem to deepen our intimacy with the substance of the work and, more valuable, to heighten our sense of how that substance is controlled. The sense of control is perhaps the highest form of apprehension; it is understanding without immersion.

The question we have here to ask then is how did Melville go about controlling his two novels, *Moby-Dick* and *Pierre?* The general, strictly true, and mainly irrelevant answer would be: haphazardly—that is, through an attitude which varied from the arrogance of extreme carelessness to the humility of complete attention. It is not that he attended only to what seriously interested him, for he was as careless of what he thought important as of what he thought trivial, but that apparently he had no sure rule as to what required management and what would take care of itself. His rule was vagary, where consequential necessities did not determine otherwise. And even there, Melville's eye was not good; he did not always see that if you took one series of steps your choice of further directions was narrowed, and that you could not step in two directions at once without risk of crippling yourself. It is perhaps his intellectual consistency, which he felt putatively omniform, that made him incorrigibly inconsistent in the technical quarter. For example, in *Moby-Dick,* after setting up a single consciousness to get inside of, he shifted from that consciousness at will without sense of inconsistency, and therefore, which is the important thing, without making any effort to warrant the shifts and make them credible. Ignorance could not have excused him, because he had the example of Hawthorne, who was adept at shifting his compositional centers without disturbing his gravity, plumb in front of him. Not ignorance, but ineptitude and failure to discriminate. For the contrary example, I can think of only three occasions of importance in *Pierre,* if we except the digressions of the author himself in his own voice, where the consciousness of the hero is not left the presumed sole register of the story. Of these occasions, two are unnecessary to the story, and the third, where in the very end the perceiving center is turned over to the turnkey in the prison, funks its job. Yet in *Pierre* the theme cried out, one would think, for as many and as well chosen centers of consciousness as possible, all to be focussed on Pierre himself, the distraught and ambiguous, otherwise not measurable: the principle being that the abnormal can only be seen as viable, as really moving in response to the normal world, if seen through normal eyes.

Meanwhile we have approached a little nearer the composition of the two novels. Melville was right, granting the theme of *Moby-Dick,* in choosing Ishmael the novice, to represent a story in which he had only a presumed and minor but omnipresent part; he was only wrong where he breached his choice without covering up. Ishmael, not otherwise ever named, is as mysterious as Ahab, but he is credible because he tells us not what he is but what he sees and what he sees other people see. The mere interposition of a participating consciousness between the story and its readers, once it has been made logical by tying the consciousness to the story, is a prime device of composition: it limits, compacts, and therefore controls what can be told and how. The only error Melville made is that he failed to distinguish between what Ishmael saw and what the author saw on his own account. If an author is to use digressions, which are confusing but legitimate by tradition, he ought to follow Fielding and put them in inter-chapters, and especially where the narrative is technically in the first person. Otherwise, as with Ishmael, the narrator will seem to know too much at a given time for the story's good; it will tend to tell itself all at once, and the necessary modicum of stupidity in the operative consciousness will be blighted by excess intelligence. As Ahab said to the carpenter who handed him a lantern: "Thrusted light is worse than presented pistols." Ishmael of course is Melville's alter ego, which explains why so much is imputed to him, but does not condone the excess.

On the whole the mode of Ishmael is a success exactly where the mode of Pierre (another alter ego of Melville) is wrong. Ishmael is looking on, and able to see; Pierre is in the center of his predicament, and lost in the action. Ishmael represents speech; Pierre represents rhetoric. Ishmael reports the abnormal, driven and demonic Ahab, either through his own normal sensibility or through the reported sensibilities of the mates and the crew. Pierre is seen principally without the intervening glass and focus of any sensibility whatever—so that he falls apart into a mere voice whenever he speaks, whereas the voice of Ahab, equally eloquent and rhetorical past belief, rings true in ears that have actually heard it.

It should be noted, curiously, that Ishmael is the only character in the book not "characterized" by Melville; he is merely situated in the center, explained a little, and let speak his part of recording angel. The curiosity is that all the other characters except Ahab and Queequeg near the beginning (the night at the inn), although given set characterizations as they appear, are far less viable and are far less *present* in the book than Ishmael. The reason may be that the other characters are only pulled out at intervals and are usually given stock jobs to do, set speeches to make, whereas Ishmael, sacking his creative memory, is occupied all the time. Which suggests two or three things: that character requires the sense of continuous action to show continuously, that the mates and crew were not *in* the book substantially but that their real use was to divide up the representation of the image of Ahab. There is nothing illegitimate about such characters, but to be successful and maintain interest they must be given enough to do to seem everywhere natural, and never obviously used, as here, *only* to make the wheels go round. One suspects, therefore, that Ahab comes out a great figure more because of the eloquence of the author's putative conception of him, and Ishmael's feeling for him, than from any representational aids on the part of the crew. The result is a great figure, not a great character. Ahab is as solitary in the book as he was in his cabin.

Pierre was in his way as compositionally isolated as Ahab; he was so situated, and so equipped as a consciousness, that he recorded his own isolation to the point of solipsism. If Pierre was real, as he was asserted to be, then nothing else properly in the novel was real except in terms of his perception or through the direct and unwarrantable intervention of the author. That is the risk attached to making the protagonist record the action in which he participates to the exclusion of other agents and while the action is going on. Melville instinctively tried to get round the difficulty by resorting to a series of dramatic scenes in which Pierre was chief interlocutor. The device was the right one—or one of the right ones—but it failed to work for a number of reasons, of which the chief was that Melville had no talent for making his dramatic scenes objective except by aid of external and unrelated force—as in *Moby-Dick* he was able to resort to the ordinary exigencies of life on a whaling ship. In *Pierre* the White Whale was entirely in the protagonist's own inadequate perception of it; and the real weight of the book—what it was really about: tragedy by unconsidered virtue—was left for the author's digressions and soliloquies to carry as it could; which is to say that the book had no compositional center at all.

Something of the same sort may also be true of *Moby-Dick.* Is it not possible to say that Ishmael, the narrator, provides only a false center? Is it not true that a great part of the story's theme escapes him, is not recorded through his sensibility, either alone or in connection with others? Then the real center would lie where? It would lie variously, I think, in the suspense attached to the character of Ahab and the half imputed, half demonstrated peril of the White Whale—the cold, live evil that is momently present. If we think of the book in that way, we may say that its compositional form is a long, constantly interrupted but as constantly maintained suspense, using as nexi or transitions the recurring verbal signs of Melville's allegory, Ahab's character, and the business of whaling. The business of whaling, including both the essays on anatomy and those on butchery, takes the most space and provides the most interest. All the reader has to do is to *feel* whaling as interest and he will recognize it as a compositional device mounting to the force of drama. Indeed we speak of the drama of whaling, or of cotton, or of gold without substantial injustice to the language; and I cannot for the life of me see why the drama of whaling should not be as efficient an agent of interest, if well felt, as the drama of who fired the second shot; and with Melville there is the additional advantage that the business of whaling points to the everlasting assassin instead of the casual and no doubt remorseful murderer. Interest is the thing of prime importance as any artist and any audience will tell you. If it takes up time and prepares for life, it does not matter how it is secured and does not fatally matter if it is overdone or vulgar in its appeal as it is in *Moby-Dick.*

> —R. P. BLACKMUR, "The Craft of Herman Melville" (1938), *The Lion and the Honeycomb: Essays in Solicitude and Critique* (New York: Harcourt, Brace & World, 1955) pp. 129–36

W. H. AUDEN

Kierkegaard defines defiant despair as follows:

> ... with hatred for existence it wills to be itself, to be itself in terms of its misery; it does not even in defiance or defiantly will to be itself, but to be itself in spite ... Whereas the weak despairer will not hear about what comfort eternity has for him, so neither will such a despairer hear about it, but for a different reason, namely, because this comfort would be the destruction of him as an objection against the whole of existence. It is (to describe it figuratively) as if an author were to make a slip of the pen, and that this clerical error became conscious of being such—perhaps it was no error but in a far higher sense was an essential constituent in the whole exposition—it is then as if this clerical error would revolt against the author, out of hatred for him were

to forbid him to correct it, and were to say, "No, I will not be erased, I will stand as a witness against thee, that thou art a very poor writer." (*Sickness unto Death*)

Of this despair, Ahab is a representation, perhaps the greatest in literature.

Before he was born there were prophecies of some extraordinary destiny, which caused his mother to name him Ahab, after the son of Omri, of whom it is written in the book of Kings that he "did evil in the sight of the Lord above all that were before him," that reared up an altar for Baal, that he made a grove, and constructed an ivory house.

He himself declares that the prophecy was that he should be dismembered. Now a prophecy is either true or false, and in either case the only thing to do is to ignore it. If it is true, then it will happen and must be accepted when it occurs, and it is defiance either to try to make it happen or to try to avoid it. If it is false, it will not happen, and if one makes it happen one is not really fulfilling a prophecy at all but doing what one has chosen to do.

As a symbol of his uniqueness, he is distinguished from the rest of mankind by a scar. About this there is a mystery. An Indian relative of Tashtego's says that Ahab was forty before he received it; the old Manx sailor, on the other hand, declares that Ahab was born with it. Ahab himself makes a mysterious statement during the thunderstorm:

> "Oh! thou clear spirit of clear fire, whom on these seas I as Persian once did worship, till in the sacramental act so burned by thee, that to this hour I bear the scar." (CXIX)

Whether he was born marked, whether he received it by chance, or in some mysterious blasphemous rite is left vague. All we know for certain is that before his encounter with Moby Dick he was an exceptional man, an aesthetic hero.

So he encounters Moby Dick and loses a leg. That this is a castration symbol is emphasized by the story of how shortly before the present voyage he was found insensible in the street "by some unknown, and seemingly inexplicable, unimaginable casualty, his ivory limb having been so violently displaced that it had stake-wise smitten, and all but pierced his groin." It is possible to attach too much importance to this as also to the sexual symbolism of the Whale as being at once the *vagina dentata* and the Beast with two backs or the parents-in-bed. The point is that the sexual symbolism is in its turn symbolic of the aesthetic, i.e., the Oedipus fantasy is a representation in aesthetic terms of the fantasy of being a self-originating god, i.e., of the ego (Father) begetting itself on the self (Mother), and castration is the ultimate symbol of aesthetic weakness, of not being an aesthetic hero.

Ahab, then, the exceptional hero, suffers a tragic fall in the Greek sense, he is reduced to being lower than the average. In a Greek story this would be a punishment by the gods for hybris, and would come at the end of the book. Here, however, it comes before the book starts, so we must take it differently. How should Ahab react? Repent of his past pride? Perhaps, but the important thing is the future. What is the catastrophe telling him to become? Here again we can only answer negatively and say, "At least, not to go on whaling." One might hazard a guess and say, "To will to become nobody in particular in an aesthetic sense," i.e., to be a happy husband and father, to enter the cloister, the actual symbol does not concern us; the decisive difference is between the kind of individuality which is *being* what others are not, and that defined as *"becoming* what one wills or God wills for one."

Ahab does turn into such an individual but in a negative sense. He neither says, "I am justly punished" if he has been guilty nor "Though He slay me yet will I trust in Him" but "Thou art guilty and shalt be punished." His nature or self certainly does not wish to go rushing off in his aged maimed state round the world chasing a whale. It wants, as he himself admits, peace, family and, above all, happiness. It is as if, knowing that this is also what God wills him to become, he, his ego, defiantly wills to be always at every moment miserable. His extra wounding of himself, mentioned above, may well have been, at least unconsciously, not an accident, but a goading of himself to remember his vow. It is interesting to note the occasion during the voyage when he breaks his leg, jumping off the *Enderby,* whose captain has also lost an arm to Moby Dick without despairing and whose doctor ascribes Moby Dick's apparent malice to clumsiness. The example of sanity with authority is too much for Ahab, and he must again goad himself to his resolution.

So in defiance he takes his vow: "I now prophesy that I will dismember my dismemberer. Now then, be this prophet and the fulfiller one. That's more than ye, ye great gods, ever were."

The defiant man and the obedient man use the same words "It is not I but Fate," but their meaning is opposite.

> The path to my fixed purpose is laid with iron rails, whereon my soul is grooved to run . . . The whole act's immutably decreed. I am the Fates' Lieutenant. I act under orders.

So too, as we follow him on his unnecessary voyage, unnecessary because he has been on it before and nothing new, as he well knows, can happen to him, only, possibly, to the whale, we watch him enact every ritual of the dedicated Don Quixote life of the Religious Hero, only for negative reasons.

His first act is to throw away his pipe, an act of ascetic renunciation. But what should be done, so as not to be distracted from the task set one by God, is done to prevent distraction from a task set by himself.

Next he sets up the Doubloon which is to be a prize for whoever sights Moby Dick first. The motive is simple enough—to inspire the crew in terms of their interests to work for his—actually, however, Ahab hasn't the slightest intention of letting anyone but himself be the first. At the same time he makes the harpooners swear an oath to pursue Moby Dick to the death.

Now an oath is an individual's commitment of his individual future. It is an aesthetic form of the ethical, for if later its fulfillment should turn out to involve violating ethics, the one who took the oath cannot release himself, which can only be done by the individual or his representative before whom the oath was made. It is right therefore to take an oath about a certain direction of the will, e.g., to vow at the altar that one will love one's wife till death. It would be all wrong to take an oath about a particular future act, e.g., that one will give one's wife a pound of candy every week, for the act which at this moment is an expression of one's love may not be tomorrow; she may get diabetes.

When it comes to persuading another to take an oath, not only must there be no coercion, the other must be completely free to refuse, but also he must understand exactly what is going on; he must have the right motive. Ahab violates these conditions both for himself and for the harpooners. He exercises his authority as captain, he weakens their will with drink, and they have no motives for taking the oath at all, nor could they understand his if he told them.

Later he goes further and baptises his harpoon itself. This is a perversion of the Knight Errant's act of dedicating his arms, so that he shall remember not to dishonor them. Ahab's act, however, is a pure act of black magic, an attempt to compel objects to do his will.

Three other acts are worth mention. He throws away the ship's quadrant with the words: "Science! Curse thee, thou vain toy; and cursed be all the things that cast man's eyes aloft to the heavens. . . . Level by nature to this earth's horizon are the glances of men's eyes; not shot from the crown of his head, as if God had meant him to gaze on his firmament." This is the defiant inversion in pride of the humility which resists the pride of reason, the theologian's temptation to think that knowledge of God is more important than obeying Him.

Next he places the child Pip in his place in the captain's cabin and takes the humble position of the lookout, an inversion of "He who would be greatest among you, let him be as the least."

Lastly, in refusing the call for help of his neighbor, the captain of the *Rachel,* whom he has known in Nantucket and who asks him to help look for his young son, he counterfeits the text:

> If any man come to me and hate not his father and mother and wife and children and brethren and sisters, yea and his own life also, he cannot be my disciple.

His whole life, in fact, is one of taking up defiantly a cross he is not required to take up. Consequently, the normal reactions to pleasure and pain are reversed for him. Painful situations like the typhoon he welcomes, pleasant and happy ones like the calm day he regards as temptations. This is a counterfeit version of the saints' acceptance of suffering and distrust of pleasure. The aesthetic hero reacts normally, in that it is pleasure that tempts him to do wrong, and if he is doing wrong, suffering will dissuade him. Thus the hero of *The Voyage of Maeldune,* who is also bent on vengeance but not for himself but for his father, is brought to his senses by suffering, i.e., by the disasters that happen to his men on each of the islands they come to. The Religious Hero, however, is related in exactly the opposite way, and if his god be his own defiant will, it is pain that tempts him further, and pleasure that could save him.

—W. H. AUDEN, "Ahab," *The Enchafèd Flood; or, the Romantic Iconography of the Sea* (Charlottesville: University Press of Virginia, 1950), pp. 133–40

LAWRANCE THOMPSON

The climactic action in *Moby-Dick* occurs in the Lear-like storm scene of "The Candles" chapter, where the simultaneously wistful and defiant prayer of Captain Ahab correlates and clarifies certain factors which have hitherto remained obscure. Thereafter, the remainder of the narrative may be considered as the falling action, because the outcome is certain, even though we as readers may not be able to anticipate the details of that outcome.

In one sense, the storm scene may be viewed as a sort of inverted religious ritual, related to Ahab's previous inverted ritual of communion, and to the inverted ritual of baptism, which occurs when Ahab forges his special harpoon and baptizes it in pagan blood and in the name of the devil. All these ritualistic actions, including the smashing of the quadrant, are indicative of Captain Ahab's quondam religiosity, somehow abandoned because experience had caused him to lose faith and become disillusioned. Until "The Candles" chapter, however, the reader has been forced to guess that Ahab himself sees some close connection between that wound-scar caused by lightning and that wound-scar caused by the White Whale. All of these separate elements are now brought together and illuminated, in the storm scene. ⟨. . .⟩

That tremendously dramatic scene, bringing together so many related motifs, also illuminates the importance of the death motif, and correlates it with the central thematic concern: ". . . and e'en for hate thou canst but kill; and all are killed." Ishmael has tried to master his death obsession by escaping to sea; Captain Ahab has tried to master his death obsession by facing his enemy and by defying him: ". . . the white flame but lights the way to the White Whale." Now the remaining ritual of action is clear in all its implications: Ahab will fight fire with fire, malice with malice, hate with hate.

The best gloss on Melville's own attitude toward that climactic scene, and toward the total action, is contained in ⟨. . . a⟩ letter to Hawthorne in which Melville outlined a strikingly similar concept of tragic, heroic, Promethean defiance. For Melville, according to that letter, the heroic human being who has penetrated the mysteries of God sufficiently to understand divine malice, assumes the attitude of a sovereign being who does not quail before these malicious indignities, "though they do their worst to him." For Melville, as for Captain Ahab, the obsession is with death as the "worst" that awaits all. Like Melville, Ahab "declares himself a sovereign nature (in himself) amid the powers of heaven, hell, and earth." Ahab knows he will perish: "To neither love nor reverence wilt thou be kind." Perceiving all this, even fearing all this, Ahab heroically and bravely and tragically defies God: "No fearless fool now fronts thee. I own thy speechless, placeless power; but to the last gasp of my earthquake life will dispute its unconditional, unintegral mastery in me." Or, as Melville said it to Hawthorne, "He may perish; but so long as he exists, he insists upon treating with all Powers upon an equal basis." In other words, Melville conceived the heroic attitude to be one which gloried in its own divine attributes so persistently that no quantity or quality of God-bullying could ever impair the sovereignty of self. All of this is summarized in Captain Ahab's climactic and (viewed from Christian doctrine) blasphemous invocation or "prayer."

In the denouement, even Ahab's last defiance of death, and of God's malice, after the three-day struggle with the White Whale, cannot match the vivid rhetoric and drama of the storm scene. In fact, Ahab's last words merely reiterate, in different form, his previous storm-scene words. The passage is brief, and some sentences in it deserve to be glossed. But first the passage as a whole. After the White Whale has rammed the *Pequod* and has left it sinking, the monster lies quiescent "within a few yards of Ahab's boat." For the last time, Ahab closes with it, knowing well that the thrust of his raised harpoon will be fatal for him, and not for the White Whale. Thus poised for the blow, he speaks his last words:

> "I turn my body from the sun. What ho, Tashtego! Let me hear thy hammer. Oh! ye three unsurrendered spires of mine; thou uncracked keel; and only *god-bullied* [italics added] hull; thou firm deck, and haughty helm, and Pole-pointed prow,—death-glorious ship! must ye then perish, and without me? Am I cut off from the last fond pride of meanest shipwrecked captains? Oh, lonely death on lonely life! Oh, now I feel my topmost greatness lies in my topmost grief. Ho, ho! from all your furthest bounds, pour ye now in, ye bold billows of my whole foregone life, and top this one piled comber of my death! Towards thee I roll, thou all-destroying but unconquering whale; to the last I grapple with thee; from hell's heart I stab at thee; for hate's sake I spit my last breath at thee. Sink all coffins and all hearses to one common pool! and since neither can be mine, let me then row to pieces, while still chasing thee, though tied to thee, thou damned whale! *Thus,* I give up the spear!"

The gloss for "I turn my body from the sun" is supplied by an earlier passage of considerable interest, in the chapter entitled, "The Dying Whale," where Ahab comments on how the dying whale turns his body toward the sun, and faces it, so that the instinctive gesture becomes an emblem of faith: "He too worships fire; most faithful, broad, baronial vassal of the sun! ... here, too, life dies sunwards full of faith; but see! no sooner dead, than death whirls round the corpse, and it heads some other way.... In vain, oh whale, dost thou seek intercedings with yon all-quickening sun, that only calls forth life, but gives it not again." This gloss indicates that Ahab's last turning away from the sun is another symbolic act of conscious, deliberate, Satanic, Promethean defiance.

The command to Tashtego to continue nailing the flag to the mast of the *Pequod,* even as she sinks, is another assertion of courageous and indomitable and tragically heroic defiance.

Ahab's reference to the ship creates a temporary and tentative trope which has been hinted at, several different times, throughout the narrative: the *Pequod* not only as an emblem of the whole world (macrocosm) but also of the whole man (microcosm), Captain Ahab: the "three unsurrendered spires of mine" thus becomes a symbol of Ahab's body, mind, soul. By extension, the "god-bullied hull" becomes a symbol of the God-destroyed body; but even as the body "sinks" and dies, the indomitable spirit of Captain Ahab is represented by the "haughty" helm and "Pole-pointed" prow, which translates her into a "death-glorious ship."

For further enrichment, the limitations of that temporary and tentative trope are immediately abandoned, and a new trope is established. Ahab is isolated from his ship, cut off, alone. "Oh, lonely death on lonely life!" With those six words in mind, the reader is able to appreciate the significance of the sentence which follows: "Oh, now I feel my topmost greatness lies in my topmost grief." Lonely death is the topmost grief; but Ahab's greatness lies in his asserting his living sovereignty, his indomitableness, his heroic defiance, alone and unaided, even in the face of death. Having brought this key conviction into sharp focus, Ahab immediately acts out that key conviction: "Towards thee I roll, thou all-destroying but unconquering whale; to the last I grapple with thee; from hell's heart I stab at thee; for hate's sake I spit my last breath at thee. . . ."

There is only one more gloss needed for this passage. Consider the overtones of *"Thus,* I give up the spear!"—Ahab's last words. Throughout *Moby-Dick,* Melville has interlocked various myths illuminating the relation of Creator and created: the Prometheus myth, the Genesis myth, the Jonah myth, the Job myth, the Faust myth, the Milton's Satan myth. The recurrent references to Job included Ishmael's taunting and extended quotation from the Forty-first Chapter; that quotation concluding, "He laugheth at the shaking of the spear." Considered realistically, Ahab's last words refer to a harpoon he holds in his hands, and his calling the harpoon a "spear" has a value which is greater as symbolic or emblematic meaning. It would seem to be one more cross-reference to Job, nicely interlocked with Ishmael's taunting. In effect, Ahab is saying that even though God may be invulnerable, the defiance behind that spear-hurling gesture is more significant than the futility of the gesture.

Perhaps Ahab's last words are so worded by Melville to interlock with Christ's last words, also. Attention has already been called to Melville's use of the term "Man of Sorrows," which occurs in Isaiah and which is sometimes interpreted as a prophetic reference to Christ. For Melville, Christ's relation to God was another significant instance of the relationship between man and God, in that it offered much food for dark thoughts, as already suggested. The Gospels conflict as to just what Christ's last words were. Melville could darkly conclude that the last words, as reported in Matthew and Mark, indicated Christ's eyes were opened, on the cross; that Christ died with the tragic self-discovery that God had double-crossed him. Luke, on the other hand, indicates that Christ's last words were ones of faith and acceptance, and "thus he gave up the ghost." In effect, Ahab inverts the meaning of these words as reported in Luke. Instead of "Father, into thy hands I commend my spirit," Ahab's action may be said to dramatize something like this, "Father, *out of my* hands I commend to you—my spear!" Thus interpreted, Ahab's final words are doubly symbolic, Satanic, blasphemous.

As the *Pequod* sinks, following Ahab's last words, Melville achieves one final emblem of blasphemous defiance, and the significance of Tashtego's continuing to nail the flag to the mast is overtly glossed, in the context itself:

> A sky-hawk that *tauntingly* [italics added] had followed the main-truck downwards from its natural home among the stars, pecking at the flag, and incommoding Tashtego there; this bird now chanced to intercept its broad fluttering wing between the hammer and the wood; and simultaneously feeling the ethereal thrill, the submerged savage beneath, in his death-gasp, kept his hammer frozen there; and so the bird of heaven, with archangelic shrieks, and his imperial beak thrust upwards, and his whole captive form folded in the flag of Ahab, went down with his ship, *which, like Satan, would not sink to hell till she had dragged a living part of heaven along with her, and helmeted herself with it.* [Italics added]

> —LAWRANCE THOMPSON, "Wicked Book," *Melville's Quarrel with God* (Princeton: Princeton University Press, 1952), pp. 229–36

MARIUS BEWLEY

In a recent book on Melville, *Melville's Quarrel with God,* Mr. Lawrance Thompson has undertaken to cast Melville in the role of God-hater. His position will provide a convenient foil for presenting its opposite. In *Moby-Dick* Melville is not attacking God; he is attempting to rescue the idea of the good, to push back from his darkening consciousness that instinctive reaction of the disillusioned American: hatred of creation itself. A large part of Mr. Thompson's argument is based on Melville's intense dislike of the Dutch Reformed Church in which he grew up, and a good many of the insults against Christianity that Mr. Thompson uncovers are delivered at the level of the Calvinism preached by that bleak institution. The trouble with using Melville's attitude to that form of Calvinism as a touchstone by which to gauge his attitude to religion generally is simply that one is compelled to simplify disastrously.

Early in his discussion of *Moby-Dick* Mr. Thompson takes up the question of Ahab's name, which derives from the wicked King of Israel in the First Book of Kings. This is a crucial problem in any interpretation of *Moby-Dick,* for it helps us

guard against that romantic exaltation of Ahab which has resulted in missing
Melville's point. A just appreciation of Melville's reasons for choosing this name,
among all others, for his monomaniac captain, will reveal a great deal about his
creative intentions. Mr. Thompson, in conformity with his general argument, sees in
Melville's choice an instance of his habit of beguiling Christian readers:

> But there is one other correlation, far more interesting, between these
> two Ahabs. Each of them is seduced to his death by a prophet, and Captain
> Ahab's misleading prophet is Fedallah. . . . Consider, however, the hint in First
> Kings as to how it happened that King Ahab was similarly victimized: 'I saw the
> Lord sitting on his throne, and all the host of heaven standing by him, on his
> right hand and the left. And the Lord said, Who shall persuade Ahab, that he
> may go up and fall at Ramoth-gilead? . . . And there came forth a spirit, and
> stood before the Lord, and said, I will persuade him. And the Lord said unto
> him, Wherewith? And he said, I will go forth, and I will be a lying spirit in the
> mouth of all his prophets. And the Lord said, Thou shalt persuade him, and
> prevail also: go forth and do so.'
>
> For Melville's anti-Christian purposes, that passage lends itself nicely to a
> correlated series of insinuations that God is a malicious double-crosser, a
> deceiver, who is not above employing a 'lying spirit' . . . to lead a man to his
> death. . . .'

Mr. Thompson's reading of the twenty-second chapter of First Kings is so
unusual that one's best alternative, in commenting on it, is to digress for several
paragraphs in the role of Biblical commentator. The meaning of *Moby-Dick* is, I
think, in deep accord with a somewhat less 'sinister' reading of the scriptural
chapter.

It may be recalled that as the chapter opens, King Jehosophat has arrived from
Judah on a social visit to King Ahab of Israel. During an early conversation, Ahab
raises the question of Ramoth-gilead, formerly a tributary city of his in the north,
but for some time since, by the power of possession, in the hands of the King of
Syria. Ahab wants it back, and persuades Jehosophat to assist him in a military
expedition. Being more devout than Ahab, Jehosophat insists that the prophets be
officially consulted to insure that Jehovah's blessing rest on the undertaking. So at
Jehosophat's insistence, Ahab summoned four hundred prophets—that is to say,
four hundred of the clergy of the Established Church—to appear and prophesy
before them in a public place. Two thrones were erected, and at the appointed
time the two Kings in full royal regalia took their places. The four hundred prophets,
passing before them, prophesied great success for their arms. One of them went
so far as to wear iron horns to suggest the way in which Ahab would crush his
enemies. It is perfectly clear from the chapter as a whole that they were not
unaware of the private expediency of their tack. In fact, ever since their day the
clergies of most countries have not found it difficult to prophesy glory for the arms
of their temporal sovereigns. But apparently Jehosophat was not deceived, for

turning to King Ahab, he asked: 'Is there not here a prophet of the Lord besides, that we might enquire of him?' Why, yes: Ahab admitted that there was, but he never had anything agreeable to say. But Jehosophat would not be put off, and so Ahab had to send a messenger to summon the prophet Micaiah. But it is clear that he instructed his messenger to have a private talk with Micaiah, for coming before him the messenger said: 'Behold now, the words of the prophets declare good unto the King with one mouth; let thy word, I pray thee, be like the word of one of them, and speak that which is good.' It was, as who should say, an order; and as an obedient subject of his temporal ruler, Micaiah obeyed. But Ahab understood well enough the way in which he had sealed the lips of his prophet. It is intriguing to speculate what compulsive drive led him to blurt out at the crucial moment, just when Micaiah had prophesied good as the King had commanded him to do through the messenger: 'How many times shall I adjure thee that thou tell me nothing but that which is true in the name of the Lord?' Nothing could be clearer than that this is an implicit confession that he hadn't believed the lying four hundred prophets in the first place, being so aware of the way he had projected his royal will into their servility. Being thus adjured to speak, not in the name of his King but of his God, Micaiah prophesied the defeat of Ahab's army, and his death. Ahab's response to this, apart from putting Micaiah into prison, was to turn to Jehosophat and enquire: Didn't I tell you he would only speak evil about me? It is the perfect picture of a man who will not admit a truth that he knows to be true. It is, then, at this point, before being led away to gaol for having prophesied truly, that Micaiah turns to Ahab and speaks that passage about the 'lying spirit' and the four hundred prophets leading Ahab to destruction—the passage that leads Mr. Thompson to speak of God as a malicious double-crosser, at least for the purposes of his critical argument. It is a little difficult to see how Mr. Thompson's reading can be accepted as plausible at any level of interpretation. Mr. Thompson had radically criticized the immaturity of meaning with which Melville invested Captain Ahab. Actually, Melville was as aware of the moral limitations of Ahab as Mr. Thompson, and a proof of it is that he chose the name Ahab for very different reasons than those Mr. Thompson attributes to him.

What, in fact, did Melville see in the Biblical King? So far from being a victim, King Ahab is one of the most petulant self-asserters among Israel's rulers. His God-defiance never really got above the level of a foot-stamping 'I won't!' Ahab didn't have a great will, but he had a leech-like will. Once he had fastened it to a purpose it was a little difficult to disengage it. With a blue-print of his own destruction in his hand he deliberately followed it to the last line and letter. He is one of the most remarkable delineations of a perverse will in sacred or profane literature, and what we see is not a Titan but a weakling. Melville's Ahab is certainly not a weakling in the usual sense—but then the King was never more typical than when he insisted on going to war with the knowledge that he would be killed, and much of his army also. This, I think, was what influenced Melville in First Kings, chapter twenty-two. The flaw in the King and the Captain is identical.⟨. . .⟩

Captain Ahab is the focus of attention in the novel, and as the symbolic embodiment of the representative nineteenth-century American the fate that over-takes him is an indication of Melville's own reaction to the American world of his day. There is no need here to argue this representative quality in Ahab. Nearly all critics are agreed on it. But perhaps it is worthwhile remarking that in nothing is Ahab more representative (I use 'representative', of course, in this context not to indicate the average but the paradigmatic) than in the transition he illustrates between the American democratic acceptance of creation, and hatred of that creation. Ahab is sometimes mistakenly identified with Melville's viewpoint in the novel, and, indeed, to some extent he represents a part of Melville's mind; and a much larger part if we consider the Melville of a year or so later. But it is Ishmael with whom we must identify Melville's viewpoint in the end; and this identification is essential if we are to discover a positive and coherent form in *Moby-Dick.*

Leviathan, I have argued, represents the *good* in Melville's universe, but through Ahab's and Ishmael's eyes we are given two different visions of him. Thus, the ambiguity that, in *Pierre,* will be rooted in the nature of reality itself, is, in *Moby-Dick,* restricted to the point of view. But beyond that point of view we sense a universe of objective values in which moral action and direction are still possi-bilities, though difficult to achieve. That Ishmael *does* achieve them constitutes the formal justification of the novel. Ishmael's solitary survival at the end of the novel is, in a sense, the validation of his vision; and it represents Melville's momentary triumph in having introduced an element of moral order into his universe, in having re-established, in the face of his growing doubts, the polarity of good and evil. I wish to consider here, as briefly as I may, the meaning of Ishmael's point of view, as opposed to Ahab's which usually gets most of the attention. For it is through Ishmael that Melville makes his positive affirmation.

The experiences in which Ishmael participates on the *Pequod* are, in a sense, his. They constitute a kind of passion play for him from which he is almost literally resurrected in the Epilogue into new life. The opening paragraph indicates the problem that faces Ishmael, and to which the action of the novel brings a cosmic solution:

> Whenever I find myself growing grim about the mouth; whenever it is a damp drizzly November in my soul; whenever I find myself involuntarily pausing before coffin warehouses, and bringing up the rear of every funeral I meet; and especially whenever my hypos get such an upper hand of me, that it requires a strong moral principle to prevent me from deliberately stepping into the street, and methodically knocking people's hats off—then, I account it high time to get to sea as soon as I can.

Though so casually expressed, Ishmael's malaise as described here represents the essence of that despair, though then greatly exaggerated, which overtook Melville in *Pierre* and *The Confidence-Man.* But in *Moby-Dick* there will be, as the opening paragraph indicates, no submission to it, but a vigorous resistance. The sea is the source of life in the world, and it is to the sea that Ishmael returns whenever he feels symptoms of this depression. Ishmael, then, hardly less than Ahab may be said to do, sets out on the voyage on a quest, but it is a different quest from Ahab's. It is a quest for spiritual health, a desire to enter into a new and deeper harmony with creation. Ishmael accepts the mystery of creation—particularly as embodied in Leviathan—which Ahab does not. Ishmael's attitude towards Moby Dick is one of respectful reverence and wonder, and although from time to time during the course of the *Pequod*'s voyage Ishmael comes under the influence of Ahab's intellectual domination, such occasions are momentary.

From the very beginning, Moby Dick is not a symbol of evil to Ishmael, but a magnificent symbol of creation itself. Creation is not a pasteboard mask for Ishmael, to be broken through in some excess of spiritual pride, as it was for Ahab, whose attempt to penetrate visible creation, not through love but hatred, could only end in a material vision. The measure of Ishmael's contrast in this respect is given in the following passage. Ishmael is paying a visit to the whaling chapel in New Bedford:

> 'Methinks that in looking at things spiritual, we are too much like oysters observing the sun through water, and thinking that thick water the thinnest air. In fact, take my body who will, take it, I say, it is not me. And therefore three cheers for Nantucket; and come a stove boat and stove my body when they will, for stave my soul Jove himself cannot.'

We are sometimes inclined to lose sight of the elementary fact that the whole complex movement of *Moby-Dick* originates in Ahab's inability to resign himself, after Ishmael's fashion as indicated here, to the loss of a leg. Ahab is guilty of that most democratic of sins—of denying hierarchy between the body and soul, eternal and temporal values. He can proceed from a severed limb to a condemned and guilty universe with the greatest of ease. We are back at John Quincy Adams once again, who discovered in Eli Whitney's cotton gin God's great betrayal of the world. Essentially, democracy is the denial of degree, and, by implication, of limit also. But the very principle of form is boundary and limitation. Thus, the democratic aspiration that would deny the hieratic element in creation ends in a monstrous negation. It is the very essence of formlessness.

The degrees of knowledge are the most important of all for they most directly reflect the degrees of order and value in the spiritual world. It is an important element in Ahab's comprehensive significance that, in Chapter CXVIII, 'The Quadrant', he symbolically destroys the instrument of knowledge by which he should determine his location—his place in creation, as it were:

> Then gazing at his quadrant, and handling, one after the other, its numerous cabalistical contrivances, he pondered again, and muttered: 'Foolish toy! babies' plaything of haughty Admirals, and Commodores, and Captains; the world brags of thee, of thy cunning and might; but what after all canst thou

do, but tell the poor, pitiful point, where thou thyself happenst to be on this wide planet, and the hand that holds thee: no! not a jot more!'

The manner in which the official hierarchy of the navy is merged here with the ordered knowledge for which the quadrant stands, is worth noting. The importance of this chapter is generally recognized; but there is still reason to insist that it is not science as such that Ahab is rejecting here. Rather, it is the idea of degree. It is precisely Ahab's *place* in the universe which he does not wish, indeed refuses, to know. And it is only his *place* that the quadrant can tell, his place with reference to the sun. Thus, the paradox of the democratic dogma that refuses to recognize anything above it exists in its being forced back on the degrees below: 'Curse thee, thou quadrant! . . . no longer will I guide my earthly way by thee; the level ship's compass, and the level dead-recoking, by log and by line; *these* shall conduct me, and show me my place on the sea.' Once the ordered framework that controlled and directed the political vision of John Adams, Cooper, and even of Jefferson, is rejected, we are confronted by a breed of nineteenth-century Titans whose offspring is ultimately degraded to the 'common man' of the twentieth century.

Ahab's attitude is the antithesis of life because it represents a rejection of creation. The analysis of this attitude forms the main substance of the novel, but its great formal achievement exists in the beautiful way that Melville placed the action in an evaluative perspective so that its final effect is one of positive affirmation. He achieved this in two ways. First, he built up the symbol of Leviathan, layer on layer, so that it became one of the most magnificent images in the language of the positive aspects of creation. Leviathan, especially in his greatest role of the White Whale, is the affirmation of all that Ahab denies. The impact of this recognition on the imagination is the greater because, if Melville leads one towards it irresistibly, we yet make the discovery in the midst of all the gargantuan suffering of the whaling ground. We learn the triumph of life that the White Whale represents only because we come to it through such seas of death. This is the most deeply Christian note that Melville ever strikes.

—MARIUS BEWLEY, "Melville" (1953), *The Eccentric Design: Form in the Classic American Novel* (New York: Columbia University Press, 1959), pp. 192–96, 205–8

JAMES BAIRD

⟨. . .⟩ Ahab of *Moby-Dick* ⟨. . .⟩ is insanity as distinguished from sapience. He is knowledgeable in nothing save his own demoniacal purpose. Opposite to Queequeg, he is a gigantic symbol of the sickness of the self, the disease of the egoist-absolutist of Christendom. If immortal health shines in the dying Queequeg, then mortal illness festers in Ahab. He is the hater of that "heartless, proud, ice-gilded world" hated, in turn, by Pierre Glendinning. True, Melville intends us to see Ahab as an ancient. In perfect consistency with the whole range of imagery in *Moby-Dick* which evokes antiquity, we are given an Ahab who had such vital strength in him when the White Whale sheared off his leg that his shipmates were forced to lace him, raving, into his hammock; and that strength lurked in his *Egyptian* chest (*Moby-Dick,* Ch. XLI). But Ahab's strength is not the strength of endurance or wisdom. It is the misspent power of a whole human history of absolute defiance of God. Long ago he had transferred to the White Whale all the maledictions of humanity. Upon the white hump of Moby Dick "he piled . . . the sum of all the general rage and hate felt by his whole race from Adam down; and then, as if his chest had been a mortar, he burst his hot heart's shell upon it" (Ch. XLI). Not one of Ahab's purposive and fully reasoned acts shows wisdom. We see him as the expression of civilized man's colossal error. Clearly *Moby-Dick,* the work, itself a vast symbol, shows here the counter-being of Queequeg. To go back to Melville's reflection as he presents Ishmael at the Spouter-Inn, "there is no quality in this world that is not what it is merely by contrast." The wisdom of Queequeg is the wisdom which is just for man. But, as Melville saw it, the master paradox of life is that we cannot know the nature of justice and nobility until folly and the over-reaching pride of the ego explain this nature by contrast.

—JAMES BAIRD, "Queequeg and the Archetypal Sage," *Ishmael*
(Baltimore: Johns Hopkins University Press, 1956), p. 251

ALFRED KAZIN

⟨. . .⟩ Ishmael is a witness not only to his own thoughts, but also a witness to the actions of Captain Ahab. The book is not only a great skin of language stretched to fit the world of man's philosophic wandering; it is also a world of moral tyranny and violent action, in which the principal actor is Ahab. With the entry of Ahab a harsh new rhythm enters the book, and from now on two rhythms—one reflective, the other forceful—alternate to show us the world in which man's thinking and man's doing follow each its own law. Ishmael's thought consciously extends itself to get behind the world of appearances; he wants to see and to understand everything. Ahab's drive is to *prove,* not to discover; the world that tortures Ishmael by its horrid vacancy has tempted Ahab into thinking that he can make it over. He seeks to dominate nature, to impose and to inflict his will on the outside world—whether it be the crew that must jump to his orders or the great white whale that is essentially indifferent to him. As Ishmael is all rumination, so Ahab is all will. Both are thinkers, the difference being that Ishmael thinks as a bystander, has identified his own state with man's utter unimportance in nature. Ahab, by contrast, actively seeks the whale in order to assert man's supremacy over what swims before him as "the monomaniac incarnation" of a superior power.

This is Ahab's quest—and Ahab's magnificence. For Ahab expresses more forcibly than Ishmael ever could something of the impenitent anger against the universe that all of us can feel. Ahab may be a mad sea captain, a tyrant of the quarter-deck who disturbs the crew's sleep as he stomps along on his wooden leg. But his Ahab does indeed speak for all men who, as Ishmael confesses in the frightening meditation on the whiteness of the whale, suspect that "though in many of its aspects this visible world seems formed in love, the invisible spheres were formed in fright." So man, watching the sea heaving around him, sees it as a mad steed that has lost its rider, and looking at his own image in the water, is tortured by the thought that man himself may be an accident, of no more importance in this vast oceanic emptiness than one of Ahab's rare tears dropped into the Pacific.

To the degree that we feel this futility in the face of a blind impersonal nature that "heeds us not," and storm madly, like Ahab, against the dread that there's "naught beyond"—to this extent all men may recognize Ahab's bitterness, his unrelentingness, his inability to rest in that uncertainty which, Freud has told us, modern man must learn to endure. Ahab figures in a symbolic fable; he is acting out thoughts which we all share. But Ahab, even more, is a hero of thought who is trying, by terrible force, to reassert man's place in nature. And it is the struggle that Ahab incarnates that makes him so magnificent a *voice,* thundering in Shakespear-ean rhetoric, storming at the gates of the inhuman, silent world. Ahab is trying to give man, in one awful, final assertion that his will *does* mean something, a feeling of relatedness with his world.

Ahab's effort, then, is to reclaim something that man knows he has lost. Significantly, Ahab proves by the bitter struggle he has to wage that man is fighting in an unequal contest; by the end of the book Ahab abandons all his human ties and becomes a complete fanatic. But Melville has no doubt—nor should we!—that Ahab's quest is *humanly* understandable. And the quest itself supplies the book with its technical *raison d'être.* For it leads us through all the seas and around the whole world; it brings us past ships of every nation. Always it is Ahab's drive that makes up the *passion* of *Moby-Dick,* a passion that is revealed in the descriptive chapters on the whale, whale-fighting, whale-burning, on the whole gory and fascinating industrial process aboard ship that reduces the once proud whale to oil-brimming barrels in the hold. And this passion may be defined as a passion of longing, of hope, of striving: a passion that starts from the deepest loneliness that man can know. It is the great cry of man who feels himself exiled from his "birthright, the merry May-day gods of old," who looks for a new god "to enthrone . . . again in the now egotistical sky; in the now unhaunted hill." The cry is Ahab's—"Who's to doom, when the judge himself is dragged to the bar?"

Behind Ahab's cry is the fear that man's covenant with God has been broken, that there is no purpose to our existence. The *Pequod* is condemned by Ahab to sail up and down the world in search of—a symbol. But this search, mad as it seems to Starbuck the first mate, who is a Christian, nevertheless represents Ahab's real humanity. For the ancient covenant is never quite broken so long as man still thirsts for it. And because Ahab, as Melville intended him to, represents the aristocracy of intellect in our democracy, because he seeks to transcend the limitations that good conventional men like Starbuck, philistine materialists like Stubb, and unthinking fools like Flask want to impose on everybody else, Ahab speaks for the humanity that belongs to man's imaginative vision of himself.

—ALFRED KAZIN, "Ishmael and Ahab," *Atlantic Monthly* 198, No. 5
(November 1956): 83

DENIS DONOGHUE

In the chapter of *Moby-Dick* called "The Symphony," far out in the fable, when we have almost despaired of Ahab's ever assenting to his membership of the human race, that first modern hero speaks to Starbuck, a man who acknowledges limits. What he says is prefigured by his sobbing, by his leaning heavily over the side of the whaler, and by Starbuck's instinctive movement toward the old man: these are good companionable signs:

> "But do I look very old, so very, very old, Starbuck? I feel deadly faint, bowed, and humped, as though I were Adam, staggering beneath the piled centuries since Paradise. God! God! God!—crack my heart!—stave my brain!— mockery! mockery! bitter, biting mockery of grey hairs, have I lived enough joy to wear ye; and seem and feel thus intolerably old? Close! stand close to me, Starbuck; Let me look into a human eye; it is better than to gaze into sea or sky; better than to gaze upon God. By the green land; by the bright hearth-stone! this is the magic glass, man; I see my wife and my child in thine eye."

Yeats wrote something like that and called it "The Circus Animals' Desertion." This act is a startling transformation in Ahab, a man who thrust his will beyond any human scale of action; who invented a mask so that he could strike through it; who cried out, "Who's over me?"; who so withdrew credence from the finite order that he could say, "Oh! how immaterial are all materials! What things real are there, but imponderable thoughts?" For once, and only provisionally, Ahab sees that he has allowed his opaque Faustian will to stand between himself and the real. To a finite, limited eye he now attributes magical powers. But for once, and provisionally; for in the same chapter, now only half-outside his will, he names God or Fate as its source and therefore its sinister cause. This is the easiest way out:

> "But if the great sun move not of himself; but is as an errand-boy in heaven; nor one single star can revolve, but by some invisible power; how then can this one small heart beat; this one small brain think thoughts; unless God does that beating, does that thinking, does that living, and not I. By heaven, man, we are turned round and round in this world, like yonder windlass, and Fate is the handspike."

It is only a matter of time, and of the "grand god's" victory, before our hero declares that "Ahab stands alone among the millions of the peopled earth, nor gods nor men his neighbors!"

I have called Ahab our first modern hero because he is the first and, as yet, one of the most extreme of those intransigent heroes who have enacted our own intransigence, our inability to conceive of Being except in a context of extremity and aggression. His spirit, like ours, is wilful, all the more so when it deems itself ill-used; it bears down upon the actual, crushing it; or denying it; or using the whip upon it, setting it to work. He is neither philosopher nor poet, as we remind ourselves by rehearsing St. Thomas' Commentary upon the first Book of Aristotle's *Metaphysics:* "Causa autem quare philosophus comparatur poetae est ista quia uterque circa miranda versatur." The sense of wonder, the "response in love to the whole of being," the genial and dynamic relation to the actual: there is no place for such motives in Ahab's dense extremity. The world of his acts is strident, assertive, full of repudiation and destruction.

—DENIS DONOGHUE, "In the Scene of Being," Hudson Review 14, No. 2
(Summer 1961): 232–33

A. R. HUMPHREYS

On the conscious level Melville has gone to great lengths to establish his novel in terms of a relatively orthodox though not specifically Christian morality of humility, charity, and acceptance. Readings which do not observe this make of it something less valuable than it is. They have some excuse, however, for if Melville has tried to preserve moral balance by slanting his vocabulary throughout to stress Ahab's malevolence (not least by giving him his loaded name), and by making Ishmael the vehicle of the story, he has invested much emotion and rhetoric on Ahab's side; as Stanley Geist puts it, "that grief and greatness were inseparable was Melville's ripest conviction." In Ahab he expresses something of what he praised in Hawthorne, the type he himself repeated in Pierre, Ethan Allen, and Moredock, the man who "declares himself a sovereign nature (in himself) amid the powers of heaven, hell, and earth." Pierre likewise, a moral extremist defying the normal codes, and "ringed ... in with the grief of Eternity," enables Melville to express something obsessionally powerful, something expressed in self-purgation. It is the purgation aspect which is ultimately the unsatisfactory thing about Ahab and Pierre. Melville knows of attitudes better than those he projects in these hero-victims, and the novels prove it. But the "unmanageable" element indulges itself, heightening the book's grandeur but its fulsomeness likewise. "We are not convinced that [Melville] is not inflating his theme, is not giving it a bulk it cannot properly bear," Dr. Tillyard observes in *The Epic Strain in the English Novel,* and one would agree.

Ahab's species, of course, is that of heroic rebel. His presentation, preluded by Ishmael's "foreboding shivers" (Melville is too little content to let his material make its own effect), is of the massive, scarred figure with the grandeur and woe of the Miltonic Satan, the Radcliffian Schedoni, the Shelleyan Prometheus, the Byronic Lara (*Lara*, I.xvii–xix, is particularly relevant), and the "Daemonic persons" Goethe describes in *Truth and Poetry:*

> a tremendous energy seems to be seated in them, and they exercise a wonderful power over all creatures and even over the elements; and, indeed, who shall say how much further such influence may extend? All the moral powers combined are of no avail against them ... and they are to be overcome by nothing but the universe itself ... *Nemo contra Deum nisi Deus ipse.*

The recurrence of this Latin tag in *Pierre,* and the Enceladus story there, suggest a direct Goethean influence, for Goethe also writes of "the Titanic, gigantic, heaven-storming character":

> Tantalus, Ixion, Sisyphus, were also my saints. Admitted to the society of the gods, they would not deport themselves submissively enough, but by their haughty bearing as guests, provoked the anger of their host and patron, and drew upon themselves a sorrowful banishment.

Ahab may owe something also to the hero of Fenimore Cooper's *Red Rover.* Melville reviewed a re-issue of this in 1850 and commented, "Long ago, and far inland, we read it in our uncritical days, and enjoyed it as much as thousands of the rising generation will when supplied with such an entertaining volume." It resembles *Moby-Dick* in, for instance, the *Royal Caroline*'s sinking, the turbulent crew chosen from many nations, Roderick the timid lad devoted to his master, and most of all the Rover himself, despotically commanding, "settled and austere," a "reckless, wayward being," with "thoughtful and clouded brow ... brooding reveries." The Rover lives up to the description the introduction gives of him:

> a nature quick in intellect, endowed with great force of will, possessing every advantage of social position and culture in early life, but wildly passionate and wayward, [and having] violently thrown off all social restraint and cast itself loose on the stormy side of life; an outlaw in spirit.

(Incidentally, the sea-fight in *The Red Rover* brings strongly to mind that in *Israel Potter,* and may well have affected Melville's narrative.) Ahab is vastly more striking than the Rover; his place is with what Mario Praz calls "the Fatal Men of the Romantics." Yet Melville greatly admired Cooper, and it would be strange if *Moby-Dick* owed nothing to the most famous previous American mystery novel of sea-adventure.

"One of Shakespeare's modes of creating characters," Coleridge observes, "is to conceive any one intellectual or moral faculty in morbid excess." Melville was reading Coleridge as well as Shakespeare, and it may be, Leon Howard suggests, that he echoes this in his comment that Ahab has "a half wilful morbidness at the bottom of his nature" and that "all men tragically great are made so through a certain morbidness . . . all mortal greatness is but disease." Ahab's moral unfolding must now be examined, to see how far his greatness is disease.

At first still linked to society, with a new-married wife and soon a son, "Ahab has his humanities." At first Ishmael feels sympathy and sorrow for him, as well as curiosity. Peleg bears witness to his resourceful seamanship when the *Pequod* was dismasted off Japan—"Life was what Captain Ahab and I was thinking of; and how to save all hands." From "a considerating touch of humanity" Ahab refrains from stumping the quarter-deck by night, and he smokes a pipe, "meant for sereneness," until in an unsociable impulse he flings it overboard. (Melville's own appreciation of the creature comforts occurs amply in his novels and letters, and in the comments of his friends.) But steadily the obsessive mania asserts itself. The objects of his defiance are twin aspects of supernatural power—the lightning which scarred him, the whale which maimed him. Fedallah, smuggled aboard with his fellows to be Ahab's director in the hunt for the whale, his auxiliary in defying God's fire, is his evil spirit, and Ahab's boat-crew when Moby Dick is attacked are secret and in effect diabolical aliens. Fedallah, "perched aloft . . . his turban and the moon companions in one sky," first sights the spout superstitiously taken to be Moby Dick's jet, though Ahab himself, eighty-two chapters later, first actually sights the whale. Along with the try-works scene, that of "The Candles" is the one which most sensationally expresses Ahab's alienation from God and man, and addiction to Satanic pride. This stage of his development needs some attention.

The "Candles" scene is influenced by, and should be seen against, the supernatural fires of Hawthorne's "Young Goodman Brown." In this story, illuminated by "four blazing pines, their tops aflame, their stems untouched, like candles at an evening meeting," a diabolically-possessed assembly of New England townsfolk joins in a witches' sabbath:

> As the red light arose and fell, a numerous congregation alternately shone forth, then disappeared in shadow, and again grew, as it were, out of the darkness. . . . [They sang] words which expressed all that our nature can conceive of sin, and darkly hinted at far more. . . . The four blazing pines threw up a loftier flame, and obscurely discovered shapes and visages of horror on the smoke wreaths above the impious assembly.

Though Hawthorne's four pines become Melville's three masts, Melville's derivation is evident. But whereas Hawthorne's effects are single, his assembly diabolic, his candles infernal, Melville's, as his other symbols, are complex, offering a differing interpretation to each nature. To Ishmael, the St. Elmo's fire is "God's burning finger" laid on the ship, to Stubb, "a sign of good luck," to Starbuck, God's warning. But Ahab takes it to symbolise supreme tyranny, and he stands against it:

> "Hand me those mainmast links there; I would fain feel this pulse; and let mine beat against it; blood against fire! So." Then turning, the last link held fast in his

left hand, he put his foot upon the Parsee; and with fixed upward eye, and high-flung right arm, he stood erect before the lofty tri-pointed flames.

God is, in effect, warning against sin; along with Ishmael, Starbuck is the most reliable focus of judgment in the book. But Ahab makes this scene one of the peaks of his defiance, his confrontation of supreme power in one of its two great aspects. Immediately before, he has destroyed the quadrant by which he observed the sun; immediately after, he outrages the codes of seamanship, the compasses are found to be reversed by the electric storm, and the log-line breaks. The corpusant flames flashing upwards from the mastheads are linked to the other symbol of "speechless, placeless power"—"the white flame but lights the way to the White Whale." Challenging the symbolic fire and the symbolic creature (whether these be agents or principals) Ahab puts himself outside (above, he would say) nature and mankind. "Though nominally included in the census of Christendom, he was still an alien to it . . . in his inclement, howling old age, Ahab's soul, shut up in the caved trunk of his body, there fed upon the sullen paws of its gloom." With "intense bigotry of purpose," "gaunt and ribbed, like the black sand beach after some strong tide has been gnawing it," Ahab, "the Fates' lieutenant," is his own law; "Ahab is for ever Ahab." The measure of his repudiation of humanity is the "unconditional and utter rejection" of the *Rachel's* appeal for help in an errand of paternal mercy (Captain Gardiner entreats him in terms of Christian doctrine and of family affection alike— "Do to me as you would have me do to you in the like case. For *you* too have a boy, Captain Ahab—though but a child, and nestling safely at home now"). Shortly afterwards Ahab confesses to Starbuck his "desolation of solitude," "whole oceans away from that young girl I wedded past fifty, and sailed for Cape Horn the next day, leaving but one dent in my marriage pillow—wife? wife?—rather a widow with her husband alive." In the strongest contrast with Ahab's rejection of parenthood and with the destructiveness of his profession (man's version of "vulturism") is the chapter on the whale-mothers and their offspring, in its reverent treatment of natural procreativeness. Yet enough of intermittent humanity diversifies Ahab's monomania to make him genuinely a tragic figure, a great man in ruin.

—A. R. HUMPHREYS, *"Moby Dick," Melville* (Edinburgh: Oliver & Boyd, 1962), pp. 63–68

JOYCE CAROL OATES

The most famous naysayer of American literature, Captain Ahab, inhabits a world of an "infinite background," which is intolerably hidden from him by the masks of physical reality. Yet it is a temptation to him because he wills it to be so; the nightmare of *Moby-Dick* (the annihilation of man by an utterly devastating nature) is not without redemption for us because we are made to understand continually that the quest, whether literal or metaphysical, need not be taken. Man chooses this struggle. The doom that overturns upon the human constituents of the drama is a doom that they, as willful human beings, insist upon: for Ahab does insist upon his doom. The choice has been made, and action may seem compulsive in the present; the weaving ball of "free will" surrenders to the fateful cry from the whaleman's lookout, yet this is still a compulsiveness that is self-inspired, a creation of the ego. And, in the end, it is not really deceived. The grandeur of human consciousness, even of futility, gives us the sense of a choice of nightmares.

When Ahab says:

> "What is it, what nameless, inscrutable, unearthly thing is it, what . . . cruel, remorseless emperor commands me; that against all natural lovings and long- ings, I so keep pushing, and crowding, and jamming myself on all the time . . . ? Is Ahab, Ahab? Is it I, God, or who, that lifts this arm?"

he is calling upon secret yet somehow knowable patterns of reality that sustain his world, and his hatred for this world. Ahab's monomania does not exclude a recognition of his confusing role in the drama—is he Ahab, or is "Ahab" someone else? What is his identity? Does he exist as an autonomous being or is he merely the acting-out of a decree of another will? His consciousness of his own futility, at times, suggests that he is a tragic hero of a new type—one who knowingly and willingly chooses his "fate," however mistaken this may seem to others. He is a romantic hero, in relation to the white whale as Milton's Satan is to God, an alternately raging, alternating despairing rebel against the supreme order. The human victim within such a tautology is a victim who demands disaster; we feel that if the personified universe did not destroy him, he would have to destroy himself. Yet an important distinction between Melville and Milton must be made: while Milton gives us the godly side of the struggle for man and leaves the reader no doubt as to the ultimate meaning of *Paradise Lost*, Melville gives us only man's side, and his constant tone is one of ambiguity. A tragedy of ambiguous meanings is a modern tragedy, in which certain classical remnants appear amid the chaos of a post-Copernican universe.

Ahab does surely say "No," and he would say it to God as well as the Devil. Unfortunately, God is no more present than the Devil—in fact, God is less present than the Devil. Ahab has created a world of an irreconcilable dualism in which he not only believes, but to which he has surrendered himself; without this terrific dualism—without his religious faith in it—he would topple from the height of a pseudo-god to the level of the merely human. The merely human is a condition in which, perhaps, the voicing of a "No" to the universe is not only futile but without meaning. Up to this point in Melville's works, and a little beyond, the emphasis upon the "No," upon the dualism and the blackness as evil, is surely legitimate. These central passions are the catalysts for the inner rage of the works, and their rela- tionship to similar themes in American literature is certainly valuable to criticism.

—JOYCE CAROL OATES, "Melville and the Tragedy of Nihilism"
(1962), *The Edge of Impossibility: Tragic Forms in Literature*
(New York: Vanguard Press, 1972), pp. 64–66

RANEY STANFORD

The rebel of pride, the Satan of Milton redrawn as hero by Blake and Byron, reaches his most striking development in Melville's Captain Ahab. Pursuing the white whale for revenge, he takes the whole crew of the *Pequod* with him, sacrifices to his unappeasable rage against the mystery of nature and the limitations of man. Ahab has been branded by nature as an exceptional man; his reaction is to wage war against the world for the sake of his ego and pride. A "false Prometheus" Richard Chase calls him, because, unlike the true one, he storms heaven and its mysteries not in order to bring a gift to man, but solely to satisfy the cravings of the insatiable romantic self and its pride. He does not set forth to battle and subdue the demonic, but to become the demonic archetype himself before the quest is ended.

The whale is many things to many men, as all readers of Melville know, but to Ahab it is

> ... the monomaniac incarnation of all those malicious agencies which deep men feel eating in them, till they are left living on with half a heart and half a lung. That intangible malignity which has been from the beginning.... Ahab did not fall down and worship it.... He pitted himself, all mutilated, against it.... He piled upon the whale's white hump the sum of all the general rage and hate felt by his whole race from Adam down; and then, as if his chest had been a mortar, he burst his hot heart's shell upon it.

Thus, in a very real sense, Ahab *does* worship the power beyond man's ken and control, for it is through assaulting it in rebellion that he achieves significance, even identity. There is no God in this world and its purpose is delusion or mystery. "All visible objects, man, are but as pasteboard masks.... If man will strike, strike through the mask! How can the prisoner reach the outside except by thrusting through the wall? To me, the white whale is that wall, shoved near to me." To assert the self in such a world is an act of lonely agony; to put the self forward as something divine is the romantic heresy that Ahab personifies at its utmost. The lonely self which sickens the Manfred and Cain of Byron, Ahab would escape by assaulting the limits of the human condition itself. He will escape lonely alienation through becoming God. "There is one God that is Lord over the earth, and one Captain that is lord over the *Pequod.*—On deck!" he barks at the rational Starbuck, who would turn back. God and Captain both stand obdurate and mad here, driving men on through a bewildering and malevolent universe, with loaded muskets from the same quarterdeck. Standing before the famous doubloon nailed to the *Pequod*'s mast, in which all men read the universe in terms of themselves, Ahab sees only himself in the mountains of Ecuador: "Three peaks as proud as Lucifer. The firm tower, that is Ahab; the volcano, that is Ahab; the courageous, the undaunted and victorious fowl, that, too, is Ahab; all are Ahab."

But Ahab is not a mere megalomaniac, and the attraction of his tumultuous quest and disastrous end is not that of watching a wild animal in a pit. He is drawn by his passionate commitment which consumes him, in the fashion which Hegel described as suitable for the "World-historical individual." "What is it, what nameless, inscrutable, unearthly thing is it; what cozzening, hidden lord and master, and cruel, remorseless emperor commands me; that against all natural lovings and longings, I so keep pushing and crowding, and jamming myself on all the time. . . . Is it I, God, or who, that lifts this arm?" The enraged and soiled pride, incensed that this question is not and cannot be answered, drives him on until he, and all with him, are committed to the irrevocable doom of the white whale, who plays and rolls with such beauteous charm in the sun-lit sea, when man does not push against him. In the unearthly light of the St. Elmo's fire that plays about the ship on her quest, Ahab announces kinship with the unearthly light, but cries in furious despair because kinship with this divine spark is *not* identity. "I own thy speechless, placeless power; but to the last gasp of my earthquake life will dispute its unconditional, unintegral mastery in me. In the midst of the personified impersonal, *a personality stands here*" (italics mine). He would join this flame: "I leap with thee; I burn with thee; would fain be welded with thee; defyingly I worship thee!"

Worship in defiance is what he must express. In Ahab, Melville has created for all time the image of the rootless man who makes the will to power his sole motivation in life. Ahab looms forever as the image of the rebel who only lives by and through rebellion—and whose drive to supremacy destroys such of the world as he can wield power over. All along the way he chooses to define himself by destruction, as W. H. Auden has noted. "What to the Greeks could only have been a punishment for sin is here a temptation to sin, an opportunity to choose; by making the wrong choice and continuing to make it, Ahab punishes himself." Revenge is his vocation, and the quest is not really for anything, but is an end in itself. Ahab probably represents the most dramatic creation of the modern man of *virtù*, the rebel as hero in post-renaissance literature. Other rebels elsewhere throughout European literature sound petulant and boring, as they voice their complaints about the status or power they do not have; for Ahab's rebellion, profound and metaphysical, is against the limits and nature of man himself. He goes even further than Faust, who signed a pact with the Devil for superhuman power. Knowing not God or any meaning at all in which a vital man may acquiesce and find peace, Ahab becomes the devil himself. "Ego non baptizo te in nomine patris, sed in nomine diaboli!" he howls at the primitive ritual in which he horrifies and fascinates the crew by consecrating his ubiquitous harpoons in blood.

But he is a hero who drives relentlessly up a road from whence there is no returning. A latter-day Achilles who would assault nature itself, he lacks even that proud warrior's humility, for reminders of mortality that bring Achilles down from his pedestal of glory to embrace old Priam and restore the body of Hector to that king, merely urge Ahab on to fresh frenzies of effort in his death-haunted quest. The hero who spends his brief life in a fury at being left alone in an inexplicable universe really seeks death; that is, seeks to make the universe beyond him as tumultuous as that within him, so that in some way his loneliness is compensated for. Such a man will destroy himself and those about him in his search for a destruction of the self on a scale satisfactory to his own pretentious ego. If this world is absurd and cannot be changed, then it should be destroyed, say Ahab and Caligula, the furious hero of Albert Camus' play of much the same theme.

Melville's triumph is to depict Ahab clearly, in all his terror as well as glory, leading his world to destruction. Other writers throughout the nineteenth century, not so fair with themselves or us, tend to present in various works what we now call hero-worship. Ahab shows us that the cult of pure ego leads to self destruction, and that the abuse of power, even to satisfy the cravings of the spirit (Ahab is an inverted idealist; he only wants power for his mission), leads to suffering and death for all about him.

—RANEY STANFORD, "The Romantic Hero and That Fatal Selfhood,"
Centennial Review 12, No. 4 (Fall 1968): 440–43

MARTIN LEONARD POPS

As Ishmael is saved because he incorporates his Shadow, Ahab is destined to die because he does not; because, unlike Ishmael, he refuses to commit himself to the only person aboard the *Pequod* whom he loves and through whom he can be saved. Only Pip possesses those "childish . . . or primitive qualities that would in a way vitalize and even embellish [Ahab's] . . . existence," for only Pip is the "real counterpart of [Ahab's] . . . conscious ego, the not or not sufficiently lived side of [his] . . . psyche." Ahab is white, Pip is black. Ahab is the Captain, Pip is the "most insignificant" of the crew. Ahab is courageous, Pip is a coward. Ahab is *head*strong, Pip is "over tender-hearted." Ahab is usually solemn, Pip is usually laughing. Ahab is an allegorist, Pip is a symbolist. Ahab craves death and risks all on the sea, Pip "loved life, and all life's peaceable securities." Ahab makes a pact with the Devil and arraigns the gods for human suffering; Pip "saw God's foot upon the treadle of the loom" and comes to feel "indifferent" about human "weal or woe."

Therefore, incorporating the Shadow would mean for Ahab what it means for Ishmael: reducing the vision of "attainable felicity," shifting his love from the quest to the family. And although Ahab *is* vulnerable where his wife and child are concerned—Pip elicits from him the tender feelings he would have reserved for them—Ahab finally, in his madness and desperation, turns not toward his good angel but toward his bad, toward Fedallah, in whom he recognizes his prophetic soul. But the tragedy of Ahab is that he is doomed regardless of what he does. By assimilating the Shadow in the personal unconscious, he must renounce the quest, for him a fate worse than death. By failing to assimilate the Shadow, he must confront Moby Dick inadequately armed in his transpersonal dimension, and that, as we know, is death itself.

If Ishmael is sexually immature, Ahab is sexually perverse, for, like Taji and Pierre, he too is parricidal and incestuous. And although it is true that Melville knew he had written a "wicked book," I very much doubt whether he was entirely aware of its deepest sexual import. Tommo effects his release by hurling a spear into Mow-Mow's throat; Taji divides the lacing of Yillah's tent with his cutlass; White Jacket rips open his water-logged jacket with his knife. These acts, symbolic of initiation, are instances of that typically American *rite de passage* in which sex is sublimated and replaced by violence—although, to a limited degree at least, they also imply that sexual energy is potentially creative. In *Pierre* and in such later works as "Benito Cereno" and *The Confidence-Man* possession and use of the phallic weapon suggests that sexual energy is unfailingly destructive. But in *Moby-Dick,* at the wavecrest of Melville's art, the connotations of the symbolic instrument, like the genital implications of the great Whale, are both creative *and* sinister.

On one hand, Queequeg rescues the drowning Tashtego from the womblike whale's head by plunging "his keen sword" again and again into it "so as to scuttle a large hole there." The he hauls him forth, and Tashtego is reborn. But on the other hand, Ahab, in his fanatically Oedipal compulsion, would penetrate the whale-wall, which bears the characteristics of the Male (even as Taji stabbed Aleema), and plunge his harpoon into Moby Dick's inner sanctum where the Female Principle inheres (where Taji cutlassed Yillah). But, as Newton Arvin, Dr. Murray, and several others agree, in *Moby-Dick* this Principle is Maternal, not Filial, and, therefore, Ahab's hidden sexual desire is not to commit "secondary" incest with the Sister, like Taji, but the more grievous offense, "primal" incest with the Mother. In this regard, W. H. Auden's comments seem to me decisive:

> In *Moby-Dick*, where Ahab's pride revolts against lack of absolute strength, against being finite and dependent, the sexual symbolism centres round incest and the Oedipus situation, because incest is the magic act of self-derivation, self-autonomy, with the annihilation of all rival power. . . .
> . . . the Oedipus fantasy is a representation in aesthetic terms of the fantasy of being a self-originating god, i.e. of the ego (Father) begetting itself on the self (Mother), and castration is the ultimate symbol of aesthetic weakness, of not being an aesthetic hero.

At the end, in the act of hurling his harpoon, Ahab yields his sex to the castrating Mother, for, as Harry Slochower asserts, Ahab

> . . . is [finally] . . . 'united' to the whale by his line. The umbilical cord is retied, and Ahab [strangled] sinks, like an infant 'voicelessly' into the ocean by the side of the mystery he has been unable to fathom.

Thus as Ahab seeks the zenith of metaphysical perversion in the quest—to stab into the realm of Absolute Reality and slay God—so here he seeks, presumably with unconscious intent, the correlative zenith of sexual perversion. Like Oedipus who confronts the Sphinx, Ahab confronts the "sphinx-like" whale, and, as, in final comprehension of his act, Oedipus blinds himself, so Ahab, "as he beholds Moby Dick about to pierce the hull of the *Pequod* . . . smites his forehead and cries out:

'I grow blind; hands! stretch out before me that I may yet grope my way. Is't night?' "
Ahab's monstrous desires, then, similarly proceed from a maddened brain and are
similarly thwarted, but they inspire *Moby-Dick* to a hell-fire intensity far more
hypnotic than the dream-like anxiety of *Mardi* or the manufactured fervor of
Pierre.

As far as the Father is concerned, Ahab's mad purpose is not only to slay but
to embrace him as well—and fatally embrace him he does. For Ahab is a kind of
maimed Fisher King—even the baptism of his harpoon in blood suggests the sexual
injury implicit in the Bleeding Spear motif—and he would restore his potency
through conjunction with the phallus-shaped, divinely erotic Jove himself. But the
Beast, like the weapons in *Moby-Dick,* is profoundly ambiguous: divine, yet malign—
and so, as Ahab finally hooks Moby Dick, so the Whale finally ravages the *Pequod,*
the oil-laden feminine vessel.

Captain Ahab is Melville's first adult quester and the first who actively challenges the Great Mother—the White Whale; and, as with Taji, there are two ways,
not just one, of evaluating his incestuous desires. In his ontogenetic character, Ahab
exhibits an Oedipal neurosis in the classic Freudian sense; but, at the same time, by
viewing him in his phylogenetic magnitude, we may locate his place in the history of
the Quester whose development is in the direction of health, not sickness. By
interpreting Ahab's Oedipal fate transpersonally, we recognize his heroic attempt
to emancipate himself from the Mother through "regenerative" incest. Oedipus,
writes Erich Neumann,

> . . . has no knowledge of what he has done and when he finds out, he is unable
> to look his own deed, the deed of the hero, in the face. Consequently he is
> overtaken by the fate that overtakes all those for whom the Eternal Feminine
> reverts to the great Mother; he regresses to the stage of the son, and suffers
> the fate of the son-lover. He performs the act of self-castration by putting out
> his own eyes.

Ahab, similarly, has no conscious knowledge that he has sought the Mother;
nor does he seem to realize it at the very end, although, interestingly enough, he
does claim to suffer Oedipus' punishment.

> The blinding [of Oedipus] is no longer a puzzle for us. It signifies the destruc-
> tion of the higher masculinity, of the very thing that characterizes the hero; and
> this form of spiritual self-castration cancels out all that was gained by his victory
> over the Sphynx. The masculine progression of the hero is thrown back by the
> old shock, the fear of the Great Mother which seizes him after the deed. He
> becomes a victim of the Sphynx he had conquered.

Thus the phylogenetic progress of the Quester is partially undercut by Ahab's
submission to the Great Mother, and this is perhaps why Melville's next protagonist,
Pierre, is, like Taji, adolescent again.

Ahab's desperate battle with the Whale coincides with that stage of ego development Neumann calls the "dragon fight," a "fight [which] has three main components: the hero, the dragon, and the treasure," that is, the Quester, the Parents, and the Captive respectively. Melville himself identifies whales with dragons in *Moby-Dick,* and the adversaries in the dragon fight are very like those in the whale-hunt. According to Neumann,

> The fight [of the Quester] with the dragon is thus the fight with the First Parents, a fight in which the murders of both father and mother, but not of one alone, have their ritually prescribed place.

But, as I noted earlier, Ahab tries not merely to slay the Father; he means to embrace him as well, and their affiliation is essential if Ahab is to succeed in killing Moby Dick:

> The slaying of the mother and identification with the father-god go together. If, through active incest, the hero penetrates into the dark, maternal, chthonic side, he can only do so by virtue of his kinship with 'heaven,' his filiation with God.

Ahab, however, fails on all counts: to embrace and slay the Father, to mate with and slay the Mother. Thus he gives his life trying to achieve

> The mythological goal of the dragon fight ... the virgin, the captive, or, more generally, the 'treasure hard to attain.' It is to be noted that a purely material pile of gold, such as the hord of the Nibelungs, is a late and degenerate form of the original motif. In the earliest mythologies, in ritual, in religion, and in mystical literature as well as in fairy tales, legend, and poetry, gold and precious stones, but particularly diamonds and pearls, were originally symbolic carriers of immaterial values.

In Melville gold and treasure—albeit "a late and degenerate form of the original motif"—are still symbolic carriers of immaterial values, of the reality of the Sacred and the Absolute.

—MARTIN LEONARD POPS, "In the Splendid Labyrinth: *Moby-Dick,"
The Melville Archetype* (Kent, OH: Kent State University Press, 1970),
pp. 82–87

ANN DOUGLAS

If Melville was performing an act of formal repression against his readers in *Redburn* and *White-Jacket,* he was also staving off open expression of his conflict with them. In *Moby-Dick* and *Pierre,* Melville allows this conflict to surface, and, in doing so, he summons and exploits all his creative energies to a degree unique in his career. The two books are, however, radically dissimilar. While Melville acknowledges his challenge to the sentimental culture of his reader in both works, only in *Moby-Dick* does he still hope to make good on it. As a result, the book operates thematically and structurally as a conversion process; Melville plots brilliantly to bring his audience to his side. *Pierre,* in contrast, is Melville's document of despair. Revenge, not conversion is his aim; Melville punishes his readers in advance for their inevitable failure of comprehension.

⟨. . .⟩ Melville specifically warned women away from *Moby-Dick*—"Don't you buy it—don't you read it." The book was written for men, or at least from a self-consciously masculine viewpoint. Early on in the story, Ishmael and Queequeg attend a chapel service for sailors where they see a number of women whose countenances suggest "unceasing grief" for their men lost at sea. When they appear in *Moby-Dick,* women are the mourners and the losers: they have no other role. Never before has Melville emphasized so heavily the acquisitive brutality of the fishing enterprise: we witness the horrible killing of an old sperm whale, we see the beating of his bloody fins. Melville's attitude is hardly simple here; yet his criticism of the whaling industry, real as it is, functions less significantly than his need to face the facts, paint the whole picture, as part of an exemplary process of disciplined total perception. Melville is giving the reader lessons in honesty, not in pity. Melville never denies in *Moby-Dick* the value of the domestic virtues of piety or morality; he does deny such virtues the right actively to justify themselves in the narrative. Their place is negative; they are what is forgotten, over-ridden, whether for good or bad. On board the *Pequod,* the first mate Starbuck constitutes himself the spokesman for the softer, more "human" values; it is he who, just before the chase of the white whale, speaks to Ahab of his own family waiting at home and of Ahab's young wife and new-born son. Ahab has a moment of weakness; he thinks of the mother he never knew, he even weeps, but he is finally adamant against all softening impulses. The most impervious and dictatorial of all Melville's captains, Ahab will not help the captain of the *Rachel* look for his lost son, he disavows the black boy Pip whom he had befriended, he turns from Starbuck. Important as the relations among various crew members are to Melville, he subordinates them, as he did not in his earlier narratives, to the phenomenon represented by his captain. Both newly embattled and released at this point in his career, Melville wishes to explore rather than challenge the meaning of masculine authority.

It is interesting that, unlike Melville's earlier protagonists, Ahab cannot be understood at all without some knowledge of Calvinism: it is essential to his masculinity. In the works preceding *Moby-Dick,* Melville dealt with the Christian religion in large part negatively, by a critique of the missionary effort; in *Moby-Dick* and the books which succeed it—all of which are essentially located in America as the earlier narratives were not—the critique continues, but it is accompanied by an intermittent yet vital exploration of the Calvinist heritage Melville's contemporaries were abandoning. As Hawthorne's comments in his Liverpool journal indicate, Melville was in no conventional sense a believer; but, as his own artistic ambition was activated in its most serious form, he apparently found it necessary to utilize the ideas and structures of Calvinism. Its hieratic form, its preoccupation with pain, defiance, and grandiosity, its complex confrontation of the human and the in-human, give Melville a suitable object for imitation, exploration, and attack. In *Moby-Dick,* when Queequeg is signed up for the *Pequod,* Bildad, one of the ship's owners, wishes to convert the pagan harpooner to Christianity. The other owner, Peleg, at once protests: " 'Pious harpooners never make good voyagers—it takes the shark out of 'em.' " One could say that in *Moby-Dick,* Melville is putting the shark back into religion.

At one point, in speaking of the white whale's beauty, Melville explains: "real strength never impairs beauty or harmony, but it often bestows it." Melville is of course defending the "sublime" against the tacit resistance of a society which es-pouses the "beautiful" and the "picturesque." He continues by comparing the "robustness" of Michelangelo's "God the Father" with "the soft, curled, her-maphroditical" Christ of later Italian painters, and—as Melville must have been aware although he does not say so here—of nineteenth-century American repre-sentations. Such pictures of Christ show "nothing of any power, but the mere negative, feminine one of submission and endurance, which on all hands it is con-ceded form the practical virtues of his teachings." Melville was never really con-cerned with Christ—certainly not the Christ of his culture; for him as for Lyman Beecher, although in a more terrifying sense, "everything was swallowed up in God." Although the God of *Moby-Dick* is hardly the specific theological entity of earlier Calvinist creeds but rather an "inscrutable thing"—the presence which Ahab defies and the white whale suggests—he is hardly less terrifying, less impressive, or even less Calvinist for his amorphousness and inaccessibility. *Moby-Dick* is, in fact, an implicit critique of liberal Protestantism. Starbuck's death, which occurs when the white whale overwhelms the *Pequod,* is a demonstration of the inefficacy of the sentimental creed. Imploring "Ye sweet powers of air," whom Melville has speci-fically linked with feminine influences, to "hug me close," Starbuck goes down to destruction ironically exclaiming "My God, stand by me now!" Melville's God is as indifferent to mortal needs and aspirations for happiness as Joseph Bellamy's. Like the God Bellamy preached whom one of his parishioners found " 'SO GREAT!' " the divine presence in *Moby-Dick,* whether malign or benign, by definition stretches the human mind almost past endurance. Ahab's acknowledged insanity is a measure of his recognition, however inadequate, of the force that rules the universe. The "class" struggle in *Moby-Dick* is no longer between crew and captain; the men back Ahab in his pursuit of the whale. But the "Marxist" struggle has been transformed, or abandoned; *Moby-Dick* concerns the archetypal conflict between the rules and the ruled, between God and man.

Moby-Dick opens with a powerful revival service conducted by Father Map-ple, a former seaman. His sermon sets the tone for the book. Ahab, damned as he is, will convert the entire crew, with the exception of Starbuck, to his Calvinist view of life, his obsession with what Melville elsewhere called "the power of blackness"; in a very real way, I believe, he will convert the reader. The crew's concern and our concern will increasingly be Ahab's confrontation with his destroyer. This is not to suggest that Melville totally approves of Ahab any more than he entirely disapproves of the domestic virtues which Ahab cannot heed. Yet it would have been so easy for Melville to turn us against Ahab; if the noble self-possessed Bulkington remained on stage longer, if Ishmael, or indeed any crew member we thoroughly respected, genuinely resented and protested Ahab's despotic lack of concern for the crew's interests, we could contextualize and distance Ahab more readily. None of these things happen. Bulkington disappears; Ishmael, despite his disapproval, is swept up by Ahab. Ishmael launches the "narrative," but only while it deals with events on shore; he tells us of his friendship with Queequeg, the preparations for sailing. Once at sea, Ishmael's voice exists in a complex counterpoint with Ahab's and is at times even supplanted by it. Ahab gives us, indeed embodies, the "story," and his voice represents the extreme of public performance and revivalist art. Ahab is probably the greatest orator, the finest preacher in American literature; if Margaret Fuller had been alive in 1851, she would have appreciated his language; if Stowe had read *Moby-Dick,* she would have understood his style and his subject.

In taking over the narrative voice, Ahab moves it from the personal to the impersonal; Ahab's mind may be diseased, but it is a sickness he caught from God, not man. Nor can the movement from the particular to the abstract be reversed. After Ahab's death, the closing paragraphs before the "epilogue," presumably given us by Ishmael, are in a narrative mode which is significantly more mannered, more grandiose, than Ishmael's opening style. Here is the start:

> Call me Ishmael. Some years ago—never mind how long precisely—having little or no money in my purse, and nothing particular to interest me on shore, I thought I would sail about a little and see the watery part of the world.

Note the frightening connotations of a plethora of undistinguishable possibilities, Ishmael's hypothetical unwanted but insistent personal perspective. Here is the (penultimate) ending:

> Now small fowls flew screaming over the yet yawning gulf; a sullen white surf beat against its steep sides; then all collapsed, and the great shroud of the sea rolled on as it rolled five thousand years ago.

The tone is detached but magisterial, even orchestrated. Certain things are no longer possible: history has happened. Ishmael is no more "important" than he ever was, but his attitude toward his task of reportage has shifted. Ishmael survives, although he inhabits a universe which stands defined as the wake of the whale and the grave of Ahab. His return is necessary, for he represents the possibility, no matter how randomly available, of taking responsibility for experience, even for experience beyond our control. He suggests if not a commitment, a continuity on the part of the author, and a lesson for the reader.

Ahab's implacability offers a clue to his literary as well as to his religious significance. His moral value is ambiguous, as I have said, but I do not think this ambiguity is central to Melville's design as, say, the uncertainty about Lord Jim's courage is essential to Conrad's. Melville is not drawing the reader close to Ahab in the sense that he is urging the reader as a man to emulate or even evaluate Ahab as a hero. The levels of Melville's literary self-consciousness here are numerous and uncannily "modern," as we like to say in praise of writers of former ages. He grasped the fact that a reader identifies with a fictional protagonist not only as he represents a "real" person, but also purely *as a fictional character*. Melville brings the reader close to Ahab because he wishes the experience of Ahab *as a hero in a book* to educate the reader not simply as a person but *as a reader*. Ishmael is not only an observer and an actor in the book, he is a model for the reader. It is important that Ahab is a deliberately old-fashioned, even anachronistic, character; his bombastic, self-consciously literary rhetoric is that of the American drama of the 1830s; his very insanity is a kind of cultural throwback; his intensely romantic view of the universe—which his "monomania" frees him to find compact with meaning, if a diabolic one—is not that of Ishmael, our contemporary. Ishmael, with his utter lack of cultural roots and his terror of a potentially empty, meaningless universe, needs to identify with Ahab as well as to survive him. Ishmael is not asked to become Ahab—finally he cannot, although he is tempted to try—but he is asked not to deny that he knew him. Melville is insisting that art is not a product to be consumed and thrown aside, as the "sketch" suggested, but an experience which can and must alter the participant's view of life and himself. Ishmael cannot regain his pre-Ahab voice because Ahab has happened. The reader is denied the usual cycle of vicarious involvement, readjustment, and rejection. *Moby-Dick* is the most powerful attempt made by an American author on the eve of the commercialization of literature as a part of mass culture both to find a wide audience and to restore the indispensability, the essentially religious dignity, of the literary work.

In an age which expected its authors to be accessible and easily assimilable, Melville advertised the difficulty of his book. When Ishmael arrives at the Spouter-Inn, he finds on the wall "a very large oil-painting" whose subject it is almost impossible to decipher. There are "such unaccountable masses of shades and shadows," such "portentous" masses, that it is "enough to drive a nervous man distracted." The painting possesses an "unimaginable sublimity" which freezes the viewer to the spot, until he "involuntarily" takes "an oath . . . to find out what that marvellous painting meant." Only by "much and earnest contemplation, and oft repeated ponderings," however, can Ishmael make out an image: that of a whale impaling itself on the three masts of a ship—a picture very close to the final scene with Moby Dick and the *Pequod*. Melville is both acknowledging and justifying the intricate sustained effort he demands of his reader: as Margaret Fuller asked of her friends, he expects his readers to be productive. The reader is asked to move from the passivity of the "sub-sub," the Irvingesque *persona* who opens *Moby-Dick* with his erudite but uncollated series of definitions, the consumer of literature who is always more a reader than a writer, toward the philosophy of Ishmael, who is preeminently engaged with experience, and finally to the passion of Ahab, whose imagination encompasses and creates the enormities of adventure. The reader is urged to deal with the ambiguities of Ahab's moral status precisely because to deal with ambiguity is, in Melville's mind, to deal with danger. Melville asks the reader metaphorically to risk his life to explore the necessities of the imagination; he invites the reader to help him write the book—if he dares.

The reader of *Pierre* is exposed to endless "ambiguities"; that is, indeed, the book's subtitle. But the danger is not educative here, for Melville allows his readers no real way into the novel; the story is an insult, not a dare. In the same letter to Sophia Hawthorne in which Melville expressed his surprise that she had liked *Moby-Dick*—"for as a general thing women have small taste for the sea"—he promised her that his next work, presumably *Pierre,* would be a "rural bowl of milk," a book for the ladies. Instead, in *Pierre,* Melville turned decisively and openly against the middle-class sentimental-minded feminized reading public he had essentially tried to evade or educate in his previous work. It is as if their interference with his creative effort has become so troubling that he must deal with it, and he does so by making it, in curious ways, the actual subject of his book.

—ANN DOUGLAS, *"Moby-Dick* and *Pierre:* The Struggle for Possession," *The Feminization of American Culture* (New York: Knopf, 1977), pp. 304–9

CAROLYN L. KARCHER

⟨. . .⟩ Pip and Ishmael have many affinities with each other, as Edgar A. Dryden has pointed out. Not only does Pip's experience of being a "castaway" prefigure Ishmael's at the end of the book, but it gives Pip insights much like those at which Ishmael arrives in contemplating the whiteness of the whale. Pip perceives in the infinite ocean where he has been abandoned the same "heartless voids and immensities of the universe" that Ishmael apprehends in the "indefiniteness" of whiteness. Similarly, Pip sees "God's foot upon the treadle of the loom" in the "wondrous depths" to which he is transported and feels God's indifference, as Ishmael does when he comes face to face with the world's "weaver-god" in a "wondrous" bower in the Arsacides and finds him so "deafened" by his weaving "that he hears no mortal voice."

Pip also holds out to Ahab the same promise of redemption through love that Queequeg holds out to Ishmael. He attracts Ahab's attention on the heels of one more ill omen that the monomaniacal captain has stubbornly refused to heed—the snapping of the log-line. Troubled by Pip's madness, Ahab reproaches the gods for having begotten this helpless black boy only to abandon him. "There can be no hearts above the snow-line," he exclaims. In identifying the "frozen heavens" with the North, as Alan Heimert has noticed, Ahab echoes the southern apologists' "ringing indictment of northern hypocrisy and indifference to the Negro's welfare." Yet when he vows that "Ahab's cabin shall be Pip's home henceforth, while Ahab lives," the captain ironically overlooks the problem of what will happen to Pip afterwards. He thus follows the example of both the gods he denounces and the numerous southern masters whose deaths plunged favorite slaves into the worst horrors of slavery.

Ultimately, of course, Ahab will forsake Pip to pursue the fanatic chase he has never considered giving up. But for the moment, he seems to be feeling the "Siamese ligature" with Pip that Ishmael learns to acknowledge toward all mankind. "Thou touchest my inmost centre, boy; thou art tied to me by cords woven of my heart-strings," he tells Pip. Pip likewise seizes Ahab's hand "as a man-rope; something that weak souls may hold by," recalling the monkey-rope through which Ishmael is "wedded" to Queequeg "for better or for worse." Like Ishmael and Queequeg, Ahab and Pip even contract a symbolic marriage. Claiming that "had poor Pip but felt so kind a thing" as the "velvet shark-skin" of Ahab's hand, he might never have been lost, Pip summons the blacksmith to "rivet these two hands together; the black one with the white, for I will not let this go." Ahab, on his part, characteristically turns the ritual into a histrionic gesture meant to vindicate his quarrel with God: "Lo! ye believers in gods all goodness, and in man all ill, lo you! see the omniscient gods oblivious of suffering man; and man, though idiotic, and knowing not what he does, yet full of the sweet things of love and gratitude. Come! I feel prouder leading thee by thy black hand, than though I grasped an Emperor's!" It is no accident, however, that Ahab's union with Pip takes place in the chapter "The Log and Line," where it is framed by the snapping of the log-line and by the old Manxman's complaints that the line is too "rotten" to mend. The same is evidently true of the cords woven of Ahab's heart-strings, which prove too fragile to hold him to Pip when he feels Moby Dick's pull. Thus Pip's description of Ahab's hand as "velvet shark-skin" may express a crazy intuition of the irredeemable sharkishness underlying Ahab's kindness towards him. Ahab, unlike Ishmael, is not saved by his marriage with his fellow man, since he does not truly commit himself to it as the alternative to the phantasmic hunt through which he carries his shipmates to their doom.

> —CAROLYN L. KARCHER, "A Jonah's Warning to America in *Moby-Dick*,"
> *Shadow over the Promised Land: Slavery, Race, and Violence in
> Melville's America* (Baton Rouge: Louisiana State University Press, 1980),
> pp. 86–88

DAVID SIMPSON

In a peculiar way, Ahab and Moby Dick are doubles; at least they are so figured by Ishmael. At first sight, Ishmael is appalled by Ahab, just as he will be by the whale. Ahab has a mark on his face which is "lividly whitish," and we are soon told "that for the first few moments I hardly noted that not a little of this overbearing grimness was owing to the barbaric white leg upon which he partly stood" (ch. 28). ⟨. . .⟩ Moby Dick's whiteness occasions a long disquisition on the horror caused by that color, or absence of color. Ahab comes to identify with the whale, "not only all his bodily woes, but all his intellectual and spiritual exasperations" (ch. 41). The reflexivity implicit in his threat, "I will dismember my dismemberer" (ch. 37), is enacted also in the mirror imaging of the body-parts that they project to the outer world. As Moby Dick shows a "wrinkled brow" (ch. 36; ch. 44) or "wrinkled forehead" (ch. 41) as the sign of his identity, so Ahab too shows a "wrinkled brow, till it almost seemed that while he himself was marking out lines and courses on the wrinkled charts, some invisible pencil was also tracing lines and courses upon the deeply marked chart of his forehead" (ch. 44). As his "snow-white new ivory leg" matches the whale's hump, so, when he goes back to the charts, it is again with a "wrinkling" of the brow (ch. 109), reading himself thus into an imitative (and thus worshipful) relation to the figure of his pursuit. It is Ahab's "unappeasable brow" (ch. 135) that Starbuck sees with his last earthly glance, as he too is mesmerized into the circle of duplication and compulsion, to his death. Thus operates the mirrorlike dialectic of fetishism.

However negatively or positively we read Ahab's relation to the white whale, it is clearly a relation dependent upon substitution and reflection rather than upon achievement and conjunction. This pertains even in death. It is the Parsee, himself always written into an almost magnetic connection with his captain, who dies the death most properly befitting Ahab himself, strapped by the harpoon line to the whale's back, his "half torn body" (ch. 135) thus disjunctively connected to the object that his master has in such a tortured way worshipped and hated for so long. Man and whale belong together, but only in a metonymic relationship, held by rope. That is the answer to the assumption of control Ahab seeks in his revenge—so suffer all men wedded to their tools—and it is itself presented *to* him rather than enacted *by* him. Ahab is thus made to see, at a distance, his own predicament of distance *imaged* in the Parsee. For Ahab himself dies in utter silence, strangled and dragged from the boat, though not before he has commented on the final disjunction or distance forced upon him, dying away from his ship, "cut off from the last fond pride of meanest shipwrecked captains." Always cut off.

This is indeed a book about substitution on the grandest scale, and not just in the personalized context of Ahab's quest. Just as the collected etymologies and the various data which preface the story do not encapsulate the whale, so none among the activities of deflection and representation taking place in the narrative ever manages to produce that apparently sought-for "full utterance"—the phrase is Conrad's ⟨...⟩. Ahab tries to integrate Moby Dick into the most familiar and apparently manageable form of social exchange and shared meanings, the money system, in offering the doubloon as the reward for the first sighting. But this gesture is at once undermined by the 'mad' discourse of the ship's boy, Pip, as he sees it nailed to the mast:

> "Here's the ship's navel, this doubloon here, and they are all on fire to unscrew it. But, unscrew your navel, and what's the consequence? Then again,

if it stays here, that is ugly, too, for when aught's nailed to the mast it's a sign that things grow desperate. Ha, ha! old Ahab! the White Whale; he'll nail ye!" (ch. 99)

Reference to the old joke, of which most editors remind us (but which in fact invites reference to the falling off of more than one body-part), high-lights the prospect of loss within the sign which asks to be taken as gain. The sighting of the whale thus threatens the dismembering of the ship and of all who sail in her. But the ship is already committed to disaster, by the fact of the nailing to the mast, the concentration of energy into a single, obsessive direction. And the doubloon is in fact not at all a principle of exchange but yet another example of Ahab redoubling himself. No other sailor manages to anticipate him in spotting the white whale, so that the reward he has offered in fact devolves on himself: "No, the doubloon is mine, Fate reserved the doubloon for me. *I* only; none of ye could have raised the White Whale first" (ch. 133). The coin is his image, the thing that purports to be outside him, but that is in fact within in its essential purposes. Thus, when he fixed his "riveted glance" on the "riveted gold coin," he too "wore the same aspect of nailed firmness" ch. 99). Within is without, for Ahab.

—DAVID SIMPSON, *Fetishism and Imagination: Dickens, Melville, Conrad* (Baltimore: Johns Hopkins University Press, 1982), pp. 80–81

TONY MAGISTRALE

Herman Melville's fiction reveals his fascination with elements from the eighteenth-century Gothic literary tradition. Merton Sealts says that Melville read Walpole's *Otranto*, Beckford's *Vathek*, and even Mary Shelley's *Frankenstein*, as well as a number of lesser known but related Gothic texts. Gothicism is concerned with fallen man, often embracing and flaunting his sinful state. The genre's characteristic association with evil, the rebellion against God and optimistic virtues, and an emphasis on disorder, chaos, and ambiguity all find a developmental place in Melville's works. The Gothic supplied Melville with a workable tradition: a theater that enabled and encouraged him to give dramatic life to conflicting and often darkly pessimistic philosophical positions. In his hands, the standard, eighteenth-century Gothic apparatus—blood bonds with evil, haunted castles, a reliance on supernatural terror—evolved to tell a more complicated story, focusing on the profoundly tragic imperfections inherent in man and his institutions.

Melville's most ambitious use of standard Gothic elements occurs in his 1851 novel, *Moby-Dick*. The environmental backdrop of the novel itself—life on board the restricted *Pequod*—possesses something of the poetic quality of the haunted house, with Ahab as the one man who is lord over it. Indeed, the ship's bond with the land-locked haunted house may be felt in nearly every description of the *Pequod:* from its weather-stained hull, its venerable bows, its spire-like masts, its worn and ancient decks, to its general atmosphere of grotesqueness and somber picturesqueness. In short, the ship holds much in common with the Houses of Usher, Udolpho, or Ortranto. Moreover, the eclectic collection of sailors on board the *Pequod* are as much Ahab's captives as any incarcerated maiden trying to gain exit from the Gothic castle.

It is, however, within the actions and personality of the *Pequod*'s mad captain Ahab that Melville's most significant debt to the Gothic genre becomes apparent. A major theme running through Gothic fiction is an association of the male villain with evil forces, most specifically, the Devil. Ahab emerges as an embodiment of the fallen angel demi-god who in the Christian myth was variously named Lucifer, Devil, Adversary, Satan. Ahab is not Satan, but a human creature possessing Satan's evil pride and energy, summing up within himself, as Irenaeus said, "the apostasy of the devil." Melville's intention to beget Ahab in Satan's image can hardly be disputed. Indeed, early in the novel Elijah warns Ishmael and Queequeg to fear for their souls because a voyage with Ahab and his "shadowy figures" is certain to involve evil:

> "Yes," said I [Ishmael], "we have just signed the articles."
> "Anything down there about your souls?"
> "About what?"
> "Oh, perhaps you hav'n't got any," he said quickly. "No matter though, I know many chaps that hav'n't got any. . . . *He's* got enough, though, to make up for all deficiencies of that sort in other chaps," abruptly said the stranger, placing a nervous emphasis upon the word *he.*

Connected to the Gothic fascination with evil is a pervasive element of blasphemy. In Lewis's *The Monk,* Ambrosio is a Catholic monk who violates on top of an altar a woman masquerading as a nun. Vathek, in Beckford's novel of the same name, makes a Faustian pact with Satan in order to experience as many depraved sensations as mortal life will afford. Ahab is a continuation of this Gothic tradition in that he is an "ungodly, god-like man" who is spiritually outside Christendom. In Ahab there is a well of blasphemy and defiance, of both rejection and scorn for the gods: " 'Who's over me?' " he asks, taunting whatever inhuman forces may animate the supernatural realm. We are also told that Ahab once spat in the holy goblet on the altar of the Catholic church at Santa. In the course of the whale voyage—a journey that ironically commences on Christmas Day—Ahab engages in three blasphemous rituals. Each unholy rite incorporates the use of a harpoon (with Ahab serving in the role of high celebrant) clearly to present a blasphemous parody of a religious ritual. In the first of these rituals, "The Quarter-Deck," Ahab pours grog into the inverted ends of hollow harpoon heads and commands the harpooners to drink from the "murderous chalices" with this oath.: " 'God hunt us all, if we do not hunt Moby Dick to his death!' " And when Starbuck suggests that perhaps Ahab's quest is blasphemous, the captain snarls in a tone reminiscent of Manfred's or Melmoth's enraged pride: " 'Talk not to me of blasphemy, man; I'd strike the sun if it insulted me. For could the sun do that, then could I do the other; since there is ever a sort of fair play herein, jealousy presiding over all creations.' "

The demonical nature of Ahab's quest is again suggested in "The Forge," when Ahab baptizes a scorching harpoon in the name of the Devil. And, finally, in "The Candles" Ahab uses his consecrated harpoon to aid him in a speech of defiance, asserting his unconquerable individuality in the face of nature: " 'Oh, thou clear spirit, of thy fire thou madest me, and like a true child of fire, I breathe it back to thee. . . . Yet blindfold, yet will I talk to thee. Light though thou be, thou leapest out of darkness; but I am darkness leaping out of light, leaping out of thee!' " Like Manfred on his mountain, lightning flashes and Ahab speaks directly to it, calling it his ancestor: " 'There burn the flames! Oh, thou magnanimous! now I do glory in my genealogy. But thou art but my fiery father; my sweet mother, I know not.' " In these scenes Melville relies on standard Gothic visual effects and soundtrack: tremendous fire, blackness, storm, and battering seas; all are present, as are high emotion, conflicting beliefs, and a clash of personalities. Ahab once more establishes his link to the male-dominated world of the Gothic genre by calling the flames his father, while denying even a knowledge of a mother's milder milk.

His nexus to evil notwithstanding, there exists another side of Melville's captain that is not entirely wicked. Like Walpole's Manfred or Lewis's Ambrosio, "Ahab has his humanities!" We are told that he thinks often of his bride and daughter, and his care of the pathetic Pip reveals his compassion. These instances serve to complicate our response to Ahab and further connect him to earlier Gothic prototypes. Despite his imperious manner and narrowed perception of reality, Ahab possesses a streak of sensitivity and melancholia that is found in a number of earlier Gothic villains. Maturin's Melmoth and Lewis's Ambrosio are two illustrations of the morbidly sensitive Gothic hero whose value system is considered warped because he refuses to conform to accepted social mores. The Gothic novel thus prefigures the romantic movement insofar as it delineates the irreconcilable gap between individual psyche and societal constraints. The Gothic hero's alienation is self-imposed and socially ordained; it remains a continual source of paradox, encompassing both a sense of pride in his rising above the moral restraints of common men and a melancholic lamentation born out of prolonged isolation.

Like Manfred's, Ambrosio's, or Melmoth's, Ahab's single name suggests a lonely and sinister independence from social ties. Ahab throws overboard, loses, or smashes several social objects in the course of the voyage. Each one symbolizes the rejection of some aspect of his connection with the rest of humanity. In chapter 30, "The Pipe," Ahab realizes that he no longer can derive any pleasure from so leisurely an activity as smoking and throws his pipe into the sea. In "The Quadrant," Ahab dashes the valuable instrument to the deck and crushes it, shouting, " 'Cursed be all the things that cast man's eyes aloft to that heaven, who live vividness but scorches him.' " In both scenes Ahab, more and more obsessed with the inhuman whale, is shown displaced from human or geographical positioning in the actual world. The unsocial nature of the *Pequod*'s voyage under Ahab is stressed in the ship's encounters with the other whaling vessels. Because of Ahab's obsession, the *Pequod* is not merely unsociable, but antisocial in the literal sense:

> "Come aboard, come aboard!" cried the gay Bachelor's commander, lifting a glass and a bottle in the air.
> "Hast seen the White Whale?" gritted Ahab in reply.
> "No; only heard of him; but don't believe in him at all," said the other good-humoredly. "Come aboard!"
> "Thou art too damned jolly. Sail on. . . ."

Not simply desirous of avoiding company, but actually of attacking the very foundation and values upon which a society is built, Ahab's quest becomes a fanatical violation of both the purpose of whaling and of respect for other human beings. Ahab's attitude bears much in common with the profoundly antisocial world of the eighteenth-century Gothic novel. A primary reason that the Gothic novel remains significant to literary history is that it initiates the destruction of the social order and stability that was characteristic of the rest of the eighteenth century. The last decade of this century—with its emphasis on the breakdown of social ties, social hierarchy, conventions, and institutions—belongs more to the romantic generation of the century to follow rather than to the enlightened world of reason and societal organization. It is, after all, the decade that followed the dramatic French Revolution of 1789. The *Pequod,* then, is analogous once more to the haunted castle where the Gothic owner spends the majority of his time avoiding social company, and tending to an assortment of perverted personal quests.

If Ahab's bonds with humanity are shown to be slowly disintegrating in the course of the voyage, his links with the satanic grow proportionately stronger. His personal crew, for example—those "shadows" that Ishmael and Queequeg see board the *Pequod,*—resemble mysterious phantoms from an old Gothic romance; indeed, they are refugees taken directly from *Vathek.* The crew has a symbolic significance reflected in Ishmael's speculation: "Such a crew, so officered, seemed specially picked and packed by some infernal fatality to help [Ahab] to his revenge." Melville's most striking use of the Gothic device is his characterization of the enigmatic Fedallah, the crew's leader: "that hair-turbaned Fedallah remained a muffled mystery to the last . . . He was such a creature as civilized, domestic people in the temperate zone only see in their dreams." Fedallah seems linked to *Macbeth*'s weird sisters, especially in his talent for surrounding himself in an air of ambiguity and in stating false prophesy. Like the forces of evil in Gothic dramas, he is never clearly defined by the author but is omnipresent, lurking mainly in the background and always weaving an air of intrigue. Also, Fedallah's "presence" on board the ship grows in proportion to Ahab's nearness to the whale. We do not see him at all early in the voyage; he and his infernal crew only emerge from the *Pequod*'s shadows when it is time to go into battle against Moby Dick. Fedallah seems to represent the darkest recesses of Ahab's own psyche, emerging more as an extension of the captain's deepening madness than as an independent source of evil.

In depicting the end of Ahab's quest, Melville uses colossal effects similar to those found throughout the Gothic realm. Mrs. Radcliffe's castles inevitably vanish into forests or tarns or the reader's imagination in the conclusions of her novels. The end of *Moby-Dick,* like so many Gothic visual climaxes in Poe's tales or Walpole's *Otranto,* overwhelms the crew of the *Pequod* as well as the reader in a vortex to such intensity that it sucks everything with it, including a "living part of heaven."

> [Tashtego] kept his hammer frozen there; and so the bird of heaven, with archangelic shrieks, and his imperial beak thrust upwards, and his whole cap-tive form folded in the flag of Ahab, went down with his ship, which, like Satan, would not sink to hell till she had dragged a living part of heaven along with her.

The tale that Ishmael lives to tell, however, ultimately succeeds in transcending the restrictive Gothic world of the late eighteenth century. The genre's scope is en-larged by Melville to include a tragic dimension: Ahab goes out not simply to avenge his accident at the jaws of Moby Dick, but to revenge a world-insult, the world-wound of existence as symbolized in his leg injury: that man is a simple creature fated to dying by his very birth. Melville adds philosophical complexities to *Moby-Dick* that finally lift it out of the Gothic cesspool. But through an adaptation of standard Gothic apparatus *Moby-Dick* attains the power and dimensionality of classical tragedy.

—TONY MAGISTRALE, " 'More Demon Than Man': Melville's Ahab as
Gothic Villain," *Extrapolation* 27, No. 3 (Fall 1986): 203–7

JOSEPH ALLEN BOONE

Of course, as every reader knows, the quest for selfhood in *Moby-Dick* does not only unfold by positive example. The encompassing, fluid identity toward which Ishmael is always moving is continually counter-balanced by Ahab's rigid self-definition, as the latter character's tragically fixed purpose and fixated personality attest. Having concentrated all his energies, both emotional and libidinal, into one singularly aggressive goal, Ahab becomes the stereotype of the destructive "male" impulse, his "deepeningly contracted" personality recalling the single-minded de-termination fueling Lovelace and Heathcliff's acts of female persecution in *Clarissa* and *Wuthering Heights;* all three men, along with *Deronda*'s Grandcourt, are obsessed by varieties of erotic domination as the only means of asserting their superiority in a world in which their identity as men depends on being recognized as separate from and above any threatening "other." In the process, Melville's mad captain has replaced the potential for human relations of love and parity with violent thrusts against an imagined foe. The aim of "quest," thus perverted by

Ahab's "narrow-flowing monomania," has become, simply, one of "conquest"—a conquest as sexually charged and as self-destructive as if the arena in which it were taking place were indeed that of patriarchal marriage.

Ahab's defiant posturing specifically reveals the self-hatred that is unleashed against others when the softening influences associated with the heart, the soul, the emotions, are lost to human nature. Thus, in a speech in chapter 38 that identifies the soul's gender as female, Ahab's first mate mourns that "small touch of the human mother" and "soft feeling of the human" which he feels that Ahab, through his assumption of absolute mastery, has "overmanned" both in himself and in his crew; a few chapters later the reader is made privy to Ahab's nightmare-ridden sleep when this very "soul" attempts to escape the "integral" of which it is part, an action metaphorically leaving Ahab a divided man. The incompletion that results from the triumph of will over feeling is also figured in the symbolic castration that occurs (in the narrative time prior to the novel's opening) when Ahab loses his leg in combat with Moby Dick. On the one hand precipitating the Captain's obsession with besting the whale, this loss of limb on the other ironically reveals that the aggressive ethos to which Ahab clings is his own worst enemy. For, before sailing on the *Pequod*, Ahab is found unconscious one night, "his ivory limb having been so violently displaced, that it had . . . all but pierced his groin." The implication is clear: the aggressive behavior fostered by a culture's phallocentricism is self-destructive, rendering one psychically and physically impotent—and, hence, like Ahab, incapable of initiating positive human contact.

The degree to which the values of hatred and tumult finally supplant in Ahab those of love and inner calm embraced by Ishmael reaches a narrative climax rife with sexual implications when Ahab declares his satanic allegiance and "right worship" to "my fiery father" and rejects the power of the mother ("my sweet mother, I know not") during the terrifying storm-at-sea episode near the end of the novel. As he establishes his supremacy by waving a lightning-lit harpoon—snatched from the "conspicuous crotch" of his whaleboat and discharging "a levelled flame of pale, forked fire"—over the heads of his terrified crew, it is obvious that phallic power has become satanic, an event clinching the psychic pattern of resemblances between Ahab and his English counterparts in "masculine" diabolism—Lovelace, Heathcliff, and Grandcourt. It should come as no surprise, then, that soon afterward in the "Symphony" chapter Ahab once again rejects the momentarily softening emotions coaxed to life within him by the surrounding environment, his "hardened" resolve resurfacing "against all natural loving." By the time the climactic three-day chase begins, Ahab's identity has become more contracted than ever, impervious to change or emotion—the man has become a nightmarish embodiment of the erotic compulsion to subjugate lying behind the traditional male ethos that makes heroes of conquerors and uses power to maintain its supremacy in a gender-divided world.

Ahab's external relationships, like Ishmael's, reveal much about his inner state of being. The consequences of his only two intimate bonds (with his crazed double, the cabin boy Pip, and the mysterious Parsee, Fedallah) are presented in two tellingly juxtaposed sequences in chapters 129 and 130. Pip's schizophrenia, the result of having internalized fears of displaying unmanly cowardice when abandoned during a sea chase, awakens Ahab's long-dormant compassion, and the captain's offer to make his cabin Pip's "home" is a symbolic drawing together, a momentary act of union, signaling his unconscious recognition that Pip's presence evokes a missing part of his own identity. But the very feelings awakened by Pip lead the captain to sever the bond because "there is that in thee, poor lad, which I feel too curing to my malady . . . and for this hunt, my malady becomes my most desired health." In contrast to the healing that Queequeg's similarly generous love brings to Ishmael's splintered heart, Ahab's diseased drive for conquest demands the expulsion of the weaker or unmanly impulse of love that Pip's presence has inspired in him. The price of Ahab's decision, however, as Pip's reply makes clear, is a denial of wholeness. "Ye have not a whole body, sir," the boy declares in one of his madly true statements that reflects on Ahab's psychic well-being as much as his physical body; "I ask no more [than that] I remain a part of ye." In the immediately following chapter, Ahab's evil alter ego, the shadow-figure Fedallah, comes to the fore as his rightful mate in an antagonistic dance of polar opposites in which, at first glance, Ahab appears as the "lord . . . [and] the Parsee but his slave," but in which Fedallah has actually gained ascendancy over Ahab's will. Fearful of the truth lying in the adage that "like cures like," Ahab turns from Pip's benign influence to an imprisoning bond that ironically reproduces the paradigm of love relationship as a struggle of opposites, and in so doing dooms himself to a fight to the death.

—JOSEPH ALLEN BOONE, "Moby-Dick: The Great American Love Story,"
Tradition Counter Tradition: Love and the Form of Fiction
(Chicago: University of Chicago Press, 1987), pp. 247–50

DAVID S. REYNOLDS

Scholars have long sought historical prototypes for several scenes and characters, but the results have often proved contradictory. Ahab, for instance, has been variously associated with the radical abolitionist William Lloyd Garrison, with Garrison's archopponent John C. Calhoun, and with the moderate politician Daniel Webster! Such historical source study can be delimiting, for the fact is that *Moby-Dick* moves beyond slavery or antislavery, protemperance or antitemperance—in short, beyond programmatic reform—to a literary realm in which subversive reform *energy* and *rhetoric*, rather than reform *message*, becomes the literary artist's central concern. In this context, a passage in Father Mapple's sermon can be taken as a gloss on Melville's attitude toward the dark-reform style. Toward the end of his sermon Father Mapple declares: "Woe to him who seeks to pour oil upon the waters when God has brewed them into a gale! Woe to him who seeks to please rather than to appal!" We have seen that from the 1830s onward, there had been a linguistic split between Conventional reformers (mainly Unitarians and rationalists), whose style was determinedly staid, and Subversive ones (particularly evangelicals and other so-called ultraists), who tried through stylistic violence to combat and overwhelm the irrationalism and ugliness of various social iniquities. Often Conventional reformers would directly lament the linguistic violence of their op- ponents, as when Lydia Maria Child wished to found a temperate antislavery paper as an antidote to "the wild spirit of ultraism" represented by Garrisonian abolition- ists, whose rhetoric she found "irrational, unphilosophic, impracticable, mischie- vous." She was praised in her efforts toward Conventional antislavery by a friend who wrote: "You are just the editor we want. We need oil upon the waves" since "we have had too much of fighting." In contrast, the Subversive reformers—from McDowall through Garrison to Mike Walsh and George Lippard—repeatedly de- nounced what they labeled "puny" or "effeminate" reformers whom they regarded as too timid to clench vice strongly and reproduce all its lurid horrors on the page. Father Mapple's real-life prototype, Father Taylor, was himself a roughneck re- former reportedly more at home jousting verbally with barroom drunkards than sermonizing to polite congregations. When Melville has Mapple lambaste those who would "pour oil upon the waters" he is aligning himself with the Subversive tradition.

The many explicit reform devices in *Moby-Dick,* therefore, are pushed to- ward literariness by Melville's devotion to the Subversive style, which formed a rhetorical sub-basis connecting *all* dark-reform writings. As a result, some of his central images seem titanic versions of dark-reform images. While it is misleading to equate Ahab either with the abolitionist Garrison or with the proslavery leader Calhoun, it is certainly possible to connect him with the suprapolitical, powerfully human volatility that linked Garrison, Calhoun, and many other clamorous reform orators as well. When Ahab is described paradoxically as an "ungodly, god-like man" or a "swearing good man," it may be useful to know that Daniel Webster had been famously satirized by one popular exposé novelist as "Gabriel Godlike," who seems noble but is in fact evil; but it is even more important to understand Ahab as the era's most fully developed oxymoronic character, attaining a kind of univer- sality from the magnitude of the contrary impulses he embodies. This amplification of reform devices is perhaps best seen in Melville's use of mythic images. We saw that in popular reform literature, mythic imagery increasingly took on an indepen- dent life. The following metaphors from an 1847 New York exposé are typical:

> The dark swelling tempest which rages over the wildest sea, is not more dissimilar from the tranquil ocean, when not a wave ripples, nor a breath fans the sails, than is the community of men, when surveyed at different times, and in varying aspects. All seems bright, and good, and glorious, to the superficial looker on, while to the experienced inquirer, and the laborious collector of facts, there is a dark understratum of guilt, and a wide expanse of material that is decayed, corrupt, offensive, and revolting . . . [as in the case of prostitutes, where] extremes meet in the same individual woman. Outward splendor covers internal sorrow. Flagrant vice walks forth in public places under the mantle and veil of virtue . . . [Apparently healthy womanhood] is but a mere

vulgar compound of paint and silk and pasteboard, an image artificially made up.

Like numerous dark-reform passages, this one verges on the literary because its supposed message (the lamentable rise of prostitution) is virtually smothered by images of the ocean, the swelling tempest, hidden corruption, cheating appearances, cosmetics, pasteboard coverings, and so forth. We should not be surprised that many of these images sound pre-Melvillian, for Melville in his early works has proved himself a uniquely flexible experimenter with dark-reform stances, preparing himself for the truly mythic subversiveness of *Moby-Dick*. The ungodly, godlike Ahab pursuing the demonic, divine white whale figuratively enacts the highly charged ironies of antebellum reform culture, in which pursuit of moral truth was often waged in a kind of divine madness, a righteous unrighteousness.

Ultimately, Melville in *Moby-Dick* is a gigantic dark reformer, towering above all reform programs but driven by the powerful reform impulse. If other reformers "lifted the veil" off social corruption or lamented the "pasteboard" artificiality of certain people, Melville has Ahab describe all visible objects as "pasteboard masks" and declare that man's highest goal is to "strike through the mask." In this sense, the object of Ahab's quest is the ultimate dark-reform mythic image, which now has been granted a full independent life and an alluringly malevolent moral will of its own. The white whale brings together all the "whales" swimming in all the turbulent "oceans" described by the image-fashioning ultraists. If reformers had regularly seen surrounding society as a "whited sepulchre" hiding submerged evil, so the white whale is invested with the most apparently benign but most ultimately subversive qualities, suggesting to Ishmael that "all deified Nature absolutely paints like the harlot, whose allurements cover nothing but the charnel-house within." If the popular reformers liberally used post-Calvinist imagery, Melville secularly enacts the Calvinist God itself, as the whole novel culminates in the destruction of Ahab and his crew by the "predestinating head" of Moby Dick, which is alive with "[r]etribution, swift vengeance, eternal malice." In the end, the liberated reform *vehicle*, released totally into mythic ambiguity, turns upon the equally liberated moral *tenor*, seeking desperately for connection with moral truth but lost hopelessly in its own paradoxes.

> —DAVID S. REYNOLDS, "Melville's Whited Sepulchres: The Stylization of Reform," *Beneath the American Renaissance: The Subversive Imagination in the Age of Emerson and Melville* (New York: Knopf, 1988), pp. 156–59

WAI-CHEE DIMOCK

Ahab is a monstrous reader, as a number of critics have suggested; his monomania threatens to reduce indeterminate text to determinate meaning. His goal is to penetrate "that inscrutable thing," the "impregnable, uninjurable wall" that is both whale and text: "If man will strike, strike through the mask! How can the prisoner reach outside except by thrusting through the wall? To me, the white whale is that wall, shoved near to me." If Ahab were to have his way, the category of the "inviolate" would exist no more, and neither doubloon, nor ambergris, nor even a literary text, could find refuge in it. That would be a blow indeed to Melville. For this, if for no other reason, Ahab is doomed never to have his way. *Moby-Dick,* in that respect, once again allegorizes the author's battle for sovereignty. It also allegorizes his revenge on the reader.

Ahab's sins, as a reader or otherwise, have been abundantly documented. My focus in this chapter, however, will not be on those sins, but on the punitive logic his author administers. To dispatch Ahab, to disarm him, to make him die not only inevitably but also deservedly, Melville needs an executory instrument, a logic that explains and justifies the fate of this character. That logic is only too easy to come by, for it is already a provision in individualism. What we might expect to find in Ahab is an individualism that afflicts its bearer, one that apprehends and incriminates, one that disciplines the self in its very freedom. And that, in fact, is what we do find.

Being a product of individualism, Ahab is by definition a free agent. But, since his individualism happens to be the negative variety, he is, also by definition, an overdetermined character. He is both doomed and free: free, that is, to choose his doom. This is a strange logic, to say the least, but within the terms of negative individualism, nothing is more reasonable, or more necessary, for such a logic—a logic that inscribes discipline in freedom—is just what makes the autonomous self governable as such. Embracing this logic, *Moby-Dick* will find itself in intimate communion with antebellum America, for both the text and the nation agree about what it means to be "doomed"—about the cause, character, and trajectory of that unfortunate condition.

The narrative of doom in *Moby-Dick* comes into play even before Ahab appears. His ship is introduced with the accompanying information that *"Pequod,* you will no doubt remember, was the name of a celebrated tribe of Massachusetts Indians, now extinct as the ancient Medes." The crucial words here are "now extinct"—and it is crucial, too, that the word should be "extinct," rather than "exterminated." "Extermination" betrays the work of an exterminator; "extinction," on the other hand, suggests a natural process, as if time alone were responsible for this fated course of events. Melville is not alone in favoring the word. As we have noted, Andrew Jackson had used the same word in his Second Annual Message (1830) to defend his Indian policy. "To follow to the tomb the last of his race and to tread on the graves of extinct nations excite melancholy reflections," Jackson admitted, but quickly added that "true philanthropy reconciles the mind . . . to the extinction of one generation to make room for another." The usefulness of the term becomes even clearer in the following observation by Benjamin Lincoln, the Revolutionary general from Massachusetts. Commenting on the imminent demise of the Indians, he predicted:

If the savages cannot be civilized and quit their present pursuits, they will, in consequence of their stubbornness, dwindle and moulder away, from causes perhaps imperceptible to us, until the whole race shall become extinct.

Dying from "imperceptible" causes, Indians obligingly solved the problem for white settlers. "Extinction" is what happens in an autotelic universe: it naturalizes the category of the "doomed," not only by recuperating it as an evolutionary category but, most crucially, by locating the cause for extinction within the extinct organism itself. If Indians die out it is their own fault. Their extinction is a function of their "stubbornness," their benighted refusal to quit their savage ways. This is the logic of blaming the victim; within the terms of our discussion, we might also call it the logic of negative individualism. The strategy here is to equate phenomenon with locus, to collapse cause and casualty into an identical unit, to make the Indian at once the scene and the agent of his own destruction. No less than the whale, the Indian too is a self-contained figure. He is both necessary and sufficient for his own condition: his impending doom refers to nothing other than his own savage self.

The Indian, as he is described by antebellum ethnographers and politicians, is therefore always the subject of a predestined narrative, in which he is responsible for, guilty of, and committed to a fated course of action, in which he appears not only as both victim and culprit, but also as a legible sign of his own inexorable end. Negative individualism could have found no better exponent. Ahab's kinship with the Indian is, under the circumstances, only to be expected. A single narrative works for both, for like the doomed savage, Ahab too is a product of negative individualism. He too is a victim of his own fault, and an instrument of his own fate. *Moby-Dick,* then, is not just a story of doom, but the story of a particular kind of doom, self-chosen and self-inflicted. As such, it has more than a little in common with another story of doom, Francis Parkman's *The Conspiracy of Pontiac,* a book also published in 1851, one written to record the "final doom" of those "destined to melt and vanish before the advancing waves of Anglo-American power."

The *Pequod* is, for that reason, a "cannibal of a craft," "apparelled like any barbaric Ethiopian emperor," and manned by a "barbaric, heathenish, and motley" crew, repulsive in the "barbaric brilliancy of their teeth" and their "uncivilized laughter." Less civilized still are the five "tiger-yellow barbarians" reserved for Ahab's whaleboat. Such barbaric trappings are obviously meant to suggest something about Ahab himself; in "The Try-Works" we are expressly told that "the rushing *Pequod,* freighted with savages, and laden with fire, and burning a corpse, and plunging into that blackness of darkness, seemed the material counterpart of her monomaniac commander's soul." Ahab, indeed, is not without savage airs of his own. He walks on a "barbaric white leg," for instance, and even though we do not ordinarily think of him as being animal-like, he has been shown on occasions to manifest a "sudden, passionate, corporal animosity," and to emit a "terrific, loud, animal sob, like that of a heart-stricken moose."

All the same, Ahab's barbarism has to do less with his "animosity" than with what Melville in *White-Jacket* has referred to as "barbarous feudal aristocracy," a condition associated with Czarist Russia, "immovable China," and to some extent England. Ahab's "dictatorship" is best understood in this context—in the equation between "barbarism" and "feudal aristocracy." Given such a definition, the repeated references to Ahab as "Khan of the plank," "sultan," and "Grand Turk" are nothing if not ominous. More verdict than tribute, such allusions hardly describe Ahab: they merely brand him as a thing of the past. At once regal and barbaric, he takes his place among other candidates for extinction. "Social czarship," "sultan's step," and "Egyptian chest" all conspire to make him a hopeless anomaly (and a sure casualty) in the age of the "Nantucket market." Barbarians are doomed, in *Moby-Dick* as in antebellum America, because they have outlived their allotted time span, because their very nobility marks them as anachronistic. The Indian (John Quincy Adams called him the "lordly savage") perished not in spite of but because of his "stateliness," his "heroic virtues," his "fine figure, commanding voice, noble beauty." Ahab perishes because he inhabits "the nameless regal overbearing dignity of some mighty woe"—because, where feudalism equals barbarism, regality *is* woe.

The constellations of terms that seal Ahab's fate are therefore exactly those that sealed the fate of the Indians. Yet seeing Ahab as an allegory of the Indian would be wrong, for the representational relation here is not so much one between the two as one encompassing both of them. Both are encompassed, that is, by a punitive representation of the self, what I have called negative individualism. Thus filiated in their genesis, Ahab and the Indians logically share a common end. We might speak of this punitive representation as broadly allegorical, for it operates through a set of signifying attributes, out of which it produces both "persons" and "destinies." Indeed, if we are right to detect in *Moby-Dick* a "hideous and intolerable allegory" (whose existence Melville denies), that allegory works, I believe, primarily as an economy of ascription, as the production of narrative through the assignment of attributes. Ahab and the Indians are both bearers of attributes. They happen to inhabit two (apparently) disparate realms, one literary and the other social, but that fact finally matters less than the attributes they share. Those attributes make them analogous characters, produce them as analogous signs, and inflict on them analogous narratives—narratives of extinction.

Ahab's archaic speech (like the eloquence so often ascribed to Indians) is therefore only another signifying attribute, another sign of his doom. At stake here is more than a question of language, for what the language embodies is actually an outmoded syntax of being. At its most memorable, this syntax takes the form of Ahab's famous resolve: to "dismember my dismemberer." This syntax of vengeance makes Ahab the coeval of "sultans" and "Khans," for vengeance is the alleged code of the primitive. "Vengeance, and fortitude ... are duties which [Indians] consider as sacred," Jedidiah Morse reported in his much-reprinted article on "America" in the American edition (1790) of the *Encyclopaedia.* In agreement, Francis Parkman noted that "revenge" was one of the "ruling passions" among Indians. It was this passion that he dwelled on, at the end of *The Conspiracy of*

Pontiac, as he imagined the "savage spirit" of Pontiac revisiting the scene of his murder and exulting in the "vengeance which overwhelmed the abettors of the crime," even as other tribes gathered to "revenge his fate." In a somewhat different vein, René Girard also suggests that "primitive societies have only private vengeance." It is this primitive obsession that sets Ahab apart, and spells his doom. Captain Boomer of the *Samuel Enderby,* a man unburdened by such primitive obsession, appears, in this regard, not only as a contrast to Ahab, but also as a salient example of doom averted:

> "No, thank ye, Bunger," said the English Captain, "he's welcome to the arm he has, since I can't help it, and didn't know him then; but not to another one. No more White Whales for me; I've lowered for him once, and that has satisfied me. There would be great glory in killing him, I know that; and there is a shipload of precious sperm in him, but, hark ye, he's best let alone; don't you think so, Captain?"

Vengeance clearly means nothing to Captain Boomer. Indeed, if he were ever to hunt Moby Dick again, it would not be for revenge, but for glory and profit— glory, in killing what no one has so far managed to kill, and profit, already beckoning in that "shipload of precious sperm." Both in what he values and in what he dismisses, Captain Boomer stands as a rebuke to Ahab. In that capacity he comically echoes Starbuck, for it is Starbuck, that eminently unprimitive character, who objects most strenuously to the idea of vengeance. What he says is this, "I came here to hunt whales, not my commander's vengeance. How many barrels will thy vengeance yield thee even if thou gettest it, Captain Ahab? it will not fetch thee much in our Nantucket market."

Vengeance is wrong because it is unprofitable, Starbuck reasons. This is not simply crass materialism, either, for in spite of the talk about "barrels," about what vengeance will "yield" and "fetch," Starbuck is concerned with profit less as an end in itself than as a signifying economy, by which things can be calibrated, their meanings affixed, and their values ascertained. Only such an economy will permit Starbuck to assess Ahab's vengeance and reject it for its deficient value. And only such an economy will permit violence to end. Starbuck's strategy, in other words, is always to resist vengeance-as-vengeance, always to position it within a system of exchange. Vengeance can be validated, according to him, only if it can be substituted—only if it can be exchanged—for a different set of terms, like its value on the Nantucket market.

Ahab, of course, has no use for substitution and exchange. His universe is one of mimetic repetition: in trying to dismember his dismemberer, he is trying to be like the whale, to do what the whale has done to him. Vengeance affirms the primacy of temporal continuity, of mimesis in time. Starbuck, with no desire to imitate a "dumb brute," rejects not only mimesis but also the very idea of "continuity." Starbuck is an Emerson in the whaling business, we might say, and Emerson's defiant wish to be "an endless seeker with no Past at my back" might have served equally well as his motto. Like Emerson, Starbuck cultivates the art of discontinuity, the art of discrete substitution. Exchanging the whale (or vengeance on the whale) with what it will "fetch," he brings together two separate terms, the whale and its market value, and substitutes one for the other. There is no resemblance, of course, between the two terms, not even a logical connection, but that is precisely the point. Substitution, even as it exchanges one term for another, affirms the primacy of discontinuity.

> —WAI-CHEE DIMOCK, "Blaming the Victim," *Empire for Liberty:*
> *Melville and the Poets of Individualism* (Princeton:
> Princeton University Press, 1988), pp. 114–20

BRUCE L. GRENBERG

Ahab's initial physical engagement with Moby Dick defines his character throughout the novel. Ahab comes to identify with the whale "not only all his bodily woes, but all his intellectual and spiritual exasperations." His "torn body and gashed soul" bleeding into each other, Ahab is made mad. Ahab's "monomania" is characterized not by an idea but by a commitment to action: he sails upon the *Pequod* "with the one and only and all-engrossing object of hunting the White Whale." This murderous singleness of purpose characterizes Ahab throughout the narrative; every word he utters goads the crew in their unknowing but willing pursuit of Moby Dick, and his every act is seen as a step toward the ultimate confrontation with his "Job's whale."

Ahab's dramatic dimensions are grand—even overwhelming—and it is easy to forget that his character is essentially unadorned. Ishmael's "poor ole whale-hunter," still moving before him in "all his Nantucket grimness and shagginess," is elemental "man acting," stripped of complex motivations. Ahab's singleness of purpose defines both his grandeur and his madness. The man who can say "the path to my fixed purpose is laid with iron rails, whereon my soul is grooved to run" holds an irresistible attraction for those facing so many paths to so many questionable purposes. He attracts the crew of the *Pequod*. And he attracts us. But the chapter in which Ahab speaks of his iron way contains the equally powerful image of the "Iron Crown of Lombardy." This crown, with its "far flashings" of dazzling, confounding power, suggests just how dear a price Ahab must pay for his single-minded dedication. Committed to his iron way, Ahab is neither spurred by sunrise nor soothed by sunset; committed wholly to one purpose, Ahab finds all other purposes meaningless: he is "damned, most subtly and most malignantly! damned in the midst of Paradise!"

Throughout the body of the narrative Ahab maintains his unswerving pursuit of his nemesis. He gives up his pipe, that thing "meant for sereneness, to send up mild white vapors among mild white hairs." He pores over his charts, plotting the course of Fate, prefiguring in his dreams his final confrontation with Moby Dick.

Sleeping "with clenched hands" and waking "with his own bloody nails in his palms," Ahab is, indeed, self-crucifying—sacrificing his common humanity to his soul-devouring purpose.

In many ways Ahab's obsessive quest for his nemesis might be viewed as a protracted suicide. Seeking what all others flee (one thinks instantly of the Town-Ho story, of Captain Boomer, and of the *Rachel*), Ahab is whittled away to the very rudiments of his manhood. At times, as in "The Candles," he seems little more than vivified apparatus, cursed with a sense of his own wearing down. But Ahab is not "technological man," and Melville is not depicting the death struggle between doomed Nature and self-destructive technology. Quite to the contrary, as the *Pequod* approaches the ocean home of Moby Dick, Ahab becomes more and more primitive in his weapons, more and more naked in his defenses.

The scenes of Ahab with Perth, the carpenter, do not subdue, but rather intensify our sense of Ahab's naked mortality. Perth, the Carpenter-God, can give Ahab only what "chisel, file, and sand-paper" allow. A perverse parody of the god Ahab both curses and worships in "The Candles," Perth is a "pure manipulator," working "by a kind of deaf and dumb, spontaneous literal process"—"living without premeditated reference to this world or the next." As such, he cannot comprehend, let alone satisfy, Ahab's order for a "complete man."

Ahab's ideal man answers to his own sense of what he lacks. Being old, crippled, and weak, he envisions a man "fifty feet high in his socks" with a chest "modelled after the Thames Tunnel." A seaman all his life, he longs for "legs with roots to 'em, to stay in one place." Most important, his ideal man would have "no heart at all, brass forehead, and about a quarter of an acre of fine brains"—no eyes to see outward, but "a sky-light on top of his head to illuminate inwards." Lacking all these, Ahab prophetically concludes, "By heavens! I'll get a crucible, and into it, and dissolve myself down to one small, compendious vertebra. So."

On at least this one issue Ahab and Starbuck see eye to eye. In "The Quadrant" Starbuck reinforces this image of the crucible with his own observation on Ahab: "Old man of oceans! of all this fiery life of thine, what will at length remain but one little heap of ashes!" And it is this compression of Ahab's character into the lowest common denominator of selfhood that gives such intensity to his final confrontation with Moby Dick. Ahab's compression of self into one all-including act of revenge compresses his entire world. Between his first meeting with Moby Dick and his second, time for Ahab does not exist. Between the place of their first meeting and their second there is no space. And thus, insofar as we identify with Ahab, the three-day chase that concludes the novel's narrative action has all the density of life itself, with its myriad unspoken truths implicit in every breath, every move. Everything we know, imagine, and surmise about Ahab is instinct in his maddened harpooning of Moby Dick. In a literal sense there is only this *one* action in *Moby-Dick*: Ahab's harpooning of the white whale and being towed to his death. The will to this one act dominates Ahab's every motion, and in turn Ahab commands the *Pequod*'s every tack. It is not only fitting therefore, but also dramatically necessary, that the *Pequod* and her crew follow Ahab—to be wrapped in "the great shroud of the sea."

—BRUCE L. GRENBERG, *"Moby-Dick:* An Utter-Wreck," *Some Other World
to Find: Quest and Negation in the Works of Herman Melville*
(Urbana: University of Illinois Press, 1989), pp. 106–8

PAMELA SCHIRMEISTER

In an obvious sense, the whole of *Moby-Dick* is a commentary on the myth of Narcissus, but that is primarily Ahab's story. That the whale is at least in part an elaborate projection of Ahab himself cannot be doubted, and his attempt to capture that projection leads quite traditionally to death by drowning. But Narcissus has many stories, and it is significant that Melville chooses the simplest of these, that of the beautiful youth who dies for love of his own image. So great is Melville's solipsistic vision, certainly as great as Emerson's, that in this book no third person appears. Tiresias, Nemesis, Ameinias, Echo—all of the figures brought to us from Ovid down through the Renaissance mythographers are absent. There is only the self and the image thereof. The focus is on the purely reflective aspect of Narcissus, on what Tzvetan Todorov has called "the questions of the 'I'" as opposed to "the questions of the 'You.'"

Questions of the "I" are essentially also questions of the eye, questions of vision. The identity of Narcissus, is, after all, constituted solely by what he sees. That Melville conceives of his characters in this image, as visualizing agents, is perhaps clearest in *The Confidence-Man,* where he reflects on character as "a revolving Drummond light, raying away from itself all round it." Not surprisingly, *Moby-Dick* too is a novel full of gazers—Ahab on deck; Ishmael on the masthead; Starbuck, Stubb, and Queequeg at the rail or before the doubloon.

In fact, the chapter entitled "The Doubloon" illustrates quite well some of the consequences of making Narcissus the presiding genius of the novel. In the simplest sense, "The Doubloon" is a study in subjectivity and relativity, each viewer interpreting the doubloon in the image of himself. But when character is stripped of all function except vision, and when what it sees is always itself, subjectivity ceases to be an adequate term. When Ahab pauses before the gold piece nailed to the mast, he reflects how each of its markings—mountain, tower, volcano—represents himself: "All are Ahab; and this round gold is but the image of the rounder globe, which, like a magician's glass, to each and every man in turn but mirrors back his own mysterious self. Great pains, small gains for those who ask the world to solve them." Expanding his capacity for vision until it encompasses all things, Ahab rightly represents himself as an actual place, first as the geographical features on the doubloon, and by extension as the world itself. But Ahab is a place in at least several senses, for the representation, as accurate as can be, shows us that the self as Narcissus is always a place, always a locus of vision, in both the Emersonian and Jamesian sense.

It is a place in which one stands and from which one sees, almost a literal point of view and no more. Melville presents Ahab as a catastrophically inverted prolepsis of Isabel Archer "motionlessly *seeing*," and what he sees can show Ahab no image but his own. That there is no world but the one projected by each man's vision is not fanciful but necessary; if the self can see only itself, the world can be reduced to the point that is the self, to the Drummond light raying itself on all things.

In theory, the equation promised between the self and the world should be commutative; it could be balanced on the side of the self or the world. But Melville carries this solipsistic reduction (perhaps expansion is the likelier trope) to an extreme that undoes the dialectic between inside and outside. The doubloon is, after all, a substitute for Moby Dick, who remains, like the rest of nature, to solve the puzzle of Ahab. Nature, or anything that Emerson would have called the "Not Me," may exist, but only insofar as it can solve or read the self for itself. Thus the central chapter on cetology: the whale is classified by the duodecimal system, made into a revision of the Book of Nature that insists that the chief subject of speculation throughout the novel, the whale, can teach us nothing that is not ourselves. The whale is a book in which we read ourselves, much as Queequeg, Ahab in "The Chart," and even the whale in "The Funeral" are texts to be read, so long as they are objects of perception, mirrors of the seeing self.

This will be true no matter what Ahab, or any Narcissus, beholds, including other texts, which can be incorporated as properties of the self no less than nature can be. Without going into the extensive and already well-considered question of Shakespearean influence in *Moby-Dick,* I would speculate that one of the reasons why Melville so blithely and obviously incorporates a Shakespearean rhetoric is that he does not privilege it over anything else. Ahab's cadences in the above passage are resoundingly those of Lear or Macbeth, but since Ahab is the world, he can certainly be a Shakespearean character as well. And like Ahab, Melville willingly takes himself and his book for the world, without any doubts about his own capacity. Melville's sense of that capacity may in fact be gauged by the very emphasis he places on Shakespeare, or any other precursor for that matter. In a letter to Evert Duyckinck, written just before *Moby-Dick* was completed, he said, "The truth is that we are all sons, grandsons, or nephews or great-nephews of those who go before us. No one is his own sire." Sadly not, and yet Melville is here arguing the negligibility of that fact. In *Moby-Dick,* his overt Shakespearizing, as he would have called it, implies a similar stance. It is almost as if Melville wished to be overdetermined, in order to show that he could become the very precursors he sought to incorporate. In later work, such as "The Piazza," Melville would learn how to criticize his project of willed overdetermination, but in *Moby-Dick* he simply takes everything as his own. This is part of the charm of the book, which would otherwise and elsewhere seem like mere rhetorical bullying (and in a sense, it is). In short, a supremely solipsistic stance precludes the possibility of anxiety, influential, or otherwise.

To be on the sea, then, or anywhere else in *Moby-Dick,* is to be in the self, even when self and sea would seem to be opposed. Traditionally speaking, water is a dangerous element for any Narcissus, and although the crew of the *Pequod* does not escape drowning, when Melville pretends to oppose sea and self, water and land, the opposition will eventually be internalized to form a revelatory union. Thus in "The Grand Armada," the chapter that presents the *Pequod* most fully as a self-sufficient world, we discover that the ship carries its own water, as if the one element that might mediate and alienate desire could be internalized. A more thoroughgoing example occurs in "Brit," which Melville opens by likening the brit-eating right whales to mowers, thus linking the sea to the land, but only so he may then say that in this respect alone are the creatures of the deep and the creatures of the shore similar. As the chapter continues, he turns the sea, the actual sea in which sharks live and shadows glide, into a monstrous antagonism against the land-creature, man. As such, "Brit" would constitute a brief meditation on the alienated object world, a sorrow typically suffered by Narcissus himself. And yet as the chapter closes, Melville modulates his figure. The sea and the land no longer oppose each other as nature and man, but as a division within the self:

> Consider all this; and then turn to this green, gentle, and most docile earth; consider them both, the sea and the land; and do you not find a strange analogy to something in yourself? For as this appalling ocean surrounds the verdant land, so in the soul of man there lies one insular Tahiti, full of peace and joy, but encompassed by all the horrors of the half known life. God keep thee! Push not off from that isle, thou canst never return.

Like many passages, this one again turns the sea into a figure for the self, but the language here is slippery. The sea is not something other that has temporarily come to stand for the self, but rather a wholly internal property, coexisting alongside other properties all *within* the self.

This paragraph presents a powerful figure for unchallenged solipsism, and yet, even as Melville rhetorically elides the natural world, he closes with a warning. The internalized union created here is illusory in that it exists solely and self-consciously in language; it is a trick of Melville's very tricky rhetoric, and Melville admits as much with his mention of analogy. More often than not, Melville attempts to maintain the illusion of perfect solipsism, but a single moment of deflation is enough to indicate his self-awareness on the matter. Here is Ishmael, on the masthead:

> At last he loses his identity; takes the mystic ocean at his feet for the visible image of that deep, blue, bottomless soul, pervading mankind and nature ... In this enchanted mood, thy spirit ebbs away to whence it came; becomes diffused through time and space; like Wickliff's sprinkled Pantheistic ashes, forming at last a part of every shore the round globe over.
>
> There is no life in thee, now, except that rocking life imparted by a gently rolling ship; by her, borrowed from the sea; by the sea, from the inscrutable tides of God. But while this sleep, this dream is on ye, move your foot or hand

an inch; slip your hold at all; and your identity comes back in horror. Over Descartian vortices you hover.

Posted on the masthead for the purpose of seeing whales, the Pantheist of Ishmael's description, a true Narcissus, becomes nothing but a seer—of the multiplicity of images that are himself. I do not argue for a hard logic but wish to reiterate what seems so often to be the case when the self has assumed a purely visionary function as it does here: it must be represented as a place. In this passage, as in much of James and Emerson, place is a figure for comprehensiveness, for limits transcended and possibility achieved. But as the first paragraph moves toward the diffusion that allows the self to be everywhere and everything at once, the second paragraph counters with contraction. By transcending its immediate location—the masthead—the self moves into a different sphere that we might rightly associate with romance, with the mental landscape, or, as Melville calls it, "true" place, which is never on any map. But no sooner has Melville arrived there than he withdraws. The masthead vision is illusion, dependent on a place in which illusion cannot be recognized as such. With one slip, with the simple perspective that comes from moving an inch to the left or right, the illusion evaporates and threatens what was once the all-seeing self with its own fragility.

In a chapter like "The Masthead"—and surely in the fate of Ahab—Melville would seem to be expressing a deep skepticism about the very premises with which he sets sail. To be on the sea is to be in the self, but to be wholly within the self is to court disaster. Not only is perfect solipsism based on illusion, but the illusion, as the old myth tells us again and again, can only bring death. When Hawthorne confronted the nature and power of illusion in "Feathertop," his conclusion was much the same. No sooner does the illusory Feathertop catch sight of himself in the mirror than, quite literally, he goes to pieces.

Generally speaking, I would think that most readers find Melville of a far more negative sensibility than Hawthorne, and yet, at least in *Moby-Dick,* his sympathies are still with the visionaries of this world, even if they are Ahabs. Very near the close of the novel, Ahab is on deck with the carpenter at night, waiting for his new peg leg to be completed. Ahab greets him as "manmaker," and, seeing that the work is good, proceeds to commission not just a leg for himself but a whole new man. A fifty-foot giant with a brass forehead, acres of brains, and no heart, this creature is no mechanical Florimell, but rather a strangely literalized version of Emerson's giant and Hawthorne's Ethan Brand. And yet the man-monster is not an entirely repellent figure. Considering the question of eyes, Ahab decides against them and commissions instead "a sky-light on top of his head to illuminate inwards." The carpenter understands nothing of what Ahab says, and Melville ironically has him call to the blacksmith for a lantern, as if literally to supply the two missing eyes of Ahab's conception. Irritated by the outward light, Ahab nonetheless praises the carpenter:

Thrusted light is worse than presented pistols.

> ... but no;—a very tidy, and, I may say, an extremely gentlemanlike sort
> of business thou art in here, carpenter;—or would'st thou rather work in clay?
> Sir?—Clay? clay, sir? That's mud; we leave clay to ditchers, sir.
> The fellow's impious! What art thou sneezing about?

Perhaps thrusted light is worse than presented pistols because it robs the self of its own true visionary function. With his preference for inner light, Ahab would thus see the carpenter as divine creator, but here and throughout the chapter the carpenter sneezes at the dust generated by his file and the bone, as if allergic to his own work. Blind to his potential role as manmaker, he is the most literal-minded of creators, working the empty materiality of bone and wood alike, incapable of sustaining even a modest illusion. The price is high. A far more negative figure than Mother Rigby, the carpenter is a man whom Melville describes as "a stript abstract; an unfractioned integral," working by "spontaneous literal process." An alternative to Ahab, who admittedly knows his own mechanical moments, the carpenter surely represents Melville's own highly ironic vision of the romancer's art.

And yet Ahab's visionary impatience prevents us from accepting the carpenter's wooden work as Melville's own. It is true that Ahab can himself generate no more than a somewhat monstrous figure, but if the mechanical operation of the spirit is the alternative to Ahab's imaginative solipsism, Melville still prefers the latter. He may not fully trust it, but in *Moby-Dick* we see him again and again "trying out" the limits and consequences of the romance that is the visionary.

—PAMELA SCHIRMEISTER, "Ahab and the Carpenter," *The Consolations of Space:
The Place of Romance in Hawthorne, Melville, and James*
(Stanford: Stanford University Press, 1990), pp. 101–7

F. O. Matthiessen

THE FATE OF THE UNGODLY GOD-LIKE MAN

Notwithstanding the depth of his feeling for 'the kingly commons,' Melville knew the strength of the contrast between the great individual and the inert mass. He expressed it in Ahab's power to coerce all the rest within the sphere of 'the Leyden jar of his own magnetic life.' Melville himself was caught and fascinated by his hero. He asserted from the outset that he was dealing with 'a man of greatly superior natural force, with a globular brain and a ponderous heart... one in a whole nation's census—a mighty pageant creature, formed for noble tragedies.' To such lengths did he go in building up his old whale hunter to the stature of a Shakespearean king. But he was struck at the same time by the obverse side, and concluded his first adumbration of the still unseen captain by adding that 'all men tragically great are made so through a certain morbidness. Be sure of this, O young ambition, all mortal greatness is but disease.'

This electric attraction and repulsion runs through Melville's whole portrayal from the moment when, in this same chapter describing Ishmael's first boarding of the ship, Captain Peleg forewarns him that Captain Ahab is 'a grand, ungodly, god-like man... Ahab's above the common; Ahab's been in colleges, as well as 'mong the cannibals; been used to deeper wonders than the waves.' He hints to the awed sailor that Ahab has had moody and savage spells since the loss of his leg; but tells him not to be afraid, for though Ahab is not a pious good man like Captain Bildad, he is a swearing good one. 'Besides, my boy, he has a wife—not three voyages wedded—a sweet, resigned girl. Think of that; by that sweet girl that old man has a child: hold ye then there can be any utter, hopeless harm in Ahab? No, no, my lad; stricken, blasted, if he be, Ahab has his humanities.'

The implications of the contrasting terms, 'ungodly' and 'god-like,' come out only as we follow the captain's subsequent career. But their very choice shows Melville's sensitiveness to what was happening in his time. Anyone concerned with

From *American Renaissance: Art and Expression in the Age of Emerson and Whitman* (New York: Oxford University Press, 1941), pp. 445–59.

orthodoxy holds that the spiritual decadence of the nineteenth century can be measured according to the alteration in the object of its belief from God-Man to Man-God, and to the corresponding shift in emphasis from Incarnation to Deification. Melville did not use those terms, but he had been responsive himself to that alteration, from belief in the salvation of man through the mercy and grace of a sovereign God, to belief in the potential divinity in every man. That alteration centered around the Crucifixion. By Melville's time, and especially in protestant, democratic America, the emphasis was no longer on God before Man, on the unique birth and Divinity of the Christ, who was killed and died back into eternal life; but on the rebel killed by an unworthy society, on Man become the Messiah, become God. That celebration of Man's triumph involved also the loss of several important attitudes: that there was anything more important than the individual; that he might find his completion in something greater than himself; that the real basis for human brotherhood was not in humanitarianism but in men's common aspiration and fallibility, in their humility before God.

The relevance of these reflections to Ahab's tragedy emerges as we see how overwhelmingly he assumes the center of the stage. At the end of the account of what the captain found symbolized in Moby Dick, of why he was intent on an audacious and immitigable revenge, Melville showed how this fixed resolve could sway all before it. There was none who could stand up against him in this crew, composed chiefly 'of mongrel renegades, and castaways, and cannibals—morally enfeebled, also, by the incompetence of mere unaided virtue or right-mindedness in Starbuck, the invulnerable jollity of indifference and recklessness in Stubb, and the pervading mediocrity in Flask.' But Ahab's absolute domination carried Melville even farther; it caused him to drop what had seemed to be one of his major themes— the relation between Ishmael and Queequeg, to abandon all development or even subsequent mention of Bulkington, the barrel-chested demigod whom he had introduced, at the Spouter Inn, as a natural seeker for truth. To a degree even beyond what Melville may have intended, all other personalities, all other human relations became dwarfed before Ahab's purpose.

Therefore, to grasp the meaning of this tragedy, it is necessary to examine Ahab's development in more detail than we did that of any of Hawthorne's characters. Not that he is more living than Hester Prynne, for the comparison reveals him to be not so much a varied human being as a state of mind. In one of the fragmentary comments in *The Confidence Man,* on the question of what is meant by an original character in fiction, Melville was virtually saying what he had intended in Ahab. He held that a writer could pick up plenty of singular characters by observation, but that the true original character was rare, that such a one, like Hamlet, was 'a revolving Drummond light, raying away from itself all round it,' and illuminating life as much as a new radical philosopher. Such a description of Hamlet shows Melville's inclination to the Coleridgean interpretation of the play, which exalts the hero and tends to ignore his social environment, as Shakespeare never did. In line with this interpretation is Melville's further remark that 'for much the same reason that there is but one planet to one orbit, so can there be but one such original character to one work of invention.' But with his belief that the creation of such a character depended on more than mere observation, on a depth of spiritual insight, Melville was none the less explicit that it could not spring merely from 'the author's imagination—it being as true in literature as in zoology, that all life is from the egg.' A concentrated view of Ahab will disclose that he was born from the matrix of Melville's age. He is an embodiment of his author's most profound response to the problem of the free individual will *in extremis.*

Melville's first detailed characterization of him stresses his apartness and his suffering, his 'infinity of firmest fortitude,' and yet the 'crucifixion in his face.' His driven mind has already lost all touch with pleasure of the senses. He can no longer relish his pipe, and tosses it moodily into the sea. He looks at the sunset, and reflects that it soothes him no more: 'This lovely light, it lights not me; all loveliness is anguish to me, since I can ne'er enjoy. Gifted with the high perception, I lack the low, enjoying power; damned, most subtly and most malignantly! damned in the midst of Paradise!' The critical danger involved in the separation between perception and feeling had been noted by Melville in another context, when he underscored Gloucester's comment on the type of man who is blind to the heavenly powers,

> that will not see
> Because he doth not feel.

This cleavage is at the root of Ahab's dilemma. He can see nothing but his own burning thoughts since he no longer shares in any normal fellow-feelings. His resolve to take it upon himself to seek out and annihilate the source of malignity, is god-like, for it represents human effort in its highest reach. But as he himself declares, it is likewise 'demoniac,' the sanity of a controlled madness. The control depends upon 'that certain sultanism of his brain,' which cunningly builds its power over the others into an 'irresistible dictatorship.' At the moment of the initial announcement of his vengeance, he rises to a staggering *hubris,* as he shouts, 'Who's over me?' Starbuck, powerless before such madness, can only think: 'Horrible old man! Who's over him he cries;—ay, he would be a democrat to all above; look how he lords it over all below!' Yet Starbuck is forced not simply to resent but to pity him, since he reads in the lurid eyes the captain's desperation. And in sleep, when alone the grip of the conscious mind has been relaxed, Ahab's tortured soul shrieks out in nightmares, in its frantic effort to escape from the drive of his obsession. At such moments Melville finds an image for his state in calling him a Prometheus whose intense thinking has created the vulture that feeds upon his heart forever. It is significant that Melville wrote on the back inner cover of the last volume of his Shakespeare, 'Eschylus' *Tragedies,*' as though intending to read them. Prometheus, whose desire to help humanity was also misdirected and led him into crime, makes a not unfitting counterpart for Ahab, for the stark grandeur of Melville's creation is comparable even to that of Aeschylus.

Ahab's tragedy also runs the course of the tragedy of Ethan Brand, whom

Melville regarded as typifying the man whose inordinate development of will and brain 'eats out the heart.' He read Hawthorne's story in the summer of 1851, too late for it to have affected the first conception of his hero, but possibly in time for it to have entered into the portrayal of Ahab's final damnation through his having lost hold, no less than Brand, 'of the magnetic chain of humanity.' Moreover, Ahab's career falls into the pattern that Hawthorne had handled many other times, since it is basically a tragedy of pride. The increasing glare in his eyes reminds you of Chillingworth. The manifestations of his arrogance become ever more excessive as he advances, 'both chasing and being chased to his deadly end.' He hates to be indebted to anyone else, even to the carpenter who makes him a new leg. His refusal of Starbuck's entreaties with the insistence that just as there is one God, there is one captain, finally mounts to the point where, denying his aid to the grief-stricken master of the *Rachel,* he declares: 'God bless ye, man, and may I forgive myself, but I must go.'

Melville typifies the fatal lengths to which Ahab has gone from normality by making him hurl the quadrant to the deck and trample on it. In this action he curses everything that elevates man's eye to the heavens and the sun; he scorns man's science, the light of his mind, as an idle toy. Incidentally, the drama of this gesture may have been suggested by that scene of *Richard II*—marked in Melville's copy of Shakespeare—where the King dashes the mirror to the ground.

Up to this point there would seem to have been small scope given to 'the humanities,' which Captain Peleg insisted were also to be found in Ahab. They rise to the surface in his relations with Pip, the conception of which reveals the most effectual connection between Shakespearean tragedy and *Moby-Dick.* To judge even from the incidental verbal echoes, *King Lear* was working more pervasively in Melville's imagination at this time than any other play. Many of the sailors' defiances of outer storms ring as close to the original as 'Split jibs! tear yourselves!' When Melville wanted to magnify the size of the ship and the perilous descent of the boats over its side for the lowering, he recalled the Shakespeare passage which creates the greatest sense of height, and said that 'the three boats swung over the sea like three samphire baskets over high cliffs.' At the time of their first meeting with another vessel, Ahab notes that when the two wakes cross, a school 'of small harmless fish,' which have been swimming for some days by the *Pequod*'s side dart off to follow the *Albatross:* ' "Swim away from me, do ye?" murmured Ahab, gazing over into the water. There seemed but little in the words, but the tone conveyed more of deep helpless sadness than the insane old man had ever before evinced.' It may not be merely fanciful to read in Ahab's pathetic attitude a recombination of Lear's twisted notion that

> the little dogs and all,
> Tray, Blanch, and Sweet-heart, see, they bark at me.

But a more significant analogy resides in the function that Melville evolved for Pip. One day, after his disastrous accident, the cabin boy wandered crazily up to the quarterdeck, from which a member of the crew started to drive him, only to have Ahab shout, 'Hands off from that holiness!' and then add: 'Here, boy; Ahab's cabin shall be Pip's home henceforth, while Ahab lives. Thou touchest my inmost centre, boy ... Come, let's down.'

What strikes Ahab most in Pip's fate is that the 'frozen heavens' created and then abandoned him: 'Lo! ye believers in gods all goodness, and in man all ill, lo you! see the omniscient gods oblivious of suffering man; and man, though idiotic, and knowing not what he does, yet full of the sweet things of love and gratitude. Come! I feel prouder leading thee by thy black hand, than though I grasped an emperor's.' That gives us another glimpse of the attraction that some of the Gnostic sects held for Melville through their insistence on a tyrannous and savage Jehovah. That Ahab's sense of the evil in God corresponds to something Melville had himself experienced is plain enough in that letter he wrote to Hawthorne while working on the concluding sections of *Moby-Dick*. He had just been discussing 'Ethan Brand,' and went on to say: 'I stand for the heart. To the dogs with the head! I had rather be a fool with a heart, than Jupiter Olympus with his head. The reason the mass of men fear God, and *at bottom dislike* Him, is because they rather distrust His heart, and fancy Him all brain like a watch.'[1] To such an extent had the grounds for Channing's 'Moral Argument against Calvinism' entered into Melville's revolt from the old strict theology. Yet unlike Channing's his attitude was ambivalent, since he continued to be absorbed with the problem of evil. How the terms of that ambivalence fought in him and demanded a solution will have to be traced from *Pierre* to *Billy Budd*.

An observant sailor finds the bond between Ahab and Pip to be that the one is 'daft with strength, the other daft with weakness.' The captain drinks a restorative philosophy from the boy's devotion to him: 'Oh! spite of million villains, this makes me a bigot in the fadeless fidelity of man! and a black! and crazy!' The 'contraries' seem to have struck Ahab much as they did Ishmael in his reconciliation to life through the comradeship of Queequeg. But at this juncture there is a crucial divergence not only from the experience of Ishmael, but also from *Lear,* where the central movement is the purgation of the headstrong and arrogant King. In that scene on the heath where he finally becomes aware of the blindness in his former pomp, where he both sees and feels the plight of other human beings, and prays for all 'poor naked wretches' whereso'er they are, he is no longer a vain monarch but a fellow man.

No such purgation transforms Ahab. He perceives in Pip's attachment the quality that might cure his own malady, but he refuses to be deflected from his pursuit by the stirring of any sympathy for others, and warns the pitiful boy: 'Weep so, and I will murder thee!' In the fixity of Ahab's eyes, domineering over the doubts and misgivings of all the crew, there now lurked something 'hardly sufferable for feeble souls to see.' Yet at moments when he thought no third glance upon him, he seemed in turn awed by the eyes of the Parsee; or again, their two figures seemed 'yoked together, and an unseen tyrant driving them.'

The only other member of his crew who dares even to try to sway him is

Starbuck. But his failure is foreshadowed from the first description of him as a steadfast, careful man who is full of awe, abiding firm in the conflict with seas or whales or 'any of the ordinary irrational horrors of the world,' yet unable to withstand 'those more terrific, because more spiritual terrors, which sometimes menace you from the concentrating brow of an enraged and mighty man.' Melville gave considerable thought to the problem presented by a character like the mate's. He observed in *The Confidence Man* how 'the moderate man' might be 'the invaluable understrapper of the wicked man,' capable of being 'used for wrong, but . . . useless for right.' To be sure, he marked in *The Seven Gables* an opposite view of the problem, the singular strength that Hepzibah was able to show in her unequal struggle against the Judge, through the sheer 'moral force of a deeply grounded antipathy.' But the obverse aspect again struck Melville when he found in Edmund's 'infernal nature . . . a valor often denied to innocence'; and that face of the matter was uppermost in his handling of Ahab and Starbuck.

Yet the further contrast between Starbuck and Stubb shows the latter even less able to come within Ahab's sphere. When they reveal themselves through the symbolical meanings that they find in the design on the doubloon, Starbuck is a man of tragic foreboding who shrinks from the blackness of truth and hopes that 'in this vale of Death, God girds us round.' Stubb reads in its signs of the zodiac the successive acts of life's comedy. He is neither valiant nor craven, but happy-go-lucky. He accepts Ahab's purpose as 'predestinated,' but concludes that a laugh is always the wisest answer, and wonders 'What's my juicy little pear at home doing now?' Melville deliberately portrays in the three mates the graduated steps of decline from spiritual insight. For Flask is utterly lacking in reverence, fearless through ignorance. He sees in the doubloon 'nothing . . . but a round thing made of gold,' worth sixteen dollars to whoever raises a certain whale. That conception runs close to Blake's in 'A Vision of the Last Judgment': ' "What," it will be Question'd, "When the Sun rises, do you not see a round disk of fire somewhat like a Guinea?" O no, no, I see an Innumerable company of the Heavenly host crying, "Holy, Holy, Holy is the Lord God Almighty." ' Flask is entirely the man of unilluminated common sense, farthest from the madness that transfigures life.

Starbuck's righteousness carried him to the point of begging Ahab to turn the ship back from its ominous course. But though Ahab rides brutally over him and threatens his life, and though Starbuck knows they are all doomed unless he acts, he cannot face the thought of killing the captain even when he comes upon him defenseless in sleep. He makes one further effort to sway him, on that day of enchanted calm just before the white whale is sighted. The innocence of the blue air has seemed to dispel for a moment the torment in Ahab's soul, and tears well into his eyes. Starbuck senses his emotion, but is careful not to betray that he does. He moves besides Ahab as he leans over the rail, the mate of thirty beside the captain of twice his age.

Ahab starts to talk of his remembrance that on just such a mild day as this he struck his first whale, as a boy-harpooner of eighteen, and that since then he has spent almost forty years on the pitiless sea, in 'the desolation of solitude.' He thinks of the poor girl he has only lately married, and says to his mate: 'Close! stand close to me, Starbuck; let me look into a human eye; it is better than to gaze into the sea or sky; better than to gaze upon God. By the green land; by the bright hearthstone! this is the magic glass, man; I see my wife and my child in thine eye.' He thinks even that he can hear her telling the boy 'of cannibal old me.' But when Starbuck seizes the occasion to talk about his own wife and boy, and to urge that the ship be headed back for Nantucket, Ahab averts his glance. He declares that 'against all natural lovings and longings,' he is recklessly driven on by his 'hidden lord and master,' by the 'cruel, remorseless emperor' that commands him. 'By heaven, man, we are turned round and round in this world, like yonder windlass, and Fate is the handspike.' To such words, which admit an irreparable cleavage between Ahab's heart and his predestinated will, Starbuck can listen no more, and moves away in despair.

By his unrelaxing energy throughout the three day's chase, Ahab towers even higher above them all, for as he himself declares, 'Starbuck is Stubb reversed, and Stubb is Starbuck; and ye two are all mankind; and Ahab stands alone.' When he snaps his ivory leg again in being thrown from his boat on the second day, he is helped back onto deck by the mate, to whom he says, 'Ay, ay, Starbuck, 'tis sweet to lean sometimes, be the leaner who he will; and would old Ahab had leaned oftener than he has.' But again, unlike Lear, though he sees his dilemma, he is not really moved, for he adds that 'nor white whale, nor man, nor fiend, can so much as graze old Ahab in his own proper and inaccessible being.'

Starbuck is driven to a further agonized plea that, with Fedallah now dead, 'thy evil shadow gone—all good angels mobbing thee with warnings:—what more wouldst thou have? . . . In Jesus' name, no more of this, that's worse than devil's madness.' But the only answer he gets, after beseeching Ahab to avoid impiety and blasphemy, is: 'This whole act's immutably decreed . . . Fool! I am the Fates' lieutenant.' In that reckless hyperbole Ahab betrays again how he has misconceived any possible human purpose, since he has insanely taken upon himself the fulfilment of decrees that could properly belong only to Fate or to God.

Yet Starbuck persists in a final attempt. As Ahab prepares to have his boat lowered on the third morning, the mate clasps his hand: 'Oh, my captain, my captain!—noble heart—go not—go not! see, it's a brave man that weeps; how great the agony of the persuasion then!' But Ahab proceeds with his orders, while the voice of Pip, who has disappeared from the scene since the beginning of the chase, cries from a low cabin-window: 'O master, my master, come back!' Even after the captain's boat is launched, Starbuck sees that the white whale has changed his course, and is swimming directly away. He calls after Ahab that it is not yet too late to desist: 'See, Moby Dick seeks thee not. It is thou, thou, that madly seekest him!'

Starbuck had not accepted the theory of Moby Dick's 'intelligent malignity.' He had declared from the start that it was insane to undertake vengeance 'on a dumb brute that simply smote thee from blindest instinct!' But the evidence from the ships they have met 'contrastingly concurred to show the demoniac indifference with which the White Whale tore his hunters, whether sinning or sinned against.' No doubt concerning this last alternative, so strangely wrenched from *Lear,* touches Ahab in the least. His antagonist remains the incarnation of evil, and must, therefore, be destroyed. His pride in his purpose rises to the final terrifying pitch when he shouts to his boat crew: 'Ye are not other men, but my arms and my legs; and so obey me.' Such *hubris* challenges instant *nemesis.* Yet Ahab keeps on even after his darted harpoon has so maddened the whale that it has rushed full against the *Pequod* itself, and shattered its bow. As he sees his ship sinking, with himself not on it, the captain turns his body from the sun to seek his 'lonely death on lonely life.' But his last resolve, his last words are: 'Toward thee I roll, thou all-destroying but unconquering whale; to the last I grapple with thee; from hell's heart I stab at thee; for hate's sake I spit my last breath at thee ... *Thus,* I give up the spear!'

Ahab's career, like that of the protagonists of many of the Elizabethan trag-edies of revenge, has revealed him as both hero and villain. Ordinary men are no match for him. His superiorities of mind and will, of courage and conviction, have exalted him above the sphere of anything petty or ignoble. Yet it is repeatedly affirmed that he is a monomaniac, and that his fixed idea, his hatred of the whale as the symbol of malignity, has carried him into the toils of a diabolical bond. The contrasting halves of his nature cannot be summed up better than in the 'ungodly, god-like' of Captain Peleg's description.

The meaning of his tragedy is involved with his conception of the rigid Fate to which he is chained. This conception runs likewise through Ishmael's comments. The *Pequod* is described as 'the sometimes madly merry and predestinated craft.' In Moby Dick's final desperate rush against its bow, he vibrated 'his predestinating head': 'Retribution, swift vengeance, eternal malice were in his whole aspect.' The problem of determinism was part of the residue of Puritanism which Melville inherited. Babbalanja had devoted one of his discourses to trying to make a fun-damental distinction between Fate and Necessity: 'Confound not the distinct. Fa-talism presumes express and irrevocable edicts of heaven concerning particular events. Whereas, Necessity holds that all events are naturally linked, and inevitably follow each other, without providential interposition, though by the eternal letting of Providence.' Melville himself became absorbed in such discussion, and recorded, for instance, how, on his passage to England in 1849 to see about the publication of *White Jacket,* he spent many evenings drinking whiskey and 'talking of "Fixed Fate, Free-will, foreknowledge absolute," etc.'[2] with a German scholar on board. In launching Ahab on his pursuit, he emphasized how, 'with little external to constrain us, the innermost necessities in our being, these still drive us on.' But though Babbalanja also declared himself a Necessitarian and not a Fatalist, neither he nor Melville was able to keep himself secure in that position.

One reason why Melville was driven to magnify the relentless power of Fate is to be found in his reaction against Emersonianism. Emerson was too easy in his distinction when he said, 'Our doctrine must begin with the Necessary and Eternal,

and discriminate Fate from the Necessary. There is no limitation about the Eternal.'
Briefly, then, in one of the key-passages in his essay on 'Fate': 'So far as a man thinks,
he is free,' since thought partakes in the Eternal. 'But Fate is the name we give to
the action of that … all various necessity on the brute myriads, whether in things,
animals, or in men in whom the intellect pure is not yet opened. To such it is only
a burning wall which hurts those who run against it.' But Melville apprehended in
Ahab a man who thought, and yet conceived the white whale as an inscrutable wall
shoved near him. The captain's insistence that 'Truth hath no confines' demanded
that he thrust through the wall. Emerson would have agreed about the illimitability
of truth, and, indeed, went on to say that Fate involves 'melioration.' For 'the one
serious and formidable thing in nature is a will.' Emerson's hero is the man of will
who moves others forward by it, since 'the direction of the whole and of the parts
is toward benefit.' But Melville's hero of formidable will swept his whole crew
destruction.[3]

The result of Ahab's Fatalism is that his tragedy admits no adequate moral
recognition. The catharsis is, therefore, partially frustrated, since we cannot respond, as we can in *Lear,* to Ahab's deliverance from the evil forces in which he has
been immersed. He is held to the end in his Faustian bond to the devil. Moreover,
unlike both the sixteenth- and the nineteenth-century Faust,[4] he never really struggles to escape from it. Although his tortured soul cries out in his sleep, during his
waking hours his mind and will are dominant, and inflexible. When talking with Pip
and Starbuck, he perceives the human consequences of his action. He is momentarily touched, but he is not moved from his insistence that his course is necessary.
In his death therefore—a death that engulfs so many others—colossal pride meets
its rightful end, and there can be no unmixed pity for him as a human being. There
is no moment of release comparable, for instance, to one that Melville marked:
when, at Antony's death, Cleopatra sees and feels herself as she is, and answers Iras'
'Royal Egypt! Empress!' with

> No more, but e'en a woman, and commanded
> By such poor passion as the maid that milks
> And does the meanest chares.

The effect of that reduction is to magnify. It endows Cleopatra with the 'august
dignity' of common humanity, which Melville proclaimed in his crew. But he does
not portray its full working in Ahab, since, though the captain sees, he does not
amply feel. He is not caught out of himself and transfigured by sympathy. As a
result, his madness is not divine like Blake's, or even like Pip's, since his burning mind
is barred out from the exuberance of love. His tragedy is that of an unregenerate
will, which stifles his soul and drives his brain with an inescapable fierceness.[5] He
suffers, but unlike Hawthorne's Hester or Miriam, he is not purified by his suffering.
He remains, like Ethan Brand, damned.

Thoughts like these may have been stirring in Melville when he said to Hawthorne: 'I have written a wicked book, and feel spotless as the lamb.' He thus

instinctively transferred the effect of tragedy from the audience to make it apply to the author as well. While still in the throes of finishing it, he had also said that 'the hell-fire in which the whole book is broiled might not unreasonably have cooked it ere this,' and had added: 'This is the book's motto (the secret one), Ego non baptizo te in nomine—but make out the rest yourself.' The whole quotation, as Ahab howled it out while christening his 'malignant iron' in the harpooners' blood, was 'Ego non baptizo te in nomine patris, sed in nomine diaboli.'[6] The strain involved in portraying Ahab's demonic nature perhaps caused Melville to feel momentarily identified with it. But when the book was done, when he had written his vision of Ahab's madness out of his system, he could feel himself purged. Even though he had composed a tragedy incomplete when judged by Shakespearean standards, he had eased his thoughts by the act of creating so prodigious an artistic structure. He had experienced the meaning of catharsis, even though his protagonist had not.

Responsive to the shaping forces of his age as only men of passionate imagination are, even Melville can hardly have been fully aware of how symbolical an American hero he had fashioned in Ahab. The length to which the captain carried his belief in the fixity of Fate makes a searching comment on the theological decay that conditioned Melville's thought. He recognized the inadequacy of transcendentalism on most of the essential problems; but when he tried to reassert the significance of Original Sin, there was no orthodoxy that he could accept. When he examined the dying Calvinism in which he had been brought up, his mind could discover there only the Manichean heresy, which its founders had staunchly repudiated. Its determinism became for him the drastic distortion that he projected in Ahab's career, wherein there was no possibility of regeneration since there remained no effectual faith in the existence of divine grace. The severe, bleak, and uninspired Presbyterian church of Melville's experience had driven him inevitably into questioning even the goodness of the Biblical God.

On the other hand, he could find no security in throwing over all the restraints of dogma, and exalting the god-like man. If the will was free, as the new faith insisted, Melville knew that it was free to do evil as well as to do good. He could not rest happy with Emerson's declaration that if he turned out to be the devil's child, why then he would live from the devil. For Melville had envisaged the fate of just such a man in Ahab. He had also seen in Ahab the destruction that must overtake the Man-God, the self-appointed Messiah. 'Man's self-affirmation leads to his perdition; the free play of human forces unconnected with any higher aim brings about the exhaustion of man's creative powers.' That sentence was to be written three-quarters of a century after *Moby-Dick,* by Berdyaev in *The Meaning of History;* but it bears unintentional relevance to what happened to Ahab. And the captain's career is prophetic of many others in the history of later nineteenth-century America. Man's confidence in his own unaided resources has seldom been carried farther than during that era in this country. The strong-willed individuals who seized the land and gutted the forests and built the railroads were no longer troubled with Ahab's obsessive sense of evil, since theology had receded even farther into their backgrounds. But their drives were as relentless as his, and they were to prove like him in many other ways also, as they went on to become the empire builders of the post–Civil War world. They tended to be as dead to enjoyment as he, as blind to everything but their one pursuit, as unmoved by fear or sympathy, as confident in assuming an identification of their wills with immutable plan or manifest destiny, as liable to regard other men as merely arms and legs for the fulfilment of their purposes, and, finally, as arid and exhausted in their burnt-out souls. Without deliberately intending it, but by virtue of his intense concern with the precariously maintained values of democratic Christianity, which he saw every-where being threatened or broken down, Melville created in Ahab's tragedy a fearful symbol of the self-enclosed individualism that, carried to its furthest ex-treme, brings disaster both upon itself and upon the group of which it is part. He provided also an ominous glimpse of what was to result when the Emersonian will to virtue became in less innocent natures the will to power and conquest.[7]

NOTES

[1] More than twenty years later Melville marked in the copy of Shelley's *Essays,* which he bought in 1873, the following passage: 'Milton's Devil as a moral being is as far superior to his God, as one who perseveres in some purpose which he has conceived to be excellent in spite of adversity and torture, is to one who in the cold security of undoubted triumph inflicts the most horrible revenge upon his enemy.'

[2] In quoting this line from *Paradise Lost,* Melville was doubtless aware that the next line added: 'And found no end, in wandering mazes lost.'

[3] This juxtaposition of some of the contrasting implications of Emerson's and Melville's texts is not meant to imply a direct reaction in *Moby-Dick* against the essay 'Fate,' since that was not printed until *The Conduct of Life* (1860)—though it had been read as a lecture at least as early as 1851. The diffused presence of transcendentalism in the work of Melville and Whitman shows that, by the end of the eighteen-forties, a man did not have to be thinking of a specific text in order to be conscious of the main doctrines of the movement. In both Melville and Whitman we can perceive a double process of assimilation and rejection of these doctrines, with the chief accent on the first by Whitman, on the second by Melville.

[4] As another possible force affecting Melville's conception of tragedy, Marlowe's *Plays* were among the books he listed as having bought in London in 1849.

[5] The most comparable character in the literature of the time is Heathcliff. I have found no evidence that Melville read *Wuthering Heights* (1847), which was generally misunderstood and attacked by contem-porary reviewers; but Emily Brontë's genuine wildness of imagination strikes an intensity akin to that of some of the scenes on the *Pequod.* Virginia Woolf has remarked that *Wuthering Heights* and *Moby-Dick* seem apart from all other novels in the way poetry pervades their entire structure.

[6] On the back fly-leaf of the final volume of his Shakespeare, the volume containing *Lear, Romeo and Juliet, Hamlet,* and *Othello,* Melville jotted down some notes, apparently designed for a story involving a formal compact with the devil, cast in modern terms, since he was to have been met 'at the Astor.' He then added:

> Ego non baptizo te in nomine Patris et
> Filii et Spiritus Sancti—sed in nomine
> Diaboli.—Madness is undefinable—
> It & right reason extremes of one,
> —not the (black art) Goetic but Theurgic magic—
> seeks converse with the Intelligence, Power, the Angel.

Charles Olson, in his essay *'Lear* and *Moby-Dick'* takes these to be 'rough jottings for *Moby-Dick.'* 'Right reason,' in the Coleridgean and Emersonian terminology, is the highest range of intuitive intelligence, the gateway to divine madness. We recall that Melville had made the Serenians declare: 'Right reason, and

Alma, are the same; else Alma, not reason, would we reject. The Master's great command is Love; and here do all things wise, and all things good, unite ... The more we love, the more we know.'

Olson is particularly interesting in the way he brings out the contrast between 'Goetic' and 'Theurgic,' the traditional terms for black and white magic, for the demonic and sacred arts. The contrast involved here may clearly have some bearing on the difference between Ahab's diabolism and Pip's innocence; as may the general contrast between madness and right reason, on the difference between both these characters and Ishmael and Bulkington, the seekers for truth. But in holding that these notes contain the key-idea for the development of *Moby-Dick,* Olson finds an 'extreme significance' in Melville's curtailing of the Latin in the book itself. Olson's point is that, 'Of necessity, from Ahab's world, both Christ and the Holy Ghost are absent ... It is the outward symbol of the inner truth that the name of Christ is uttered but once in the book and then it is torn from Starbuck, the only possible man to use it.' But without seeking very far you can find the old Manx sailor saying, 'O Christ! to think of the green navies and the green-skulled crews!' and Ishmael remarking on 'the celebration of the Passion of our Lord.'

These notes project one phase of Melville's speculation, but it does not seem fruitful to try to make them a formula for Ahab's tragedy, which, as we have seen, is too richly complex to be so reduced. I have been stimulated by Olson's vigorous and imaginative essay to take issue with it on many other points of fact and interpretation, particularly concerning the relation between Ahab and Pip.
[7] The tendency that Melville prefigured in his creation of Ahab has also been described by Berdyaev in *The Fate of Man in the Modern World:* 'Liberty was discovered to be protection of the rights of the strong, leaving the weak defenceless. This is one of the paradoxes of liberty in social life. Freedom turned out to be freedom for oneself and slavery for others. He is the true lover of liberty who desires it for others as well as for himself. Liberty has become the protection of the rights of a privileged minority, the defence of capitalistic property and the power of money ...' You do not have to accept Berdyaev's solution, the mysticism of the old Russia, of the Greek Orthodox church, in order to profit from the trenchancy of his analysis.

Maurice Friedman

CAPTAIN AHAB:
MODERN PROMETHEAN

Captain Ahab, we are told, is a godly, ungodlike man. Like every hero, he is a mixture of the divine and the demonic. His very opposition to the order of things gives him a certain grandeur and nobility; he is to some extent in the line of Milton's Satan in *Paradise Lost,* of Byron's Manfred, and, of course, Prometheus, all of whom win our admiration by grandly defying.

Ahab's Modern Prometheanism is both set in perspective and foreshadowed by the sermon that Ishmael hears when, at the beginning of the story, he wanders into a strange chapel, the pulpit of which is constructed like the prow of a whaling boat. "The Sermon" that Father Mapple, the old whaling preacher, gives from this pulpit-prow is about Jonah, the man who fled before the Lord's word to go to Nineveh, who is thrown off the ship in a storm, and who is swallowed for forty days in the belly of the whale. In it there are prophetic overtones of Captain Ahab in the service of the Lord, Ahab as the rebellious prophet refusing the message of the Lord. But Father Mapple's image of man is actually not Biblical but Calvinist. In contrast to the Book of Jonah, his sermon is founded on a stern, transcendent God, a sinful world, and the moral duty of self-denial. This is the God the Gnostics and Doctor Faustus call the redeemer God, and it really is the world of the Gnostics and Doctor Faustus rather than the world of the Hebrew Bible that we see here. The basic contrast here is between the dark wrath below and the redemption above. Here is man "deepening down to doom," sinking down in "black distress" into the "opening maw of hell" and the redeemer God coming as a "radiant dolphin" shining "bright as lightning" to deliver the helpless and undeserving sinner.

The two "lessons" that Father Mapple draws from the story of Jonah show consequences of this dualism that could not have followed from the original context. In the Book of Job, Job neither commits himself to God with blind faith, nor does he feel that in order to exist as an "I" he must destroy God, like the Modern Promethean—Dostoievsky's Kirilov, Nietzsche's Superman, or Sartre's Orestes. He

From *Problematic Rebel: An Image of Modern Man* (New York: Random House, 1963), pp. 178–211.

finds his very existence in the relationship with God, and at the same time he rebels within that relationship, contending, standing his own ground, meeting God from his own unique position. In Father Mapple's sermon the relationship of this "I" to God has essentially changed. Man's self can no longer exist in Job's sense—as a partner, standing in dialogue with God. Now at the core of the self is sinful man, man born in depravity, man who must choose between affirming himself and affirming God. This already points us toward Ahab, who makes that same choice. Both must choose: there is no room any longer for both self and God, for the self is sinful and to obey God it must disobey itself. This is the first lesson that Father Mapple draws from Jonah: "It is in disobeying ourselves that the hardness of obeying God consists."

Father Mapple finds a second moral in Jonah. Jonah is not an ordinary man but a prophet who finally did the Almighty's bidding, and the bidding of the Almighty was "to preach the truth in the face of falsehood."

> "This, shipmates, this is that other lesson; and woe to that pilot of the living God who slights it! Woe to him whom this world charms from Gospel duty! Woe to him who seeks to pour oil upon the waters when God has brewed them into a gale! Woe to him who seeks to please rather than to appall! ... who, in this world courts not dishonor! *Woe to him who would not be true, even though to be false were salvation.*" (Italics mine.)

The truth as given by God, and Jonah, as the mouthpiece of God going forth to speak the truth, this truth a clear line of division between good and evil and this world an evil world against which the prophet must witness, the temptation to let this world charm one from Gospel duty and the consequent hostility to this world— this is the view of truth and of the prophet of truth in Father Mapple's sermon.

This is, at first glance, just a further extension of the first lesson, since Jonah does not want to obey God and to obey God he must disobey himself and preach God's word to the Ninevites. Yet without any clear transition another note enters in: "Woe to him who would not be true, even though to be false were salvation." It is one thing to say that one must be true and not give in to the charms of this world. It is quite another to say that one must be true *even* at the cost of salvation and set these two in opposition to each other. Although it is unthinkable that a Calvinist preacher would mean this, Father Mapple's words seem to suggest a certain absoluteness of truth that transcends even salvation—man's relation to God. As Father Mapple continues, moreover, it begins to appear that quite a different self is here than that of his first lesson. "But oh! shipmates! on the starboard hand of every woe there is a sure delight ... Delight is to him—a far, far upward, and inward delight—who against the proud gods and commodores of this earth, ever stands forth his own inexorable self." The self that a moment before was to be denied and disobeyed in obedience to God is now suddenly enthroned in the highest place, identified with truth or with the serving of truth. This is Prometheus, enduring endless agonies, yet standing forth his own inexorable self, against Zeus— the proud god of this world.

"Delight is to him when the ship of this base, treacherous world has gone down beneath him," adds Father Mapple. The relationship to God means the denial of the world. God is no longer the creator. The world is given over to the evil God, and the redeemer God redeems man not *in* the world but *from* the world. The paradoxical result of this dualism between man's relation to God and his relation to the world is that this "prophet" at once enjoys the profound humility of disobeying himself to obey God and the equally profound pride of being the spokesman of God who stands forth his own inexorable self against all the world. This "pilot of God" "gives no quarter in the truth and kills, burns, destroys all sin though he pluck it out from under the robes of senators and judges." "Delight,—top-gallant delight is to him, who acknowledges no law or Lord but the Lord his God and is only a patriot to heaven." The world is evil, and he, the bearer of truth, has the sanctified task of destroying evil, giving no quarter in the truth. Yet he does not even bear a word of truth, as does Jonah, a word of God that calls men to turn back to true existence. Rather, he simply takes it on himself to attack and destroy in the name of God.

When Ahab, unlike Father Mapple's Jonah, cuts himself off from God and identifies himself with truth, this sanctification of the task of destroying evil remains. "The Sermon" is not merely a moral and Biblical framework within which to judge the sinfulness of Captain Ahab—an unrepentant Jonah who takes on himself the vengeance which should belong to God and does not know the mercy for God's creation that the God of the Book of Jonah has for his creatures. It also contains the Promethean note which, when it is freed from the relationship to God, can sound forth, in Ahab, in that absolute affirmation of self which identifies the truth and the good with oneself, the false and the evil with what stands opposite one.

Not too long after Ishmael reports that "reality outran apprehension; Captain Ahab stood upon his quarter-deck," and immediately following the destruction of the young Platonist by an infinite that his finiteness cannot endure, we arrive at the central dramatic incident from which all the rest flows—Ahab's announcement in "The Quarter-Deck" (XXXVI) that the true goal of the voyage is the chase of Moby Dick. Here is the first real drama of the book; here the meaning is not merely symbolic but derives from the total situation—Ahab's coming on deck, his rousing the men, the Black Mass in which the harpooners drink from their inverted harpoons,[1] his almost magical success in bringing the crew along with him in his purpose, the clash with Starbuck, the one man who tries to stand against him.

Starbuck, the first mate, is a right-minded man representing mere unaided virtue. He is a strong man and he is a good man, but he lacks Ahab's passion and power, his depth and intensity. Therefore, his mere right-mindedness cannot stand against the demonry of Ahab. "Vengeance on a dumb brute! that simply smote thee from blindest instinct! Madness!" cries Starbuck. "To be enraged with a dumb thing, Captain Ahab, seems blasphemous." It seems blasphemy to Starbuck because he assumes, first, that this "dumb brute" is part of the natural world and second, that nature is the creation of God and therefore is essentially good. He recognizes that whales can bring death to men, but he cannot recognize that there could be any personal malice in Moby Dick's sheering off Ahab's leg. He cannot see Moby Dick, as Ahab does, as an incarnation of the ultimately hostile non-human power that confronts man.

Just before he speaks of blasphemy, Starbuck makes quite a different statement: "I came here to hunt whales, not my commander's vengeance. How many barrels will thy vengeance yield ... it will not fetch thee much in our Nantucket market." Here everything is turned into dollars and cents, everything is measured by the cash premium. "My vengeance will fetch a great premium here!" replies Ahab, smiting his chest. Starbuck, after all, has no intrinsic values to oppose to Ahab's. His fear of blasphemy and his concern for barrels of oil all too comfortably fit together in the God-fearing, money-earning Puritanism from which he comes. No reverence for the whale as a part of God's creation enters into Starbuck's attitude toward killing whales for money. Here "creation" becomes merely a collection of natural objects which are there for man to exploit without limit. There is no suggestion of the wonder before the independent otherness of creation that runs through the Book of Job and in particular the speeches of the Lord, who brings "rain on a land where no man is, on the desert in which there is no man; to satisfy the waste and desolate ground." In its place we find the mid-nineteenth-century rapacity of the American frontiersman, of which the American whaling industry was one of the greatest examples. "Duty and profit hand in hand!" says Starbuck at the time of the first lowering for a whale.

One of the mysteries of this chapter is how Ahab gets the rest of the crew to go along with him and "hunt his vengeance," rather than the oil they came out for. Ahab brings the whole ship and the whole crew into his demonic inner world, into his maddened consciousness; it is a powerful, an archetypal world, but it is his own personal world. Aside from observer Ishmael's, there is essentially only one point of view from now on, and that is Ahab's. There are feeble attempts to resist Ahab's spell, Starbuck making his occasional protest, Ishmael from time to time falling into doubt. But there is not really another active and positive standpoint which can compete with Ahab's. Even the parade of ships that exchange greetings with the *Pequod* only serve to throw Ahab's attitude into symbolic relief. These ships are other worlds, indeed, with sharply contrasting attitudes toward Moby Dick; nonetheless, with the exception of the *Rachel*, they are only "ships that pass in the night." The world of *Moby-Dick* is the *Pequod*, and Ahab is both its captain and its soul. "There is one God that is Lord over the earth, and one Captain that is lord over the Pequod," Ahab says to Starbuck.

But where a single point of view dominates, truth becomes identical with it and with him who holds it. Ahab's response to Starbuck's charge of blasphemy indicates a decisive new stage in the relationship between truth and reality. "Hark ye yet again,—the little lower layer," says Ahab. Ahab also has his Platonism; like the "sunken-eyed young Platonist," he too sees all visible things as only symbols of the reality behind them: "All visible objects, man, are but as pasteboard masks." But unlike the symbols of the young Platonist, they do not relate integrally to what they symbolize. Rather, they are, like pasteboard masks, thin, empty, flimsy things that cover a very different reality; they remind us, indeed, of that sunken-eyed young Platonist himself, fallen through the pasteboard mask of a fair day, a beautiful sky, and a summer sea, to his horrible death. Despite Ahab's famous transcendentalist cry, "O Nature, and O soul of man! how far beyond all utterance are thy linked analogies," Ahab's symbolism is not one of correspondence but of antagonism between the appearance and the reality that lies behind it: "In each event—in the living act, the undoubted deed—there, some unknown, but still reasoning thing puts forth the mouldings of its features from behind the unreasoning mask." The mask is not the face of reality but the façade; it is the *persona*—the mask that the characters wore in ancient plays. What really acts and moves behind it one can never know.

The horror that "the little lower layer" opens to Ahab is that what seems irrational is really rational yet unknowable, that it is both inscrutable and malicious. "Inscrutable malice" brings together two meanings of evil that are played on again and again in the course of this book: on the one hand, the personal malignancy that lies behind the seemingly impersonal or ordinary natural reality; on the other hand, the impersonal, and therefore the inhuman and anti-human, reality that confronts us in the world if we see it as it is, and not through the sunken eyes of the young Platonist. The only thing one can do in the face of this hostile reality is to strike out at it.

> If man will strike, strike through the mask! How can the prisoner reach outside except by thrusting through the wall? To me, the white whale is that wall, shoved near to me. Sometimes I think there's naught beyond. But 'tis enough. He tasks me; he heaps me; I see in him outrageous strength, with an inscrutable malice sinewing it.

Ahab's sense of impotence, after his leg is cut off and he himself is tied down to his bunk for many months, is given full expression here. He feels himself suffocated by this mask "shoved near" to him; the only way he can live is to break through it and destroy it. "That inscrutable thing is chiefly what I hate; and be the white whale agent, or be the white whale principal, I will wreak that hate upon him." Whether Ahab is striking through the whale at God or whether there is "naught beyond," it is Ahab's hatred of the inscrutability of reality that compels him to sail around the world to pursue Moby Dick even though, as Starbuck says to him, "The white whale seeks thee not."

"Talk not to me of blasphemy, man," Ahab continues. "I'd strike the sun if it insulted me. For could the sun do that, then could I do the other; since there is ever a sort of fair play herein, jealousy presiding over all creations." The Prometheanism of that passage is rather like that of the original Prometheus of Aeschylus: a defiance not of the order but in the name of the order—the "fair play" that jealously presides over the whole. But in his next statement Ahab goes beyond the

Aeschylean Prometheus: "But not my master, man, is even that fair play. Who's over me? Truth hath no confines." Ultimately there is not even an order which is over Ahab!

Here is the essential breakthrough to the Modern Promethean. Ahab arrogates to himself all the authority of truth which resided before either in God and our relationship to God, as it does for Father Mapple, or in the Platonic or idealistic absolute, as it does for Bulkington and the young Platonist. For modern man neither of these truths is any longer possible, since "God is dead." The "death of God" means the death of both the Biblical image of man face to face with God and the Greek-Platonic image of an absolute order and an absolute good in harmony with which man can live. In the face of a basically inscrutable reality, the only way left to man to find any meaning in his existence is to identify truth with himself and with his attack on the reality that appears to be fair and beautiful and is really malignant and hostile to man.

"I, Ishmael, was one of that crew," says Ishmael at the beginning of "Moby Dick" (XLI). "My shouts had gone up with the rest, my oath had been welded with theirs. A wild, mystical, sympathetical feeling was in me; Ahab's quenchless feud seemed mine." Ishmael and the crew are now entirely involved in Ahab's purpose. "With greedy ears," Ishmael confesses, "I learned the history of that murderous monster." This highly subjective statement turns out to be merely the prelude to what seems at first an entirely objective history, a scientific account of whales and sperm whales and even of the White Whale himself. Ishmael puts every intimation off on "crazy old Ahab," yet he ever more powerfully suggests that maybe there is something to it after all. Each section of the chapter tells the reader something of sperm whales or Moby Dick and then says, in closely similar formulations of the same idea, "Small wonder, then, that men react to it thus."

As the sea surpasses the land in its dangers, so the whale fishery surpasses every other sort of fishery, the sperm whale every other sort of whale, and Moby Dick every other sort of sperm whale. In this one animal, therefore, we have reached the apex of the danger man encounters when he sets out to face the hostile reality of the universe. Moby Dick, we are told, is a sperm whale of uncommon magnitude and malignity, great ferocity, cunning and malice. "No wonder, then, that ever gathering volume . . . the outblown rumors of the White Whale did in the end incorporate themselves with all manner of morbid hints, and half-formed foetal suggestions of supernatural agencies, which eventually invested Moby Dick with new terrors unborrowed from anything that visibly appears." It is "the invisible spheres" attaching themselves to Moby Dick that help to build up such wild "suggestings" and "unearthly conceits" as that of his ubiquitousness—that he is to be found at the same time in two different places. To some he seems "not only ubiquitous, but immortal." "Though groves of spears should be planted in his flanks, he would still swim away unharmed." What particularly invests the White Whale with terror, however, is "that unexampled, intelligent malignity which . . . he had over and over again evinced in his assaults."

Now that his ubiquity and immortality are combined with his malignity and intelligence, Moby Dick can be characterized by that very quality which Ahab says he cannot bear in "The Quarter-Deck"—"inscrutable malice." Due to his "treacherous retreats" and his "infernal aforethought of ferocity," the dismemberings and deaths that he caused were "not wholly regarded as having been afflicted by an unintelligent agent."

> Judge, then, to what pitches of inflamed, distracted fury the minds of his more desperate hunters were impelled, when amid the chips of chewed boats, and the sinking limbs of torn comrades, they swam out of the white curds of the whale's direful wrath into the serene, exasperating sunlight, that smiled on, as if at a birth or a bridal.

Here the horror is not only the maiming and death itself, but also the contrast between the appearance of serenity and beauty and the horrible reality. "Linked analogies" notwithstanding, "nature" does not correspond here to what is happening to man; or rather, one part of nature—the intelligent malignity of Moby Dick—destroys, while the rest of nature looks on with "benign indifference," to use Camus' phrase in *The Stranger*.

In the face of this malignity and indifference of nature, Ahab is, indeed, Promethean and defiant, but rather pitifully so. We are told of one captain who, like an Arkansas duelist, blindly sought "with a six-inch blade to reach the fathom-deep life of the whale." That captain was Ahab, we learn, and we sense again the impotence that lies behind Ahab's need to strike through the wall that is suffocating him. Having lost his trust in existence, Ahab's only choice is either to go down submitting or to go down defying. It is this blind Prometheanism of Ahab's that leads to Moby Dick's "reaping away" his leg: "No turbaned Turk, no hired Venetian or Malay, could have smote him with more seeming malice." It was not to Ahab alone that the White Whale seemed malicious, but to everybody, and this suggestion of social objectivity is reinforced by the recurrence here of the same formula as that used in the more "objective" accounts of sperm whales and of Moby Dick—"no wonder then," "judge then": "Small reason was there to doubt then that ever since . . . Ahab had cherished a wild vindictiveness against the whale, all the more fell for that in his frantic morbidness he at last came to identify with him not only all his bodily woes, but all his intellectual and spiritual exasperations."

Now Ishmael tells us exactly what Moby Dick symbolizes to Ahab, and, prepared by the whole of what has gone before, we cannot dismiss it as merely the aberration of a distracted, inflamed mind: "The White Whale swam before him as the monomaniac incarnation of all those malicious agencies which some deep men feel eating in them, till they are left living on with half a heart and half a lung." The next statement, certainly, is made as an entirely objective one even if at the end it is linked with Ahab:

> That intangible malignity which has been from the beginning; to whose dominion even the modern Christians ascribe one-half of the worlds; which the

ancient Ophites of the east reverenced in their statue devil;—Ahab did not fall down and worship it like them; but deliriously transferring its idea to the abhorred White Whale, he pitted himself, all mutilated, against it.

Ishmael in no way suggests that "that intangible malignity" itself exists only in the mind of Ahab or that it is a merely psychological phenomenon. On the contrary, "it has been from the beginning," and even the modern Christian, like the ancient Gnostic, sees that evil as at least as powerful as good, and probably more powerful. The Gnostic Ophites drew the logical conclusion that it is the devil, or snake, that should be worshiped and propitiated, not God. We do not find here, as in Zoroastrianism, the almost equal conflict of good and evil, with good bound to win out in the end with the aid of the free and rational decision of man. Rather, as in Gnosticism, evil is radically real, more real, in fact, than good on the plane of this world.

By the time that Ishmael has built up the White Whale for us, it is not an unworthy or inadequate symbol of that metaphysical evil with which Ahab identifies it.

All that most maddens and torments; all that stirs up the lees of things; all truth with malice in it; all that cracks the sinews and cakes the brain; all the subtle demonisms of life and thought, all evil, to crazy Ahab, were visibly personified and made practically assailable in Moby Dick.

The protagonists have now clearly reached mythical and metaphysical dimensions. As Moby Dick represents all evil in life, so Ahab represents all of humanity: "He piled upon the Whale's white hump the sum of all the general rage and hate felt by his whole race from Adam down." Ahab's identification of himself with truth now manifests itself in his belief that he is man fighting what is hostile to man, protesting for the sake of his own humanity before it goes down to inevitable defeat.

The entrance of the *Pequod* into "The Pacific" (CXI) heralds the encounter with Moby Dick. The "serene Pacific" lulls the "meditative Magian rover" into the ocean pantheism of the young Platonist: "Lifted by those eternal swells, you needs must own the seductive god, bowing your head to Pan." But to Ahab the Pacific is not a votive offering to Pan but the approach to the hated White Whale that swims within its waters. "In his very sleep, his ringing cry ran through the vaulted hull, 'Stern all! the White Whale spouts thick blood!'" As the book picks up momentum, the choice has crystallized into the polar opposites of a pantheistic illusion or a Promethean "woe that is madness." Just when we might wish to give ourselves to the seductive sea and sky and the fragrant musk from the Bashee isles, Ahab's cry suddenly sweeps us beyond all moderation and balance into the final stages of the chase in which, with ever heightened pace, the drama rolls unrelentingly to its end.

In "The Quadrant" (CXVIII) Ahab throws down and tramples on his quadrant, saying that if God had meant man to look upward, he would not have put our eyes level with the horizon. Ahab, who has been defying the world of nature all along, suddenly wants to follow the natural way, or so it would seem. At this very point we see pass over the Parsee's face "a sneering triumph that seemed meant for Ahab, and a fatalistic despair that seemed meant for himself." This incident gives us the clue to the difference between the Prometheanism of Ahab and that of both the original Prometheus and his Renaissance counterpart, from Doctor Faustus on. Ahab's defiance is based neither on an order which will eventually bear him out, nor on the mastery of "fire," that power stolen from the gods through which man builds his civilizations. On the contrary, not only in the case of the quadrant, but finally in that of the compass and all his other guides, Ahab throws away science, that form of co-operation with nature which man has used to gain his greatest dominion over it. "Science! Curse thee, thou vain toy," shouts Ahab as he flings down the quadrant. Science, the very essence of man's Prometheanism in the modern world, science, the key symbol of man's unlimited power since the Renaissance, no longer suffices to assure Ahab of his victory over nature and the gods. As Ishmael himself says in "Brit" (LVIII):

> However baby man may brag of his science and skill, and however much, in a flattering future, that science and skill may augment; yet for ever and for ever, to the crack of doom, the sea will insult and murder him, and pulverize the stateliest, stiffest frigate he can make.

Ahab abandons the central belief of Bacon and Renaissance man that the way to the realization of one's humanity is through the knowledge that gives one power over nature.

For Ahab, co-operation with the impersonal world means submission to it. Ahab's Modern Prometheanism, in contrast to Greek and Renaissance Prometheanism, means the defiance of the impersonal in the name of the personal, as he himself makes explicit in his "worship" of the fire when the masts are set ablaze with the "corpusants," or "St. Elmo's fire," in "The Candles" (CXIX).

> Oh! thou clear spirit of clear fire, whom on these seas I as Persian once did worship, till in the sacramental act so burned by thee, that to this hour I bear the scar; I now know thee, thou clear spirit, and I now know that thy right worship is defiance. To neither love nor reverence wilt thou be kind; and e'en for hate thou canst but kill; and all are killed. No fearless fool now fronts thee. I own thy speechless, placeless power; but to the last gasp of my earthquake life will dispute its unconditional, unintegral mastery in me. In the midst of the personified impersonal, a personality stands here. Though but a point at best; whencesoe'er I came; wheresoe'er I go; yet while I earthly live, the queenly personality lives in me and feels her royal rights.

Here then is the secret of Ahab's defiance: he is what this "clear spirit of fire" can never be—a person, and as a person he is conscious and aware of himself, as the fire is not. "Thou knowest not how came ye, hence callest thyself unbegotten; certainly knowest not thy beginning, hence callest thyself unbegun. I know that of me, which thou knowest not of thyself, oh, thou omnipotent." This fire resembles an absolute, in fact the absolute just as it is described by the Buddha—"unborn, unbegotten, uncreated"—but it is something short of absolute after all. This ostensible absolute that has confronted us throughout the book—the absoluteness of Moby Dick, of the sea, of the indifferent universe—turns out to lack one essential dimension, and that is personality. Personality is not only consciousness of oneself as a self; it is also the ability to stand as a person and hold one's ground in the face of the reality confronting one, as Ahab defies the fire and as Job contends with God.

Ahab has found something in man which gives him that inwardness, that stance from which to relate to the outer, that makes him not just a helpless atom in an infinite world, not just little Pip cast away on the immense, indifferent ocean. Ahab's fight as the representative of the human against all that "heaps" and maddens man now becomes the fight for man as person against the vast, seemingly omnipotent impersonal. Ahab knows of something that stands at the origin of both the person and the impersonal, something which man can face as a person, something which gives him the power to defy the impersonal. "There is some unsuffusing thing, beyond thee, thou clear spirit, to whom all thy eternity is but time, all thy creativeness mechanical. Through thee, thy flaming self, my scorched eyes do see it."

There is another absolute, after all, which is really absolute in a way in which this seeming absolute of nature is not. There is an eternity which is something more than an infinity of time. There is a creativity which is something more than this enormous, seemingly unlimited power. The very nature of that eternity is such that while it gives birth to the personal and impersonal there is a closer, more "integral" kinship between it and the personal. It bears up the person in the face of the impersonal even when physically he is so helpless, so limited, so easily destroyed. Ahab does not respect the courage of Stubb, because it partakes of the nature of the impersonal. "Ay, thou art brave as fearless fire, and as mechanical," Ahab says to Stubb during the final chase, taking us back to his speech to the corposants in "The Candles." Stubb, like them, is a "personified impersonal," a creature that wears the mask of personality but lacks its real creativity.

This is the one point in the book where the overall dualism seems to be qualified by the glimpse of something which perhaps, after all, underspans and overarches the gap between the human personal and the nonpersonal. Yet a dualism is implicit here too—between Ahab's "fiery father" whom he recognizes in the "clear spirit of clear fire" and his "sweet mother" whom he knows not. Since the "fiery father" seems to stand for the ineffable source of personality, there is also implicit here a Gnostic dualism between darkness and light, wrath and love, the evil "creator God" and the good "redeemer God" of the Marcionites and other Gnostics. Thus Ahab says to the fire:

> "To neither love nor reverence wilt thou be kind; and e'en for hate thou canst but kill; and all are killed . . . War is pain and hate is woe. Come in thy lowest form of love, and I will kneel and kiss thee; but at thy highest, come as mere

supernal power; and though thou launchest navies of full-freighted worlds, there's that in here that still remains indifferent. Oh, thou clear spirit, of thy fire thou madest me, and like a true child of fire, I breathe it back to thee."

Man is a child of nature as well as spirit, but he may use his natural force to defy nature; he may, and Ahab does, "fight fire with fire."

In his speech in "The Candles," Ahab seems to acknowledge a transcendent with which he identifies himself in his fight against the hostile world. If Ahab resembles the Gnostics in this and other respects, it is not because Melville is under Gnostic "influence," as some critics think.[2] Melville is a modern man who makes use of Gnostic symbolism to say something essentially different from what the Gnostics were saying: different, first, in that the "creator God" he is accusing is much closer to the power of nature, absolutized and personified, than to the God of the Bible, even in the grossly caricaturized form given him by the Gnostics; second, in that, unlike the Gnostics, he does not appeal to transcendent spirit but to the personality, as no ancient Gnostic would.[3] Man, to the Gnostic, is a fallen creature made in the image of the evil creator God, and man's body and psyche, in other words most of what goes into making up his personality, are corrupt and evil as well. Only the pneuma, the hidden, essentially impersonal spirit, still retains kinship with the transcendent redeemer God. Ahab is not an ancient Gnostic but the late continuation of the Renaissance man, now disillusioned in the essential Renaissance belief that man fulfills himself as a person through his knowledge of and control over nature. Ahab can no longer affirm himself as a person except in defiance of the impersonal.

As the novel takes its inexorable course, however, we realize that the personal is precisely what Ahab more and more gives up and betrays until he ends by utterly denying it and making himself a part of the very impersonal that he has here defied. Ahab takes his heroic stance at the meeting point of the personal with the impersonal. But he goes too far. He sacrifices the meeting of person and person through which alone he could remain a person. Ahab fights evil and becomes it, as has been remarked so often. He becomes it because he gives up the one ground on which he could fight it—his real human existence as a person in actual relation to other persons.

As a consequence, even the "personality" that he affirms is not, in him, a whole person but only one aspect of a person—a heroic ego rather than a self, as Newton Arvin points out, a "proud and defiant will" rather than "a human being in all his wholeness and roundness."[4] In "The Deck-Ahab and the Carpenter" (CVIII) Ahab moves from likening the carpenter who fashions him a new wooden leg to "that old Greek, Prometheus, who made men" to his own Promethean prescription for "a complete man after a desirable pattern," an image of man which leaves out not only everything unique and personal in man, but the heart itself.

> Imprimis, fifty feet high in his socks; then, chest modelled after the Thames Tunnel; then, legs with roots to 'em, to stay in one place; then, arms three feet through the wrist; no heart at all, brass forehead, and about a quarter of an

acre of fine brains; and let me see—shall I order eyes to see outwards? No, but put a sky-light on top of his head to illuminate inwards.

Ahab's "complete man" fills us with all the horror of the Golem or Frankenstein monster that it resembles. Yet the pseudo-human image that Ahab's monster wears makes us suspect that this "man" is for Ahab not only instrument but ideal—illuminated inward, without real contact with others, of superhuman intelligence, devoid of heart—a self-portrait, in fact; Ahab as he has increasingly become and as he wants to be! That Melville intends Ahab's image of man as a reflection of Ahab's own loss of humanity becomes eminently clear when we recall that Ishmael has described Ahab as "a Prometheus" whose "intense thinking" has created a vulture that feeds forever upon his heart. This is not Prometheus the noble rebel but Prometheus the exile, exiled by his very rebellion which cuts him off from his own self. "I stand for the heart," writes Melville. "To the dogs with the head! I had rather be a fool with a heart, than Jupiter Olympus with his head."[5]

Ahab is "queenly," indeed, but not a person in the full sense of the term. Yet, unlike his monstrous model and despite his overweening will, Ahab has a great heart, and from his first description of Ahab as "a man of greatly superior natural force, with a globular brain and a ponderous heart," Melville never lets us forget it. In Ahab, Melville created a demonic romantic figure who appeals, and is meant to appeal to us, through his noble suffering and dark grandeur. "Moody stricken Ahab stood before them with a crucifixion in his face; in all the nameless regal overbearing dignity of some mighty woe," recounts Ishmael, describing Ahab's first appearance. "Oh, my captain, my captain!—noble heart," says Starbuck in his last appeal. "See, it's a brave man that weeps; how great the agony of the persuasion then!" Starbuck still hopes that a brave man's tears can reach that "noble heart." Ahab himself contrasts his wild suffering with the lesser woe of the blacksmith: "Thy shrunk voice sounds too calmly, sanely woeful to me. In no Paradise myself, I am impatient of all misery in others that is not mad." That this distinction between superior and inferior suffering is shared by Melville is made clear beyond doubt by his comment on the Ahab who lies crushed and broken at the bottom of Stubb's boat after the mishaps of "The Chase—First Day" (CXXXIII):

> Far inland, nameless wails came from him, as desolate sounds from out ravines. But this intensity of his physical prostration did but so much the more abbreviate it. In an instant's compass, great hearts sometimes condense to one deep pang, the sum total of those shallow pains kindly diffused through feebler men's whole lives. And so, such hearts, though summary in each one suffering; still, if the gods decree it, in their life-time aggregate a whole age of woe, wholly made up on instantaneous intensities; for even in their pointless centres, those noble natures contain the entire circumferences of inferior souls.

We must distinguish between two types of "heart"—the romantic-demonic and the human. The former remains strong in Ahab till the end; the latter disappears. Ahab mistakes romantic defiance, as a result, for the affirmation of human personality. The hedonistic and sadistic Stubb is characterized by Fleece as "more of shark dan Massa Shark hisself." Ahab is above any vulgar enjoyment or mere meanness. "Gifted with the high perception, I lack the low, enjoying power," he says of himself. Just for this reason, it is he, and not Stubb, who recognizes sharkish, cannibalistic nature as evil and goes forth to attack it. Yet he does not really recognize any independent "other." His "woe" goes over to madness just at this point, when he projects all evil onto Moby Dick. Ahab is not mad merely in any prosaic sense; he is romantically mad. "I'm demoniac," he boasts, "I am madness maddened! That wild madness that's only calm to comprehend itself!" Prophet and fulfiller in one, he is more than the great gods ever were. "I laugh and hoot at ye, ye cricket-players, ye pugilists . . . ye've knocked me down, and I am up again; but *ye* have run and hidden." The gods themselves cannot swerve Ahab from his fixed purpose. Like a giant locomotive, "over unsounded gorges, through the rifled hearts of mountains, under torrents' beds, unerringly I rush!" Thus in Ahab the image of man finally becomes the image of a locomotive! This is the ultimate irony of Ahab's "iron way."

In "The Candles" Ahab speaks of a personal existence that he does not live. In "The Symphony" (CXXXII) he lives it—for a brief moment—in a relation to Starbuck that is, for once, person-to-person, rather than captain-to-mate. In the opening of "The Symphony" the dualism that is so often suggested throughout *Moby-Dick* is replaced by a dialectic. Until now the very substance of a terrifying dualism, the gentle air and cannibalistic sea become partners in a male-female dialectic, and their antagonism disappears in their harmonious sexual intercourse. But Ahab appears on the scene with his own dualism intact: "Tied up and twisted; gnarled and knotted with wrinkles; haggardly firm and unyielding; his eyes glowing like coals, that still glow in the ashes of ruin; untottering Ahab stood forth in the clearness of the morn; lifting his splintered helmet of a brow to the fair girl's forehead of heaven." Yet even Ahab, as he leans over the deck, is not entirely impervious to the caressing of the "glad, happy air" and "winsome sky." For a moment the lovely aromas seem to dispel "the cankerous thing in his soul." From beneath his slouched hat he drops a tear into the ocean, and Starbuck, who stands near, hears "in his own true heart the measureless sobbing that stole out of the centre of serenity around him."

This is another Ahab, not the "grand, ungodly godlike man" of whom Captain Peleg, the ship's owner, speaks to Ishmael, but the Ahab whom Peleg characterizes, "Stricken, blasted, if he be, Ahab has his humanities!" This is the Ahab who says to the shoals of fishes who swim away from the *Pequod* when its wake crosses with a stranger ship, "Swim away from me, do ye?" in a tone which we are told, "conveyed more of deep helpless sadness than the insane old man had ever before evinced." "I feel deadly faint, bowed, and humped," Ahab says to Starbuck in "The Symphony," "as though I were Adam staggering beneath the piled centuries since Paradise." Ahab, the self-appointed representative of mankind in its fight against the hostile nonhuman world now acknowledges himself, for once, the frail human being burdened beyond his endurance: "God! God! God! crack my heart!—stave my brain!—mockery! mockery! bitter biting mockery of grey hairs, have I lived enough to wear ye, and seem and feel thus intolerably old?"

Ahab asks Starbuck to stand close and says, "Let me look into a human eye, it is better than to gaze upon sea and sky, better than to gaze upon God." Ahab now longs for the personal and in the only way in which it can really be present—person in relation to person, eyes looking into eyes, face responding to face. "By the green land; by the bright hearth stone! this is the magic glass, man; I see my wife and my child in thine eye." This link with Starbuck is also a link with the land and with all that Ahab has of humanity in him. Starbuck takes advantage of the moment to plead: "Oh, my Captain! my Captain! noble soul! grand old heart, after all! why should anyone give chase to that hated fish!" But Ahab's glance is averted. The moment of openness is followed by bitterness, irony, despair, and defeat. "Like a blighted fruit tree he shook, and cast his last, cindered apple to the soil!" From now on Ahab will only be the old man on the chase—with this difference; that he has, for once, acknowledged weakness. Ahab's sense of the futility of his life quickly turns into a sense of fate—at first his own inner compulsion, but later the external, "predestined" universe. Since Ahab does not now identify himself with this compulsion, he sees it as external to him and projects it onto fate and to God, the judge who "himself is dragged to the bar" for creating the evil of the world.

> "If the great sun move not of himself; but is as an errand-boy in heaven; nor one single star can revolve, but by some invisible power; how then can this one small heart beat; this one small brain think thoughts; unless God does that beating, does that thinking, does that living, and not I. By heaven, man, we are turned round and round in this world, like yonder windlass, and Fate is the handspike."

"The mild, mild wind" and the fragrant air make Ahab think of mowers sleeping among new-mown hay in the Andes, but he ends with a bitter reflection on death: "Aye, toil we how we may, we all sleep at last on the field. Sleep? Aye, and rust amid greenness: at last year's scythes flung down, and left in the half-cut swaths." No sooner is the sweet moment of peace experienced than man is caught up again in the flow that inexorably takes him on to his death. It is the sense that he cannot rest in any such moment that is the bitterness which drives Ahab on, that hands him back helpless to his compulsion. What in Goethe's *Faust* is romantically meaningful and itself the guarantee of salvation—that Faust will not rest in any moment but "ever strives"—in "The Symphony" is a dreadful fate that drives man mercilessly to his end.

"The Symphony" is the only real break that we see in Ahab's mad progress toward destruction. Does this mean that there is a real chance for Ahab to turn back? No, for all his strength lies in the demonic side of his character, while the human is weak and unrealized. Ahab's "humanity" is more passive emotion than active attitude. The one moment of freedom, of real dialogue with another person, quickly dissolves into the monologue of a man who can never really listen and respond to another person. Starbuck steals away "blanched to a corpse's hue with despair" and Fedallah, Ahab's Mephistophelian *alter ego,* is left looking up at Ahab from where his eyes are reflected in the water.

F. O. Matthiessen has called Melville's account of the three days of the actual chase of Moby Dick "the finest piece of dramatic writing in American literature."[6] The first essential of the drama is the appearance of Moby Dick himself. In "The Chase—First Day," "the grand god revealed himself" with all the "terrors of his . . . trunk" and "the wrenched hideousness of his jaw."

> A gentle joyousness—a mighty mildness of repose in swiftness, invested the gliding whale . . . Not Jove, not that great majesty Supreme! did surpass the glorified White Whale as he so divinely swam.

The other essential of this archetypal drama is the legendary hero, the Prometheus who not only withstands but goes forth to attack this leviathanic Zeus. Once "The Symphony"'s moment of weakness is passed, Ahab resumes his defiance, and these last chapters resound with the leitmotif of Ahab's unconquerable soul. Although Ahab confesses to Starbuck that it is "sweet to lean sometimes," yet "even with a broken bone" he claims himself "untouched": "Nor White Whale, nor man, nor fiend, can so much as graze old Ahab in his own proper and inaccessible being." When Stubb laughs at a wreck of a boat, Ahab exclaims, "What soulless thing is this that laughs before a wreck? Man, man! did I not know thee brave as fearless fire (and as mechanical) I could swear thou wert a poltroon." But when Starbuck draws near and says, "Aye, Sir, 'tis a solemn sight; an omen, and an ill one," Ahab rejects Starbuck's omen with the same scorn as Stubb's "soulless laughter": "If the gods think to speak outright to man, they will honorably speak outright; not shake their heads, and give an old wives' darkling hint." Men who look for omens are men who passively resign themselves to fate, and this will never be Ahab—the man who converts the omen-fraught terror of the corposants into his own magic fire with which he welds the crew once more to his purpose. "Begone! Ye two are the opposite poles of one thing; Starbuck is Stubb reversed, and Stubb is Starbuck, and ye two are all mankind." Mankind is made up, on the one hand, of those fearless dolts who are able to act because they have no true sense of what they are confronting and, on the other, of those solemn, passive beings who are afraid to act at all because they see man at the mercy of fate and wish, like Shakespeare's Brutus, to blame their being "underlings" on their stars. Ahab insists on both full awareness of the hostile reality that confronts man and fully active confrontation of it. As a result, "Ahab stands alone among the millions of the peopled earth, nor gods nor men his neighbors! Cold, cold—I shiver!" Here stands the lonely Superman, the Titan Prometheus towering over the lesser breed of men.

When Starbuck pleads with Ahab to abandon the chase in "The Chase—

Second Day" (CXXXIV), Ahab replies: "Starbuck, of late I've felt strangely moved to thee, ever since that hour we both saw—thou know'st what, in one another's eyes." The dialogue with Starbuck that recalled his own humanity is still present to Ahab, but while the chase continues this dialogue can have no significance for him. It cannot affect or even in the slightest way deflect his onrushing course: "In this matter of the whale, be the front of thy face to me as the palm of this hand—a lipless, unfeatured blank." The confrontation with what is not man transcends and submerges the dialogue with man. It does not even preserve man's personality from what threatens to destroy it, as in "The Candles." If Ahab's next statement to Starbuck is the Promethean "Ahab is forever Ahab, man," it is followed by a total surrender to the impersonal power that he was originally fighting:

> "This whole act's immutably decreed.[7] 'Twas rehearsed by thee and me a billion years before this ocean rolled. Fool! I am the Fate's lieutenant; I act under orders. Look thou underling! that thou obeyest mine."

Even mad little Pip, whom Ahab has befriended, can no longer reach Ahab when he calls to him and warns him against the sharks. "Ahab heard nothing; for his own voice was high-lifted then." Ahab is the most thoroughgoing example of the "monological man" that one can find, short of the psychotic. He can hear no other human voice because his own is "high-lifted." In the end it is just this that most drastically betrays the destruction of his own humanity. "Ye are not other men," says Ahab to his crew, "but my arms and my legs and so obey me." There can be no human dialogue because there is only one person, one consciousness present, and this consciousness exists only in relation to the impersonal. "They were one man, not thirty . . . the individualities of the crew . . . were all directed to that fatal goal which Ahab their one lord and keel did point to." This is humanity at its height and at its depth—standing bravely confronting what is not man, yet denying the individuality and the free interrelationship of men in so doing.

Ahab's betrayal of the personal for the impersonal is an integral part of his denial of dialogue in favor of that overweening monologue in which all people and things become subsumed under his own ego. To this world-subjectivizing individualism Ahab clings to the last. The crew are only part of his consciousness and purpose: Starbuck must not die because he reminds Ahab of his wife and child; Moby Dick must be destroyed because he did not passively submit to being converted into oil. When Ishmael says in "The Monkey-Rope," "Another's mistake or misfortune might plunge innocent me into unmerited disaster and death," his "innocent me" is ironic. He knows that human existence is essentially, and not just secondarily, interdependent and reciprocal. Ahab's "innocent me" is paranoid—the inverted idealist's accusation against the world that does not conform to his inwardness and subject itself to his purposes. When the carpenter makes a new leg for Ahab, the latter bewails:

> "Here I am, proud as a Greek god, and yet standing debtor to this blockhead for a bone to stand on! Cursed be that mortal interindebtedness which will

not do away with ledgers. I would be free as air; and I'm down in the whole world's books." (CVIII)

Ahab's monological consciousness is nowhere more evident than in his reaction to the encounter with other worlds that have not come under the domination of his mad chase as has the little world of the *Pequod*. This encounter takes the form of the *Pequod*'s nine "gams"—its meeting and exchange of greetings with the succession of symbolically named whaling ships that pass it in the course of the book's action—the *Albatross*, the *Town-Ho*, the *Jeroboam*, the *Virgin*, the *Rose-Bud*, the *Samuel Enderby* of London, the *Bachelor*, the *Rachel*, and the *Delight*. Ordinarily, we are told, the meeting of two whaling ships at sea, one perhaps outward bound, the other coming home after a long voyage, is the occasion for "friendly and sociable contact," exchange of letters and news, exchange of visits—in short, a "gam." Ahab's unsociability and his singleness of purpose stand out all the more starkly in the face of this natural and customary sociability, "for . . . he cared not to consort, even for five minutes, with any stranger captain, except he could contribute some of that information he so absorbingly sought." When the *Pequod* meets another ship, Ahab's one question is, "Hast seen the White Whale?"

The captain of the *Samuel Enderby* has not only seen the White Whale, but has lost his arm as a result of him. But he refuses to lower for Moby Dick again, not wishing to give him another arm. " 'There would be great glory in killing him, . . . but, hark ye, he's best let alone; don't you think so, Captain?'—glancing at the ivory leg." But to Ahab it is just that which makes Moby Dick irresistible: "He is. But he will still be hunted, for all that. What is best let alone, that accursed thing is not always what least allures. He's all a magnet!" Moby Dick's evil magnetism cannot hold the English captain, who will not even go along with Ahab as to the character of Moby Dick: "What you take for the White Whale's malice is only his awkwardness." To such superficiality and levity Ahab can only turn his back: "In vain the English captain hailed him. With back to the stranger ship, and face set like a flint to his own, Ahab stood upright till alongside of the Pequod." But the *Samuel Enderby* at least has encountered Moby Dick. The jolly *Bachelor*, like jolly Stubb, will not even take him seriously. The *Bachelor*'s captain stands erect on his quarter deck enjoying "the whole rejoicing drama" of his "glad ship of good luck." Ahab, in "striking contrast," stands on the quarter-deck of "the moody Pequod," "shaggy and black, with a stubborn gloom."

> "Come aboard, come aboard!" cried the gay Bachelor's commander, lifting a glass and a bottle in the air.
> "Hast seen the White Whale?" gritted Ahab in reply.
> "No; only heard of him; but don't believe in him at all," said the other good-humoredly. "Come aboard!"
> "Thou art too damned jolly. Sail on." (CXV)

Perhaps the finest single symbol of Ahab's monological life is the doubloon which he nails to the mast as a prize for the first man who raises the White Whale.

When one after the other Ahab, Starbuck, Stubb, Flask, and the Manxman read the markings on the doubloon, "to each and every man in turn," it "but mirrors back his own mysterious self," as Ahab says himself. But only Ahab sees it as himself. "Look here,—three peaks as proud as Lucifer. The firm tower, that is Ahab; the volcano, that is Ahab; the courageous, the undaunted, and victorious fowl, that, too, is Ahab; all are Ahab." Each sees reality from his own perspective, as little Pip indicates with his grammatical recitation, "I look, you look, he looks; we look, ye look, they look." But only Ahab identifies himself with reality to such an extent that he can recognize no independent "other." It is fitting that it is Ahab himself who first raises Moby Dick and claims the doubloon for his own, and he does not fail to draw the proper conclusion from this happening:

> "I saw him almost that same instant, Sir, that Captain Ahab did, and I cried out," said Tashtego.
> "Not the same instant; not the same instant; not the same—no, the doubloon is mine, Fate reserved the doubloon for me. I only; none of ye could have raised the White Whale first." (CXXXIII)

If Ahab sounds more like a grasping child here than a noble hero, he leaves us in no doubt that his natural superiority to all men is destined by "Fate" itself. The passage in "The Chase—Second Day" in which he characterizes himself as "Fate's Lieutenant" not only begins with "Ahab is forever Ahab," as we have seen, but ends with "Ahab's hawser tows his purpose yet." Ahab is Fate's lieutenant, not its underling. If, after "The Symphony," he no longer has the strength to fight the nonhuman in the name of the human, he now finds in "Fate" the support for the Promethean self-affirmation that enables him to pit himself against the hated White Whale. Fate is no longer, for him, the merely external power that it was in "The Symphony." Rather, it is the larger order with whose purposes he co-operates, even as he once saw Fate as co-operating with his purposes when he said, in "The Sunset" (XXXVII), "The path to my fixed purpose is laid with iron rails, whereon my soul is grooved to run."

Ahab obeys Fate, but he still defies the Whale. When Moby Dick finally turns to destroy the ship that is harassing him, "retribution, swift vengeance, eternal malice" are "in his whole aspect," recalling all the hints about his inscrutable malice that are piled up in earlier chapters as well as the accounts of other sperm whales destroying large ships with "judicious" malice and "decided, calculating mischief." Ahab, certainly, does not look on the White Whale at the last as his partner in a predestined drama. His relation to him, more intensely personal even than that with Starbuck or any other human being, is one of pure hatred. "To the last I grapple with thee; from hell's heart I stab at thee; for hate's sake I spit my last breath at thee . . . while still chasing thee, though tied to thee, thou damned whale! *Thus,* I give up the spear!" Ahab goes down defying to the last. Unlike the dying whale who even as a representative of the "dark Hindu half of nature" still turns his body toward the natural sun, Ahab turns his body *from* the sun. He denies his link with nature even while he sinks his harpoon into the whale who the next moment carries him down to his death. "Towards thee I roll, thou all-destroying but unconquering whale," Ahab cries in this same speech. The whale, like the fire, has the power to destroy, but it cannot conquer Ahab; it cannot conquer that personality that he still retains to the last, if only in his defiance.

It is not nature alone that Ahab is cut off from, however, but all mankind. "Oh lonely death on lonely life!" says Ahab. "Oh, now I feel my topmost greatness lies in my topmost grief." There is no positive sense in which Ahab can be called great—even for Melville he cannot be an image of man in the full sense of the term—but he is great in his grief, in his proud aloneness, in his Promethean defiance. He is a man who pours all his life's searching and fighting into this one moment, who insists on giving his death the very meaning his life has had.

If Moby Dick is "all-destroying," he is still "unconquering." In Ahab's final hate-spitting, "from hell's heart"-stabbing defiance of the White Whale to whom he is tied, the note of self-affirmation rings out clear and undaunted. That Ahab responds to the hostility of the world with defiance does not represent a moral choice on his part in any ordinary sense of the term: he has to defy to exist. Ahab is the last stage of the romantic hero who turns his defiant despair into a barricade against God and man alike and settles down to live in the heightened reality of his own agonized self with its narrow intensity of meaning. His isolation is not that of the albino who is ejected by his fellows from the herd but, in Melville's own image in "The Cabin-Table" (XXXIV), that of the grizzly bear who shuts himself up in sullen self-reliance:

> Though nominally included in the census of Christendom, he was still an alien to it. He lived in the world, as the last of the Grisly Bears lived in settled Missouri. And as . . . that wild Logan of the woods, burying himself in the hollow of a tree, lived out the winter there, sucking his own paws, so, in his inclement, howling old age, Ahab's soul, shut up in the caved trunk of his body, there fed upon the sullen paws of its gloom!

Ahab is not only the best example in literature of Kierkegaard's "demonic shut-inness."[8] He is also the best example of Martin Buber's "second stage of evil," in which man reaches the threshold of self-deification and absolute self-affirmation. The man in this stage denies all order and reality that might call him to account and says, "What I do is good because I do it" and "What I say is true because I say it."[9]

Here the final stage of the isolated romantic hero merges with the end-term of the Modern Promethean who, as the only means of overcoming man's alienation and recovering his creative freedom, denies any reality that transcends him. Ahab is a proud romantic figure, Milton's Satan[10] and Byron's Manfred, but he is also a tragic and pitiable figure shivering in the cold on his outpost on the jutting cliff. Behind the lineaments of the romantic rebel we can dimly discern the face of the Modern Exile; behind the noble despair lurks the quotidian.

Through Ishmael, Melville is able to express with some precision the sense in which he does and does not identify with Ahab. Ishmael's warning to those who discover the dark side of life and plunge remorselessly on in their knowledge of it expresses Melville's own reservations as to his hero Ahab. "Give not thyself up, then, to fire," concludes Ishmael in "The Try-Works" (XCVI), "lest it invert thee, deaden thee; as for the time it did me. There is a wisdom that is woe; but there is a woe that is madness." Somewhere between the foolish optimist and the too-wise madman, Ishmael, and without question Melville too, hoped to find the truly wise man who could face the evil and suffering of the world without being overwhelmed by it: "There is a Catskill eagle in some souls that can alike dive down into the blackest gorges, and soar out of them again and become invisible in the sunny spaces." One must have the wisdom that is woe to be man, really to be man, and yet one has to stop short of immersing oneself in that woe, stop short of madness. Man cannot prove himself man through the attitude of a "jolly Stubb," who grins at Moby Dick and will not take him seriously. But neither can he authenticate himself in the way of Ahab, who, like an inverted idealist, turns the natural rebellion of the whale against being killed into a universal, metaphysical evil; who captures the crew within his own inner world and his own purpose; and who refuses, even on encountering other ships, to recognize any reality other than that of his monomaniac hunt.

If one must choose, however, between the superficial optimist and the man who looks only into the depths of life, Ishmael and Melville choose the latter: "Even if he for ever flies within the gorge, that gorge is in the mountains; so that even in his lowest swoop the mountain eagle is still higher than other birds upon the plain even though they soar." The fire is a symbol not only of evil, but also of suffering, of the search for truth, of the full and intense use of man's spiritual energies, and of that elemental sphere in which the human mind cannot long sojourn without madness. There is an admiration here for the Promethean hero, the seeker for truth, reminiscent of the apotheosis of Bulkington in "The Lee Shore." There is admiration for the profundity, for the courage, heroism, and defiance of the mad Ahab. But there is also a word of warning. Ahab's defiance is not a romantic pose. Ahab acts as he does because no other relation to existence is open to him.

Moby-Dick abounds with evidence that Melville intended Ahab to be seen within the context of tragedy. He proclaims that "democratic dignity" which enables him to "ascribe high qualities" and "weave tragic graces" around "meanest mariners, and renegades and castaways." Although Ahab lacks the "outward majestical trappings" of emperors and kings, he is still fit subject for "the tragic dramatist who would depict mortal indomitableness in its fullest sweep": "Oh, Ahab! what shall be grand in thee, it must needs be plucked at from the skies, and dived for in the deep, and featured in the unbodied air!" Ahab, "a poor old whale-hunter," can occupy the throne of the tragic hero that in ancient times might only be held by kings and those of noble blood.

The mediator between Ahab and the tragic hero of old, and the patent of Ahab's tragic nobility, is the romantic hero with his titanic suffering and his dark morbidity. In almost his first, oblique reference to Ahab in "The Ship" (XVI), Ishmael leaves us in no doubt that Ahab is cast in the dimensions of the romantic tragic hero:

> When these things unite in a man of greatly superior natural force, with a globular brain and a ponderous heart; who has also by the stillness and seclusion of many long night-watches in the remotest waters . . . been led to think untraditionally and independently; receiving all nature's sweet or savage impressions fresh from her own virgin voluntary and confiding breast, and thereby chiefly . . . to learn a bold and nervous lofty language—that man makes one in a whole nation's census—a mighty pageant creature, formed for noble tragedies. Nor will it at all detract from him, dramatically regarded, if either by birth or other circumstances, he have what seems a half wilful over-ruling morbidness at the bottom of his nature. For all men tragically great are made so through a certain morbidness.

Nor does Melville fail to provide us with Ahab's tragic flaw: "In his fiery eyes of scorn and triumph, you then saw Ahab in all his fatal pride." Melville's intention is also evident in modes and motifs from Shakespearean tragedy, in particular *Lear* and *Macbeth*, with which the final chapters are permeated, as well as in the heightened tone throughout, which enables Melville to "spread a rainbow" over Ahab's "disastrous set of sun."

Ahab, for all that, is not a tragic hero in the traditional Aristotelian sense of the term. There is too little real fate, despite Ahab's reference to it; there is too much that grows, almost arbitrarily, out of Ahab himself. Nor can we identify with Ahab as with the Greek tragic hero. Despite the fact that "Ahab has his humanities" in his relation to Starbuck and mad Pip, toward the end he becomes almost inhuman. Our rare glimpses of his human emotions only reinforce the sense of the dominance of the inhuman will in which they are submerged. Ahab ends his dialogue with Starbuck with his statement that, in the predestined matter of the whale, Starbuck's face is to him but as the palm of his hand, "a lipless, unfeatured blank." When Ahab refuses to help hunt for the son of the *Rachel*'s captain, his language still contains a touch of the human—"God bless ye, man, and may I forgive myself"— but it begins with "I will not do it. Even now I lose time," and ends with "I must go." Pip's offer in "The Cabin" (CXXIX) to serve as Ahab's leg touches Ahab and threatens to melt his stern determination. But he puts Pip away from him with all the more energy therefore, even while blessing him:

> "Lad, lad, I tell thee thou must not follow Ahab now. The hour is coming when Ahab would not scare thee from him, yet would not have thee by him. There is that in thee, poor lad, which I feel too curing to my malady. Like cures like; and for this hunt, my malady becomes my most desired health . . ."
>
> " . . . Sir; do ye but use poor me for your one lost leg . . ."
>
> "Oh! spite of million villains, this makes me a bigot in the fadeless fidelity of man!—and a black! and crazy! . . ."

"...I will never desert ye, Sir...I must go with ye."

"If thou speakest thus to me much more, Ahab's purpose keels up in him. I tell thee no; it cannot be...Weep so, and I will murder thee! have a care, for Ahab too is mad ... Thy hand!—Met! True art thou, lad, as the circumference to its centre. So: God for ever bless thee; and if it comes to that,— God for ever save thee, let what will befall."

Ahab's "Weep, so, and I will murder thee!" is, in reality, his final word to little Pip, who dies shut up in Ahab's cabin because Ahab has gone to hurl his harpoon at Moby Dick. Although the reader may feel Ahab's humanity in "The Symphony" and "The Cabin," it is difficult for him to identify with the Ahab of the final chase or experience at Ahab's death the catharsis of "pity and terror" that the spectacle of the tragic hero's downfall is traditionally supposed to induce.

Even if this were not the case, there could be no emotional catharsis and no tragic resolution in Aristotle's sense of the term. Ahab does not in any way become reconciled to the order of the universe as the Greek tragic hero, including Prometheus, invariably does: instead, as we have seen, he goes down defying to the last. What is more, for Melville himself there is no order with which man can become reconciled, even through tragic suffering and death. The very heart of *Moby-Dick,* indeed, is the denial of just this order. Ahab's defiance of Moby Dick is succeeded by the tranquil indifference of the sea that at the end, when the other two protagonists have disappeared, looks on with detachment just as it has all along. If the sea at the end of *Moby-Dick* is a tranquil rather than a raging one, it is, nonetheless, the "masterless ocean" that "overruns the globe." Although the final picture of the sea rolling on "as it rolled five thousand years ago" suggests an attitude of acceptance, there is here no true tragic reconciliation. The aesthetic enclosure is that provided by the artistic form: it does not answer any of the questions that the book has raised, but it holds in powerful equilibrium the still unsilenced torment of the Modern Promethean.[11]

Yet Ahab *is* a tragic figure, for he possesses true tragic grandeur. We cannot dismiss him as merely romantic, merely psychotic, merely a mid-nineteenth-century American individualist, no matter how we study Melville's sources, describe the social history of the time, and psychoanalyze Melville and his characters. If ancient Greek tragedy is based on the positing of an order and man's reconciliation with it, a truly modern tragedy must be based on the modern view of the world, and not Aristotle's—a fact largely ignored by those literary scholars who dutifully carry over Aristotle's world view, along with his *Poetics,* to every analysis of modern tragedy. The modern tragedy must mean the recognition of the absence of any such order, and it *may* also mean the hero's defiance in the face of a hostile world. Ahab is not simply the victim of psychological determinism, like Lavinia in Eugene O'Neill's *Mourning Becomes Electra* and Blanche in Tennessee Williams' *Streetcar Named Desire.* His defiance grows out of freedom as well as compulsion, and in this sense at least, he is, in his very character as a Modern Promethean, a modern tragic hero.

NOTES

[1] Cf. M. O. Percival, *A Reading of* Moby Dick (Chicago: University of Chicago Press, 1950), pp. 9–13. Percival rightly points out the organic link between this scene and the later one where Ahab baptizes his own new-forged harpoon "non . . . in nomine patris, sed in nomine diaboli!" ("The Forge," CXIII).

[2] Cf. William Brasswell, *Melville's Religious Thought: An Essay in Interpretation* (Durham, N.C.: Duke University Press, 1943), p. 62.

[3] In the modern Gnostic personalism of the existentialist philosopher Nicholas Berdyaev, however, the personal is identical with a transcendent spirit dualistically divided from the external world of "objectification."

[4] Newton Arvin, *Herman Melville,* The American Men of Letters Series (New York: William Sloane Ass., 1950), pp. 176f.

[5] Letter to Nathaniel Hawthorne, Pittsfield, June ? 1851, Willard Thorp, *Herman Melville, Representative Selections,* American Writers Series, ed. Harry Hayden Clark (New York: American Book Co., 1938), p. 392.

[6] F. O. Matthiessen, *American Renaissance* (London and New York: Oxford University Press, 1941), p. 421.

[7] That on occasion Ishmael, and perhaps Melville too, shares this Calvinist attitude toward predestination is suggested by Ishmael's statement in "The Town-Ho's Story" (LIV): "Gentlemen, a strange fatality pervades the whole career of these events, as if verily mapped out before the world itself was charted."

[8] W. H. Auden, *The Enchafèd Flood, or the Romantic Iconography of the Sea* (London: Faber & Faber, 1951); M. O. Percival, op. cit., pp. 16–18, 34–36, 42, 100–102. Cf. Sören Kierkegaard, *The Concept of Dread* and *The Sickness unto Death.*

[9] Martin Buber, *Good and Evil: Two Interpretations* (New York: Charles Scribner's Sons, 1953) II. "Images of Good and Evil," trans. Michael Bullock, Part Two and Part Three, Chaps. IV, V, pp. 99–114, 133–143. Cf. Maurice Friedman, *Martin Buber: The Life of Dialogue* (New York: Harper Torchbook, 1960), "The Nature of Evil," Chap. XV.

[10] Cf. Henry F. Pommer, *Milton and Melville* (Pittsburgh: University of Pittsburgh Press, 1950), pp. 96f.

[11] "If Ahab persists in the face of an obvious dilemma, and is thereby destroyed, the dilemma is the same as Melville's own, and Melville has not resolved it for himself . . . Ahab's fury is the last stage of Melville's malaise. Actually, no final condemnation is possible. The largest paradox in *Moby-Dick,* prior to any moral judgment, is the necessity of voyaging and the equal necessity of failure." "Just as the method of *Moby-Dick* is a paradox, the theme of the book is an unresolved question." (Charles Feidelson, Jr., *Symbolism and American Literature* [Chicago: University of Chicago Press, 1953], pp. 34f, 185.)

Robert Zoellner

AHAB'S ENTROPISM
AND ISHMAEL'S CYCLICISM

From beginning to end, *Moby-Dick* is dominated by the shark's saw-pit of mouth and charnel of maw. Into that gaping, apparently bottomless rictal void everything must go. All things are, finally, *consumed*. It is this sense of both cosmic activity and life process as a hideously predacious, devouring kind of business, that makes *Moby-Dick* the supremely horrible book that it is. Moreover, Ishmael's increasing identification with the whale, while it meliorates certain of his hypos, exacerbates this one. It is not entirely consoling to realize that one's fraternal congenerity with alien Leviathan rests in part on a shared susceptibility to life's cormorant rapacity. "Oh, horrible vulturism of earth!" Ishmael exclaims, "from which not the mightiest whale is free" (69: 262).[1] It is in the figure of *self*-consumption, however, that Ishmael's hypos achieve their agonized climax. Certainly the most frightful passage in a frightful novel is Ishmael's description of sharks, disemboweled by random thrusts of the cutting-spades, ravenously devouring their own entrails (66: 257). These are, however, relatively obvious matters. What is not so obvious is that the auto-cannibalism of the sharks finds its parallel in the *Pequod*'s Captain. If, on a physical level, sharks in their frenzy devour themselves, on a congruent metaphysical level Ahab in his frenzy devours himself. The point is important because the self-consumption of Ahab—who at one point even refers to himself as "cannibal old me" (132: 444)—provides him with a paradigm of natural process which is radically different from the one which Ishmael gradually develops. There is a subterranean connection between the sharkishness of the *Pequod*'s world and the differing cosmologies of Ahab and Ishmael.

The motif of auto-consumption extends to the whale himself. When the try-works fires are first lighted, they are fed only for a short time with precious wood. After a certain point the residue of the rendering process, the "crisp, shrivelled blubber, now called scraps or fritters," is sufficient to sustain the flames

From *The Salt-Sea Mastodon: A Reading of* Moby-Dick (Berkeley: University of California Press, 1973), pp. 191–205.

without the addition of other fuel. Ishmael cannot resist the obvious analogy: "Like a plethoric burning martyr, or a self-consuming misanthrope, once ignited, the whale supplies his own fuel and burns by his own body" (96: *352–53*).The reference to misanthropic Ahab is obvious and inevitable, and Ishmael has already exploited it. "For a long time, now," he observed just before the *Pequod*'s encounter with the Grand Armada, "the circus-running sun has raced within his fiery ring, and needs no sustenance but what's in himself. So Ahab" (87: *319*). Such images of combustive self-expenditure are repeatedly associated with Ahab. The *Pequod*'s Captain is a man "consumed with the hot fire of his purpose" (46: *182*). Ahab himself asserts that the fire by which he lives represents an irreversible expenditure of self. The crew-members are "so many ant-hills of powder," and he must be, to achieve his purpose, their igniting match."Oh, hard!" he bitterly exclaims, "that to fire others, the match itself must needs be wasting!" (37: *147*). Life for Ahab is not a process of regeneration or renewal or rebirth. It is instead a steady declension into nothingness and annihilation. Starbuck makes this point near the end of the novel: "I have sat before the dense coal fire and watched it all aglow, full of its tormented flaming life; and I have seen it wane at last, down, down, to dumbest dust. Old man of oceans! of all this fiery life of thine, what will at length remain but one little heap of ashes!" (118: *412*).

It is, however, the images of auto-cannibalism, rather than of auto-combustion, which relate rapacious Ahab most precisely to the self-devouring shark and the cosmic processes of which the shark is symbol. Ahab is, Ishmael tells us, the victim of "all those malicious agencies which some deep men feel eating in them, till they are left living on with half a heart and half a lung" (41: *160*). Of his own insane choice, Ahab is "Gnawed within . . . with the infixed, unrelenting fangs of some incurable idea" (41: *162*). He is like the hibernating bear whose winter-life is based on self-consumption: "And as when Spring and Summer had departed, that wild Logan of the woods, burying himself in the hollow of a tree, lived out the winter there, sucking his own paws; so, in his inclement, howling old age, Ahab's soul, shut up in the caved trunk of his body, there fed upon the sullen paws of its gloom!" (34: *134*). "God help thee, old man," Ishmael exclaims, "thy thoughts have created a creature in thee; and he whose intense thinking thus makes him a Prometheus; a vulture feeds upon that heart for ever; that vulture the very creature he creates" (44: *175*). The "horrible vulturism" which so appalls Ishmael is not confined to external nature. Ahab's internal self also embodies it.

But there is more to the self-consumption of Ahab than a simple pattern of imagery. A fundamental concept of certain cosmologies is *entropy,* which articulates the hypothesis that all motion and activity simply reflect an inexorable downhill process, the steady degradation of matter and energy to a state of inert uniformity. Inevitably, entropy predicts, the last temperature gradient will disappear, the last star will blink out, the last world cease to spin, the primal darkness and the primordial frigidity once again enveloping everything. Entropy thus proposes a view of microcosmic and macrocosmic activity as irreversible *expenditure*. The concept is useful here because it furnishes an analogue for Ahab's sense of his own life-process, a kind of ontological entropism. This is the philosophical thrust of the imagery of self-consumption, and this is what he means when, Starbuck having reported to him a leak in some buried oil-cask deep in the *Pequod's* hold, he flatly rejects the request to "up Burtons and break out." "Begone!" he tells the first mate, "Let it leak! I'm all aleak myself. Aye! leaks in leaks! . . . Yet I don't stop to plug my leak; for who can find it in the deep-loaded hull; or how hope to plug it, even if found, in this life's howling gale?" (109: *393*).

Such a sense of ontological "leak" makes the life-process degenerative rather than regenerative; Ahab's living is only dying. What seems to have brought him to this pervasive pessimism was not the loss of his leg to Moby Dick, but rather the consequent injury to his groin, his regenerative faculty, which occurred when he fell and was "stake-wise smitten" by his new ivory leg (106: *385*). It is well to remember that Ahab, as Peleg tells Ishmael, "has a wife—not three voyages wedded—a sweet, resigned girl" (16: *77*). M. O. Percival touches on the general significance of this "agonizing wound": "In this incident we find that Moby Dick—present in the ivory stake—had bitten into the very center of [Ahab's] being, leaving a wound that was to prove incurable."[2]

Ahab regards the groin injury as the "direct issue" of the mutilation inflicted by the White Whale. This sense of *consequence* leads him to speculate on the preponderance of woe over joy. Evil, he at first thinks, regenerates itself equally with good: "the most poisonous reptile of the marsh perpetuates his kind as inevitably as the sweetest songster of the grove; so, equally with every felicity, all miserable events do naturally beget their like." Such a formulation is *not* entropic; it suggests rather an even-handed balance of light and dark in life. But Ishmael, who is once again—as in the "Surmises" chapter—imaginatively inferring Ahab's thoughts, immediately cancels this equivalence:

> Yea, more than equally, thought Ahab; since both the ancestry and posterity of Grief go further than the ancestry and posterity of Joy. For, not to hint of this: that it is an inference from certain canonic teachings, that while some natural enjoyments here shall have no children born to them for the other world, but, on the contrary, shall be followed by the joy-childlessness of all hell's despair; whereas, some guilty mortal miseries shall still fertilely beget to themselves an eternally progressive progeny of griefs beyond the grave; not at all to hint of this, there still seems *an inequality* in the deeper analysis of the thing. (106: *385–86;* italics mine)

Ahab has moved now from ontological entropism to a much more immediate psychological and moral entropism. Grief, in the nature of things, preponderates over and will finally annihilate Joy; the "inequality" is inescapable. But there is more. Entropic inequality touches not only the whole cosmos, but ultimately whatever divinity stands behind the cosmos: "To trail the genealogies of these high mortal miseries, carries us at last among the sourceless primogenitures of the gods; so that, in the face of all the glad, hay-making suns, and soft-cymballing, round harvest-moons, we must needs give in to this: *that the gods themselves are not for ever glad*" (106: *386;* italics mine). Ahab thus arrives at the ultimate formulation: *theological entropism.* Even the beatitude and joy of divine being, which we mortals know by their reflection in the ecstatic beauty of the natural world, are forms of deific expenditure which, like all other active principles, must be terminal by nature. The death of the cosmos will be the death of God.

When Ishmael speaks of "dark Ahab" (47: *187;* 48: *189*), then, he means Entropic Ahab. "So far gone am I in the dark side of earth," the *Pequod*'s Captain confesses, "that its other side, the theoretic bright one, seems but uncertain twilight to me" (127: *433*). For Ahab, death is more fundamental than life, dark more fundamental than light, stasis more fundamental than any activity. He expresses this entropic despair when, the day after the *Pequod* gams with the *Bachelor,* four whales are slain just before sunset, one of them by Ahab. Once again, as in the "Sunset" chapter (37: *146–47*), Ahab contemplates the "lovely sunset sea and sky," and watches as "sun and whale both stilly died together," noting that "strange spectacle observable in all sperm whales dying—the turning sunwards of the head, and so expiring" (116: *409*). "He turns and turns him to it," Ahab exclaims, "how slowly, but how steadfastly, his homage-rendering and invoking brow, with his last dying motions. He too worships fire; most faithful, broad, baronial vassal of the sun!" But the whale's sun-faith is, Ahab thinks, futile: "see!" he ponders, "no sooner dead, than death whirls round the corpse, and it heads some other way." The final motion of the whale is entropic, toward dark rather than light:

> "Oh, thou dark Hindoo half of nature [Ahab exclaims], who of drowned bones hast builded thy separate throne somewhere in the heart of these unverdured seas; thou art an infidel, thou queen, and too truly speakest to me in the wide-slaughtering Typhoon, and the hushed burial of its after calm. Nor has this thy whale sunwards turned his dying head, and then gone round again, without a lesson to me." (116: *409*)

The lesson is that all life is subject to irreversible entropic decay. The sun, which appears to be a life-source, and is so worshipped by the whale, is really a death-source, since the bringing forth of life but augments the ultimate quantum of cosmic death, of which, for Ahab, the "unverdured" sea itself is the macrosymbol:

> "Oh, trebly hooped and welded hip of power! Oh, high aspiring, rainbowed jet!—that one striveth, this one jetteth all in vain! In vain, oh whale, dost thou seek intercedings with yon all-quickening sun, that only calls forth life, but gives it not again. Yet dost thou, darker half, rock me with a prouder, if a darker faith. All thy unnamable imminglings float beneath me here; I am buoyed by breaths of once living things, exhaled as air, but water now." (116: *409*)

It is no accident that in the next chapter but one, Ahab at high noon smashes the quadrant in a gesture symbolic of his rejection of natural fire, natural guidance, and natural life, nor that, in the very next chapter, we find him defying the unnatural fire of the corpusants. Even at the moment of his death he sustains this rejection. In the closing chapter, as the *Pequod* starts to sink and Ahab realizes that all is lost, he makes, like the dying whale, a last gesture of entropic despair: "I turn my body from the sun," he exclaims (135: *468*).

This analysis makes possible a more precise reading of Ahab's confrontation with the corpusants than might otherwise be possible. At the height of the typhoon, in the blackness of night, "God's burning finger" is suddenly laid upon the *Pequod*. "All the yard-arms were tipped with a pallid fire; and touched at each tri-pointed lightning-rod-end with three tapering white flames, each of the three tall masts was silently burning in that sulphurous air, like three gigantic wax tapers before an altar" (119: *415*). This trinitarian manifestation Ahab addresses as "thou clear spirit of clear fire." He acknowledges its "speechless, placeless power," but asserts that the "right worship" of such a deific phenomenon is "defiance." Ahab can risk such defiance, he thinks, because the worst the fire can do is kill, "and *all* are killed" (italics mine). Ahab, it becomes evident, includes God Himself in this "all" which will be killed. "There is," he tells the fire, "some *unsuffusing* thing beyond thee, thou clear spirit, to whom all thy eternity is but time, all thy creativeness mechanical" (italics mine). This is unmistakably entropic: the fiery deity which Ahab addresses is "suffusive," an active principle and creative force which, by virtue of that active creativity, must eventually suffer termination. This is to say that there must be an inactive, non-creative, hence "unsuffusing" principle anterior to God and therefore superior to God, an entity which will outlast God Himself. Ahab recognizes that God exists in eternity, and this would appear to imply the impossibility of termination. But as Ahab—chopping his logic with condensed subtlety—uses the term, eternity is nothing more than infinite time, and time is process, and process must end. Hence eternity is not eternal, nor the God of eternity timeless. Behind both stands something even more fundamental, absolute timelessness and total stasis. This is the "unsuffusing thing" superior to creative deity: the Final Darkness. "Light though thou be," Ahab tells his fiery Trinity, "thou leapest out of darkness; but I am darkness leaping out of light, leaping out of thee!" Such a dark-light-dark sequence renders the entropic paradigm: light coming out of darkness, doomed to return to darkness. Because "dark Ahab" is "darkness leaping out of light," he is—and this is the ultimate statement of his rampant egotism in all of *Moby-Dick*—superior to God. This is the demonic consequence of his entropic theology. This is also what is meant when the barbed tip of Ahab's own harpoon is suddenly invested with the same "levelled flame of pale, forked fire" which burns upon the masts. Ahab seizes the harpoon, brandishes its burning tip over the heads of the importunate Starbuck and the terrified crew, and then "with one blast of his breath he extinguished the flame" (119: *418*). This is the supreme entropic gesture: defiant Ahab snuffs out, like a mere candle, the suffusive God of Light.

There is, however, an unresolved element in all of this. Ahab's dark faith has answered all his questions but one. Concerning the genealogy of God there is for Ahab no problem: God is, must be, the deified child of the Final Darkness. Because entropic stasis is the ultimate nothingness, and that which is nothing cannot be known, God cannot know his own source. "Thou knowest not how came ye," Ahab tauntingly tells the corpusants, "hence callest thyself unbegotten; certainly knowest not thy beginning, hence callest thyself unbegun." In this respect too Ahab thinks himself superior to God; he knows *his* paternity. "I am darkness . . . leaping out of thee!" But this, he thinks, is only half the story. If the trinitarian God is his Father—and all Ahab's Quaker and Biblical background reinforces such a concept—*then he must also have a mother.* "But thou art but my fiery father," he says to the corpusants; "my sweet mother, I know not. Oh, cruel! what has thou done with her? *There lies my puzzle*" (119: *417*; italics mine). In terms of the final meanings of *Moby-Dick,* this is a crucial admission. Despite Ahab's subtlety and demonic brilliance, one essential element remains beyond his ken, unaccounted for. It is this single crack in the otherwise seamless monolith of his dark denial which suggests that Ahab's reading of cosmic process may not be the final reading, either for Ishmael or for Melville himself.[3]

It is only six chapters—some eight or ten pages—after Ahab tells the corpusants that "thou canst but kill; and all are killed" (119: *417*), that he is confronted with the startling possibility that death may not be the entropically terminal entity he thinks it is. Steering south-eastward on the White Whale's own grounds, a man is lost overboard. When the life-buoy—an iron-bound wooden cask which hangs at the *Pequod*'s stern—is dropped, it proves so badly weathered that it follows the doomed sailor to the bottom. There is no time to fashion another cask; Queequeg therefore suggests that the coffin which the carpenter had made for him and of which, as it turned out, he had no need, be used as a replacement. "A life-buoy of a coffin!" cries Starbuck, starting. "Rather queer, that, I should say," observes Stubb. Queer though it is, Starbuck orders the task accomplished. The carpenter reluctantly obeys: "Some superstitious old carpenters, now," he grumbles, "would be tied up in the rigging, ere they would do the job." Yet he perceives, if only dimly, that the change from coffin to life-buoy is not a *conversion,* but only an *obversion,* an alteration in aspect but not in essence: "It's like turning an old coat; going to bring the flesh on the other side now" (126: *429–31*). While he is busy nailing down the lid and calking the seams, Ahab appears, demanding to know what he is about. "Aye, sir; I patched up this thing here as a coffin for Queequeg; but they've set me now to turning it into something else." Ahab, perceiving a signification which in these penultimate hours he can ill afford to contemplate, reacts violently: "Then tell me; art thou not an arrant, all-grasping, inter-meddling, monopolizing, heathenish old scamp, to be one day making legs, and the next day coffins to clap them in, and yet again life-buoys out of those same coffins? Thou art as unprincipled as the gods, and as much of a jack-of-all-trades" (127: *432*). This is the irritable petulance of the puzzled, secretly uncertain man confronting a possibility which threatens everything for which he stands. Deeply shaken, Ahab demands that the carpenter "get these traps out of my sight," but just for a moment he is arrested by the possibility that his entropic despair is without foundation, and that death may have a meaning he does not grasp:

> "There's a sight! There's a sound! ... Here now's the very dreaded symbol of grim death, by a mere hap, made the expressive sign of the help and hope of most endangered life. A life-buoy of a coffin! Does it go further? Can it be that in some spiritual sense the coffin is, after all, but an immortality-preserver! I'll think of that. But no. So far gone am I in the dark side of earth, that its other side, the theoretic bright one, seems but uncertain twilight to me." (127: *432–33*)

But although Ahab cannot accept the concept of immortality, much less the idea of death as something which "preserves" immortality, *Moby-Dick* is nevertheless full of just this idea. Paradoxically, it is the shark himself who suggests the existence of a vitality, a dynamism, which is *not* terminated by death. When, during the shark massacre, one brain-spaded monster was hoisted to the *Pequod*'s deck for the sake of his skin, he "almost took poor Queequeg's hand off, when he tried to shut down the dead lid of his murderous jaw." Ishmael offers a brief but important explanation for this apparent manifestation of life after death: "A sort of generic or Pantheistic vitality seemed to lurk in [the shark's] very joints and bones, *after what might be called the individual life had departed*" (66: *257*; italics mine). The shark, in other words, suggests the possibility of a dynamistic residue which exists independently of, and transcends the death of, the individual. As the dead shark epitomizes this dynamism in the animal world, Ahab is made to epitomize it in the human world. For although Ahab yet lives, a major part of him has already died. One leg, presumably, has suffered dissolution in the belly of Moby Dick. But that dead leg nonetheless lives. At one point, the carpenter is busy making a new whalebone leg to replace the one which Ahab accidentally splintered in his haste to leave the congenial decks of the *Samuel Enderby*. "Well, then," Ahab asks the long-suffering old man, "will it speak thoroughly well for thy work, if, when I come to mount this leg thou makest, I shall nevertheless feel another leg in the same identical place with it; that is, carpenter, my old lost leg; the flesh and blood one, I mean."

> "Truly, sir [the carpenter replies], I begin to understand somewhat now. Yes, I have heard something curious on that score, sir; how that a dismasted man never entirely loses the feeling of his old spar, but it will be still pricking him at times. May I humbly ask if it be really so, sir?"
> "It is, man. Look, put thy live leg here in the place where mine once was; so, now, here is only one distinct leg to the eye, yet two to the soul. Where thou feelest tingling life; there, exactly there, there to a hair, do I." (108: *391*)

Ahab thus experiences in a uniquely personal way—though its significance escapes him—that same phenomenon which Queequeg encountered in the dead shark. There is, apparently, a dynamistic element at work behind life-process which is not and cannot be accounted for by entropic Ahab's dark faith. "Is't a riddle?" Ahab asks the carpenter.

It *is* a riddle, the key to which lies in the carpenter's hint that the coffin-to-life-buoy sequence is an obversion rather than a conversion. For obversion suggests, as conversion cannot, a single entity, a unitary phenomenon, which is seen *alternately,* first under one aspect, and then under another. The obversive viewpoint, in other words, is best articulated by an essentially alternative, *cyclic* conceptual framework. Such a cyclic way of seeing the world shapes almost every page of *Moby-Dick.* Back-and-forth images, to-and-fro images, up-and-down images, images of circularity, are the cornerstone of an idiom which gradually brings into focus a dynamistic Ishmaelian cosmology radically different from Ahab's entropic world-view. In its most rudimentary form, this cosmic dynamism is rendered as a simple to-and-fro rocking motion. A turn at the mast-head, Ishmael asserts, puts one in mystic consonance with the languorous rhythms of the entire universe. "There you stand," he tells us, "lost in the infinite series of the sea, with nothing ruffled but the waves. The tranced ship indolently rolls; the drowsy trade winds blow; everything resolves you into languor." These rhythms then interpenetrate the spiritual rhythms of thought so that man and nature become one. As a consequence, "lulled into such an opium-like listlessness of vacant, unconscious reverie . . . by the blending cadence of waves with thoughts, . . . at last [the mast-head stander] loses his identity; [and] takes the mystic ocean at his feet for the visible image of that deep, blue, bottomless soul, pervading mankind and nature" (35: *136–37, 140*). Ishmael endows this cyclic dynamic with cosmic breadth, extending without interruption from the barnacled hull of the *Pequod* to the very throne of deity: "There is," he continues, "no life in thee, now, except that rocking life imparted by a gently rolling ship; by her, borrowed from the sea; by the sea, from the inscrutable tides of God" (35: *140*). Such imagery occurs in *Moby-Dick* with repetitive emphasis:

> It was my turn to stand at the foremast-head [says Ishmael on another occasion]; and with my shoulders leaning against the slackened royal shrouds, to and fro I idly swayed in what seemed an enchanted air. No resolution could withstand it; in that dreamy mood losing all consciousness, at last my soul went out of my body; though my body still continued to sway as a pendulum will, long after the power which first moved it is withdrawn. (61: *241*)

The other two sailors at the other two mast-heads are similarly overcome by the systole and diastole of cosmic activity, "So that at last all three of us lifelessly swung from the spars, and for every swing that we made there was a nod from below from the slumbering helmsman. The waves, too, nodded their indolent crests; and across the wide trance of the sea, east nodded to west, and the sun over all" (61: *242*). It is this natural vibration which soothes Queequeg toward the death which he only at the last moment rejects. The imperturbable savage "quietly lay in his swaying hammock, and the rolling sea seemed gently rocking him to his final rest, and the ocean's invisible flood-tide lifted him higher and higher towards his destined heaven" (110: *396*).

But that toward which Queequeg moves, urged by the to-and-fro movement of universal cycle, is *not* a death in the terminal sense that Ahab would recognize. For there is that in Queequeg, Ishmael asserts, something in his luminous eyes, which constitutes a "wondrous testimony to that immortal health in him which could not die, or be weakened." As a consequence, Queequeg's approaching death is for Ishmael, not an end, but rather an *"endless end"* (110: *395*; italics mine). It is this simple oxymoron which furnishes the requisite clue to the significance of the cyclic imagery in *Moby-Dick*. Ahab's entropic view of cosmic activity is declensive, retrograde, and intractably terminal. Conversely, the cyclic view of cosmic process—Ishmael's view—is regenerative, autovitalistic, and non-terminal. In the ebb and flood of cosmic cycle, at the completion of such isochrone, at both the nadir and zenith of natural activity, an obversion rather than a termination occurs: flex becomes reflex, death becomes life, dark becomes light, stasis becomes movement. All of this stands as a direct repudiation of Ahab's entropic despair. No end is terminal. All ends are really endless. The cyclic structure of universal activity endows all being—and that activity itself—with immortality. "Oh! the metempsychosis!" exclaims Ishmael, "Oh! Pythagoras, that in bright Greece, two thousand years ago, did die, so good, so wise, so mild; I sailed with thee along the Peruvian coast last voyage—and, foolish as I am, taught thee, a green simple boy, how to splice a rope!" (98: *358*).

The clearest expression of Ishmael's "endless end" occurs in the cycle become specifically circular, returning always upon itself.[4] In that same passage where Ishmael describes how the sea rocks dying Queequeg, he also remarks a symbolic circularity in the cannibal's fading expression: "And like circles on the water, which, as they grow fainter, expand; so his eyes seemed rounding and rounding, like the rings of Eternity" (110: *395*). Repeatedly, key ideas in *Moby-Dick* are expressed in such circular terms. The ship itself stands as symbol for such activity. She is, for Ishmael, the "circumnavigating Pequod" (87: *319*). Ahab shouts to the *Goney* that "This is the Pequod, bound round the world!" (52: *203*), and reiterates this idea at the conclusion of the gam: "Up helm! Keep her off round the world!" Ishmael makes the obvious point: "Round the world! There is much in that sound to inspire proud feelings; but whereto does all that circumnavigation conduct? Only through numberless perils to the very point whence we started, where those that we left behind secure, were all the time before us" (52: *204*).

These conventional uses of circularity fade into insignificance, however, in comparison to the gradual evolution of the vortex image in *Moby-Dick*. For both Ishmael and Melville, the vortex is a void surrounded by a cycle. Through the vortex, and through the Cartesian cosmology associated with it,[5] Ishmael achieves a brilliant fusion of cosmic activity and cosmic stasis, of the universal *something* and the universal *nothing,* and of the way in which matter and the void stand in a relation of reciprocal definition. Initially, the concentration is not on the substance and activity of the cosmos, but on the frightening metaphysical vacuity which that substance and its activity articulate. While standing a mast-head watch and being gently rocked into ontological somnolence by the cosmic tides, one is in mortal danger: "But while this sleep, this dream is on ye, move your foot or hand an inch; slip your hold at all; and your identity comes back in horror. Over Descartian vortices you hover. And perhaps, at mid-day, in the fairest weather, with one half-throttled shriek you drop through that transparent air into the summer sea, no more to rise for ever. Heed it well, ye Pantheists!" (35: *140*). It is this sense of the vortex-as-void which Melville uses for humorous effect in *Pierre,* in speaking of the impoverished "Apostles." "Their mental tendencies," he remarks, ". . . are still very fine and spiritual . . . since the vacuity of their exchequers leads them to reject the coarse materialism of Hobbes, and incline to the airy exaltations of the Berkeleyan philosophy. Often groping in vain in their pockets, they can not but give in to the Descartian vortices."[6] Nullity is, for both Ishmael and Melville, the *primary* signification of the vortex.

But in *Moby-Dick* the vortex is redeemed—as so many things are redeemed—by great Leviathan. During the *Pequod*'s encounter with the Grand Armada (87: *318–28*), Ishmael stresses the fact that the gallied whales form an incredible Leviathanic vortex. "In all directions expanding in vast irregular circles, and aimlessly swimming hither and thither, by their short thick spoutings, [the whales] plainly betrayed their distraction of panic." As the whale dragging Ishmael's boat penetrates the herd, he notes that "as we went still further and further from the circumference of commotion, the direful disorders seemed waning." Finally they reach the quiet center: "And still in the distracted distance we beheld the tumults of the outer concentric circles, and saw successive pods of whales, eight or ten in each, swiftly going round and round, like multiplied spans of horses in a ring; and so closely shoulder to shoulder, that a Titanic circus-rider might easily have over-arched the middle ones, and so have gone round on their backs." The Armada is a tremendous system of outer "revolving circles" and the "contracting orbits [of] the whales in the more central circles." But Ishmael does not find at the center of this Leviathanic vortex that ontological nullity which he perceived behind the cenotaphs of the Whaleman's Chapel, and which the Cartesian vortex gives visual rendering. In *this* vortex, at its very heart, Ishmael finds peace and life rather than terror and death:

> And thus [he concludes], though surrounded by circle upon circle of consternations and affrights, did these inscrutable creatures at the centre freely and fearlessly indulge in all peaceful concernments; yea, serenely revelled in dalliance and delight. But even so, amid the tornadoed Atlantic of my being, do I myself still for ever centrally disport in mute calm; and while ponderous planets of unwaning woe revolve round me, deep down and deep inland there I still bathe me in eternal mildness of joy. (87: *322–26*)

The Grand Armada is a partial, essentially cetological resolution for Ishmael's hypo concerning the void.

In the "Epilogue" of *Moby-Dick*, the cyclic vortex again appears. Ishmael, tossed from Ahab's boat, witnesses the destruction of the *Pequod* and the death of Ahab and his entire crew:

> *So, floating on the margin of the ensuing scene, and in full sight of it, when the half-spent suction of the sunk ship reached me, I was then, but slowly, drawn towards the closing vortex. When I reached it, it had subsided to a creamy pool. Round and round, then, and ever contracting towards the button-like black bubble at the axis of that slowly wheeling circle, like another Ixion I did revolve. Till, gaining the vital centre, the black bubble upward burst; and now, liberated by reason of its cunning spring, and, owing to its great buoyancy, rising with great force, the coffin life-buoy shot lengthwise from the sea, fell over, and floated by my side. Buoyed up by that coffin, for almost one whole day and night, I floated on a soft and dirge-like main. (470)*

At the heart of this final vortex, Ishmael once more finds, not the void, but rather life in the guise of death, rebirth in an "immortality preserver." The "Epilogue" is the ultimate statement of the redemptive cyclicism of *Moby-Dick*, and the final repudiation of Ahab's entropism.

NOTES

[1] The number before the colon in all parenthetical references in the text indicates chapter, which will be the same for most American editions of *Moby-Dick;* the italicized numbers after the colon indicate page in the Norton Critical Edition of *Moby-Dick,* edited by Harrison Hayford and Hershel Parker (New York: W. W. Norton & Company, 1967).

[2] *A Reading of* Moby-Dick (Chicago: U. of Chicago Press, 1950), p. 18.

[3] The complexities of the corpusant scene, and Ahab's address to the fire, have received considerable attention. Useful for background is C. C. Walcutt's "The Fire-Symbolism in *Moby-Dick,*" *Modern Language Notes,* 59 (1944), 304–10, as well as Paul W. Miller's "Sun and Fire in Melville's *Moby-Dick,*" *Nineteenth-Century Fiction,* 8 (1958), 139–44. Thomas Vargish's "Gnostic Mythos in *Moby-Dick,*" *PMLA,* 81 (1966), 272–77, is a tightly reasoned discussion of Melville's (and Ishmael's) possible knowledge of the doctrine that the God of Matter, the Demiurge or Creator, was the inferior of a Supreme Being who ruled the spiritual worlds. Ahab's query concerning his "sweet mother" is seen by Vargish as a reference to "the Gnostic myth of the fallen mother [Sophia]—she who fell from overweening love of the Supreme Being." Finally, William Braswell, in *Melville's Religious Thought* (Durham: Duke Univ. Press, 1943), suggests that Melville became familiar with the Paulicians, the Manichees, and the Gnostics through cross reference reading in Bayle. "Here Melville may have become acquainted with the Gnostic theory that the Creator of the Universe is an inferior Deity." This, Braswell argues, could be the source of Ahab's defiance. "In primitive Christian times the Gnostics urged rebellion against the Creator of the Universe. They taught that He is an emanation from a higher power, that He is ignorant of His genealogy, and that He tyrannically governs the world in the belief that He is the Supreme God" (pp. 52, 62). In any case, whatever the sources of the "Candles" chapter, Melville was capable of conceiving of a God both less than ultimate and less than omnicompetent. "We incline to think that God cannot explain His own secrets," he remarked in an 1851 letter to Hawthorne, "and that He would like a little information upon certain points Himself." See *The Letters of Herman Melville,* ed. Merrell R. Davis and William H. Gilman (New Haven: Yale Univ. Press, 1960), p. 125.

[4] A valuable counterpoint to my discussion of Ahab's entropism and Ishmael's cyclicism is John Seelye's "diagrammatic" analysis, in which the *line* is associated with Ahab because of the linear and absolutist structure of his unifocal quest, while the *circle* is associated with Ishmael because of the relativistic,

reiterative, and polyfocal nature of the Ishmaelian sensibility. See *Melville: The Ironic Diagram* (Evanston: Northwestern Univ. Press, 1970), pp. 6–7 and Ch. V, "*Moby-Dick:* Line and Circle," pp. 60–73.

[5] Descartes, starting from the theories of Copernicus and Galileo, developed the idea that all motion was circular, and that the cosmic material tended to form vortices—a pre-Newtonian attempt to account for the spherical shape of all major celestial bodies, their rotational motion, and their circular orbits. James Baird suggests that in Melville the vortex represents "descent into water, the emblematic essence of God," an interpretation which does not quite meet the implications of the void at the center of all vortexical activity. See *Ishmael* (Baltimore: Johns Hopkins Univ. Press, 1956), pp. 266–73. For a suggestive discussion of the vortex in Hindu thought, see H. B. Kulkarni, *Moby-Dick: A Hindu Avatar* (Logan, Utah: Utah State Univ. Press, 1970), esp. pp. 48–49.

[6] Northwestern-Newberry *Pierre; or, The Ambiguities*, p. 267.

Bainard Cowan

READING AHAB

The chapter "Moby Dick" attests to the difficulty of going beyond Ahab's interpretation of the white whale. Ishmael describes the unifying power of Ahab's word:
"My shouts had gone up with theirs ... my oath had been welded with theirs ...
Ahab's quenchless feud seemed mine." Caught in the force field of Ahab's will, the
individual almost loses all hope of forming an "original relation to the universe" or
of seeing anything other than what the scheme of vengeance will allow. This force
leads Ishmael to relinquish his attempt to imagine Moby Dick: "I gave myself up to
the abandonment of the time and place," he admits, and all during this early stage
of the voyage he "could see naught in that brute but the deadliest ill."[1] His attempt
to pass beyond the screen of Ahab's discourse results in the magnificent and
terrifying effort of the next chapter, "The Whiteness of the Whale," which begins
with that explicit purpose: "What the white whale was to Ahab, has been hinted;
what, at times, he was to me, as yet remains unsaid" (p. 163). Yet it concludes with
no real difference in attitude from the previous chapter: "Wonder ye then at the
fiery hunt?" (p. 170). The progression of images in this chapter is not dictated by
any inherent logic but by attraction and repulsion: "a colorless, all-color of atheism
from which we shrink" (p. 159, emphasis added). Ahab asserts his presence in this
chapter by these terms of force, for, though wholly absent from the images, he has
gained control over what would seem most private: the unconscious imaginary
order of Ishmael's thought. The terms from magnetism and electricity that repeatedly describe the captain make this point.

Stubb's nighttime encounter demonstrates this dream power. Ahab's pacing
on the deck above his sleeping crew at night causes such a "reverberating crack and
din" that "their dreams would have been of the crunching teeth of sharks" (p. 112).
When Stubb requests the captain to stop and is intimidated by him, he reflects on
those brief events as on a dream encounter and is only able to talk in mad similes:

From *Exiled Waters:* Moby-Dick *and the Crisis of Allegory* (Baton Rouge: Louisiana State University
Press, 1982), pp. 95–106.

"his eyes like powder-pans! . . . his brow . . . flashed like a bleached bone" (pp. 113–14). He feels "turned inside out" afterward, and muses, "I must have been dreaming, though—How? how? how?" The "Queen Mab" chapter that follows finds Stubb recounting the actual dream he has had afterward, in which Ahab appears as a pyramid impervious to Stubb's kicks. "So confoundedly contradictory was it all," says Stubb; yet Ahab everywhere presents a monolithic power to his crew, a power that cannot be broken down and analyzed any more than it can be assailed. Nonetheless the dream symbol itself may provide the key to Ahab's decomposition, if anyone could read it: for Moby Dick is described as having a "high, pyramidical white hump" (p. 159). The image may suggest that Ahab is a double of the white whale itself and that all his power only comes from the object of his vengeance, which can by its movements dictate his every move. The white whale, as Ahab's double, decodes him, converting him from enigma to readable text.

Though Ahab is himself controlled by his own object, his power to control others is not thereby annulled but paradoxically multiplied. His quarter-deck speech to the crew seals their purpose with the aid of inverted sacramental symbolism. Turned upside down the harpoon sockets become "murderous chalices" to hold the liquor he passes among his crew. As *symbola* they annul differences by calling for an unconscious assent. The inversion of the harpoon points indicates their displacement from their cultural function, the purpose for which they were designed, and their reappropriation as imaginary objects, or images, operating in a realm where signifiers no longer exist in a conscious system of exchange but manifest the power of the other over the self, conveying the force of desire and enthrallment rather than any specific meaning. The harpoons' inversion is thus a double one: as chalices from holy to unholy, and as weapons from tool to charm.

The sailor Ishmael, who feels the strong pull of this "quenchless feud," is countered by the retrospective narrator, who can see through Ahab's maneuvers as "more or less paltry and base." He recognizes that all of Ahab's gestures of dignity or charismatic power are mere "external arts and entrenchments," and that his resorting to them differentiates his kind eternally from "God's true princes of the Empire" (p. 129). These remarks, which already suggest a more or less complete reading of Ahab's character, are made in the chapter ending in the narrator's question of how he can present Ahab—"But Ahab, my Captain, still moves before me in all his grimness and shagginess." As a character Ahab still exerts his enchantment on Ishmael, and only a heroic effort can capture his nearly ineffable nature: "Oh, Ahab! what shall be grand in thee, it must needs be plucked at from the skies, and dived for in the deep, and featured in the unbodied air!" (p. 130). What *shall be* grand—the task for author Ishmael thus parallels the one for sailor Ishmael: to read, and to write, Ahab. Chapter 33 chiefly succeeds in telling what Ahab is not—a "true prince"; his nature remains vague, "shaggy." The process against which his own pyramidical will militates in his decomposition into separate levels of discourse and of existence—an interpretation which would be one with an allegorization of him.

The discovery of two levels in Ahab already begins implicitly in the "Quarter-

Deck" chapter that so firmly asserts his unity. Describing his very unity, however, already frames Ahab in a potentially dualistic scheme: his thought, Ishmael notes, seems to be "so completely possessing him, indeed, that it all but seemed the inward mould of every outer movement" (p. 141). This construction sets up the categories of inside and outside, thus providing the possibility of a future discernment of a discrepancy between appearance and reality in Ahab. Stubb follows suit: "'The chick that's in him pecks the shell. 'Twill soon be out.'" Both these remarks suppose a continuity between the two levels discerned: as the inner, so the outer, or first in, then out.

In the speech itself this duality continues to be paired with an assertion of continuity between levels. When Starbuck objects, "I came here to hunt whales, not my commander's vengeance," Ahab replies, "Thou requirest a little lower layer." He repeats this phrase in his great monologue:

> "Hark ye yet again,—the little lower layer. All visible objects, man, are but as pasteboard masks. But in each event—in the living act, the undoubted deed—there, some unknown but still reasoning thing puts forth the mouldings of its features from behind the unreasoning mask. If man will strike, strike through the mask! How can the prisoner reach outside except by thrusting through the wall? To me, the white whale is that wall, shoved near to me. Sometimes I think there's naught beyond." (p. 144)

The metaphors of layer, mask, and wall each insist on a two-leveled model of reality. Ahab's analysis of himself discloses an ostensible motive of vengeance which is simply the outward expression and consequence of that deeper motivation, a hatred of the "inscrutable thing" that with seeming malice masks itself and presents a wall to man. The mask and the wall, however, mark discontinuities between appearance and the reality of that "unknown but still reasoning thing." To know this reality Ahab seeks to prove himself in a "living act" that will force the hidden thing to show its hand, to "put forth the mouldings of its features." The impression made on the mask of appearance is, like a stamp on wax, a negative one. Here is no symbolic unification of subject with object; here no analogical order insures the image of reality in appearance; instead a wall exists between the two, and the ultimate reality can only be known by the traces that it leaves showing where it is not.

Critics have noted that Ahab's view of the whale is an allegorical view, of the kind seen in Prudentius' *Psychomachia* where good agents war with evil agents.[2] But it cannot be said that Ahab partakes of the allegorist's mind, even though he does in a sense preserve the biblical typological view of the world by inverting it. To the Jews the epoch-making movements in their history were moments in which God intervened in secular reality to reveal Himself as other than that reality. Ahab also sees the world as significant only when an alien force intrudes to show itself; yet that force is evil. "I see in him outrageous strength, with an inscrutable malice sinewing it. That inscrutable thing is chiefly what I hate; and be the white whale agent, or be the white whale principal, I will wreak that hate upon him" (p. 144). Hatred does not lead to history, however: Ahab does not see time as patterned meaningfully by the white whale's appearance but sees its intervention in his life as a hateful originary moment. The desire to make coherent sense of one's life through retrospective interpretation is supplanted in Ahab by an obsessive, repeated return to the horrendous moment of his loss, which stands outside of time to him.

An inversion of the Jewish attitude toward God in history, Ahab's conviction is thus connected only negatively to the dim inheritance of Judaeo-Christian typology left behind on the shores of New England. He is haunted by the suspicion that there may in fact be "naught beyond." The physical world already has no significance in itself, but that lack has seemed to be in the service of some higher worth. If in fact no higher truth exists, then significance cannot return to the world but disappears entirely, making the world a pure interplay of "unreasoning" forces. This is of course the vision of the world opened up by the impact of scientific discoveries on the modern mind—Arnold's "darkling plain . . . Where ignorant armies clash by night." But it induces a deep-rooted cynicism and dishonesty in Ahab.

To judge from the way he presents himself to the crew in his quarter-deck speech, Ahab's deeper reality is undeceivingly bound up with his appearance. Further, he knows he must keep up appearances—and the principle of appearances disclosing reality—to his crew if he expects them to act confidently and obediently. Ishmael expresses this faith in a congruence between inside and outside near the end of the chapter, describing a sudden stillness that allows several ominous signs to be heard and felt at once, only to disappear just as quickly. "Ah, ye admonitions and warnings!" he exclaims, "why stay ye not when ye come? But rather are ye predictions than warnings, ye shadows! Yet not so much predictions from without, as verifications of the foregoing things within. For with little external to constrain us, the innermost necessities in our being, these still drive us on" (p. 145).

This is the retrospective narrator, commenting on the Aeschylean unity of character and fate in the completed drama. For the drama in progress, however, that unity is by no means assured, for the narrator has yet to go beyond Ahab's presentation of himself to an independent, analytic assessment of him. He has not yet shown Ahab's "innermost necessities."

He can only hope to do so by "furious tropes." Chapter 41's probing of Ahab's mind sums up, "If such a furious trope may stand, his special lunacy stormed his general sanity, and carried it, and turned all its concentred cannon upon its own mad mark" (p. 161). No explanation other than a psychomachia seems able to account for his combination of madness and sanity. Yet the narrator is still aware that "Ahab's darker, deeper part remains unhinted." Furthermore, he resorts to an elaborate two-leveled figure of the human psyche to explain his inability to expose Ahab fully:

> Winding far down from within the very heart of this spiked Hotel de Cluny where we here stand—however grand and wonderful, now quit it;—and take your way, ye nobler, sadder souls, to those vast Roman halls of Thermes; where far beneath the fantastic towers of man's upper earth, his root of

grandeur, his whole awful essence sits in bearded state ... aye, he did beget ye, ye young exiled royalties; and from your grim sire only will the old State-secret come. (p. 161)

In this magnificent passage, reminiscent of Keats's *Hyperion,* man's conscious and everyday life is like a palimpsest written over an *Urtext,* not representing but concealing the ruined sovereign that is the original image of man.[3] Presumably Ahab has found the "old State-secret" from this deposed power within himself. The scene is allegorical not only in personifying an element in the human psyche but in referring to a past state of being which, when found, reveals one's present state to be not a plenitude but an exile. At the heart of human existence is something that Ahab has probed and that prevents Ishmael the narrator from saying explicitly what it is, because it is "vain to popularize profundities, and all truth is profound." This something, roughly phrased, consists of the realization that man in his present state not only is alienated from his original kingly image but has even forgotten this alienation. The reason for both alienation and forgetting is the too great suffering attendant on the dethronement of original man. What Ahab has come up against is the heart of what Romantic allegory realizes—that worldly existence is related only negatively to a prior, more authentic experience of being. Ishmael expands this moment into an allegorical tableau in which life is characterized as a forgetting of an exile from a dethronement—a triple removal from that royal existence that would mean participation in true being.

But what this moment actually leads to in Ahab is a total break between inner motive and outer means. And the text reflects this break: Ahab is not fitted smoothly to the picture of the ancient king but is only indicated as roughly cognizant of the whole problem it denotes. "Now, in his heart," the narrative continues, "Ahab had some glimpse of this, namely: all my means are sane, my motive and my object mad." But if this is the extent of Ahab's understanding then it is poor indeed in comparison to the depths of insight which would seem to be required of one who winds his way down to the "vast Roman halls" of the psyche. The chief thing that Ahab has discerned is the discontinuity between his means and ends, because they too exist on two levels simply superimposed on one another. If his "motive and object" are to break out of the prison mentioned in his quarter-deck speech and restore himself to his throne, this end in itself is not mad but seems the natural response to a sympathetic vision of the old king. What is mad, paradoxically, is the resort to "sane" means—that is, means wholly within the control of the practical intellect—to accomplish this transcendent end. So Ahab's glimpse of himself, seen from the standpoint of the old-king allegory, actually reverses sanity and madness.

Nonetheless, Ahab is aware of the discontinuity inherent in his project. It is a discontinuity that leads him to dissemble: "Yet without power to kill, or change, or shun the fact; he likewise knew that to mankind he did long dissemble; in some sort, did still." His attempt to mask his transcendent purpose and deny the discontinuity of his actions thus manifests that discrepancy only more surely and more dangerously.

Ishmael begins now as narrator to be aware of the gap in Ahab's character, and in Chapters 43 and 44 he presents allegorical masques of the discrepancies between the levels of his endeavor. Chapter 43 ("Hark!") makes use of the ship's two-level structure as a possible allegorical distribution. On the top level sailors are standing in a line on the deck directly above Ahab's cabin, silently passing buckets of fresh water from one of the ship's casks to another. One sailor suddenly hears a noise beneath them, coming from Ahab's cabin, that "sounds like two or three sleepers turning over" (p. 170). He is led to speculate that Ahab is hiding someone in his cabin, and thus the ostensible purpose of the chapter—suspense—is accomplished.

But the spatial, diagrammatic quality of the scene provokes a further reading. To begin with, it takes place on two levels. At the top level the chain of sailors and the exchange going on between them, always of the same buckets, suggests the circulation of an economic system and has literal ties with that system, since they are filling the ship's scuttle-butt in the interests of fulfilling their commercial mission. It is all a clear, rational, and mundane proceeding, and its continuity achieves precisely the effect Ahab looks for in his command. Below them, however, something unknown is going on, something hidden that can be discerned only vaguely but that sounds like a turning and suggests some darker purpose of Ahab's. Thus Ahab's pretense of business as usual on board a whaling ship is carried out with only momentary misgivings by the sailors; Archy, who has heard that brief hint, must drop his speculations when he is told—look to your bucket: do your job. But the murmur in that smooth-flowing circulation, even if brief, cannot be erased. It has happened, and the chapter's title reflects the moment of that break. Ahab's own darker purpose—his turning—has put forth the mouldings of its features from behind his well-constructed mask.

Chapter 44 ("The Chart") presents a further two-level look at Ahab. At the beginning of the chapter the reader is asked to follow him down to his cabin from the quarter-deck, where "that wild ratification of his purpose with his crew" took place. Once alone, he takes out "a large wrinkled roll of yellowish sea charts," evidence that Ahab's change of scene is a transfer from public to private and from oratory to writing. As an allegory of reading his language, the scene in his cabin reveals a level of thorough calculation masked by the power and spontaneity of his rhetoric. Already in the "Quarter-Deck" chapter he is portrayed as a man traced upon—"his ribbed and dented brow" marked by "the footprints of his one un-sleeping, ever-pacing thought." Now, while he writes he is seen as written upon on another level, a level not inherent to himself and one of which he is unaware: "The heavy pewter lamp suspended in chains over his head, continually rocked with the motion of the ship, and for ever threw shifting gleams and shadows of lines upon his wrinkled brow, till it almost seemed that while he himself was marking out lines and courses on the wrinkled charts, some invisible pencil was also tracing lines and courses upon the deeply marked chart of his forehead" (p. 171).

In this chapter, for the first time, Ishmael takes the measure of Ahab. Previously the captain has appeared as a legend, a figure of power—and before any of these, as a difficult subject for narrating, who presents a problem for portrayal. Ahab must enter the domain of writing in order to execute his purpose. His speech could pretend the unity of his project just as it sought to effect his crew's solidarity with him, but he cannot long sustain this level. At the heart of his project are discontinuities, capable of being graphed only by the movement of his pencil. Yet as this scene implies, to write is to leave oneself open to be written on. Ahab's wordless tracing is a direct transcription of his will onto space and time, yet the very entry of his project into an explicit dimension of time reveals to Ishmael that Ahab's action has been graphed at a level beyond his own control. The shadow writing of the lamp on Ahab's forehead is a glimpse of the anagoge, a foreshadowing of Ahab's ultimate place in the temporal chart of the world.

The vision of Ahab on two levels leads at the end of this chapter to his portrayal as a double figure. He becomes increasingly allegorical as he realizes that his charting can do little to catch Moby Dick: "And have I not tallied the whale, Ahab would mutter to himself . . . tallied him, and shall he escape? His broad fins are bored, and scalloped out like a lost sheep's ear!" (p. 174). The word *tallied* suggests both the numerical enterprise of his charting and the knife wound, like a notch, he gave Moby Dick in their first encounter. Suddenly he realizes that the grid of his chart, net though it be, is not sufficiently fine to capture the whale, who will perpetually elude any systematic attempt to possess him.

And here the old biblical language enters to indicate the point at which Ahab's scientific, systematic enterprise falls short. The whale as "lost sheep" suggests Ahab as a demonic inversion of the Good Shepherd, who in this case would find his charge only to destroy it. But despite the biblical archetype implied here Ahab cannot return the escaped beast to the fold. The whale's elusion of all preconceived systems appears inevitable to the imagination at the very point where scientific language is dropped and biblical metaphors taken up.

Ahab's muttering in this scene leads to his greater anguish at night, the torment of a man who "sleeps with clenched hands; and wakes with his own bloody nails in his palms." If the image of Christ is suggested as a play on the word "nails" here, it marks Ahab as a Romantic antitype, the would-be harrower of heaven rather than of hell, who nonetheless has his own agony in the garden. His suffering is staged within him, however, largely hidden from the conscious Ahab, revealing itself only at the threshold between sleep and waking, a continually fruitful moment for allegory in that it suggests two parallel worlds both conjoined and disjoined, able to bring out the disjunctures and doublings within the supposedly integral self. Ahab's "exhausting and intolerably vivid dreams of the night" goad him on until "a chasm seemed opening in him" and a "hell in himself yawned beneath him." When he bursts out of his stateroom into the open, Ishmael speculates that the tormented thing before him is a double (or, more accurately, one half) of Ahab, not "the scheming, unappeasedly steadfast hunter of the white whale" but "the eternal, living principle or soul in him" which "in sleep, being for the time dissociated from the characterizing mind . . . spontaneously sought escape from the scorching contiguity of the frantic thing, of which, for the time, it was no longer an integral" (p. 175).

This double Ahab is now a thoroughly conceptualized character, become so nearly an allegorical type that he can be identified, in the closing image of the chapter, with Prometheus, the *locus communis* of defiant striving. No longer an ineffable, magnetizing presence to the mind of the narrator, he has become identifiable and dissoluble into dyadic models. The fact that his decomposition can be accomplished only by an allegorical fiction, however, means that Ishmael's understanding of him cannot be the univocal possession of knowledge but only a series of dualistic schemes, in which the two components remain incommensurable with each other and ultimately inexplicable. Two chapters after "The Chart," Ahab is shown more clearly than ever in Chapter 46 to be a conniving manipulator. He considers his men "tools" that are merely "apt to get out of order" and need adjusting, and judges that "the permanent constitutional condition of the manufactured man ... is sordidness" (p. 183). Thus he must hold up to them his promise of "cash" as a sop to their lower natures, meanwhile "observ[ing] all customary usages" of a normal whaling voyage to keep them from recalling his announced purpose and perhaps mutinying. How this debased and spiritually desolate condition squares with his terrible magnificence, Ishmael does not venture to say.

NOTES

[1] Herman Melville, *Moby-Dick,* ed. Harrison Hayford and Hershel Parker (New York, 1967), 163. Page numbers in parentheses in the text refer to this edition.

[2] Charles H. Cook, Jr., "Ahab's 'Intolerable Allegory,'" *Boston University Studies in English,* 1 (Spring–Summer, 1955), 45–52.

[3] Although no hard evidence exists that Melville read Keats, it is difficult to believe that his attentive study of the major and minor English Romantics, increasing steadily over the years, would leave out such a major figure. Merrell Davis points out several close parallels in *Mardi* to *Endymion, Lamia,* and other poems (*Melville's* Mardi: *A Chartless Voyage* [New Haven: Yale University Press, 1952], p. 75, 75n, 76, 132n, 141n). It may be that whereas Melville is compelled to mention Coleridge's prior text when writing of the unmediated experience of seeing an albatross, his obviously allegorical scene here needs no spell-breaking reference to give token of its textuality. On traces of allegory in Romantic symbolic experience, see Gayatri Spivak, "Allégorie et histoire de la poésie: Hypothèse de travail," *Poètique,* No. 8 (1971), 431–35.

Michael Paul Rogin

MOBY-DICK AND THE
AMERICAN 1848

v

The sea devours and dissolves the object world; commodities provide humans with their sense of power over nature. Instead of being consumed, humans consume commodities. The white whale reverses that process. It drives Ahab back to the original human helplessness against which commodity creation defended. When Moby Dick shears off Ahab's leg, it reopens the wounds of nature's antagonism. Ahab is, his wound forces him to see, vulnerable to nature's power. Capitalist appropriation has failed him (as it failed Allan Melvill), returning him to the devouring danger of mother nature.

The assault on Madame Leviathan and her babies initiates the commoditization of the whale. Ahab's dismemberment, the "bridal" which gives "birth" to his monomania, reverses that process. "Amid the chips of chewed boats, and the shrinking limbs of torn comrades," Ahab "swam out of the white curds of the whale's direful wrath into the serene, exasperating sunlight that smiled on, as if at a birth or a bridal." Then Ahab attacked the whale with his "six-inch blade," and Moby Dick, "sweeping his sickle-shaped lower jaw beneath him . . . reaped away Ahab's leg. . . ."[1] The merchant-captain fails to appropriate Leviathan's body. Instead, Moby Dick "devoured, chewed up, crunched" (74) Ahab's leg.

Ahab went crazy from his dismemberment, became delirious and directionless, and "his mates were forced to lace him fast, even there, as he sailed, raving in his hammock. In a straitjacket, he swung to the mad rocking of the gales." (154–55) Filled even more than most mariners with "half-formed foetal suggestion of supernatural agencies," (151) cradle-rocking Ahab formed his project of revenge. Returned to infancy, Ahab was reborn a monomaniac. He reinhabited the primitive desire to destroy the early source of all nurture and all disappointment. "His narrow-flowing monomania" abandoned "not one jot of Ahab's broad madness"; (155) instead it focused Ahab's delirium on an object. Ahab's obsession defended

---

From *Subversive Genealogy: The Politics and Art of Herman Melville* (New York: Knopf, 1983), pp. 115–40.

him against chaos, against the panic of rage without a target. Whiteness dissolves the "visible spheres," Ishmael explains, and leaves only a void. Ahab organizes the object world, and saves his self, by attributing a constricted, determined purpose to Moby Dick.

That purpose also organizes the text. Like the *Pequod*, *Moby-Dick* is unified by emblems rather than by the social action of realistic characters. In a Balzacian, realist plot, insists Georg Lukács, every cog is human; when power is attributed to emblems, and they do human work, the writer has succumbed to animism. Allan Melvill, the textile importer, succumbed to the animistic emblem of clothing. But his son, to repeat the metaphor Melville used both in *Moby-Dick* and about it, wove his own text. Melville's symbolic method does not signify his failure as a realist. It rather reconstitutes an atomized society of isolated individuals, whose religious and political life remained under the sway of Puritan typology.[2]

Emblems may acquire power at human expense. But humans symbolize by nature, and that activity comes into focus once the idea of a reality that preexists human language is discredited. Symbols empower the storyteller, and Ishmael uses them to make sense of his world. His symbolizing method both depends on, and departs from, the allegorizing approach of Captain Ahab.

Uncontrolled symbolization proliferates meanings endlessly, and that is what happens when the *Pequod*'s crew examines the doubloon. Their various interpretations destroy any confident ground, either in a reality beneath the symbol or in a shared experience of it. When mad Pip looks at the doubloon he sees only the viewer. His "I look, you look, he looks; we look, ye look, they look" (335) raises the specter of solipsist subjectivism.[3]

Only Queequeg is untroubled by the meaning of objects, for he participates in nature unselfconsciously. Queequeg's text is written on his body; tattooed with hieroglyphics he cannot read, his skin and his clothing are one. In *Redburn* and *White-Jacket,* at the end of *Moby-Dick* and in *Billy Budd,* the button is a locus of signification. Normally in Melville's fiction the button is a doubloon; Queequeg seems to take the doubloon for "an old button." (368) Queequeg does not read texts symbolically. He is still a mirror of nature; the other men on the *Pequod* are separate from it. Pip, like Ishmael's Platonist fallen from the masthead, has lost his identity in the objectless void. He looks at the doubloon and sees the other lookers. Ahab sees only himself in the doubloon, and imposes that self on the crew.

Pip's ego is disintegrated; Ahab's is fetishized. Pip—"tied to me by cords woven of my heart-strings" (394)—is Ahab's mirror self. Unlike Ishmael, Ahab cannot afford to read natural and social texts symbolically, weaving together their various, linked meanings. Instead he projects a single, allegorical meaning on the white whale. The allegorist inhabiting a secure universe knows that his allegory is only a representation and not the thing itself. Ahab, defending against chaos, forces the whale to become what it is not. But Ishmael needs Ahab, for only Ahab's allegory gives *Moby-Dick* its narrative.

Ishmael narrates a romance action, rather than a realistic social action. Realist characters lack the power, in a disintegrated world, to generate a meaning-giving order. Ahab, the allegorist, succeeds where they would fail. Ishmael tells a story, whose symbolist pattern reworks the lived world, but the story which forces coherence on the text is Ahab's. The early chapters of *Moby-Dick* are divided between empirical descriptions of whaling and whales, and invocations of Ahab's monomania. The book becomes unified as it approaches apocalypse. On the one hand, the bloodiest whaling scenes occur toward the end of the narrative, as if orchestrated by Ahab's growing frenzy. On the other hand, as Ahab acquires for himself the ferocity distributed throughout nature, the natural world grows more benign. By making the white whale its target, Ahab's malevolence unifies the text. Naturalistic description and Ahab's monomania join together seamlessly in the final chase. Ahab succeeds where a realistically drawn character would fail, and makes possible a narrative in *Moby-Dick.*[4]

During one peaceful moment before the *Pequod* sights the white whale, "the rover softly feels a certain, filial, confident, land-like feeling toward the sea." The rover, Ishmael, was cast out from the land onto the ocean. Now, for a moment, he feels at home. The experience also returns Ahab to his family and childhood. He soliloquizes:

> "Would to God these blessed calms would last. But the mingled, mingling threads of life are woven by warp and woof: calms crossed by storms, a storm for every calm. There is no steady unretracing progress in this life; we do not advance through fixed gradations, and at the last one pause:—through infancy's unconscious spell, boyhood's thoughtless faith, adolescence' doubt (the common doom), then skepticism, then disbelief, resting at last in manhood's pondering repose of If. But once gone through, we trace the round again; and are infants, boys, and men, and Ifs eternally. Where lies the final harbor, whence we unmoor no more? In what rapt ether sails the world, of which the weariest will never weary? Where is the foundling's father hidden? Our souls are like those orphans whose unwedded mothers die in bearing them: the secret of our paternity lies in their grave, and we must there to learn it." (374–75)

As warp and woof weave the mingled threads together, Ahab takes all of life in. He inhabits a circular, eternal return of the stages of the life cycle, rather than the monomaniacal, linear direction of his imposed design. Becoming alive to experience, he feels, in a perfectly undefended way, the overwhelming force of loss. Ahab feels that flux and that loss at moments, but they threaten to unman him. Riven inside, he responds to loss with vengeance. Repudiating Ishmael's passive, symbolic whole, Ahab imposes a forced unity on the world.

Ahab's wound has awakened his anxiety over separation, and therefore has intensified his inner division as well. Prudent entrepreneurs keep separate market and family, body and soul, bourgeois (in Marx's terminology) and citizen. But when "Ahab and anguish lay stretched together in one hammock, rounding in mid winter that dreary, howling Patagonian Cape; then it was, that his torn body and gashed soul bled into one another; and so interfusing, made him mad." (154) Normal men in the marketplace protect themselves by dividing body from soul. Ahab's longing for a merged dual-unity splits him within. His interfused body and soul give "unbidden and unfathered birth" to an "independent being" within him—a Promethean vulture who feeds on his heart, a grizzly who gnaws on his paws. (168, 131) Ahab "wakes with his own bloody nails in his palms." The "eternal living principle or soul" in the body of Captain Ahab ties him to the white whale. He is alive only in his bond to Moby Dick. But that bond is not life-giving, and it cannot make the world whole, for what animates Ahab is his desire to destroy. Without his self-tormenting spirit, Ahab is a "formless, somnambulistic being," a "blankness." His obsession gives Ahab an "object to color"; it twins him with Moby Dick. (167–68)

> The White Whale swam before him as the monomaniac incarnation of all those malicious agencies which some deep men feel eating in them, till they are left living on with half a heart and half a lung. . . . all evil, to crazy Ahab, were visibly personified, and made practically assailable in Moby Dick. He piled upon the whale's white hump the sum of all the general rage and hate felt by his whole race from Adam down; and then, as if his chest had been a mortar, he burst his hot heart's shell upon it. (154)

"[A]ll my means are sane, my motive and my object mad," Ahab recognizes. (155) "The conduct may be in some respects regular, the mind acute, and the conduct apparently governed by the rules of propriety, and at the same time there may be insane delusion, by which the mind is perveted." Lemuel Shaw, in *Commonwealth* v. *Rogers,* was describing a newly recognized form of insanity. Monomania began attracting notice early in the nineteenth century; it was the disease specific to a society of uprooted and driven men. The monomaniac, explained Shaw, knew the difference between right and wrong, but was possessed by a power which drove him to violence. He no longer controlled his own actions. In Melville's description of Ahab, "That before living agent, now became the living instrument." (155) "The mind broods over *one idea,* and cannot be reasoned out of it," in Shaw's. Shaw was, Henry Nash Smith has shown, characterizing the madness of Ahab.[5]

The criminal who was innocent by reason of insanity, before *Rogers,* could not distinguish right from wrong. Shaw's purpose was to extend the insanity defense. Modifying the Enlightenment belief in the autonomy of the will, Shaw acknowledged powers that overwhelmed moral judgment. He was making law for individuals less governed by reason and contract, more driven by forces beyond their control. He was responding to what Henry Adams would later characterize as the shift from eighteenth-century will to nineteenth-century force.[6]

Shaw did not permit monomania as an insanity defense, however, unless the criminal thought he was called by God. Those who acknowledged the Father went to the asylum; those who rebelled against him went to the gallows. Shaw rescued only the madmen who still felt themselves possessed by the voice of legitimate authority. They were society's victims, in his distinction, not its destroyers.[7]

The same year he decided *Rogers*, 1844, Shaw freed the slave, Robert Lucas, from the *United States*. The *Lucas* and *Rogers* decisions protected those who were still in the power of their masters. They offered no solace to Gansevoort Melville, who repudiated the political allegiances of Shaw and his father in 1844, and then went mad and died. Herman Melville returned home in 1844. Seven years later, while he was writing *Moby-Dick*, Shaw sent Thomas Sims back to slavery. Sims, unlike Lucas, had escaped from his master. The distinction Shaw made between Lucas and Sims was the one he had made in *Rogers*. Claims to freedom, by slaves against masters and monomaniacs against God, cost them the paternal protection of the law.[8]

"Ego non baptizo te in nomine patris, sed in nomine diaboli!" (373) Ahab baptized his hickory harpoon not in the name of the Father but of the devil. The secret motto of *Moby-Dick*, Melville wrote Hawthorne two months after *Sims*, was "Ego non baptizo te in nomine—but make out the rest yourself." Melville stopped, Charles Foster has pointed out, before "patris." The word called attention to the fathers, Shaw and God, whom the motto repudiated.[9]

Two years earlier, Melville had written the same motto in his Shakespeare volume which contained *King Lear*. He followed it with "Madness is undefinable—It & right reason extremes of one." As mad Ahab would strike through the paste-board mask of Moby Dick, so (in the "Mosses") "Lear the frantic king tears off the mask, and speaks the sane madness of 'vital truth.'" Ahab's madness did not speak the entire truth. But his rebellion penetrated the defenses of law-abiding men, and reached the derangement at the heart of America. "[M]an's insanity is heaven's sense," Ishmael says of Pip. (322) Melville's father-in-law exculpated human madness that was obedient to heaven; Melville valorized madness as either satanic rebellion or heavenly truth. Shaw confined the God-fearing monomaniac. "Truth has no confines," says Ahab. "How can the prisoner reach outside except by thrusting through the wall?" (139) Shaw's philanthropy kept the madman at a distance, and placed him under the judge's power. Ahab refused that condescension and claimed power for himself. "Delight is to him," preached Father Mapple, who "kills, burns and destroys all sin, though he pluck it out from under the robes of Senators [like Webster] and Judges [like Shaw]." (57) Ahab accepted Father Mapple's mission, and turned it against the fathers. "Where do murders go, man! [asks Ahab.] Who's to doom, when the judge himself is dragged to the bar?" (410) Neither the products of Allan Melvill's marketplace nor the walls of Judge Shaw's asylum insulated society from the madman or Ahab from the whale.[10]

V I

Capitalism transforms its environment, writes Joseph Schumpeter, by a process of "creative destruction." It proceeds not by the bookkeeper's mentality of rational cost-accounting, but by the spirit of risk and adventure. Starbuck, the owners' representative on the *Pequod,* speaks for the Nantucket market. His world is neatly divided between family at home and moneymaking at work. From Starbuck's perspective, Ahab has nothing in common with the economic man of the marketplace. For those sharing that view, Ahab's vengeance is merely a black version of the religious dreams of the citizen. But Ahab's "hark ye yet again,—the little lower layer," correctly points to a deeper motive than the rational pursuit of gain, not a higher one. Ahab carries to its extreme the egotistic, bourgeois desire for power, to be alone in the world and to possess it.[11]

Starbuck's appeals were not simply inadequate to stop Ahab. They were inadequate to capitalism's historical task. Ahab, like other merchant-adventurers, has broken loose from the process that generated him. But he has done so by carrying its social logic to its limit. The capitalist transformation of America began about the time Melville was born, and it swallowed up his father. Allan Melvill had opposed the "universal joint stock company" of "Equality" in the name of an American "aristocracy."[12] Ahab refuses the "joint stock world" (67) of "mortal inter-indebtedness" (361) in the name of the self-made man.

The heroic captain of industry, impatient of all limits, wants to ingest the world and build it anew. He is impatient of all restrictions on his egotistic freedom. He stands at the juncture of capitalism and imperialism, "never satisfied by the fulfillment of a concrete interest," in Schumpeter's words, but possessed by an "objectless disposition . . . to unlimited forcible expansion." He claims the power of Aladdin, in the oft-repeated metaphor, to bring a new world into being. Appropriating nature's life-giving power, he makes the elements respond to his commands. There is unacknowledged defiance in those aspirations. Praising the humanly created miracle of the telegraph, Lewis Cass boasted, "We can now answer the sublime interrogatory put to Job: 'Canst thou send lightnings that may go and say unto thee, here we are?' Yes, the corruscations of Heaven man has reduced to obedience, and they say to him, here we are!"[13]

Ahab, like Cass, reduces lightning to obedience. He orders the *Pequod's* lightning rods kept above board during a storm. Then, seizing the links, he holds the lightning in his hand. Cass claimed God's power as if he were making no challenge to God. At the same time (this was 1847), he warned that if America did not expand, it might face the turmoil of the "crowded communities" of Europe. Resistance to the American dream of freedom cast a shadow over Cass's optimism. Ahab wears the mark of that resistance—the "livid brand" of lightning—on his body. "A slender rod-like mark, lividly whitish," forms a "birthmark on him from crown to toe." (110) Father Mapple's "Father!—chiefly known to me by Thy rod" (57)—has coruscated Ahab. "The lightning flashes through my skull; my eye-balls

ache and ache," he cries. (384) "Fire . . . wasted all [Ahab's] limbs." (110) He took
the lightning inside him, and defied the "fiery father" whose scar he bore.

"Canst thou draw out Leviathan with a hook? or his tongue with a cord which
thou lettest down? . . . Canst thou fill his skin with barbed irons? or his head with fish
spears?" Ishmael alluded to these verses from Chapter 41 of Job; (279) Melville's
Chapter 41 is "Moby Dick." Ahab understood the blasphemy, and the cost, of
Cass's answer to God. He reveals the rebellion and the desire for domination
entangled in the wish to be free.[14]

Ahab's desire for mastery has lost its ground in any concrete, material aim, and
taken possession of his self and his ship. He appears in America when the dream
to have no master encounters resistance. The resistance which allowed Melville to
create Ahab (like the anxiety underneath Cass's boast) came from slavery. American freedom was originally founded on the subjugation of peoples of color. *Moby-
Dick* registers the dependence of American freedom on American slavery, and the
threat of American slavery to destroy American freedom.

The capitalist world system began in the sixteenth century when Europeans
seized the land and labor both of peasants at home and of the world's peoples of
color. Marx gave the name of primitive capitalist accumulation to that process of
forcible expropriation.

> The discovery of gold and silver in America [wrote Marx], the extirpation,
> enslavement and entombment in mines of the aboriginal population, the be-
> ginning of the conquest and the looting of the East Indies, the turning of Africa
> into a warren for the commercial hunting of black-skins, signalized the rosy
> dawn of the era of capitalist production. These idyllic proceedings are the chief
> moments of primitive accumulation.[15]

Capitalism, imperialism, and slavery were, at the origins of capitalism, symbiotically
intertwined. Capitalist imperialism spawned merchant-adventureres, who lived
both inside and outside of civilized society, and who were fascinated by the primi-
tives they destroyed. American capitalism—the absorption of the mass of the
population into commodity markets and the significant spread of wage labor—was
also imperialist and enslaving at its origins. The antebellum market revolution depended upon people of color.

Indian removal from 1814 to 1840 opened the West for land speculation,
settlement, and commercial agriculture. Cotton, grown by slave labor on land
recently expropriated from Indians, paid for the growth of American industry.
Profits from the Asian trade supplied capital for New England railroads, and mo-
bilized commercial elites in favor of westward expansion. Asian commerce, Indian
land, and black labor promoted the spread of industry and the rise of wage labor
in antebellum America.[16]

The harpooners on the *Pequod,* writes Alan Heimert, "are representatives of
the three races on which each of the American sections, it might be said, had built
its prosperity in the early nineteenth century." Stubb, who speaks in the Western

idiom, has an Indian for his squire. Little Flask is perched on Daggoo's shoulders, as the Southern economy rested on the Negro. And Starbuck, loyal to the New England commercial code, has a native from the Pacific islands to harpoon his whales.[17] The sectional, racial division of labor promoted capitalist development and political harmony in the early nineteenth century. That harmony exploded in the wake of the Mexican War.

Moby Dick, writes Melville, was not the first whale to be singled out for destruction. Others which had wreaked havoc were "systematically hunted out, chased and killed by valiant whaling captains ... much ... as in setting out through the Narragansett Woods, Captain Butler of old had it in his mind to capture that notorious murderous savage Annawon, the headmost warrior of the Indian King Philip." (170) King Philip's War, 1675–1678, broke the power of the Indian tribes of New England. Cotton Mather and William Hubbard interpreted that war, for the Massachusetts Puritans, as the biblical "hunting of the beast." In Richard Slotkin's summary, "The Indians are serpents, 'generations of the dragon,' and giants. . . . King Philip is compared to Og, to the Python, to a 'great Leviathan sent to [the victors] for a *thanksgiving-feast*.' "[18]

Melville has Captain Butler hunt the "murderous savage Annawon." He did not. Butler was the American officer who pursued "the monster Brant" after the siege of Fort Stanwix. That Mohawk chief was Colonel Gansevoort's enemy, and Melville was reading about Butler's pursuit of him in Brant's biography. Shortly after he finished *Moby-Dick,* referring to that biography, Melville named his second son Stanwix. Consciously or not, he was collapsing Captain Benjamin Church's chase after Annawon, in 1678, with Butler's pursuit of Brant in 1778. He was passing that heritage on to his son, and to Ahab.[19]

The line running from King Philip's War through the siege of Fort Stanwix pointed backward to the Puritan extermination of the Pequod Indians. The Puritans justified the Pequod war as the elimination of those idolatrous tribes who occupied the promised land before God's chosen came from Egypt. The line from the Pequods through Fort Stanwix pointed forward—by way of Andrew Jackson, New Orleans, and Indian removal—to the war against Mexico. "What was America in 1492 but a loose fish, in which Columbus struck the Spanish standard by way of waifing it for his royal master and mistress?" asks Ishmael. "What at last will Mexico be to the United States?" (309–10) Mexico may have been an ordinary whale; Great Britain was something more. England was the "Sea-beast Leviathan" to Western expansionists in the 1812 War. Thirty years later they saw England behind Mexico, fomenting slave uprisings and Indian war on the Southwestern frontier. These charges were made against the mother country during the Revolution, and repeated during the War of 1812. "A conspiracy of five monarchs," warned Allen of Ohio, again threatened American freedom. "Has our blood already become so pale that we should tremble at the roar of the King of Beasts?" asked Congressman McClernand. "If he crosses our path ... his blood will spout as from a harpooned whale."[20]

Opponents of the Mexican War turned to the Bible, as had Cotton Mather before them. The message they found there reversed his. Theodore Parker attached a "Scripture Lesson" to his 1848 sermon on the Mexican War. It was the lesson of the fate of King Ahab, who coveted Naboth's vineyard. When Naboth refused to sell Ahab his land, the king had him killed. Elijah prophesied Ahab's doom, and Parker ended his biblical quotation with the appearance of Elijah before the king. Parker's audience already knew the American implications of that story. It had been used first against the seizure of Indian land, and then applied to Texas and California. *The Taking of Naboth's Vineyard* was the title of one pamphlet against Texas annexation.[21]

Both the biblical Ahab and his American counterpart coveted native land. Their greed placed them at odds with the religion of their fathers; it turned them, in biblical exegesis and Whig propaganda, into the pagans they were out to replace. From that perspective, Melville's Ahab led his primitive tribe of "mongrel renegades, and castaways, and cannibals" (156) against the people of God.

"Those aboriginal whalemen, the Red-Men," sallied forth from Nantucket "to give chase to the Leviathan" before the *Pequod.* (27) "Your true whale-hunter is as much a savage as an Iroquois," says Ishmael (naming Joseph Brant's nation). "Long exile from Christendom and civilization inevitably restores a man to that condition in which God placed him, i.e., what is called savagery." (219) The *Pequod* was "a cannibal of a craft, tricking herself forth in the chased bones of her enemies." (72) Just as cannibals acquired the power of their enemies by ingesting them, so it was with the *Pequod.* Her name expressed this reversion to barbarism. "None but a Pequod Indian," wrote Theodore Parker, could condone American "butchery" in Mexico. The Pequods were reputedly a bloodthirsty tribe. Half a century after the Puritans exterminated them, Captain Benjamin Church (in the incident alluded to by Melville) tracked down and captured the satchem Annawon at the end of King Philip's War. Annawon gave Church his wampum and headdress, writes Richard Slotkin, symbolically crowning him the new king of the woods. Slotkin calls the conquest of savages and the acquisition of their power regeneration through violence. That was how Andrew Jackson, defeating the Creek Indians during the 1812 War, acquired the name and the authority of Old Hickory. Melville, naming Ahab's ship the *Pequod,* paid ironic homage to the process.[22]

The Indianization of the American Ahab corresponded to the paganization of the biblical Ahab. Ahab embodied the dangers facing America in 1850, and Theodore Parker returned to him in another sermon. "If I am rightly informed, King Ahab made a law that all the Hebrews should serve Baal, and it was the will of God that they should serve the Lord," preached Parker. "If they served Baal, they could not serve the Lord. . . . We are told that Elijah . . . came unto all the people, and said, 'If the Lord be God, follow him; but if Baal, follow him!' Our modern prophet says, 'Obey both. . . .'" Parker's modern prophet was the Massachusetts Judge Peleg Sprague. "Judge Peleg Sprague," sermonized Parker, "supposes a case: that the people ask him, 'Which shall we obey, the law of man or the law of God?' He says,

'I answer, obey both. The incompatability which the question assumes does not exist.' . . . Such is the difference between Judge Elijah and Judge Peleg."[23]

Elijah and Peleg are present on the Nantucket docks, when Ishmael boards the *Pequod*. Captain Peleg and Captain Bildad (who has the name of one of Job's comforters) sign Ishmael on for the cruise, and Peleg first tells him of Ahab. When Ishmael remembers Elijah's prophecy, that the dogs will lick Ahab's blood, Peleg assures him it is safe to serve the captain. Ishmael returns to the ship with Queequeg, and Bildad, giving the "Pagan" a missionary tract, tells him to "Spurn the idol Bell, and the hideous dragon." (87) Ishmael and Queequeg meet Elijah when they leave the *Pequod,* and he warns them against the voyage. Like Parker, and for the same purpose, Melville collects Ahab, Elijah, Peleg, and Baal together in America.

Melville knew the contemporary, political implications of an American Ahab, and of the prophecies of his destruction. The prophets appeared in ancient Israel when Solomon sultanized the Jewish kingship. They protested his transformation of the Jewish state into an Egyptian liturgical state, with royal favorites, priests, and foreign harem-women. Queen Maachah, alluded to in "The Cassock," made an idol of the phallus; her son deposed her and cut it down. Ahab, whose story is told in the next chapter of Kings, reinstituted the worship of the excluded Canaanite divinities. He married Jezebel, a Phoenician Baal-worshiper, and she and her priests brought idol-worship to the Jews. They arranged vegetation rituals. They engaged in orgiastic celebrations of the old nature and mother deities. Their idolatry invested objects with powers that belonged only to Jehovah. Elijah called, against King Ahab, for a return to the ways of the fathers.[24]

Were *Moby-Dick* an orthodox prophetic book, it would side with God and with the Hebraic and Puritan fathers against the worship of Baal. Melville actually tells a more complicated story. He baptized his "wicked book" in the name of the devil, not the Father. And his Ahab does not worship Baal; he seeks vengeance both against the God of his fathers and (like them) against the pagan deity of nature.

The biblical Ahab attended to the prophets of Baal. Melville's Ahab also brings false prophets on board the *Pequod,* Fedallah and his crew, and, as in the Bible, Elijah warns against them. As captain of an Indian-named ship, the American Ahab is tied to Baal, for American Indians had been seen as idol- and Baal-worshipers since Puritan times. The Asian people of color inherited that attribution, but Fedallah worships fire, not animal and vegetable life. The biblical Elijah called fire down upon Ahab's prophets of Baal,[25] but fire is Captain Ahab's instrument, and he uses it in the hunt against Baal. Baal-worship, as the nineteenth century imagined it, was materialist and orgiastic. It set up androgynous or female gods, or (like Queen Maachah) appropriated the phallus-idol for women. "The abhorred white whale" was an androgynous, pagan, animal God, but "Ahab did not fall down and worship it." (154) His marriage pillow is but thrice dented because he has repudiated the family, not for an orgiastic celebration, but for an ascetic hunt.

"The Israelites during the absence of Moses to the mount made a golden calf and fell down and worshipped it; and they sorely suffered for their idolatry," warned Andrew Jackson. His golden calf was the "monster Hydra" United States Bank, "coiling, like a huge sea-Serpent, its leviathan folds" around America. "Providence has power over me," said Jackson, "but frail mortals who worship Baal and the golden calf can have none."[26]

"The flourishing cities of the West," warned Thomas Hart Benton, "are in the jaws of the monster!" "They may be devoured by it at any moment. . . . One gulp, one swallow, and all is gone." Jackson aimed to rescue America from the power of Baal. He promised "to draw every tooth and then the stumps" of the "mother Bank." (The *Pequod*'s harpooners "drag out" a sperm whale's teeth. [263]) "I have it chained, the *monster must perish*," boasted Jackson. He believed he was returning the children of Israel to the virtues of their fathers, and slaying the demons of mammon and corruption. Ahab's appropriation of Old Hickory's rhetoric, however, suggests the indebtedness of such iconoclasm to the paganism it opposed. Ahab's hunt signals not a repudiation of idolatry, but its inversion.[27]

The Protestant ethic, glorifying visible signs of grace, located saving power in material objects rather than in God. This fetishism of commodities replaced pagan idol-worship with a modern form of animism. It endowed material objects with magical, redemptive power, detaching them (in a Marxist view) from the human labor that produced them and (in a Protestant perspective) from the power of God that lay behind them. Possession of commodities, in bourgeois idol-worship, signified individual power and worth. Ahab, like a disappointed fetishizer of commodities, strikes through the visible signs of grace to destroy the governing, inscrutable power. He has fetishized the whale, assigning to it a power reserved (in the Calvinist view) to God. The monsters of antebellum politics, like Jackson's Bank and Ahab's whale, were centers of hidden power, which explained the bourgeois's failure to master the world. They have the power he wants, and the sensual materiality he experiences as resisting his will, and so he makes war against them.

Moby Dick may be the leviathan to whom Job's God speaks a love poem, letting Job know that such a grand object of desire is beyond his reach. It may be "a grand god" of the pagan world—"the white bull Jupiter, swimming away with ravished Europa clinging to his graceful horns." (412) Refusing to be the submissive Job who accepts God's power, Ahab will end as the ravished Europa instead.[28]

VII

As the biblical Ahab seized Naboth's vineyard, so America engrossed half of Mexico. But this triumph brought retribution. The *Pequod,* named for a tribe the Puritans exterminated, fell "into the hidden snare of the Indian" (140) in the end. The snare is prepared in the black communion, when Ahab's savage harpooners enlist the crew in their captain's mad hunt. Ahab arranges that ceremony under the sway of Fedallah's false promises. They reassure the captain that Moby Dick cannot kill him, and draw him on to his doom. Fedallah's body, lashed to Moby Dick, still precedes Ahab on the chase's final day.

Manifest Destiny lured America across the continent and to the shores of Fedallah's Asia. The agents of westward expansion, removing the Indians in their path, promised a life of egoistic independence. The snare into which Indians led white Americans was baited with independence; it trapped them in slavery. Manifest Destiny twinned whites with Indians and promised them freedom. That claim to freedom, in the wake of the Mexican War, twinned them with slaves.

Indians signified freedom in part because they could be gotten out of the way. Indian removal, unlike black-white relations, offered escape from dependence on others. Indian existence was also envied as itself free from restraint. As Tocqueville put it, "The savage is his own master as soon as he is capable of action. Even his family has hardly any authority over him, and he has never bent his will to that of any of his fellows; no one has taught him to regard voluntary obedience as an honorable subjection, and law is unknown to him even as a word. He delights in this barbarous independence and would rather die than sacrifice any part of it."[29]

The opposite image was applied to slaves. "The Negro has lost even the ownership of his own body," to quote Tocqueville again. "If he becomes free, he often feels independence as a heavier burden than slavery itself, for his life has taught him to submit to everything."[30] Seeking the masterlessness of the imagined Indian, Americans feared they were placing themselves in the determined and dependent position of the slave.

The emergence of the controversy over slavery paralyzed American politics, for it posed the gravest of threats to the country. The issue endangered the Union, raised the specter of slave insurrection, and called attention (in proslavery apologetics) to the social question in Northern "free society."[31] As the citizen demand for freedom infected the European social order, so it threatened the organization of labor in the South. The American 1848 brought to the surface the buried connections between American slavery and American freedom.

Slavery, Edmund Morgan has argued, insulated the colonies from the dangers posed by the European poor. One reason whites could claim natural rights in 1776 was because the bulk of propertyless American workers were in chains. Black slaves could not apply the Declaration of Independence against their rulers at home.[32] To attack slavery, in the American 1848, was to endanger both Southern society and the Union. To leave it alone, once it was an issue, was to acknowledge that freedom for some Americans required the enslavement of others. Perhaps that symbiosis was more than a political arrangement, necessary to save the Union. Perhaps it spoke to the character of American freedom itself. *Moby-Dick*, rooting Ahab's freedom in the enslavement of his crew, raised that possibility.

Ahab "did more to provoke the Lord God of Israel to anger than all the kings of Israel that went before him." His rule, according to interpretations of the first book of Kings, initiated a line of wicked rulers; God punished the Jews for their wickedness with the Babylonian captivity. Nebuchadnezzar, the ruler of Babylon, carried the Jews into slavery, and the scholarship of Melville's day identified the Babylonian Bel with the Phoenician Baal. Melville made the same connection in

Clarel, describing the enslavement of Israel. The suffix of Jezebel's name, together with her licentious reputation, cemented the connection between Baal and Bel, Ahab and Babylon. Abolitionists like Theodore Parker identified slavery with Baal-worship and America with Babylon. The "whore of Babylon," target of the American children of Israel since Puritan days, had seized power in Parker's America. Melville's Ahab hunts Baal, but he rules over an ascetic Babylon.[33]

Solomon himself enslaved those Hittites whom the Jews had not destroyed; the Puritans who sold the Pequod remnant into slavery were following his example. Melville connected those two bits of history in *Clarel,* his epic poem of a pilgrimage to Jerusalem. He compared the modern, Palestinian Arabs to the Hittites and Pequods; they were, thought the American, converted-Jewish pioneer, Nathan, "slaves meriting the rod." Melville implied that the punishment of the Hittites and Pequods made the biblical and Puritan fathers no different from their foes. Most Americans were blind to that possibility. But many did find worrisome another biblical precedent, the Pharaoh's enslavement of the Jews. They feared that the slaveholding nation of Israel was following Egypt's path.

Negroes were "the children of Israel," said Abraham Lincoln, held in "Egyptian bondage." The question of slavery, complained Thomas Hart Benton, was like one of the biblical plagues Jehovah visited on Egypt. Benton elaborated, "You could not look upon the table but there were frogs, you could not go to the bridal couch and lift the sheets but there were frogs." Ishmael insists that his own description of a whale's power to sink ships is meant seriously, and Benton could have said, with him, "I had no more idea of being facetious than Moses, when he wrote the history of the plagues of Egypt." (171) But Benton's wish that the "black question" would go away allied the American pioneers, his "children of Israel," with the Pharaoh. Benton may not have been aware of one biblical exegesis, in which the frogs bit off Egyptian phalluses. Like the Egyptians, nonetheless, he feared the emergence of "this black question forever on the table, on the nuptial couch, everywhere," from the watery social depths.[34]

The frogs, like the white whale, called to account a nation which held slaves. But Ahab, unlike Benton, refuses to wish away the monster that had chewed off his leg. Instead of avoiding the leviathan, he pursues it. He thereby appropriates for himself, and enforces on the *Pequod,* the power he attributes to Moby Dick. Ahab's demand for freedom enslaves his crew. It leads not to anarchy but to order. Ahab's obsession unifies a society fragmented by human claims to power. The whaling industry disintegrated leviathans, but it could not restore wholeness to the world. Ahab creates, from leviathan's natural body, the *Pequod's* organic, communal, social body.

VIII

Ahab is the first and only captain with commanding personal authority in all Melville's fiction. Mutiny or desertion is central to the action of *Typee, Omoo, Mardi, White-Jacket, Benito Cereno,* and *Billy Budd*—every other tale of the sea but *Redburn.* Mutiny takes place offstage in *Moby-Dick,* on the *Town-Ho,* as if to contrast the subversive threat from democratic man on that ship with Ahab's power on the *Pequod.* Two-thirds of the crew typically deserted from a whaling ship. Sailors deserted on Tom Melvill's four whalers, whose routes roughly paralleled the *Pequod's.*[35] But the *Pequod* never touches land once it leaves Nantucket. No one abandons the *Pequod* but Pip, and the punishment which drives him mad is to be abandoned in return. A perfectly ordered and isolated shipboard society— the dream of Alexander Mackenzie and Guert Gansevoort—sails alone in nature on its westward quest—the dream of Gansevoort Melville. Society (the traditional domain of the novel) and the sea (subject of romance) join together in diabolic harmony.

Steelkilt and his mutineers are "sea-Parisians" on the *Town-Ho.* Behind their "barricade," they reenact the June days of 1848. (204) White-Jacket's natural rights, claimed against an arbitrary *Town-Ho* officer and his whip, generate an ugly revolution. Ahab recontains shipboard class divisions, as we shall see, by calling up primitive racial instincts. He mobilizes destructive impulses in the service of authority, thereby avoiding the dangers consummated on the *Town-Ho,* of servile insurrection and civil war.

Political authority, in liberal theory, derived from social contracts among equal and independent men. Such compacts, as 1848 in Europe and America brought forcefully home, were insufficient to bind either individuals or individual states into a body politic. Liberalism split off community from its marketplace model of economic and political life, into the citizen ideal on the one hand and familial bonds on the other. The process of making a product on the *Pequod* undercut that liberal image of society. Melville placed work and hierarchical authority, not contractual agreements among equals, at the center of economic life. He showed that value derived from the appropriation of nature, not from commodity exchange. Ahab's power originated from the human hierarchy on the whaler, and the ship's domination of nature. But Ahab was no ordinary captain. He made transcendent the two sources of maritime authority rooted in civil society and insufficient by themselves to command obedience—the familial structure of formal naval rank, and the marketplace contract for a percentage of the whaling voyage profits. Ahab placed Guert Gansevoort's institutional hierarchy in the service of Gansevoort Melville's democratic expansion.

Ahab fused the two paths taken from the breakdown of the eighteenth-century paternal family order—that of democratic equality, and that of familial hierarchy. To avert disunion and slave revolt, the return to the fathers required new social bonds, not merely a disembodied citizen ideal. Ahab created from the contradictory impulses of political life a new, meaning-giving, communal order. He went back to the Protestant, covenantal roots of the liberal social contract, and made them demonic. He thereby reformed the splintered fragments of Jacksonian Democracy into an organic whole.

The Mexican War shattered the Jackson–Van Buren alliance between Northern Democrats, Southern planters, and Western farmers. It split Jacksonian Democracy in four parts—into Free-Soilers, secessionists, Young America expansionists, and conservative, proslavery Unionists. Calhoun had run for Vice President with Jackson in 1828, broken with him soon after, and then used his position in the Tyler administration to promote Texas annexation. Van Burenites blamed Calhoun for depriving their leader of the 1844 Presidential nomination. Gansevoort Melville, sabotaging Van Buren in Jackson's name, could thus be seen as transferring Old Hickory's mantle to Calhoun. From that point of view, which is Alan Heimert's, Jackson, Calhoun, Gansevoort Melville and Ahab cohere. Calhoun, however, was no expansionist by 1848, since he feared contamination by newly acquired peoples of color. Moreover, Free-Soilers, who also claimed descent from Jackson, were twinned with the secessionists they opposed. Like the "monomaniacs" of the South, the "fanatics" of the North made slavery their obsession. The two factions, wrote Thomas Hart Benton, were twin blades of the shears that together would cut up the Union.[36]

Young America, burying slavery under westward expansion to preserve the Union, was faithful to Jackson's memory. But once the slavery issue had surfaced in the West, the rhetoric of Manifest Destiny was as explosive as that of secession and Free-Soil.

Each fragment of Jacksonian Democracy offered a partial and divisive solution to the American 1848, and Ahab derived from no single one alone. Rather he reunited them all into a new, communal body, which also contained within it the industrial core of patriarchal New England Whiggery—Webster and Shaw—and then led that ship of state to its doom. Political figures who exposed one connection between American slavery and American freedom suppressed another. Ahab stands as a reproach to and culmination of them all.

Like the slaveowner and Indian-fighter Andrew Jackson, Ahab acquired authority over his white equals by appropriating the power of people of color.[37] The intimate, violent bonds of race shattered conventional limits on the *Pequod;* Ahab's "pagan kinsmen" (141) sanctified his rule. They did so in two ceremonies, one early in the tale and the other near its end. The first ritual formed an "indissoluble league" (141) on the *Pequod,* shifting the purpose of the voyage from profit to revenge. The second blessed the weapon the new community will use.

Ahab "revive[s] a noble custom of my fisherman fathers" in the first ritual. He forms a circle with his crew, and passes around a flagon of grog, "hot as Satan's hoof," from which all drink. The mates cross their lances and Ahab, reversing the worldly hierarchy, appoints them "cup-bearers to my pagan kinsmen." Harpooners and mates drink communion from the "murderous chalices" of the harpoon sockets, and swear death to Moby Dick. (140–41)

Ahab christens his hickory harpoon in savage fire and blood in the second ritual. He welds it in the Parsee's "fire" and baptizes it, in the name of the devil, in the harpooners' "baptismal blood." (372–73) Melville transferred Andrew Jackson's Old Hickory baptism in "the fire and blood at New Orleans" from Polk to Ahab. The hickory pole was, thanks to Gansevoort Melville, the emblem for Polk. It was carried in Democratic parades, raised at Democratic rallies, and hoisted aloft in Democratic barbecues. It appeared everywhere in what Herman Melville, writing to Polk, called "the memorable general election" of 1844. Melville was reminding the President of the "signal services" his dead brother had rendered Young Hickory.[38] He appropriated those services for Ahab.

Redburn split Gansevoort Melville between the aristocratic brother ashore and the savage Jackson at sea. Ahab was Jackson's inheritor, but Ishmael's "inseparable twin-brother" (253) on the *Pequod* was the real savage, Queequeg. "You would a good deal rather not sleep with your own brother," remarked Ishmael, when he was offered Queequeg's bed to share at the Spouter-Inn. Melville must have shared his bed with Gansevoort one night in 1839, for after he woke, he wrote his brother, "What the Devil should I see but your cane along in bed with me." Gansevoort's cane supported his bad leg; Jacksonian politics cured it. Melville gave Ahab two canes on the *Pequod,* the whalebone leg and the hickory harpoon, and Ahab baptized the latter in the devil's name. Ahab's false leg is "a cane—a whalebone cane," (114) and his harpoon supports him, too. "The point of a hickory pole," in congressional oratory, bedeviled the British leviathan. "The sound of his ivory leg, and the sound of the hickory pole" (373) rang together when Ahab walked the decks of the *Pequod.*[39]

The hickory harpoon, in Herman Melville's imagery, is to strike through Moby Dick. It replaces Ahab's "flesh and blood," sensate, vulnerable, "old lost leg." (361) "From the keen steel barb" of that harpoon, "lashed in conspicuous crotch, so that it projected beyond the whale-boat's brow," there issues forth a "pale, forked fire" during a lightning storm. Ahab seizes the burning harpoon and waves it like a torch. "All your oaths to hunt the white whale are as binding as mine," he shouts, and blows out the flame. (385) The mincer adorns himself with the "pantaloon-leg," whaleskin phallus to cut up leviathan. At once invulnerable phallus and leg, he can safely do violence to the body of the whale. The role played by "the cassock" in the production of sperm oil is played by the hickory harpoon in Ahab's revenge. At the cost of giving up his own body-part, Ahab acquires a seemingly invulnerable weapon. The sensuous leg belonged to Ahab; the weapon possesses him. It fetishizes the instinctual, savage sources of Ahab's authority.

"Thou just Spirit of Equality," not ancient lineage or noble status, "pick[ed] up Andrew Jackson from the pebbles; [and] . . . thunder[ed] him higher than a throne!" Ahab, like Jackson, is a "champion" selected "from the kingly commons." (105) Proponents of Manifest Destiny after Jackson, like Polk, Stephen Douglas, Thomas

Hart Benton and Lewis Cass, also spoke for equality. But these Western men of the people lacked Old Hickory's kingly stature. Benton opposed the extension of slavery and the others tolerated it, but all wished the issue would go away. They inherited the racial roots of Jackson's politics without his ability to exploit them.

Young America expansionists, following Jackson, tried to bury slavery under Manifest Destiny. Cass and Douglas insisted that the slave question was political rather than social, and favored leaving it to popular sovereignty. Desperately separating the political question of freedom (to vote) from the social question of work, their rhetoric betrayed the explosive connection between them.

"Our fathers" made a revolution, said Cass, for the right of territorial self-government. Cass called the effort to prohibit slavery in the territories "a revival, almost in terms, of the discussions between the parent country and the colonies" which "led to our revolutionary struggle and to our separation from England." It "carries us back to some of the worst doctrines of the middle ages—to those feudal times"—"as if the rights of sovereignty were anything and the rights of man nothing."[40]

Europeans as well as Americans were demanding popular sovereignty, and Cass connected the territorial right to vote on slavery with the revolutions of 1848. Cass was a leading supporter of the European revolutions. He introduced a motion recalling the American minister from Austria, to protest the Hapsburg suppression of Hungarian independence. The debates over American slavery and European revolution were carried on side by side in Congress, and, like other speakers, Cass used the occasion of one subject to speak on the other. Opposing the prohibition of slavery in the territories, he explained,

> The doctrines we have heard advanced upon this subject are precisely those which are at war with human freedom in Europe, and which have achieved a temporary triumph in Hungary, in Italy, and in Germany; and they are maintained and illustrated by the same, or kindred arguments.... *We are sovereign ... and thence it follows that these unfortunate communities may be sold into slavery,* and so on to the end of the chapter, from Poland to Oregon. And human rights are thus frittered away and sacrificed.[41]

Cass demanded the "human right" to choose whether to hold slaves. A community denied that right was itself (the emphasis is his) *"sold into slavery."* "Almighty God," said Cass, "gave us our rights, and ... gave to our fathers ... the will to assert them." Now "despotic power" in Europe and America threatened political freedom. The return to the fathers' revolution, for which Cass called, enshrined the freedom to hold slaves.[42]

Cass apotheosized the Declaration of Independence in the name not of black emancipation but of the white right to enslave. Ahab acquires that freedom in dominating his crew. Cass refused to acknowledge the nature of a social order in which freedom rested on slavery. Melville shows us that order in *Moby-Dick.* There is, of course, no popular sovereignty on board ship, just as there was none for slaves. Instead, freedom for the master to pursue his goals mobilizes the crew in his service.

Cass claimed the protection of the Constitution against those fanatics who would sink the ship of state. He insisted that, "Like the cliffs of eternal granite which overlook the ocean and drive back the ceaseless waves that assault its base, so will the Constitution resist the assaults that may be made upon it." But Cass sensed, in spite of himself, that the right to vote on slavery would not protect the Union, and that he was salvaging a constitutional right from its wreckage. He continued, "We shall cling to this Constitution as the mariner clings to the last plank when night and the Tempest close around him." Popular sovereignty was not just too fragile to withstand the storm; it invited it. Applied in Kansas, Cass's doctrine forced slavery into the open, and led to the Civil War. Like the secessionists and abolitionists against whom he contended, Cass was sailing the ship of state into catastrophe.[43]

Far from defeating "Disunion's Gorgon Crest," as Sam Houston promised, popular sovereignty drew America toward it. Californians had adopted "as the emblem of their land, Minerva springing full-armed and mature from the head of Jove." The *Southern Quarterly Review* approved that choice, but it hoped that the new state would not place "the repulsive, Gorgon-bearing aegis" on Minerva's shield. Minerva represented the miraculous, virgin birth of California, its genesis in the discovery of gold. But the *Review*'s wish betrayed its fear—that the new state had short-circuited political pregnancy and labor unsuccessfully, and that Minerva would bring the Medusa head of slavery in her wake. There is no escape from Medusa on the *Pequod*. Ahab captains "a heathen crew that have small touch of human mothers in them. Whelped somewhere by the sharkish sea, the white whale is their demigorgon." (143) The gorgon, in this juxtaposition of Starbuck's, replaces the sailors' mothers. Ahab is "Cellini's cast Perseus" (109), who stands on Medusa's naked body and holds aloft her severed head. "Perseus . . . the first whaleman" also "harpooned the monster" leviathan and rescued Andromeda. (283) But Ahab fails to slay his leviathan. As Minerva with the gorgon shield, California stood at once for the dream of total freedom and the social fact of slavery. Moby Dick is the gorgon who gives birth to Ahab's vengeance and will destroy his crew.[44]

Southern fire-eaters welcomed the destruction of the American ship of state. They made the Wilmot Proviso, which would have prohibited slavery in all the formerly Mexican territories, into a cause for secession. "Everywhere in the slave States, the Wilmot Proviso became a Gorgon's head," wrote Thomas Hart Benton, "the synonyme of civil war and the dissolution of the Union." "They shout hosannas to the 'Union,'" responded Alabama Congressman S. W. Inge. "They know it is a word of inspiration to every American citizen . . . a word of idolatrous worship, engraved upon the altar of our political temple. As the Persians fall prostrate before the rising Sun, so we are expected to bow to the omnipotence of a word." Secessionists were iconoclasts, moreover, in the name not only of slavery, but of their own right to be free. "I am a Southern man, and slave-holder," said Calhoun. "I would rather meet any extremity upon earth than give up one inch of our

equality. . . . What, acknowledge inferiority! The surrender of life is nothing to sinking down into acknowledged inferiority!"[45]

"He would be a democrat to all above; look how he lords it over all below!"
Starbuck says of Ahab. (143) The "free citizens of slave states," charged Thaddeus
Stevens, were "despots" over slaves. Master on his plantation, like Ahab on his ship,
the planter felt victimized by external forces—abolitionist conspiracy, nationalist
state, corrupt terms of trade—enslaving him from a distance. Knowing from experience that "acknowledge[d] inferiority" meant slavery, the master refused to
submit to anyone. At the same time, he defended slavery as an organic, hierarchical
social relationship. In June 1848, under the pressure of efforts to prohibit slavery in
the territories, Calhoun attacked the Declaration of Independence. All men were
not created equal, he insisted, and he blamed that false doctrine both for the
present "anarchy" in Europe and for the attacks on American slavery. Nevertheless,
the "political equality" of masters required constitutional guarantees of their right to
hold slaves. Calhoun demanded the freedom of slaveholders to take their "property" to the West.[46]

Calhoun opposed the 1850 Compromise because it refused to guarantee
slavery everywhere. He died in that struggle, the Compromise was passed, and it
seemed to save the Union. Ahab's *Götterdämmerung,* Alan Heimert believes, is
derived from Calhoun's. One need not entirely accept that view to recognize the
South Carolinian as a major source for Ahab. "The influence of his mighty mind
over his weak physical structure" struck those who heard the old man speak against
the Compromise. His "skeletonlike" hands and his "emaciated body," Heimert
shows, reappear in Ahab. Melville had already satirized Calhoun, as the figure of
Nulli in *Mardi.* Nulli's eyes, like "twin Corpusant balls," derived from Calhoun;
Calhoun's "eyes, bright as coals," "in action fairly emitting flashes of fire," reappear
in Ahab. "His eyes glowing like coals, that still glow in the ashes of ruin; untottering
Ahab," on the final day of the chase, "lifted his splintered helmet of a brow to the
fair girl's forehead of heaven." Calhoun, too, in his dying battle against the Compromise and the Union, struggled "to overcome the infirmities of a sinking body: *It
was the exhibition of a wounded eagle with his eyes turned to the heaven in which
he had soared, but into which his wings could never carry him again.*"[47]

Calhoun's power, his contemporaries agreed, came from his logical, abstract
intelligence. The physical resemblance between Ahab and Calhoun is seated in their
war of mind against body. Calhoun, the "cast-iron man, who looks as if he had
never been born, and could never be extinguished," reappears in Ahab's wish that
the carpenter make him a man "fifty feet high . . . no heart at all, brass forehead, and
about a quarter of an acre of fine brains." (360) Calhoun was a "mental and moral
abstraction" because he had to divide the political mind from the social body. He
resolved the contradiction between political equality and property in slaves by
radically separating politics from society. Society, for Calhoun, was the realm of
force. Social subordination was necessary, he argued, to protect the freedom of
those in the political arena. "Mr. Calhoun regards slavery as the only secure foun-

dation for Republican institutions," commented Horace Greeley's New York *Tribune*. "Outside of this insane idea he cannot reason, and whatever he says is tinged with it as the fundamental notion of his mind. It was necessary to remember this when listening to his speech [against the Compromise], in order to avoid the impression that he was actually crazy."[48]

Ahab shared Calhoun's monomania. By mobilizing the workers on the *Pequod* in the service of his obsession, he exposed the deranged symbiosis between political masterlessness and social slavery. That symbiosis was a familiar abolitionist target. Abolitionists graphically depicted the red and black bodies sacrificed to the expansion of slavery. "That young giant, strong and mocking, sits there on the Alleghenies," intoned Theodore Parker, "bustling with romantic life."

> His right hand lies folded on his robe; the left rests on the Bible's open page, and holds these sacred words—All men are equal. . . . That stripling giant shouts amain: "My feet are red with the Indians' blood; my hand has forged the Negro's chain. I am strong; who dares assault me? I will drink his blood, for I have made my covenant of lies, and leagued with hell for my support."[49]

Nevertheless, abolitionists also opposed the 1850 Compromise and assaulted the Union. "If this Union, with all its advantages, has no other cement than the blood of slavery, let it perish," said John Hale in 1848. Like Alabama's Inge, Hale would smash the idol of the Union in the name of the right to be free. Southerners demanded that slavery go everywhere, complained Benton, Northerners that it go nowhere. "So true is it that extremes meet, and that all fanaticism, for or against any dogma, terminates at the same point of intolerance and defiance." "Those who plotted the dismemberment of the great Republic," charged Representative Charles Ezra Clarke of New York, were "monomaniacs, who, in hot pursuit of one solitary idea, rush furiously over a communion table." "The Ship of State," warned one supporter of the Compromise, "approaches the awful maelstrom of disunion."[50]

"All the time, when Mr. Webster was telling us the ship of State was going to pieces," responded Parker, "he was calling on us to throw over to Texas—that monster of the deep which threatened to devour the ship of State—fifty thousand square miles of territory, and ten millions of dollars; and to the other monster of secession to cast over the trial by jury. . . ." Parker, for his part, would make war on those monsters. As he imagined it,

> Slavery, the most hideous snake which Southern regions breed, with fifteen unequal feet, came crawling North; fold on fold, and ring on ring, and coil on coil, the venomed monster came; then Avarice, the foulest worm which Northern cities gender in their heat, went crawling South. . . . At length they met, and twisting up on their obscene embrace, the twain became one monster, Hunkerism.[51]

"Where shall I find a parallel with men who will do such a deed?" asked Parker, referring to the return of the fugitive Thomas Sims to slavery. "Come, brood of monsters, let me bring you up from the deep damnation of the graves," he intoned. "Bring up the greatest monster of the human race," and his infamy would be less than those who reenslaved Sims.[52]

The "monster of the deep" who sent Thomas Sims back to Georgia was Lemuel Shaw. His decision against Sims, the first to return a fugitive slave from Massachusetts, was also the first to declare constitutional the 1850 Fugitive Slave Law. It saved the Compromise and (many thought) the Union, at the expense of reenslaving free men. Parker appealed against *Sims* to "our fathers [who] fought and bled on yonder Hill." He indicated Bunker Hill, where Melville's grandfather had fought; his own was a veteran of Lexington. Parker called on Boston, in the name of the fathers, to slay the monster of slavery. He preached like Father Mapple. Ahab assaulted leviathan in the name of the devil, not of the Father. Although Parker claimed to speak for authority, unlike Ahab, his appeal to the fathers threatened to destroy their Union.[53]

Parker called, in his sermon, for the destruction of the Baal-worshiping slave-master, King Ahab. He imagined himself as the Elijah who had prophesied Ahab's doom. But that very apocalyptic appeal made Parker himself into an Ahab. "It is not possible to suppress the idea of freedom" the minister insisted, "but it is possible to destroy a State." "You may make your statutes; an appeal always lies to the higher law," Parker told supporters of the Fugitive Slave Law. "Your statutes cannot hold him," he continued, reminding his audience of God's invocation of leviathan in his answer to Job. "While it is calm, you may laugh, and say, 'Lo, I have chained the ocean!' and howl down the law of Him who holds the universe as a rosebud in His hand." The rosebud, in Parker's metaphor (like the ship of that name in *Moby-Dick*), was at the mercy of God and the sea. Whether Parker called upon God's ocean, or presented himself as a monster-slayer, he spoke as a prophet of destruction.[54]

Parker shifted the idea of freedom from a political right for whites to a civil right for slaves. That made him not merely the prophet of servile insurrection and civil war, but their instigator. (Within a decade, he would help finance John Brown's raid at Harper's Ferry.) European 1848ers joined political freedom to nationalism; but the freedom demanded by the European poor divided the nation, for it set one class against another. Abolitionists, applying the Declaration of Independence against slavery, played that divisive role in America.

Parker opposed the "despotic idea . . . that one man has a natural right to overcome and make use of some other man for his advantage." That may seem to make him a critic of shipboard masters like Ahab, as well as of lords of the lash. But at the same time that Parker opened up the social question in the South, he buried it in the North. Southerners were beginning to expose the coercive character of so-called free society. The capitalist had the natural right to buy labor, wrote George Fitzhugh, the propertyless worker to sell it. Parker pretended there were no labor relations in the North. He contrasted the slaveowner's power over men to the free man's power over nature. "Instead of kidnapping a man who can run away," he explained, the North "kidnaps the elements, subdues them to its command, and makes them do its work. . . . It lays hands on fire and water, and breeds a new giant." Science freed men from "slavery to the elements," and built "iron vassals" to serve them. Parker was proposing the same domination over nature that the master exercised over his slaves. Northerners created and ruled over artificial men, in Parker's images, not real ones. Parker, Cass, and other enthusiasts for technology imagined it would replace human labor.[55]

Far from separating the exploitation of nature (in the West) from control over men (in society), as Parker imagined was possible, Ahab showed how the one facilitated the other. In a "joint stock world," Ishmael imagines Queequeg thinking, "we cannibals must help those Christians." (67) It is an unsettling set of juxtapositions. The joint stock company points backward to Allan Melvill's milieu, those eighteenth-century commercial relationships in which partners shared unlimited liability. Carried forward to work relations among a nineteenth-century international proletariat, such partnerships become the model for the monkey rope that will tie Ishmael to "his own inseparable twin-brother, Queequeg," "in a joint-stock company of two." (253) But mutual dependence is risky (as Melvill's fate showed his son), since one flawed human must rely on another. "Men may seem detestable as joint stock companies; they are heroic in the ideal," comments Ishmael. (215) He is speaking for Ahab. Ahab curses "that mortal interindebtedness which will not do away with ledgers." (361) "The Guinea-Coast slavery of solitary command" (408) has prepared Ahab to mistrust interdependence and seek domination. He does so by infusing the traditional prerogatives of master over slave with the modern magic of technology.[56]

Work relations on the *Pequod* point away from isolated independence and toward fraternity. Ahab resists fraternity by manipulating mechanical power. "My one cogged circle fits into all their various wheels, and they revolve," he exults, after he has sworn the crew to hunt Moby Dick. (142) Ahab has gained "magnetic ascendancy" over the sailors, (175) for he has "shocked them into the same fiery emotion accumulated within the Leyden jar of his own magnetic life." (141) Later, Ahab refuses to navigate with scientific instruments, and throws away the quadrant. That is because he has acquired its power for himself.

Ahab exploits the technological sublime, the terrifying, awe-inspiring power of man-made inventions. In so doing, however, he shows that he is in the power of the machine. "The path to my fixed purpose is laid with iron rails, whereon my soul is grooved to run," he says. (142) The image is the negative of American hopes that technology would empower free men.[57]

The telegraph, wrote Oliver Wendell Holmes, gave America a "network of iron nerves which flash sensation and volition backward and forward to and from towns and provinces as if they were organs and limbs of a single living body." Nationalist expansion was justified in organic terms ("Contiguous territory, however remote, must eventually melt into one government . . . as in the human body, where the heart and the head govern all the members"), and railroads would provide a "vast system of iron muscles which, as it were, move the limbs of the mighty organism."[58]

Such images short-circuited historical time and geographic distance. They made the eighteenth-century Newtonian machine into an organism, and brought it to life. A mechanistic vocabulary spoke to contractual relations among individual property-owners. Organic, corporate images sanctified nineteenth-century industrial capitalism. Ahab transformed the traditional shipboard society of master and slave into a modern, industrial body.

For Southern Unionists, the "STEAM-ENGINE . . . [was] the most powerful instrument by far of pacification and commerce, and therefore of improvement and happiness, that the world has ever seen." It "promised . . . to make the whole Christian world, at least, one great family." But the home of industrial capitalism was Northeastern Whiggery. Daniel Webster, a "steam engine in trousers," was its spokesman.[59]

Although both Northern and Southern Unionists hoped that technology would harmonize the sections, Northerners went further. Fearful that a centralized, national state would upset slavery, Southerners insisted on the constitutional compact among the states as the basis for political obligation. Northerners like Webster proposed new, organic, national ties. The Kentuckian Clay defended the Compromise as a mutually advantageous sectional bargain. Webster had already, in his 1830 speech against nullification, shifted the Union's bonds from a contract among states to a national sentiment. As sectional conflict deepened, so did Webster's emotional appeal. He called for a Union which went beyond the "compact" to "fraternal feeling." He repudiated the "bonds of legal corporation" for the "unseen, soft, easy-sitting chains that result from generous affections and from a sense of common interest and common pride."[60]

Webster's "unseen, soft . . . chains" would not bind the Union. They became visible around the Massachusetts courthouse, even as he spoke, to prevent anti-slavery mobs from freeing Thomas Sims. Judge Shaw stooped beneath "the chain on the neck of the Commonwealth," as Parker called it, to decide the fate of the slave. "See the court-house in chains," preached Parker. These chains were unsanctified, for neither Webster's pieties nor Shaw's obeisance to the state had the force to hold the Union together. Melville imagined a demonic reunification instead. Webster and Shaw still grounded their state in relations among individual property-owners. Spokesmen for that sort of capitalism—Peleg, Bildad, Starbuck—have lost political power on Ahab's ship. Drawing on his destructive intimacy with nature, on the savage's instinctual power, and on a transforming, technological magic, Ahab merged his "thirty isolatoes" into a communal body.[61]

Sailing east from New England, the *Pequod* inherited and reversed the mission of the *Arbella*, which had sailed west to the New World two centuries earlier. "Christ and his church make one body," preached John Winthrop on board the *Arbella*. His "spirit and love knits all" the disordered limbs together. The members of Winthrop's community formed "one body in Christ"; Ahab formed his crew into members of his own body. The "thirty isolatoes" "federated along one keel" (108) when the *Pequod* leaves Nantucket, like the "crown of thirty stars" on Theodore Parker's giant Young America, equal the number of states in the federal union before California. "They were one man, not thirty," when they sighted Moby Dick. "All the individualities of the crew, this man's valor, that man's fear; guilt and guiltiness, all varieties were welded into oneness, and were all directed to that fatal goal which Ahab their one lord and keel did point to. . . . 'Ye are not other men, but my arms and legs; and so obey me.'" (418–19, 427) By hunting the beast, Ahab created—in the opening words of Hobbes's *Leviathan* (which Melville quoted in the opening extracts of *Moby-Dick*)—"that great Leviathan, called a Commonwealth, or State—(in Latin, Civitas)—which is but an artificial man."[62] (14)

NOTES

[1] Herman Melville, *Moby-Dick* (New York, 1956 [1851]), pp. 153–54. Subsequent page numbers in the text refer to this edition.

[2] Cf. Georg Lukács, *Realism in Our Time* (New York, 1962), pp. 11–14; Charles Feidelson, *Symbolism and American Literature* (Chicago, 1953), pp. 77–118.

[3] Erich Heller, *The Disinherited Mind* (Cleveland, 1959), pp. 210–11; Angus Fletcher, *Allegory: The Theory of a Symbolic Mode* (Ithaca, N.Y., 1964), pp. 352–56; Feidelson, pp. 8–9, 27, passim.

[4] Cf. Richard H. Brodhead, *Hawthorne, Melville and the Novel* (Chicago, 1976), pp. 134–51, 146; Charles H. Foster, "Something in Emblems: A Reinterpretation of *Moby-Dick*," *New England Quarterly*, XXXIV (March 1961), 30–33; Fletcher, p. 69; Leo Marx, *The Machine in the Garden* (New York, 1964), pp. 286–87, 299–300.

[5] Henry Nash Smith, "The Madness of Ahab," *Yale Review*, LXVI (Autumn 1976), 16–20. Cf. Leonard W. Levy, *The Law of the Commonwealth and Chief Justice Shaw* (Cambridge, Mass., 1957), pp. 206–16.

[6] David Brion Davis, *Homicide in American Fiction* (Ithaca, N.Y., 1957), pp. 64–66, 112–16; Henry Adams, *The Education of Henry Adams* (Boston, 1973 [1918]), pp. 426–27.

[7] Davis, pp. 64, 92.

[8] See below, and *Commonwealth v. Sims*.

[9] Merrell R. Davis and William H. Gilman, eds., *The Letters of Herman Melville* (New Haven, 1960), p. 134; Foster, *New England Quarterly*, XXXIV, 14.

[10] Davis and Gilman, p. 133n; Smith, *Yale Review*, LXVI, 29; Herman Melville, "Hawthorne and His Mosses" (1850), in Jay Leyda, ed., *The Portable Melville* (New York: 1952), p. 407; Michel Foucault, *Discipline and Punish* (New York, 1979), pp. 19, 29–31, 73–81.

[11] Cf. Joseph Schumpeter, *Capitalism, Socialism, and Democracy*, 3rd ed. (New York, 1950), pp. 81–86.

[12] Jay Leyda, ed., *The Melville Log*, 2 vols. (New York, 1951), p. 27; Hershel Parker, "Melville and Politics: A Scrutiny of the Political Milieux of Herman Melville's Life and Works," unpublished Ph.D. dissertation, Northwestern University, 1963, p. 21.

[13] *Congressional Globe*, 29th Congress, 2nd Session (1847), Appendix, p. 213 (hereafter cited as CG-A); Joseph Schumpeter, *Imperialism and Social Classes* (New York, 1951), pp. 6–7. Schumpeter wants to separate capitalism from imperialism, but he is drawn, in spite of himself, to the symbiotic relationship between them. Cf. *Imperialism*, pp. 89–90, 96, 104–07, 124–30.

[14] Michael Gilmore, *The Middle Way* (New Brunswick, N.J., 1977), p. 147.

[15] Karl Marx, *Capital*, 3 vols. (Chicago, 1906–09 [1867, 1885, 1894]), I, 784–848 (quoted, p. 823). Cf. Immanuel Wallerstein, *The Modern World System* (New York, 1974); Stephen Greenblatt, *Renaissance Self-Fashioning from More to Shakespeare* (Chicago, 1980), pp. 157–221; Rosa Luxemburg, *Accumulation of Capital* (New York, 1964 [1913]), pp. 368–418; Michael Paul Rogin, *Fathers and Children: Andrew Jackson and the Subjugation of the American Indian* (New York, 1975), pp. 165–69.

[16] Douglass C. North, *The Economic Growth of the United States, 1790–1860* (Englewood Cliffs, N.J., 1961); Rogin, pp. 165–69, 251–55.

[17] Alan Heimert, "*Moby-Dick* and American Political Symbolism," *American Quarterly*, XVI (April 1963), 501–02.

[18] Richard Slotkin, *Regeneration through Violence* (Middletown, Conn., 1973), pp. 154–55, 177–78.

[19] Charles Feidelson, ed., Herman Melville, *Moby-Dick* (Indianapolis, 1964), p. 276n; Davis and Gilman, pp. 140–41; William L. Stone, *Life of Joseph Brant-Thayendanegea …*, 2 vols. (New York, 1838). Settlers called the Iroquois leader "the monster Brant" because of Indian devastation of the Mohawk Valley; the phrase is in Stone, II, 458.

[20] T. Walter Herbert, Moby-Dick *and Calvinism* (New Brunswick, N.J., 1977), p. 106; Heimert, *American Quarterly*, XVI, 507; Major L. Wilson, *Space, Time and Freedom* (Westport, Conn., 1974), pp. 113, 129; Norman Graebner, ed., *Manifest Destiny* (Indianapolis, 1968), p. xvii.

[21] Heimert, *American Quarterly*, XVI, 503–05; Theodore Parker, *A Sermon of the Mexican War …* (Boston, 1848), p. 1.

[22] T. Parker, p. 54; Slotkin, pp. 169–79, passim; Rogin, pp. 144–57.

[23] Heimert, *American Quarterly*, XVI, 511–12; Theodore Parker, "The Chief Sins of the People" (1851), *Works*, 14 vols. (Boston, 1907–13), IX, 25–26.

[24] Nathalia Wright, *Melville's Use of the Bible* (Durham, N.C., 1949), pp. 61–69; Gilmore, pp. 138–49; Martin Green, *The Von Richthofen Sisters* (New York, 1974), pp. 146–47; Feidelson, ed., *Moby-Dick*, p. 536n; Herbert, p. 106; Henry N. Murray, "In Nomine Diaboli," *New England Quarterly*, XXIV (Dec. 1951), 442–43.

[25] Wright, p. 64.

[26] Rogin, p. 290; Heimert, *American Quarterly*, XVI, 516.

[27] Rogin, p. 289–91.

[28] Murray, *New England Quarterly*, XXIV, 444–49.

[29] Alexis de Toqueville, *Democracy in America*, J. P. Mayer, ed. (Garden City, N.Y., 1969 [1835, 1840]), pp. 318–19. Cf. Rogin, pp. 114–25; Bernard W. Sheehan, *Seeds of Extinction* (Chapel Hill, N.C., 1973), pp. 89–116.

[30] Toqueville, Mayer, ed., p. 318.

[31] Holman Hamilton, *Prologue to Conflict: The Crisis and Compromise of 1850* (Lexington, Ky., 1964), p. 87. Southerners made that argument during the Compromise debate. Its classic statement is George Fitzhugh, *Cannibals All* (Cambridge, Mass., 1960 [1854]).

[32] Edmund P. Morgan, *American Slavery, American Freedom* (New York, 1975).

[33] Gilmore, pp. 148–50; Wright, pp. 69–71; Heimert, *American Quarterly*, XVI, 511–12; Herman Melville, *Clarel*, Walter E. Bezanson, ed. (New York, 1960 [1876]), pp. 346–47.

[34] Melville, *Clarel*, pp. 62, 570n; Abraham Lincoln, "Speech at Springfield, Ill.," June 26, 1857, in Roy P. Basler, ed., *Abraham Lincoln, Collected Works*, 9 vols. (New Brunswick, N.J., 1953–55), II, 409; David M. Potter, *The Impending Crisis 1848–1861* (New York, 1976), p. 39; Richard L. Rubenstein, *The Religious Imagination* (Boston, 1968), p. 74; CG-A, 26th Cong., 1st Sess. (1839–40), p. 71. Kathleen Moran called my attention to Benton's biblical reference and its Talmudic exegesis.

[35] Jay Leyda, "Ishmael Melville," *Boston Public Library Quarterly*, I (Oct. 1949), 121–34.

[36] Heimert, *American Quarterly*, XVI, 513–14; Thomas Hart Benton, *Thirty Years View*, 2 vols. (New York, 1856), II, 695.

[37] On Jackson, see Rogin, pp. 38–205.

[38] Heimert, *American Quarterly*, XVI, 507–08; New York *Morning News*, Aug. 21, Sept. 9, Oct. 7, 1844; Davis and Gilman, pp. 30–31.

[39] Davis and Gilman, pp. 16, 29; Heimert, *American Quarterly*, XVI, 507.

[40] CG-A, 31-1, pp. 58–59.

[41] CG-A, 31-1, p. 73; cf., e.g., pp. 84–91.

[42] CG-A, 31-1, p. 73.

[43] CG-A, 29-2, p. 213.

[44] CG-A, 31-1, p. 98; "California Gold and European Revolution," *Southern Quarterly Review*, XVII (July 1850), 306–07.

[45] Benton, II, 695; CG-A, 31-1, p. 103; John C. Calhoun, "Resolutions on the Slave Question," Feb. 19, 1847, in *Works*, Richard Crallé, ed., 6 vols. (New York, 1851), IV, 348.

[46] CG-A, 31-1, p. 142; John C. Calhoun, "Speech on the Oregon Bill," June 27, 1848, in *Works*, IV, 489–81, 506–12.

[47] Heimert, *American Quarterly*, XVI, 523–26.

[48] Ibid., p. 523; Richard Hofstadter, *The American Political Tradition* (New York, 1948), p. 95; Louis

Hartz, *The Liberal Tradition in America* (New York, 1955), pp. 145–71; New York *Tribune,* March 6, 1850, p. 1.

[49] Heimert, *American Quarterly,* XVI, 511–12; Theodore Parker, "A Sermon of War" (1846), *Works,* IV, 30–31.

[50] Potter, pp. 44n, 45; Heimert, *American Quarterly,* XVI, 500, 513–14; Daniel Webster, "Speech at Capon Springs, Va.," June 28, 1851, in *Writings and Speeches,* 18 vols. (Boston, 1903), XII, 439.

[51] Theodore Parker, "Discourse Occasioned by the Death of Daniel Webster" (1852), *Works,* VII, 331, 336–37. Parker delivered this speech after Melville published *Moby-Dick.* It is evidence of a shared symbolism, not a borrowed one.

[52] Parker, "Chief Sins," *Works,* IX, 37.

[53] Ibid., *Works,* IX, 42; Pittsfield *Sun,* April 10, 17, 1851.

[54] Parker, "Chief Sins," *Works,* IX, 44; Theodore Parker, "The State of the Nation" (1850), *Works,* XII, 126–27.

[55] Parker, "The State of the Nation," *Works,* XII, 104–07; L. Marx, p. 201; Fitzhugh, *Cannibals All.*

[56] Cf. C. L. R. James, *Mariners, Renegades, and Castaways* (New York, 1953), pp. 2–4, 54–60; Stephen C. Ausband, "The Whale and the Machine: An Approach to *Moby-Dick,*" *American Literature,* XLVII (May 1975), 197–211.

[57] L. Marx, pp. 195–208, 294–95.

[58] George Forgie, *Patricide in the House Divided* (New York, 1979), p. 103; Graebner, ed., p. 99.

[59] H. S. Legare, "The Steam Engine," *Southern Literary Messenger,* XVII (Jan. 1851), 24; Foster, *New England Quarterly,* XXXIV, 29.

[60] Wilson, pp. 99–100; Irving H. Bartlett, *Daniel Webster* (New York, 1978), pp. 114–20; Webster, *Writings and Speeches,* XIII, 389.

[61] Parker, "Chief Sins," *Works,* IX, 41–42.

[62] John Winthrop, "A Model of Christian Charity," in Edmund S. Morgan, ed., *Puritan Political Ideas* (Indianapolis, 1965), p. 84; Heimert, *American Quarterly,* XVI, 501; Parker, "The State of the Nation," *Works,* XII, 130.

William B. Dillingham
AHAB'S HERESY

The story of Ahab is one of self-warring. There are two Ahabs as there are two Ishmaels, but the two sides hidden within the single body of Ishmael recognize and understand each other. In Ahab, one self—that characterized by God-hunger—battles with a tendency within that self, a tendency toward what may be called atheism or nihilism. Concurrently, this same self is at war on another front with an enemy it does not even recognize, a hooded knight that turns out to be another aspect of Ahab's complex personality, the side that is godlike and so proud of its specialness that it hates the other side, the yearning for a higher God. The nature of the combatants and the great final battles of this self-war that occupy the foreground of *Moby-Dick* were the subjects of the previous chapter; what precipitated the breach to begin with that led to hostilities is the subject of this one.

If one factor can be said to be primarily responsible for the division of self that finally destroys Ahab, it is his preoccupation with the subject of evil. "Some deep men," Melville says in chapter 41 ("Moby Dick"), are prone to "feel eating in them" the troublesome mystery of iniquity.[1] They simply cannot help probing to the furthest possible extent the question of evil, its nature and especially its source. Where, they ask over and over, does this "intangible malignity" come from? With such deep and obsessive thinkers, several answers and subsequent courses of action based on those answers are possible.

After delving into the problem of evil to discover its source, some probers of this sort may conclude that it has no supernatural origins, that it is merely the absence of good, not, in its own right, a positive force at all. But to Ahab the evidences in his own experience of universal malignity have been far too great for him to be able to accept this answer. He reads signs, and the signs point to a real and powerful evil. Others may deny the presence of supernatural evil by denying the presence of *any* supernatural force: there is no devil because there is no God. The evil in the world, they may decide, derives from social injustices, from poor

From *Melville's Later Novels* (Athens: University of Georgia Press, 1986), pp. 91–124.

environmental conditions and conditioning, and from psychological abnormalities. But Ahab by his very nature is a God-seeker, and he engages in fierce combat with any tendency to blot out all supernatural forces.

Being as he is, unable to deny the reality of evil or its supernatural origins, Ahab in his pursuit of truth seems to have three options. First, he could recognize evil as being the overwhelming power of the universe and become its subject. Again, Ahab's God-hunger, his love of balance and justice, are too much a part of his nature to allow him to become a devil-worshipper. As a second possible course, he could follow the traditional way for a nineteenth-century American of religious bent and become an ardent Christian like Father Mapple, who recognizes the supernatural presence of evil but feels that God is stronger and allows evil to exist for purposes He alone understands but we in our limited finite minds cannot. No matter how hard they try to do this, however, some deep, questioning souls who are preoccupied with rightness and fair play cannot understand why God allows children to die in their cribs, innocent women to be violated, or whole populations to be wiped out by famine, earthquakes, tidal waves, or senseless wars. They are told by Christians that all is for the best, that God is on his throne, and that He sees every sparrow that falls. Such a person as Ahab cannot accept this orthodox Christian God who is responsible for evil and who allows it to flourish. Nevertheless, Ahab must have some God; he will fight to have God.

The third option for Ahab is another way of thinking about evil and God, one that Melville knew about, one that he was strongly attracted to himself, and one that he has Ahab embrace as both the answer to his questions and the cause of his destruction—the ancient heresy of Gnosticism. Precisely how much Melville knew about this Christian heresy that arose in the first century, flourished in the second, and gradually died out, is impossible to determine. A few scattered references to the Gnostics do occur in his writings from each period of his career, but there is no direct evidence that he made any deep and systematic study of them. He did know at least the basic outlines of Gnostic beliefs, and this was enough to impress him profoundly because these fundamental concepts were startingly congenial to his own temperament. If he read no more on Gnosticism than in books he is known to have owned, he would have been supplied with all the basic tenets of the heresy.[2] He could not but be struck with how like himself those ancient thinkers were.

Two sets of reference books that he owned contain multiple entries on the Gnostics. In Pierre Bayle's *A General Dictionary, Historical and Critical,* which Melville obtained in 1849, he found discussions of Gnostics and related sects, including the Cainites, the Paulicians, the Marcionites, and the Manacheans. Millicent Bell has argued conclusively for Melville's fondness for Bayle and for the influence of the *Dictionary* on many aspects of *Moby-Dick.* Bell correctly perceives that "Melville must have discovered a state of mind remarkably like his own."[3] What she is referring to is the concern of both men for the question of evil. Whatever Bayle happens to be writing about, he likely will get around to the perplexing problem of evil. "Bayle was a man tossed between the will to believe and the compulsion to doubt. He denied that he was an atheist but, truly, one can say of him what Hawthorne was to say of Melville . . . : 'He can neither believe nor be comfortable in his unbelief.' "[4] Bayle chose to write several entries on the Gnostics because he was, in spite of his rejection of their solutions, obviously fascinated with them and attracted to their unorthodox handling of the thorny question of evil.[5] Melville was likewise.

Melville received more of an objective and systematic outline of the fundamentals of Gnosticism from his copy of Ephraim Chambers's *Cyclopaedia; or, An Universal Dictionary of Arts and Sciences* (1728). He acquired this two-volume reference work in 1846, a gift from his uncle Herman Gansevoort. It contains substantial entries not only on the general subject of "Gnosticks," but also on the individual sects, including the Valentinians, Simonians, Carpocratians, Nicolaitians, and others. No Gnostic outlook with which Melville furnished Ahab would need to have come from any source outside Chambers and Bayle, though it is likely that Melville did pick up knowledge of the subject here and there in his extensive reading elsewhere.

Biographers and critics have been uncharacteristically slow in recognizing both Melville's affinity for the Gnostics and his awareness of their beliefs. William Braswell perceptively but briefly pointed out Melville's reference to the Gnostics in *White-Jacket,* suggested that Melville "must have been stimulated by the heretical ideas of those early rivals of Christianity" as Pierre Bayle described them, and explicated a few of Ahab's speeches in Gnostic terms.[6] Braswell's groundbreaking work of 1943 was not really continued until much later and then only partially, although Millicent Bell did direct herself in 1951 to the single question of the Gnostic position on evil as described by Bayle. Building on Braswell's suggestion that Ahab reflects certain Gnostic ideas, Thomas Vargish published an article on the subject of Melville's interest in Gnosticism.[7] Vargish admirably outlines many of the intricacies of the heresy (more perhaps than Melville was actually acquainted with). In order to account for Melville's knowledge of Gnosticism, Vargish conjectures that he must have read Andrew Norton's *The Evidences of the Genuineness of the Gospels,* published in 1844. If Melville had, indeed, read these three volumes, he would certainly have been something of an expert on the Gnostics, for they are the major target of Norton's inquiry. It is possible that he was acquainted with Norton's work, but there is no direct evidence that he was and some suggestion that he was not.[8] Nevertheless, the article remains a pioneering piece of scholarship that has not been followed up.[9] The purpose of this chapter is to do that, to argue (with Braswell, Bell, and Vargish) that Melville was acquainted with Gnostic beliefs, that he found them compelling, and that he used them in his creation of Ahab. In addition, I wish to suggest that Ahab's destructive split, his war within, results from Ahab's heretical beliefs.

The most obvious characteristic of the Gnostics' behavior is also the most obvious aspect of Ahab's. The Gnostics believed that they were very special people, superior not only to the heathens and barbarians of the world but also to other Christians. In a fashion vaguely similar to Calvin's view of the Elect, they spoke of their own favored status. Ephraim Chambers wrote in his entry on the "Gnosticks" that they acted "as if they were the only Persons who had the true knowledge of Christianity: Accordingly, they look'd on all the other Christians as simple, ignorant, and barbarous Persons, who explained, and interpreted the Sacred Writings in too low, and literal a Signification."[10] The Gnostics could not have described themselves better than did Ishmael when he pointed to the differences between the ordinary masses and the "true princes of the empire," the "choice hidden handful of the Divine inert." These and many other expressions in *Moby-Dick* are so close to Gnostic belief and imagery that they could have been taken directly from the pages of the heresiarchs themselves.

The Gnostics believed they were the Elect because they felt that they had within them what Ahab refers to as royal essence ("queenly personality"): Ishmael's eloquent description of Ahab as a many-layered person is a description the Gnostics would have given of themselves, for they believed in a pristine, unfallen Adamic Man within, which they frequently described as a royal personage, a queen, a king, or the son of a king, held captive by the body and the world. Knowing that the Gnostics considered themselves by their very natures the most special and favored people on earth, Melville wrote passage after passage in *Moby-Dick* that startlingly reproduce the imagery they used. Ishmael says that if one could go down through the layers of being in Ahab, like the layers of civilizations uncovered in the Hotel de Cluny in Paris, one would come to a royal personage held there, a "captive king" (p. 161). The Gnostics considered themselves the chosen because they were descended from the royal Godhead.[11] When they were not describing this divine spark or spiritual gift within them as a link in royal lineage they were using other similar images, such as uncorruptible gold in the midst of corruption.[12] The extent to which like temperaments and like thinking can produce ideas clothed in the same metaphors is to be seen in Melville's use of gold as the emblem of Ahab's self-concept. In the solid gold doubloon that he nails to the mainmast, Ahab sees his deepest and purest self, "nailed amidst all the rustiness of iron bolts and the verdigris of copper spikes, yet, untouchable and immaculate to any foulness" (p. 359). Though Starbuck, Stubb, and the others who gaze at the doubloon read a variety of meanings into it, Ahab sees there "his own mysterious self."

Ahab's specialness, which is projected in images of royalty and gold, makes him stand out in his own and in Ishmael's mind clearly above two other classes of men in *Moby-Dick*. Ahab believes that he has within him that which is "divinely inert," that is, a spiritual element that is of the same substance as God and is thus immune to the corrupting influences around it. Like gold, it cannot be oxidized. In his various estimates of his mates and seamen, he places most of them in a category well below himself. He refers to this class in general as "manufactured man." By this he seems to mean that such men are more like machines—"androids" we would call them today—than like created human beings with an indwelling spirituality or soul. He applies the term *mechanical* to Stubb at one point (p. 452), and he uses the term later to describe most of his crew (p. 459).

Ishmael's thinking often parallels Ahab's in the matter of human categories. They are as one in their view of the ship's carpenter as an example of "mechanical" man. Ishmael compares him to an intricate tool, "one of those unreasoning but still highly useful . . . Sheffield contrivances" (p. 388). He is, Ishmael says, "a pure manipulator" (p. 388). Though he seemed not to possess a soul, he did have some sort of "cunning life-principle in him; this it was, that kept him a great part of the time soliloquizing; but only like an unreasoning wheel, which also hummingly soliloquizes" (p. 389). The point in using this pattern of imagery to refer to the ordinary mass of mankind is to convey the idea that unlike Ahab, who according to Elijah has enough soul "to make up for all deficiencies of that sort in other chaps" (p. 86),[13] the carpenter and those like him are "soulless," as, indeed, Ahab says of Stubb at one point (p. 452).

Ahab has a much higher regard for Starbuck, in whom he confides near the end that he feels like "Adam, staggering beneath the piled centuries since Paradise" (p. 444). Though Starbuck comes close to influencing Ahab to turn back, he cannot finally reach the old man, and Ahab remains in the isolation of his self-conceived "grand, Lama-like exclusiveness." To Ahab, Stubb and Starbuck represent the two types that are generally encountered in mankind. "Ye two are the opposite poles of one thing; Starbuck is Stubb reversed, and Stubb in Starbuck; and ye two are all mankind" (p. 452). Not *all* mankind, though, for Ahab and the few choice hidden handful like him represent a third type that stand above "the millions of the peopled earth, nor gods nor men . . . [their] neighbors!" (p. 452). In Ahab's mind Starbuck is higher than the "soulless" Stubb and the millions of mechanical-like people because Starbuck does have a soul. But Ahab realizes whenever he converses with Starbuck that his first mate lacks the depth of spiritual insight, the "specialness" that he himself possesses.

This hierarchical view of humankind, which Ahab and to a large measure Ishmael express, is precisely that espoused by the Gnostics. No belief of these early Christian heretics was better known than this or more frequently referred to in books Melville would have read. Chambers's *Cyclopaedia* includes the following information about the Gnostics: "On the like Principle they also distinguished three Sorts of Men; *Material, Animal,* and *Spiritual:* The first, who were Material, and incapable of Knowledge, inevitably perished. . . . The third, such as the *Gnosticks* themselves pretended to be, were all certainly saved: The Psychic, or Animal, who were the middle between the other two, were capable either of being saved, or damned according to their good, or evil Actions."[14] Earlier, Chambers refers to the favored third type as "Pneumatic," which means "spiritual."

Ahab's sense of superiority is the result of the same conviction that made the Gnostics feel special. He thinks that he is the only one aboard the *Pequod* who truly knows what is going on. He has been blessed with special insight, or so he believes. He is one of the few who has "the true Knowledge," as Chambers expressed the

Gnostics' attitude toward themselves. That insight places him far above the masses of vulgar and stolid material men and even above psychics like Starbuck. In his entry on the Gnostics, Chambers explains that "the Word *Gnostic* is formed of the Latin *Gnosticus*" and from two Greek words, which mean "enlightened" and "I know."

Coming to know was for the Gnostics—as it was for Ahab—a form of initiation, and once initiated, the Gnostic felt above and apart from the unknowing masses. But this knowledge could not be gained from study. Gnosticism was not a philosophy but a form of intuitive conviction. The Gnostics' insights about good and evil and about God and mankind came not through the intellect, not through the ordinary processes of learning, but through something like a mystical experience, which they referred to as "the call." In a single moment one would be awakened and *know* one's true spiritual self.

Because of this mystical element in their beliefs, the Gnostics acquired the reputation, from the time of Simon Magus onward, as practitioners of magic.[15] Certain sects were noted for their creation of amulets, which they wore on their spiritual quests.[16] Chambers's *Cyclopaedia* claims for the Basilidians the invention of "certain Amulets, to which they attributed great Virtues."[17] Though he does not wear it or create it himself, Ahab seems to regard the doubloon in some magical way. Fascinated with the figures on it, its "cabalistics" (p. 359), he rubs it against his jacket before he nails it to the very center of the ship. While he is rubbing it, he produces a sound that is "strangely muffled and inarticulate" (p. 142). Indeed, Ahab is not only a believer in such things of the world of magic as Fedallah's riddle-prophecy, but he is something of a magician himself.[18] Melville probably read in his copy of Chambers the entry on the "Simonians," another sect of Gnostics who "made profession of Magic" and believed in the "Uses of Magic" as a means of enlisting the spiritual aid of certain supernatural forces or beings that were "the Mediators between God and man."[19] Ahab's control over his crew in "The Quarter-Deck" (chapter 36) is little less than magical. They are "magnetically" attracted to their strange captain, and "the three mates quailed before his strong, sustained, and mystic aspect" (p. 146). Ahab arranges the crew in a kind of magical circle and performs a ritualistic ceremony replete with overtones of magic. Later in the novel, he declares himself "lord over the level loadstone" and repairs the compass needle. The crew members stare in "servile wonder," and "with fascinated eyes they awaited whatever magic might follow" (p. 425).

Ahab's belief in and practice of magic, however, is merely a single aspect, and not a major one at that, of his Gnostic tendencies as Melville understood Gnosticism from his reading in such volumes as Chambers and Bayle. Of more significance is Ahab's "Knowledge"—in the Gnostic sense—of the Creator. In the chapter entitled "The Candles," Ahab observes Fedallah, a Zoroastrian,[20] kneeling before the phenomenon of Saint Elmo's fire, and he indicates that he, too, once worshipped as does this "Persian" the Creator who manifests Himself through nature. " 'Oh! thou clear spirit of clear fire, whom on these seas I as Persian once did worship, till in the sacramental act so burned by thee, that to this hour I bear the scar; I now know thee, thou clear spirit, and I now know that thy right worship is defiance" (p. 416). Ahab is not saying that he is a converted Zoroastrian[21] but that the Creator he once worshipped—or tried to worship—was, like the one Fedallah is worshipping, a personal God that responds directly to mankind, one whose presence is manifested in nature and in the activities of the world. He no longer kneels before that God, however, because the Creator is responsible for the evils that have been visited upon him.[22] He has learned the nature of this personal, intervening God who takes part in the affairs of humankind, and he knows that in order to be true to a higher power, the "right" thing to do is defy the Creator. His blasphemy against the Creator is worship of the God—the real and true God—that is above the Creator.

It is clear from what he says, then, that Ahab has accepted fully the Gnostic belief that there is a Supreme God separate and apart from the inferior Jehovah of the Biblical Old Testament who created the world and all in it except for the royal, divine spark that exists in some people, those favored true princes of the empire. That core of spirituality is a part of the highest God, not the Creator. In his entry on the Gnostic Cainites, Pierre Bayle describes this view of the Creator: "A Sect of Heretics which appeared in the second Century, and had this name by reason of their great respect for Cain." Cain, too, believed that the proper way of responding to the Creator was through defiance. Bayle continues: "These people had drawn their abominable dogms out of the sinks of the Gnostics, and were the spawn of Valentinus, of Nicolaus, and of Carpocrates. . . . They carried their boldness so far as to condemn the Law of Moses, and to regard the God of the Old Testament as a Being who had sown tares in the world, and subjected our nature to a thousand disasters; so that, to revenge themselves, they did the direct contrary of what he had prescribed."[23] Bayle is careful to point out, however, that the Gnostics did not believe that the Creator was purely evil but that He was merely a subordinate God and a somewhat careless and unperceptive one who was unaware that a Higher Power existed. They believed "in particular that the Jewish nation had been directed by a mischievous Being"[24] who was responsible for the evil in the world as practiced by still another subordinate supernatural being, Satan. The Supreme Power had no part in the creation of the world or man, but saw to it that part of Himself emanated into the fallen world, entered the Elect, and would be someday gathered and taken from the control of the Creator back to the true and highest God.[25] This is what the Gnostics "knew," and this is what Ahab knows when he states to the Creator: "Thou knowest not how came ye, hence callest thyself unbegotten; certainly knowest not thy beginning, hence callest thyself unbegun. I know that of me, which thou knowest not of thyself, oh, though omnipotent. There is some unsuffusing thing beyond thee, though clear spirit, to whom all thy eternity is but time, all thy creativeness mechanical" (p. 417).[26]

One of the books of the Bible that Melville marked up most extensively in his copy was Isaiah,[27] which happened also to be the book of the Old Testament that the Gnostics used most often to show the limitations, the blindness, and the unjustified arrogance of Jehovah, the Creator, as opposed to the true Supreme Being. And it is to Jehovah's words as expressed in Isaiah that Ahab is directly responding in the above passage. Through Isaiah, Jehovah declares: "I am the Lord, and there is none else, there is no God beside me: I girded thee, though thou hast not known me. That they may know from the rising of the sun, and from the west, that *there is* none beside me. I *am* the Lord, and *there is* none else. I form the light, and create darkness: I make peace, and create evil: I the Lord do all these *things*" (45:5–7). The Gnostics found here an inferior God, one who is unaware that there was a higher God and one who admits openly to the responsibility for evil in the world, for He says: "I make peace, and create evil." A true God, the highest God, could have no part in the creation of evil, they argued. Gnostic Ahab mocks the Jehovah of Isaiah, accuses Him of claiming that He is unique and unbegotten merely because He is blind that there is a power beyond Him "to whom all thy eternity is but time, all thy creativeness mechanical." The extent to which Ahab is defying the Creator in this passage is suggested by two other verses in the same chapter of Isaiah: "Woe unto him that striveth with his Maker! Let the potsherd *strive* with the potsherds of the earth. Shall the clay say to him that fashioned it, What makes thou? or thy work, He hath no hands? Woe to him that saith unto *his* father, What begettest thou or to the woman, what has though brought forth?" (45:9–10). Consciously ignoring this warning, Ahab *is* striving with his maker, and he *is* asking him, "What makest thou?"—the forbidden question.[28] Moments like this in *Moby-Dick* have led many readers to assume that Ahab has taken up arms against God. It is again necessary to realize that in Ahab's view there is God and there are gods. The Creator, to whom he speaks defiance in "The Candles," is merely one of the gods, though He did make man and the earth. He is not truly lord over them, however, though He thinks He is. "There is one God" that is truly Lord, Ahab, says of the Supreme Being (p. 394).

Ahab's view of the highest God reflects the Gnostic belief that He is not a personal god as is the Creator, for His only connection with the world is through that piece of Himself that exists in some human beings, the pneumatics. These chosen few do not communicate directly with the Supreme Being, for He, unlike Jehovah, is unnamed, unknowable, unapproachable. The Elect sense his glory, power, and goodness only by sensing these qualities *in themselves*. In describing one of the chief Gnostics of the second century, Carpocrates, Chambers writes that "he own'd with them [the Gnostics], one sole Principle and Father of all Things, whose Name, as well as Nature, was unknown."[29] This unknown First Principle did not create the world, which is thoroughly corrupt. Matter, including man, was made by the Creator and his helper gods or angels, who are "vastly inferior to the first Principle."[30] Of this real and truly mysterious God, then, Ahab knows nothing except that it is "some unsuffusing thing beyond" the God of the Old Testament, the Jehovah that Jews and Christians worship, to whom all the Creator's "eternity is but time," all the Creator's "creativeness mechanical." This is the Most High God, given by the Gnostics several names to set Him apart from the God of Genesis: the

Abyss, the uncreated, or "the Silence invisible and incomprehensible."[31] It is the unknown God that Melville spoke of in *Pierre* where he describes the attempt to find the true God through reason and philosophical inquiry: "That profound Silence, that only Voice of our God, where I before spoke of; from that divine thing without a name, those impostor philosophers pretend somehow to have got an answer; which is as absurd, as though they should say they had got water out of stone; for how can a man get a Voice out of Silence?"[32]

Once recognizing that this true God was not responsible for evil, which lies at the door of the Creator, Ahab could rebel against Jehovah as the father of all unfairness and as the somewhat blind author of corruption without violating his fundamentally religious nature. Gnosticism was the only way for him to go. Now he could glory in his self-sufficiency and power without being irreverent, for the Gnostics believed that those qualities of the inner man derived from a spark of the Unknown God present in the Elect. *Gnosis* or Knowledge—of the nature of Isaiah's God, of his own nature as pneumatic, of the world as inferior and evil—freed him from the usual restrictions and laws imposed upon mankind by Jehovah and his host of subordinate gods to keep the human race subservient and ignorant of the truth.

These laws and restrictions are not merely those of Moses and the Old Testament but the seemingly unalterable system of nature itself, the planetary movements, the laws of reproduction, and all the rest.[33] Ahab—and the Gnostics—believed that man is caught in this vast machine. Jehovah, or Ialdaboath as He was sometimes called, "had forcibly taken possession of the seventh Heaven," as Chambers explained in the entry on the Nicholaitians. While orthodox Christians looked upon nature with wonder and awe as a mirror of God's harmony, the Gnostics saw it as a pernicous and degrading machine controlling and enslaving mankind. Beyond the seventh Heaven, the planetary system of which the earth is a part, is a higher Heaven, the Gnostics believed, what Chambers calls in the entry on Eon as the "Pleroma," and this is the true spiritual home of the pneumatics.[34] They must break through the Zodiac and go beyond. It is in this context of Gnostic freedom and destiny that Ahab breaks his quadrant, declares himself master of the loadstone, and speaks of striking the sun. And it is in this context that the "cabalistics" on the doubloon take an added significance. Though Melville was describing literally an actual coin of Ecuador, he chose one that also symbolizes generally the Gnostic view of man's entrapment in nature and the proper reaction to this situation. "Arching over all" on the doubloon "was a segment of the partitioned zodiac . . . and the keystone sun entering the equinoctial point at Libra" (p. 359). This overarching span of the Zodiac seems to bear down upon the scene below it, to shut it in, dominate, and control it.[35] However, a volcano seems to be erupting below and on two other mountain peaks is a proud tower and "a crowing cock" (p. 359). These signs of defiance represent the Gnostic spirit of rebellion, and in them Ahab sees his deepest self.

But Ahab is not victorious; he is destroyed by divided and warring selves. The reasons for his defeat are precisely those that account for the demise of Gnosticism as a historical movement. The most basic of the reasons that Ahab in particular and the Gnostics in general could not survive is that Gnosticism does not satisfy the most fundamental needs of humankind. Through the centuries, orthodox Christianity proved more durable than Gnosticism and finally conquered. Gnosticism gave the elitist a few answers to troubling questions about evil and the nature of the true God, but it created psychological chaos—as it does in Ahab—simply because it was incompatible with basic human nature. Arthur Darby Nock has observed that Christianity was successful in its struggle with Gnosticism because of its "perfect because unconscious correspondence to the needs and aspirations of ordinary humanity."[36]

Ahab is a heretic in the true sense of the word. Chambers's *Cyclopaedia* defines a "real Heretic" as "properly he who maintains a false Opinion out of a Spirit of Obstinacy." Yet he is not an infidel but one who professes to believe in God. What makes such a person a heretic is not what he does but what he believes that deviates from orthodoxy. "A man does not become a Heretic by doing a Thing condemned, or forbidden by the Gospel, and, of Consequence, repugnant to the Christian Faith; but by a stiff adherence to an Opinion opposite to some Article of the Christian Faith, whether it regard Speculation or Practice."[37] Ahab's probing, sensitive nature leads him to the troubling questions about evil and God; his personal misfortunes make him deeply resentful and rebellious; he becomes a heretic—he adopts with tenacity the beliefs of Gnosticism; these heretical notions play havoc with him psychologically; then all of this is manifested in his actions.

Melville's portrayal of Ahab reveals that he clearly recognized the Gnostic dilemma. Gnostic answers satisfy the intellectual hunger of those who cannot accept the seemingly illogical positions of Christianity. But orthodox Christianity is far more in tune with emotional and spiritual cravings.[38] Gnosticism may make more sense, but Christianity is better for the whole man. Gnosticism was created by the head; Christianity was created by the heart.

Father Mapple's sermon projects the reasons why he survives as a whole person and Ahab does not, why orthodox Christianity survived and Gnosticism did not. The God of Father Mapple is a father figure who personally takes a hand in the activities of His children and threatens to punish them when they disobey Him. He is not some unknown and unknowable force. He uses nature as an instrument to teach and chastise His children. He created nature (as well as man); therefore it is not an alien and repugnant realm to Him. The God that most closely corresponds with man's deepest spiritual needs is one that he can talk with, a personal God, the God of Father Mapple. We may not always understand Him—why he allows evil in the world, why he created imperfection—but children cannot always understand their earthly fathers either. Father Mapple says, and Christianity says, that we must simply love, accept, obey—not understand. These are the uncomplicated answers that have endured because they are among other things tailored to human nature. And herein abides one of the great ironies of Christian belief. Father Mapple teaches: "If we obey God, we must disobey ourselves; and it is in this disobeying ourselves, wherein the hardness of obeying God consists" (p.45). In a superficial sense this is true. We must overcome temptations of the flesh in order to live a Christian life. But in a far more significant sense, Father Mapple is wrong, for Christianity is a system devised for obeying ourselves, our true, most fundamental selves that bring peace and health when not violated. Ahab the heretic violates his own nature by adopting Gnostic beliefs, and by disobeying himself he becomes divided, tormented, blinded.

What saved Melville himself from the same fate was his ability always to return to and act on this fundamental truth that any attitudes that violate the deepest aspects of human nature are psychologically destructive. I say "return to" this truth because he often strayed from it and, like Ahab, was tempted by many of the beliefs of Gnosticism. Indeed, his life was marked by a vacillation between the Gnostic ideas he shows Ahab succumbing to and others that are more in keeping with a healthy inner life. Two illustrations will reveal something of his personal affinities for Gnostic beliefs. He wrote to Hawthorne in November of 1851: "I feel that the Godhead is broken up like the bread at the Supper, and that we are the pieces."[39] This statement reflects one of the principal tenets of Gnosticism, that in the pneumatics of the world a segment of the true God exists which sets them apart from the masses as a chosen group. Melville seems to embrace the same position in his review of Hawthorne's *Mosses from an Old Manse.* Throughout, he sets up a distinction among men, especially writers. Hawthorne, he says over and over, is special and not to be understood by "the world" but only by those like himself who have the intuitive ability to recognize what lies under the surface: "You cannot come to know greatness by inspecting it; there is no glimpse to be caught of it, except by intuition; you need not ring it, you but touch it, and you find it is gold."[40] The Gnostics liked to refer to this specialness as the "gold in the mud." The gold that Melville was finding in Hawthorne—to be equated with the pieces of the Godhead he referred to in his letter—he was also finding in himself: "I cannot but be charmed by the coincidence; especially, when it shows such a parity of ideas . . . between a man like Hawthorne and a man like me."[41] Again he returns to the conviction that there exists an elect of writers; he calls them "men of genius" who together make up the "commanding mind."

These statements about his and Hawthorne's specialness do not in themselves prove that Melville was attracted specifically to Gnostic doctrines, but they do reveal the kind of mind that would be highly susceptible to such a set of beliefs. That Melville was, indeed, susceptible and that he fully realized the destructive powers of Gnosticism on the mind are evident in a number of his short stories. Several deal with narrators who are exposed to Gnostic insights and are driven to the brink of madness. The Gnostic view of God's chosen creatures existing in an evil and alien world is particularly evident in "Cock-A-Doodle-Doo!" Melville never created a more poignant statement of this theme. Nature is described in the story as a force foreign and abhorrent to the narrator: "It was a cool and misty, damp, disagreeable air. The country looked underdone, its raw juices squirting out all round."[42] He thrusts a stick in the "oozy sod" and notes that the "humped hills" resemble "brindle kine in the shivers." All in all, the imagery is calculated to arouse emotions of disgust with the natural world: "The woods were strewn with dry dead boughs, snapped off by the riotous winds of March. . . . Along the base of one long range of heights ran a lagging, fever-and-anguish river, over which was a duplicate stream of dripping mist, exactly corresponding in every member. . . ." It is a disagreeable and depressing world, but the world of mankind is no better. The narrator dwells on the chaos that characterizes man's activities, the ugliness of society matching that of nature. Revolts have been taking place, trains have been wrecked, steamers have blown up: "A miserable world! Who would take the trouble to make a fortune in it, when he knows not how long he can keep it, for the thousand villains and asses. . . ."[43] He sneers at "Great improvements of the age" and summarizes his overall attitude both toward the world of man and the realm of nature when he describes himself as in the act of climbing a hill in a bent and toiling posture, "as if I were in the act of butting . . . against the world."[44]

The narrator is a perfect candidate for a Gnostic call, and it comes in the form of a crowing cock, who brings him the message of his own specialness and his ultimate salvation; of the true God, who is not responsible for the pitiful state of society and the external world; and of the proper way for him to respond to his alien surroundings.[45] It is a message, delivered in a flashing instant, of profound inspiration and hope. The problem is that it leads to such arch-arrogance that he is himself crowing like a cock.[46] By the end of the story he has lost his compassion for others and feels such contempt for everything in the world that he is totally unable to function in it. As is frequently the situation, Melville obviously admires the man's heroic revolt but recognizes what great price it costs. So frequently does Melville indulge in this kind of characterization that one is led to believe that whenever he was greatly tempted to embrace the Gnostic vision, he developed a hero who was destroyed by it. He often needed to remind himself that it was better to live among fools—without becoming one of them—than to alienate himself from them for a realm of what may be the truth but a truth that leads to psychological hell. He revealed this conviction in the brief poem "A Spirit Appeared to Me":

> A Spirit appeared to me, and said
> "Where now would you choose to dwell?
> In the Paradise of the Fool,
> Or in wise Solomon's hell?"
>
> Never he asked me twice:
> "Give me the fool's Paradise."[47]

The Gnostic God, the unknown and unknowable, is so far removed from ordinary human emotions and activities that allegiance to Him—as opposed to Jehovah (or the Demiurge)—leads ultimately to severe self-ostracism, as the narrator of "The Lightning-Rod Man" illustrates. The God he worships has nothing to do with the war that is going on against mankind, which is suggested in the story by the battle imagery to describe rain, thunder, and lightning. This is a war without purpose waged by an inferior deity in which a "servant girl [is] struck at her bed-side with a rosary in her hand," struck by lightning sent by the very Demiurge she is worshipping.[48] The lightning-rod salesman is a priest of this inferior deity—the Jehovah of the Old Testament—who preaches fear and the strict obedience to a set of strict rules. Those likely to be struck down, the salesman explains, are "tall men," which means the extraordinary few who rebel against this capricious and blindly arrogant maker and ruler of earth ("*Mine* is the only true rod"). In the fashion of Ahab, the narrator of the story will not worship or tremble in fear of this god of other men. He believes in the "returning-stroke," sending back lightning to the Demiurge. He throws himself "into the erectest, proudest, posture" he can command while the preacher of fear and obedience to the author of lightning attempts to proselyte him. When in great anger and rebellion the narrator explains that he worships the only true God who has no part in the evil of the world and then bodily throws out his adversary, the salesman does not accuse him of being a religious fanatic but, in effect, a heretic with wrong notions about God.

It is not really the views of Gnosticism that Melville wants to espouse, however, in "The Lightning-Rod Man"; nor does he wish to emphasize the motivations, especially fear, that move ordinary men to worship Jehovah, though there may be great truth and nobility in the one and great shallowness and cowardice in the other. What he seems most to be interested in is the mind of the narrator, the course it has taken as a *result* of his Gnostic proclivities. As is true with the narrator of "Cock-A-Doodle-Doo!" rebellion has become a way of life with him. His ostensible enjoyment of the lightning is actually a manifestation of his fearless scorn of it and what it can do. In fact, his most obvious and most frequently displayed emotion is that which inevitably results from a Gnostic orientation—contempt. He is contemptuous of the storm and the force that produces it, of the salesman who tells him that he can be reduced to offal unless he bow down in trembling and obedience to the laws of this force, and of ordinary men, who do so. The story is a brief but poignant depiction of how the Gnostic differs from orthodox positions and how he becomes so proud and fearless in his contempt of all the world and the world's God (the Demiurge) that he ends up alienated and mentally twisted. Though the narrator seems amused at his visitor and plays a cat-and-mouse game with him, and though the story has itself been singled out for its humor, one cannot ignore the fact that there is something strikingly unusual about this narrator, something strange and disturbing in his baiting of the salesman, a quality of unhealthy glee that resembles Montresor's tone in Poe's "The Cask of Amontillado." In the end he says that he tried to warn others that the salesman was a false prophet, but they would not listen. It is he who remains the alienated heretic drowning is his flood of contempt. It is not that the salesman is right and he is wrong—he is presented as a more heroic and noble figure than the lightning-rod man—but that his truth leads to madness whereas the salesman's does not.

The same dilemma is the substance of several other stories: in them, a character cannot accept on the one hand the orthodox religious views of God, nature, and mankind because they violate his deepest sense of justice and contradict his own collective experience; but if he embraces a set of beliefs, heretical in nature, that gives him better answers to his questions, he faces destruction. The answers the world gives are wrong, but many of these characters cannot survive the alternative. Bartleby is a prime example of one caught in this dilemma. His self-imposed separation from ordinary human activities, his refusal to take heed of the needs of his body, and his determination to break off communication with the world all are characteristic of one large segment of the ancient Gnostics, those who practiced extreme asceticism.[49] The motive behind their behavior was fundamentally the same as Bartleby's—a desire for independence from the corruption that surrounded them. Enveloped in matter, which is evil, the ascetic Gnostics believed, as does Bartleby, that the most appropriate form of rebellion, the most effective way of insuring independence and purity, was to prefer not to; for earthly activity only leads away from the true heaven.[50] Though I believe it has not been pointed out before, a poem Melville wrote probably long after "Bartleby" is closely related to it and suggests the scrivener's motivation for withdrawal and starvation. "Fragments of a Lost Gnostic Poem of the Twelfth Century"[51] reveals Melville's perceptive awareness of the Gnostic mind:

> Found a family, build a state,
> The pledged event is still the same:
> Matter in end·will never abate
> His ancient brutal claim
>
> . . .
>
> Indolence is heaven's ally here,
> And energy the child of hell:
> The Good Man pouring from his pitcher clear,
> But brims the poisoned well.[52]

Though the poem may seem to reflect a futile or nihilistic view, it is rather a statement of the Gnostic's belief in the evil of all matter, in the unimportance of worldly activities, and in a willful withdrawal as the best way to cope with the enslaving laws of nature and to remain in tune with the real God and higher heaven. "Bartleby" is the story of a man who believes this and acts upon it. The spectacle of his doing so is not that of a heroic victory—though there is this element present as in Ahab's destruction—but that of fearsome tragedy. Without being, by any means, didactic, "Bartleby" is another elaborate reminder by Melville to himself of where the seductive Gnostic vision, to which he was by temperament strongly drawn, could lead.

To dwell on the psychological ravages of the Gnostic vision is one way to avoid being seduced by it. Another way is quickly to close one's eyes and mind to it when it presents itself. Melville's narrator in the second part of his bipartite story "The

Paradise of Bachelors and the Tartarus of Maids" does just that. What this man sees when he goes deep into the bowels of the earth is the Gnostic view of nature and mankind's horrible enslavement to the physical laws of the universe.[53] The paper machine that so shocks him that he almost faints is a symbol of universal nature. It is, to be sure, suggestive of the womb, as many readers have noticed, but the womb and the process of reproduction in general represent in turn all of the physical laws by which pitiful mankind is ruled.[54] No tenet of Gnosticism is more different from orthodox Christian belief than this position on nature and natural laws. To the Gnostic, the world was an alien place, but the Christian goes to the "garden," as a popular hymn reads, and hears the "voice" therein of the true God.[55] This attitude toward nature is nowhere more clearly presented than in another Christian hymn, "This Is My Father's World" (1901):

> This is my Father's world,
> And to my listening ears
> All nature sings, and round me rings
> The music of the spheres.
>
> This is my Father's world:
> I rest me in the thought
> Of rocks and trees, of skies and seas;
> His hand the wonders wrought.
>
> This is my Father's world:
> The birds their carols raise,
> The morning light, the lily white,
> Declare their Maker's praise.
>
> This is my Father's world:
> He shines in all that's fair;
> In the rustling grass I hear Him pass,
> He speaks to me everywhere.[56]

The narrator of "The Tartarus of Maids" encounters a different nature from this one—a cold and merciless world of horrible regularity in which emasculated mankind acts as handmaiden. Whether this Gnostic view of nature is the true one is a subordinate issue in the story. More significant is the fact that the narrator (called a "seedsman") is prone to see the external world in this way, to associate an actual place and a real paper factory with the overall realm of nature and its physical laws, and to be psychologically and physically imperiled *because* of the vision. His quick retreat back into the other nature, that of "This Is My Father's World" (the paradise of the fool, though it may be), is all that saves him. He is fortunate, for many of those characters in Melville's fiction who are tempted by the Gnostic heresy succumb to its substantial magnetism and are destroyed. The dilemma rests in the question, "How can the truth lead to hell?" Ahab is Melville's carefully delineated answer. Noble though he is, Ahab exists in a living hell brought about through his envelopment in a set of convictions that pit one part of himself against the other without his even realizing it.

What I have attempted to show in this chapter is that Ahab's division of self ⟨...⟩ is largely the result of his Gnostic orientation. Melville saw clearly that Gnosticism produces three devastating effects. First, and most important, it leads to the formation of two distinct and rivaling selves in a single personality—that which seeks to find and merge with God and that which arrogantly loves itself and leaves no room for God.[57] Second, it fails to satisfy in a God-seeker the deep hunger for a personal God whom one can go to directly for guidance, comfort, and rewards for faith. The Unknown Father that Ahab speaks of is a cold divine stranger, ill-suited to satisfy the cravings of the human heart.[58] Consequently, the Gnostic is cut off, psychologically speaking, from one of the healthiest aspects of Christianity and experiences a sense of isolation. Third, this separation from a caring and controlling Creator is painful enough, but the Gnostic must face as well alienation from the realm of nature, for the world must be rejected as totally corrupt. No beauty is to be seen in nature, no higher harmony in its laws. With a sneer, the Gnostic must reject the appeals of rivers, trees, and flowers; the suggestion of order and rightness in the changes of the seasons; and all the natural affinity a human being feels for the lush supportive world around him because all of matter comes from the inferior Demiurge.

In a characteristically brilliant insight, Melville indicated in *Clarel* that modern Christianity has managed to get around the problem of evil, not by confronting the issue directly and accusing Jehovah, as did the Gnostics, but by gradually and subtly replacing Him with Jesus Christ as the Supreme Being. In that way the personal Savior is combined with the perfect God—innocent of all evil—and the best of two visions is fused without the ill effects that come from Gnosticism or the emptiness of unanswered questions that sometimes results from straight Christian doctrine. The strange usurpation, Melville says, has taken place without Christians even admitting it:

> 'Twas averred
> That, in old Gnostic pages blurred,
> Jehovah was construed to be
> Author of evil, yea, its god;
> And Christ divine His contrary:
> A god was held against a god,
> But Christ revered alone. Herefrom,
> Less frank: none say Jehovah's evil,
> None gainsay that He bears the rod;
> Scarce that; but there's dismission civil,
> And Jesus is the indulgent God.   (III.v.39–45, 56–59)

Such is the quiet and unadmitted way in which Christians have absorbed a part of Gnosticism without suffering its consequences. The true Gnostic, however, must ultimately end up an alien to himself, to God, to the external world, and to his fellow man. This Melville clearly knew, as reflected in his portrayals of Ahab and other characters, and though he was mightily drawn to these bold, rebellious, free-thinking, arrogant ancients, he knew they beckoned him to self-destruction; so he made a conscious choice not to leave the "Paradise of the Fool" for "wise Solomon's hell." Hell is hell, no matter with whom you share it.

NOTES

[1] *Moby-Dick*, ed. Harrison Hayford and Hershel Parker (New York: Norton, 1967). All references to *Moby-Dick* are to this edition.

[2] It is difficult not to assume, however, that he would have seen various other materials on the Gnostics, for the nineteenth century saw a great surge of interest in them. In tracing the rise and fall of Gnosticism, Hans Jonas writes: "The last of the major heresiologists to deal extensively with the Gnostic sects, Epiphanius of Salamis, wrote in the fourth century A.D. From then on, with the danger past and the polemical interest no longer alive, oblivion settled down on the whole subject, until the historical interest of the nineteenth century returned to it in the spirit of dispassionate inquiry." *The Gnostic Religion: The Message of the Alien God and the Beginnings of Christianity* (Boston: Beacon, 1958), pp. xiv–xv. The new interest that Jonas speaks of is evident in the periodicals of the time. The religiously oriented *Ladies' Repository* warned its readers against the seduction of the Gnostic vision in an article by George Waterman, Jr. ("Gnosticism," 3 [October 1843]: 292–93). Waterman charges the Gnostics with holding "the God of the Jews in supreme contempt—esteeming him as a malicious being, whom Jesus came to destroy. They supposed all sin to consist in matter" (p. 293). Even earlier in the century, a writer for the *Edinburgh Review* severely criticized George Waddington's *History of the Church from the Earliest Ages to the Reformation* (London, 1835) for its neglect of the Gnostics. In doing so, the reviewer gives a clear impression of the current fascination with Gnosticism: "At a period when some of the most gifted individuals on the Continent of Europe are turning their attention to the subject of the Gnostics, as one of the most interesting and important that can attract the notice of the historian, the philosopher, or the divine, and when philosophical societies are holding out prizes which bring forth such works as that by Professor Matter of Strasburg, such is the very different conclusion to which Mr. Waddington, in the simplicity of his heart, arrives. We are far indeed from undervaluing the advantages to be derived from an acquaintance with the Gnostics." Gnosticism, he continues, "presents to us the human mind in some of its most interesting attitudes,—mourning over the introduction of moral evil into the universe,—wasting itself in unavailing efforts to scale the inaccessible heights that carry up from the finite to the infinite—prying into the mysterious links that connect the will of the Omnipotent with the existence of the visible Universe,—and when the voice of the Eternal 'calls for "things that are not," ' vainly endeavoring to discover *how or whence* 'they come.' Even in their wildest excesses they exhibit the imperishable longings of the soul of man after the vast, the unknown, the infinite; they show us the extent—if they instructively teach us the limits also of the human faculties;—and in illustrating the vanity of the desire after perfect *gnosis*, they may convince us of the wisdom of resting in simple *faith* in the fundamental principles of natural and revealed religion." *Edinburgh Review* 62 (October 1835): 152–53.

[3] Millicent Bell, "Pierre Bayle and *Moby-Dick*," PMLA 66 (1951): 627.

[4] Ibid., p. 629.

[5] See, for example, Bayle's entry on the Paulicians. He argues that the Paulician explanation for evil "would probably have made a greater progress still, had it been explained in a less gross manner," and he proceeds to debate at length the question of evil.

[6] William Braswell, *Melville's Religious Thought: An Essay in Interpretation* (Durham: Duke University Press, 1943), pp. 52, 62–63.

[7] Thomas Vargish, "Gnostic *Mythos* in *Moby-Dick*," PMLA 81 (1966): 272–77.

[8] In so establishing his argument, Vargish writes: "In *Moby-Dick* itself, Melville's single direct reference is to a Gnostic sect called the 'Ophites.' In Chapter xli, he pictures them worshipping their 'Statue-Devil' and *compares* [italics mine] them with Ahab who had personified all the 'subtle demonisms of life and thought' in the white whale. From Norton's *Evidences* we learn that . . . the Ophites took the part of the serpent and represented him as having given good counsel to Adam and Eve" (p. 273). Consequently, the Ophites were not truly worshipping evil, for they saw the serpent as a symbol of goodness, of,

indeed, the Divine. If Melville had read Norton he would have known this, but he apparently did not. He does not "compare" Ahab with the Ophites, as Vargish indicated, but *contrasts* him with them. Ishmael says that Ahab saw in the white whale "that intangible malignity which has been from the beginning; to whose dominion even the modern Christians ascribe one-half of the world; which the ancient Ophites of the east reverenced in their statue devil" (p. 160). Melville has the Ophites worshipping evil when they actually worshipped goodness, as Norton carefully explains. Ishmael continues, "Ahab did not fall down and worship it [evil] like them; but deliriously transferring its idea to the abhorred white whale, he pitted himself, all mutilated, against it." Melville had to be unaware of the true beliefs of the serpent-worshipping Ophites to have written this passage, and had he read Norton, as Vargish argues he had, he would never have made the contrast between Ahab and the Ophites. It is likely that he merely picked up somewhere in his reading the misleading information that the Ophites had worshipped serpents, did not realize that the Ophites were actually an unusual brand of Gnostics, and erroneously concluded that they were devil-worshippers.

[9] William H. Shurr deals with the subject briefly but knowledgeably in *The Mystery of Iniquity: Melville as Poet, 1857–1891* (Lexington: University Press of Kentucky, 1972), pp. 164–66, 255.

[10] Ephraim Chambers, *Cyclopaedia; or, An Universal Dictionary of Arts and Sciences* (London: Knapton, 1728), I:165.

[11] In the Gnostic Acts of Thomas, the chosen are admonished to "Get up and sober up out of your sleep. . . . Remember that you are a king's son. You have come under a servile yoke. Think of your suit shot with gold." Werner Foerster, *Gnosis: A Selection of Gnostic Texts,* ed. R. McL. Wilson (Oxford: Clarendon, 1972), I:357.

[12] In his description of Gnostic beliefs, the second-century church father Irenaeus writes: "For even as gold, when submersed in filth, loses not on that account its beauty, but retains its own native qualities, the filth having no power to injure the gold, so they affirm that they cannot in any measure suffer hurt, or lose their spiritual substance, whatever the material actions in which they may be involved." *The Writings of Irenaeus,* trans. Alexander Roberts and W. H. Rambant (Edinburgh: Clark, 1868), I:26. This is volume 5 in the *Ante-Nicene Christian Library: Translations of the Writings of the Fathers Down to A.D. 325,* ed. Alexander Roberts and James Donaldson, 24 vols. (Edinburgh: Clark, 1867–72). Werner Foerster comments that "the totality of Gnosis can be comprehended in a single image. This is the image of 'gold in the mud.'" Introduction to *Gnosis,* I;2.

[13] Elijah raises the significant question to Ishmael and Queequeg as to whether their souls will be in danger if they ship with Captain Ahab. He then conjectures that they may not even have souls to lose (p. 86).

[14] Chambers, I:165.

[15] Evelyn Underhill comments on the Gnostics' "attempted fusion of the ideals of mysticism and magic." *Mysticism: A Study in the Nature and Development of Man's Spiritual Consciousness* (London: Metheun, 1911), p. 149. J. P. Arendzen states that "it is markedly peculiar to Gnosticism that it places the salvation of the soul merely in the possession of a quasi-intuitive knowledge of the mysteries of the universe and of magic formulae indicative of that knowledge." "Gnosticism," in *The Catholic Encyclopedia,* 1909.

[16] Campbell Bonner points out that magical amulets were "intended to bring death or serious harm to an enemy." "Magical Amulets," *Harvard Theological Review* 39 (1946): 52. Herbert Loewe states that "amulets were regarded as potent charms to . . . assist the wearer to obtain his desire. The charms were usually written on parchment or *engraved on a precious metal"* (italics mine). *Encyclopaedia of Religion and Ethics,* ed. James Hastings (New York: Scribner's, 1915), 7:626. For other discussions of the nature and uses of amulets and talismans see the following: Bonner, *Studies in Magical Amulets* (Ann Arbor: University of Michigan Press, 1950); C. W. King, *The Gnostics: Their Remains, Ancient and Mediaeval* (London: Nutt, 1887); and George Frederich Kunz, *The Magic of Jewels and Charms* (Philadelphia: Lippincott, 1915).

[17] Chambers, I:89.

[18] Charles Olson discusses the distinction Melville makes between "goetic" and "theurgic" magic and refers to Ahab as "Conjur Man." *Call Me Ishmael* (San Francisco: City Lights Books, 1947), pp. 53, 55–56. The distinction Olson alludes to occurs in a note Melville wrote in his copy of Shakespeare's plays: "—not the (black art) Goetic but Theurgic magic—seeks converse with the Intelligence, Power, the Angel." Douglas Robillard suggests that Edward Bulwer-Lytton's *The Last Days of Pompeii* (1834) may have furnished Melville with the terms *Goetic* and *Theurgic.* "A Possible Source for Melville's Goetic and Theurgic Magic," *Melville Society Extracts,* no. 49 (1982): 5–6. Richard Cavendish explains the nature of the higher magic—that practiced by Gnostics: "There is a useful rough distinction between high magic

and low magic. High magic is an attempt to gain so consummate an understanding and mastery of oneself and the environment as to transcend all human limitations and become superhuman or divine." *A History of Magic* (New York: Taplinger, 1977), p. 12. According to A. E. Waite, "the central doctrine of the high theurgic faith . . . was that by means of certain invocations, performed solemnly by . . . mentally illuminated men, it was possible to come into direct communication with those invisible powers which fill the measureless distance between man and God." *The Magical Writings of Thomas Vaughan* (London: Redway, 1888), p. xxi. In a sense, Ahab appears to be practicing a form of theurgy in his very pursuit of the white whale. In his revealing to Starbuck a "little lower layer," he speaks of the importance of "the living act, the undoubted deed" as a way of "thrusting through the wall" to some great and eternal truth (p. 144). E. R. Dodds comments on this form of theurgic practice and quotes Iamblichus: "Theurgic union is attained only by the efficacy of the unspeakable *acts* performed in the appropriate manner, acts which are beyond all comprehension, and by the potency of the unutterable symbols which are comprehended only by the gods. . . . Without intellectual effort on our part the tokens by their own virtue accomplish their proper work." *The Greeks and the Irrational* (Berkeley and Los Angeles: University of California Press, 1951), p. 287. Though theurgic magic is supposedly the door to truth, it leads more often to error. What begins as God-hunger can end in personal fragmentation. Joseph Ennemoser recognized this truth: "To this white magic belongs the power of working miracles, of perceiving and using the signatures of natural things, of foretelling the future, and of uniting the spirit fully with God through love, and thereby becoming an immediate partaker in the being and the word of God. . . . It is difficult to arrive, however, at this beautiful idea of magic in the highest degree, since there requires for it a genuine holiness; and where pious minds strive honestly after it, yet they easily stray . . . and thence lose themselves in . . . frantic darkness." *The History of Magic,* trans. William Howitt (London: Bohn, 1854), 2:219–20.

[19] Chambers, I:79.

[20] Fedallah has been frequently depicted by critics as a kind of fanatical religious figure, but it is probable that Melville was interested in him because of his indulgence in magic, prophecy, and superstitions and because of a vicious and treacherous nature thought popularly to be characteristic of the Parsees. To give one example of this widely held view, I quote a review of George Buist's *Annals of India for the Year 1848* (1849): "It is by this look, and by the character of which it is the expression, that the true Parsee shows that he traces back his origin to a northern country. More than a thousand years ago, faithful to a religion which for ages they had respected undisturbed, the Parsees, flying before Moham-medan persecution, left their native Persia, carrying with them their sacred, unextinguished fire. Guided by the bright emblem of their God, they found shelter on the western coast of India. Here they established themselves, and during succeeding centuries, preserving always traces of their ancient customs and faith, keeping as far as possible out of frequent quarrels and wars which have been the curse of the native races of India, taking no historical part in the affairs of the country . . . they have spread and prospered. . . . *The nobler qualities of character, those alone which give a people an honorable place in the history of the world, are almost as rare among them as among other Oriental races. . . . Whatever may have been the character of their religion in ancient times, it is now nothing better than a disjointed superstition . . . and possessing no moral influence over the lives of its professed adherents"* (italics mine). The review charges that Parsees appear mannerly but that this is actually "a suspicious suppleness," which is a "cover of falseness and deceit." It is far more likely that writings like this in current periodicals influenced the characterization of Fedallah than research into the heart of Zoroastrian religion. The review appears in the *North American Review* 73 (1851): 135–52.

[21] Vargish states that "Ahab once worshipped the fire as a Persian" (p. 276). For various other inter-pretations of the "Persian" passage, see Charles Child Walcutt, "The Fire Symbolism in *Moby-Dick,*" *Modern Language Notes* 59 (1944): 304–10; Bell, "Pierre Bayle and *Moby-Dick*"; Dorothee Metlitsky Finkelstein, *Melville's Orienda* (New Haven: Yale University Press, 1961), pp. 236–39; and Mukhtar Ali Isani, "Zoroastrianism and the Fire Symbolism in *Moby-Dick,*" *American Literature* 44 (1972): 385–97.

[22] To Gnostics, the Demiurge was inextricably linked with fire, and fire, in turn, was associated with blindness. Hans Jonas writes: "To ignorance in the mental realm corresponds in the physical realm the fire, which like its archetype is not so much an element among elements, as a force active in all of them. . . . But what to the Stoics is thus the bearer of cosmic Reason, to the Valentinians is with the *same* omnipresence in all creation the embodiment of Ignorance. When Heraclitus speaks of 'the everliving fire,' they speak of fire as 'death and corruption' in all elements. Yet even they would agree that as far as *cosmic* 'life' so-called and *demiurgical* 'reason' so-called are concerned these are properly symbolized in fire, as indeed in many gnostic systems the Demiurge is expressly called the god of fire; but since that

kind of 'life' and of 'reason' are in their true nature death and ignorance, the agreement in effect amounts to a subtle caricature of the Heraclitean-Stoic doctrine" (p. 198).

[23] Pierre Bayle, *A General Dictionary, Historical and Critical* (London: Bettenham, 1736), 4:19, 20.

[24] Ibid., 4:20.

[25] Versions of how man and the universe were created vary a good deal among the many sects of Gnostics. Often, the creation is the result of an unexplained fall or a fall motivated either by erotic feelings or by a spiritual desire to be more like the Supreme Being. The fallen one is generally a female entity, an aspect of the Most High. From this fallen female, Ialdabaoth, or the Creator, is formed, and he in turn makes man. Sometimes the fallen one is called Prunikos (Lust), sometimes Sophia (Wisdom). More often Sophia is the mother of Prunicos or Achamoth (Lover of Wisdom) and, with the consent of the Supreme Being, scatters the divine seed on the newly created earth into selected men—the pneumatics—without the Creator knowing about it.

[26] What Ahab does not know, however, is the source within himself of the feminine principle. He recognizes that he is part of a royal lineage that goes back to the Unknown Father, the true God, that "unsuffusing thing" beyond the Demiurge, the Creator. But he says: "my sweet mother, I know not. Oh, cruel! what has thou done with her? There lies my puzzle" (p. 417). Despite his Gnostic insight into the reality of a true God beyond Jehovah, therefore, Ahab still feels incomplete at this moment, though he goes on to say that the Demiurge's puzzle is greater than his own, for the Creator is *completely* ignorant of His heritage. Vargish feels that in this passage Ahab is invoking Sophia, whom he clearly recognizes as his Divine Mother, the "champion of the spiritual in man against the Creator of material evil." Vargish, p. 275. This seems to me unlikely since Ahab says he is ignorant altogether of the mother or feminine principle and confesses, "There lies my puzzle."

Braswell quotes this passage with the prefacing comment that "Ahab brings what seems to be a definitely Gnostic accusation against God when he [speaks] . . . to the symbolical corposants" (p. 62). Braswell feels, however, that the Gnostic theme in *Moby-Dick* "remains undeveloped" (p. 63).

[27] Nathalia Wright, *Melville's Use of the Bible* (Durham: Duke University Press, 1949), p. 10.

[28] Irenaeus states that Gnostics were instructed to address themselves boldly to the Demiurge in the following manner: "I am a son from the Father—the Father who had a pre-existence, and a son in Him who is pre-existent. . . . I derive being from Him who is pre-existent, and I come again to my own place whence I went forth. . . . I am a vessel more precious than the female [Achamoth] who formed you. If your mother is ignorant of her own descent, I know myself, and am aware whence I am." *Writings*, pp. 83–84. By this bold statement of divine identity and a direct show of power to the Demiurge and His companion gods, the Gnostics believed that they could escape enslavement by the seven heavens and throw the subordinate gods into a state of agitation and confusion.

[29] Chambers, vol. I, entry on "Carpocratians."

[30] Ibid.

[31] Jean Doresse, *The Secret Books of the Egyptian Gnostics* (New York: Viking, 1960), p. 17.

[32] *Pierre; or, The Ambiguities*, ed. Harrison Hayford et al. (Evanston and Chicago: Northwestern University Press and the Newberry Library, 1971), p. 208.

[33] The "mud" of the Gnostic view, in which the gold is caught, is "that of the world: it is first of all the body, which with its sensual desires drags man down and holds the 'I' in thrall. . . . The hostility to the body is only part of a more far-reaching hostility to *the world*. The gnostic has no appreciation for the beauty of this earth, for him 'the whole world lies in wickedness,' and this because it is dominated not only by the power of sense but, beyond and including it, by the power of Fate" (Foerster, pp. 2–3).

[34] Chambers, I:318.

[35] According to Werner Foerster, "Fate presented itself in that period above all in the world of the stars, especially in the seven planets which the ancients counted (Sun, Moon, Mercury, Venus, Mars, Jupiter, Saturn), but also in the twelve signs of the Zodiac; the 'seven' and the 'twelve' are therefore marked in a special way as the power of evil which enslaves mankind" (pp. 3–4). The soul, writes J. P. Arendzen, "had to pass the adverse influence of the god or gods of the Hebdomad before it could ascend to the only good God beyond. This account of the soul through the planetary spheres to the heaven beyond . . . began to be conceived as a struggle with adverse powers, and became the first and predominant idea in Gnosticism" (p. 593). R. M. [Robert] Grant comments that "Gnostics were ultimately devoted not to mythology but to freedom. Speculation and mythology were aspects of this freedom, which involved freedom from astral spirits, from the god of the Old Testament, from the tyranny of the creation, from Old Testament law or any law" (p. 12). *Gnosticism and Early Christianity* (New York: Columbia University Press, 1959).

[36] Quoted in Elaine Pagels, *The Gnostic Gospels* (New York: Random House, 1979), p. 149. Accounting further for the survival of orthodox Christianity over Gnosticism, Pagels comments that "while the gnostic saw himself as 'one out of a thousand, two out of ten thousand,' the orthodox experienced himself as a member of the common human family, and as one member of a universal church" (p. 147).

[37] Chambers, I:241.

[38] One reason for this is that orthodox Christianity sets out clear laws of conduct whereas by its nature Gnosticism seeks freedom from laws and leads to a lawlessness within. As Hans Jonas observes: "For all purposes of man's relation to existing reality, both the hidden God and the hidden pneuma [what Melville calls "the Captive King"] are nihilistic conceptions: no *nomos* emanates from them, that is, no law either for nature or for human conduct as a part of the natural order" (p. 271).

[39] *The Letters of Herman Melville,* ed. Merrell R. Davis and William H. Gilman (New Haven: Yale University Press, 1960), p. 142.

[40] "Hawthorne and His Mosses," in *The Norton Anthology of American Literature,* 2d ed., ed. Nina Baym et al., 2 vols. (New York: Norton, 1985), I:2164.

[41] Ibid., p. 2173.

[42] "Cock-A-Doodle-Doo! or, The Crowing of the Noble Cock Beneventano," in *The Complete Stories of Herman Melville,* ed. Jay Leyda (New York: Random House, 1949), p. 119.

[43] Ibid., p. 121.

[44] Ibid., p. 119.

[45] The Gnostic concept of the call is described succinctly by Werner Foerster: "The central factor in Gnosis, the 'call,' reaches man neither in rational thought nor in an experience which eliminates thought. Man has a special manner of reception in his 'I.' He feels himself 'addressed' and answers the call. He *feels* that he is encountered by something which already lies within him, although admittedly entombed. It is nothing new, but rather the old which only needs to be called to mind. It is like a note sounded at a distance, which strikes an echoing chord in his heart. Here is the reason why the basic acceptance of Gnosis can and should take place in a single act" (p. 2).

The distinguished interpreter of Gnosticism Hans Jonas has observed that "the first effect of the call is always described as 'awakening,' as in the gnostic versions of the story of Adam." The three elements that I have named as the content of the message the narrator of "Cock-A-Doodle-Doo!" receives are precisely those which, according to Jonas, make up the Gnostic call: "the *reminder* of the heavenly origin [of the one called]...; the *promise* of redemption...; and finally the practical *instruction* as to how to live henceforth in the world, in conformity with the newly won 'knowledge' and in preparation for the eventual ascent" (p. 81).

[46] Irenaeus described Gnostics in the following manner: "But if anyone do yield himself up to them like a little sheep, and follows out their practice and their 'redemption,' such an one is puffed up to such an extent, that he thinks he is neither in heaven nor on earth, but that he has passed within the Pleroma; and having already embraced his angel, he walks with a strutting gait and a supercilious countenance, possessing all the pompous air of a cock" (I:322). This is a perfect description of the narrator of "Cock-A-Doodle-Doo!" at the story's end. With his new sense of freedom and severe contempt for the world, he indulges himself fully in sensuous experience (overeating, drinking, and so forth) and thereby becomes a clear illustration of what the church fathers termed "libertine" Gnosticism, one of the two main branches. The other, which is its opposite, is asceticism, *withdrawal* from sensuous experience. Both, however, derive from the same fundamental view, as Hans Jonas points out: "Opposite as the two types of conduct are, they yet were in the gnostic case of the same root, and the same basic argument supports them both. The one repudiates allegiance to nature through excess, the other, through abstention. Both are lives outside the mundane norms. Freedom by abuse and freedom by non-use, equal in their indiscriminateness, are only alternative expressions of the same acosmism" (pp. 274–75). Irenaeus accused the libertine Gnostics of great excesses of all "kinds of forbidden deeds of which the Scriptures assure us that 'they who do such things shall not inherit the kingdom of God' " (I:26).

[47] *Collected Poems of Herman Melville,* ed. Howard P. Vincent (Chicago: Hendricks House, 1947), p. 390. In *Moby-Dick,* Ishmael says that the "world hath not got hold of unchristian Solomon's wisdom yet," establishing the dichotomy that is in the poem between a fool's paradise and the hell Solomon can lead you to. Solomon's Ecclesiastes, says Ishmael, is the "truest of all books," but it is also "the fine hammered steel of woe. 'All is vanity.' All" (p. 355).

[48] "The Lightning-Rod Man," in *Complete Stories,* p. 216.

[49] Bartleby's world view seems parallel to what Hans Jonas calls the Gnostic "acosmic position" that "comes to express itself in a general morality of withdrawal, which develops its own code of negative

'virtues' " (p. 276). The principle involved was "not to complete but to reduce the world of the Creator and to make the least possible use of it" (p. 144). Jonas explains that "turned into a principle of practice, this conception engenders an extreme quietism which strives to reduce activity as such to what is absolutely necessary (p. 232).

Curiously, some understanding of why Bartleby acts as he does results from a study of the syndrome peculiar to (but not restricted to) some teenage girls, anorexia nervosa. Several of the underlying motives of those suffering from this form of starvation are surprisingly close to those of the acosmic Gnostics and, apparently, to those of Bartleby. A seventeenth-century physician, Richard Morton, is credited with first observing the disorder. He reported two cases of young women who developed an abhorrence of food and who withdrew from ordinary activities. In the nineteenth century, W. W. Gull observed the same syndrome, labeled it "anorexia," and attributed it to psychological causes. See Salvador Minuchin et al., *Psychosomatic Families: Anorexia Nervosa in Context* (Cambridge: Harvard University Press, 1978), pp. 11–12. What those suffering from this disorder have in common with Bartleby is evident in a statement Hilde Bruch has made concerning the motivation of anorectics: they are waging "a desperate fight against feeling enslaved and exploited. . . . They would rather starve than continue a life of accommodation." Besides manifesting a high degree of will in resisting appetite, such persons also develop "narcissistic self-absorption" and regress "to earlier levels of mental functioning." Hilde Bruch, "Psychological Antecedents of Anorexia Nervosa," in *Anorexia Nervosa,* ed. Robert A. Vigersky (New York: Raven Press, 1977), pp. 1, 2. These are clear characteristics of Bartleby as well. Though known chiefly as a disorder growing out of modern society, "in a strange way, anorexia still represents the triumph of the will over bodily needs, bringing back centuries of learned argument on the dichotomy of body and soul" (Minuchin, p. 232). What the anorectic has in common with Bartleby, then, is that they both "consider self-denial and discipline the highest virtue and condemn satisfying their needs and desires as shameful self-indulgence." Hilde Bruch, *The Golden Cage: The Enigma of Anorexia Nervosa* (Cambridge: Harvard University Press, 1978), p. x. No desire is more deeply felt in the anorectic—and in Bartleby—than the desire to rebel against the forces that enslave and to be free. They are all taking what Hilde Bruch calls the "misguided road to independence" (*Cage*, p. xii). Melville of course knew nothing of this disorder from which a growing number of modern young women suffer, but he did understand their profound drives that most of them consciously do not—the will to prefer not to, the desire to defeat the world through denial of self, drives that anorectics share with the ancient acosmic Gnostic.

[50] Commenting on Gnostic asceticism, Hans Jonas writes: "The *asceticism* thus prescribed is strictly speaking a matter not of ethics but of metaphysical alignment. Much as the avoidance of worldly contamination was an aspect of it, *its main aspect was to obstruct rather than promote the cause of the creator; or even, just to spite him*" (p. 144, italics mine). Jonas quotes Hippolytus as saying that Marcion "believes that he vexes the Demiurge by abstaining from what he made or instituted" and Jerome as indicating that the "perpetual abstinence" from food is "for the sake of destroying and condemning and abominating the works of the creator" (p. 144).

[51] Although Gnosticism flourished in the second century and began its decline in the third, certain sects survived for centuries. In his excellent commentary on this poem, William H. Shurr suggests that Melville has in mind the Paulicians, about whom Bayle wrote: "The Paulician movement was exceptionally long-lived, enduring from the fifth century well into the Middle Ages, even though its advocates were constantly persecuted by the church" (p. 165).

[52] *Timoleon* (New York: Caxton Press, 1891), p. 40.

[53] In Gnostic terms, this is *heimarmene,* universal Fate, "a concept taken over from astrology but now tinged with the gnostic anti-cosmic spirit. In its physical aspect this rule is the law of nature; in its psychical aspect, which includes for instance the institution and enforcement of the Mosaic Law, it aims at the enslavement of man." Jonas, p. 43.

[54] Hans Jonas writes that "a genuine and typical *gnostic* argument . . . [is] that the reproductive scheme is an ingenious archontic device for the indefinite retention of souls in the world" (p. 145).

[55] According to R. M. Grant, "ultimately, the difference between Christian and Gnostic philosophical theology seems to lie in their attitudes toward the world. For any Gnostic the world is really hell. For Christians the world is one which God made, a world whose history he governs" (p. 150).

[56] Maltbie D. Babcock, "This Is My Father's World," in *The Hymnbook* (Richmond: Presbyterian Church in the United States, 1965), hymn 101.

[57] This condition derives from the Gnostic desire to *be* God. This aim is set forth in a document both Gnostic and Hermetical in origins, the second-century *Poimandres:* "Such is the blissful goal of those who

possess knowledge [*gnosis*]—to become God." *Gnosticism: A Source Book of Heretical Writings from the Early Christian Period,* ed. Robert M. Grant (New York: Harper, 1961), p. 217. "The potential divinity of man," points out Richard Cavendish, is the theme of both alchemy and Gnosticism. "If you do not make yourself equal to God," you cannot find God (p. 18).

[58] The Gnostic Unknown God, according to Hans Jonas, is He "whose acosmic essence negates all object-determinations as they derive from the mundane realm; whose transcendence transcends any sublimity posited by extension from the here, invalidates all symbols of him thus devised; who, in brief, strictly defies description" (p. 288).

Larry J. Reynolds

MOBY-DICK, NAPOLEON, AND THE WORKERS OF THE WORLD

Once one recognizes the strong conservative reflections elicited from Melville by the French revolution of 1848, it becomes possible to trace both the short- and long-term effect it had upon his thought and his art. Although he responded to America's renewed spirit of chauvinism (caused by events abroad) with passages freighted with messianic nationalism,[1] he also expressed new hostility toward the mass of mankind and admiration for superior individuals who stood above the mass. This elitism can be discerned in *White-Jacket* (1850),[2] and it is prevalent in *Redburn* (1849) as well. The novel he wrote between the spring of 1850 and the summer of 1851, however, is of far more importance than these "two jobs,"[3] as he called them: *Moby-Dick* (1851), his masterpiece, viewed in the new light of the French revolution of 1848 and in the rekindled light of the first French Revolution, reveals its political features with new clarity.

Although *Moby Dick* has often been read as a political allegory, it has invariably been linked to political figures and events in America.[4] In their major studies of the politics of Melville's fiction, James Duban and Paul Michael Rogin, for example, use and extend earlier interpretations that identify Ahab and Ishmael with American political figures and issues. Duban agrees with earlier critics that Ahab is modeled on spokesmen for expansionism and slavery such as Lewis Cass and John Calhoun, and he identifies Ishmael as "an unwitting post facto accomplice to his captain's worst nationalistic transgressions." Rogin, whose interpretation of the novel is Marxist, sees Ahab not only as a representative of American expansionism and slavery, but also of American industrial capitalism. For him, the crew of the *Pequod* is a "multiracial proletariat" enslaved by Ahab, who reunites all fragments of Jacksonian Democracy—"Free-Soilers, secessionists, Young America expansionists, and conservative proslavery Unionists"—into "a new, communal body, which also contained within it the industrial core of patriarchal New England Whiggery—Webster and Shaw—and then led that ship of state to its doom."[5]

From *European Revolutions and the American Literary Renaissance* (New Haven: Yale University Press, 1988), pp. 108–24.

Studies such as these offer useful observations, for Melville indeed paid close attention to the American political scene; nevertheless, they use a closeup lens where a wide-angle is needed. Melville's political interests, like those of the magazines and newspapers of his day, were international as well as national (and historical as well as current). Thus, to focus upon American political developments in an attempt to capture the political meanings of the novel can result in an incomplete reading. To his credit, Rogin, in his chapter "*Moby-Dick* and the American 1848," offers a number of suggestive observations (to which this study is indebted) on political developments in Europe in 1848 that preceded Melville's writing of the novel in 1850 ("the American 1848"); he views these developments, though, as but illustrative parallels, not as formative influences in their own right, which they were.

Before turning to the international dimensions of *Moby-Dick*, I wish to acknowledge how much greater the work is than any examination of its parts can show. Lewis Mumford once identified *Moby-Dick* as "a symphony," and Henry A. Murray, in a classic essay, echoed him by calling it "Beethoven's *Eroica* in words," citing the "masterly orchestration of harmonic and melodic language, of resonating images and thoughts in varied meters. . . . the spacious sea-setting of the story; the cast of characters and their prodigious common target; the sorrow, the fury, and the terror, . . . and finally the fated closure, the crown and tragic consummation of the immense yet firmly welded whole."[6] Melville's inspiration for his symphony came, of course, from almost countless sources. Dante, Milton, Shakespeare, Goethe, Carlyle, Hawthorne, Byron, the Bible have all been identified as major influences upon him, while the characters convincingly identified as Ahab's prototypes include Prometheus, Satan, Lear, Macbeth, Hamlet, Faust, Teufelsdröckh, Ethan Brand, Manfred, Cain, Adam, Job, King Ahab, and even Christ. But though the richness of the novel and the extent of its sources have long been recognized, the influence of revolution in France upon the novel as a whole and of the figure of Napoleon upon the characterization of Ahab has yet to be demonstrated. Such a demonstration will show that Murray's comparison of the novel with the *Eroica* is far more apt than even he realized, given the circumstances of that symphony's composition and the fate of its dedication.[7]

In *Heroes and Hero-Worship,* Carlyle explains how a new king naturally emerges from revolutions, because of their natural movement from chaos toward order. "There is not a *man* in them, raging in the thickest of the madness," he writes, "but is impelled withal, at all moments, towards Order. . . . While man is man, some Cromwell or Napoleon is the necessary finish of a Sansculottism."[8] Although the revolution Ahab rages at the center of during the voyage of the *Pequod* is primarily metaphysical rather than political, and although his cause, like Lucifer's, appears anarchical and destructive, he is at heart a man impelled toward order. This can easily be seen in his military bearing and in his touching insistence that life should be governed like a boxing match, by rules of fair play. Ahab's quarrel, in its most heroic form, is not with the clarity, harmony, and integrity of creation, but rather with "all that most maddens and torments; all that stirs up the lees of things; all truth with malice in it; all that cracks the sinews and cakes the brain; all the subtle demonisms of life and thought."[9] And these, of course, are what Moby Dick personifies for him, and why this imperial, godlike creature is the object of his hatred.

While Ahab's military bearing and affinity for order link him to the king who emerged from the last phase of the first French Revolution, these are only two of many subterranean linkages. In profound ways, Napoleon served as a prototype for Ahab, and Napoleon's political development served as a paradigm for Ahab's own. Melville, like Beethoven and others, viewed Napoleon as the heroic representative of the French Revolution who ultimately betrayed the democratic ideals that revolution embodied, and this, in part, is the role assigned to Ahab in *Moby-Dick*.[10] Moreover, because Melville, like many of his contemporaries, saw history repeating itself in France during and after the revolution of 1848, especially with another Napoleon rising to the head of state, he also incorporated a damning commentary on current French political radicalism into the novel.

Allusions to the first French Revolution appear throughout *Moby-Dick*, at times to bind apparently unrelated material to the main narrative. "The Town-Ho's Story," for example, is a polished set piece which seems only loosely connected to Ahab's quest; however, in it Melville introduces and develops the theme of revolution integral to the book as a whole. As Ishmael tells this story of injustice and violence, images of upheaval in Paris provide key elements of the setting. Steelkilt's origins, of course, are thoroughly American; he is an Erie Canaller, a "man of violence," "abundantly and picturesquely wicked" (215). In his rebellion against Radney and his Captain, however, Steelkilt acquires the attributes of a French revolutionary. After he staves in Radney's jaw, he and his men become "sea-Parisians," slewing large casks in front of them and entrenching "themselves behind the barricade." Steelkilt also exhibits the theatrical behavior found in revolutionary iconography as he leaps "on the barricade, and striding up and down there, defied the worst the pistols could do" (216). Betrayed by his own comrades and flogged by his cowardly adversary, Steelkilt nevertheless has his revenge, with help from Moby Dick, and he and his men, after "seizing a large double war-canoe of the savages" reach Tahiti, where they embark, appropriately, on two ships "about to sail for France" (223). Melville thus allows his readers to speculate that Steelkilt's violent, rebellious character fulfills its destiny abroad, perhaps in the "red year Forty-Eight."

Although "The Town-Ho's Story" seems curiously out of place in the novel, by treating a violent rebel whose adversary seems intent upon demeaning him, it encapsulates Ahab's situation, a situation likewise tied to revolution in France through a series of linked allusions and images. To begin with, Ishmael, in a famous phrase, calls the crew of the *Pequod* "an Anarcharsis Clootz deputation from all the isles of the sea, and all the ends of the earth" (108). Because Baron Cloots led his ragtag group of Parisians before the French National Assembly in June 1790 to symbolize the support of the human species for the French Revolution, the allusion places the voyage of the *Pequod* within the context of historic revolutionary action. Ahab strengthens the association between his quest and the course of the French Revolution when he uses the red banner of revolt as the flag of his ship; and when Ishmael notices that the *Pequod* has a complexion "darkened like a French grenadier's, who has alike fought in Egypt and Siberia" (67), the Napoleonic nature of the voyage and Ahab's resemblance to that future king are strongly suggested. Ahab himself reenforces the identification when he imagines upon his head the Iron Crown of Lombardy, which Napoleon placed upon his own head when he declared himself king of Italy in 1805. And consonant with Ahab's role as a military commander, the three mates, Starbuck, Stubb, and Flask, are introduced as "captains of companies" due to "that grand order of battle in which Captain Ahab would probably marshal his forces to descend on the whales" (106).[11]

Whaling is linked with the great battles of Napoleon through indirect allusions as well as such direct ones. Commenting on Garneray's engravings of whaling scenes, Ishmael declares, "Go and gaze upon all the paintings of Europe, and where will you find such a gallery of living and breathing commotion on canvas, as in that triumphal hall at Versailles; where the beholder fights his way, pell-mell, through the consecutive great battles of France; where every sword seems a flash of the Northern Lights, and the successive armed kings and Emperors dash by, like a charge of crowned centaurs? Not wholly unworthy of a place in that gallery, are these sea battle-pieces of Garneray" (230).

Melville had visited Versailles in the fall of 1849 and there found hundreds of paintings of Napoleon dominating the gallery, as he knew they would. Dr. Augustus Kinsley Gardner, "perhaps the most stimulating of all of [Melville's] acquaintances" in the Duyckinck circle,[12] had written about Napoleon and the gallery in his book *Old Wine in New Bottles; or, Spare Hours of a Student in Paris* (1848), which he gave to Melville in the spring of 1848 before the latter went to France.[13] Here are vivid pictures of the principal battles where he triumphed," Gardner declared. "Wagram, Austerlitz, Marengo, and Moscow, are exhibited with a power and faithfulness, which, while they chill the blood at the sight of so much suffering and carnage, exalt the consummate general who achieved them, and stands out the most conspicuous object in the groups. The effect of these paintings is wonderful." Telling how the paintings affect an observer, Gardner related, "I defy the greatest advocate of peace that lives, to look upon these paintings calmly; to view with cool composure the brown coat, the cocked hat, the white horse, the calm features of the man of destiny, who subdued all—even himself and his own feelings,—for ambition—for glory—for France. Had I lived in those tempestuous times, my heart tells me, how easily I could have shouldered the musket, and drawn the trigger, under the auspices of that glorious commander."[14]

Melville, even before he went to Paris (where he stayed in lodgings recommended by Dr. Gardner)[15] and visited Versailles, had heard much about Napoleon and had probably developed strong feelings toward him. His father, Allan, we know, had followed the emperor's career with great interest. In 1818, Allan informed his wife in a letter from Paris that his arrival on the French coast had reminded him of what he had seen there some fifteen years before. "Here were those veteran Legions," he wrote, "who had spread dismay throughout Europe, assembled for the invasion of England in 1803 most of whom I had seen reviewed in Paris by the projector of this mighty enterprise, who is now in hopeless exile, while on the same spot where his soldiers were encamped, I saw in 1818 [the present] British Troops who were quartered in the vicinity."[16] From his Uncle Thomas, another eyewitness to Napoleon's career, Melville sought and received impressions of the emperor's glory. In the memoir of his uncle, he recalled how Thomas "often at my request described some of those martial displays and spectacles of state which he had witnessed in Paris in the time of the first Napoleon. But I was too young and ignorant then, to derive the full benefit from his pictorial recollections."[17] Thomas admired the emperor so ardently that he even named his second son Napoleon, and members of the Melville family apparently shared Thomas's enthusiasm for the man. Among the recently discovered Melville family papers, there is a letter from Melville's beloved younger brother Tom who, as he was about to go to sea in 1846 at the age of sixteen, wrote home (in care of his sister Helen), "Before I come back I will proberably visit the France of Napoleon, that beacon of Modern history and you may tell Miss Lizzy Shaw that I will fetch her a peace of one of the willows (that droope their heads over the spot honnoured by being chouse as the rasting place of one of the greatest men that ever lived) to put in her collection of ods and ends."[18] (One of the two curios Melville himself purchased while in Paris three years later was a medallion of Napoleon and Josephine, which may have been, like Tom's prospective willow leaf, for Lizzy, who had become Herman's wife. He also acquired, perhaps on the same trip, a striking engraved bust of Napoleon).

Napoleon—admired by the Melvilles, brought to mind by the revolution of 1848 and the rise of his nephew, viewed in all his glory in the paintings of Versailles—surely strode naturally to the front of Melville's imagination as he created the "mighty pageant creature" (71) of *Moby-Dick*. Nevertheless, for many of the details of Ahab's character, especially those that distinguish him from traditional tragic heroes and make him a modern (that is, nineteenth-century) protagonist, Melville I think drew upon a particular account of Napoleon, that of Emerson in *Representing Men,* a book Melville probably read in the Hawthorne's small sitting room during a September morning in 1850.[19]

Emerson, fascinated in spite of himself by Napoleon, describes him as a representative of the "class of industry and skill," someone able to "carry with him the power and affections of vast numbers," because "the people whom he sways are little Napoleons."[20] Unlike the effete kings he defeated, Napoleon was, according to Emerson, "a worker in brass, in iron, in wood. . . . He knew the properties of gold and iron, of wheels and ships, of troops and diplomatists, and required that each should do after its kind" (228–29). He "would not hear of materialism" (250), however, and fondly indulged in abstract speculation, especially concerning religion and justice. Although Emerson attributes to Napoleon a deadly "absorbing egotism" (257) and admits he had no scruples, he nevertheless defends him from the charge of cruelty, claiming he must not "be set down as cruel, but only as one who knew no impediment to his will; not bloodthirsty, not cruel,—but woe to what thing or person stood in his way! . . . He saw only the object: the obstacle must give way" (234).

Once one considers Ahab in the light of Emerson's Napoleon, the similarities become striking. And in fact, if one listens closely, echoes of Emerson's observations on Napoleon can be heard throughout the novel, in Ishmael's comment on "Ahab's iron soul" (438), in Ahab's boast that "naught's an obstacle, naught's an angle to the iron way!" (147), in Starbuck's lament that "flat obedience to thy flat commands, this is all thou breathest. Aye, and say'st . . . all of us are Ahabs."[21] The unique link between Ahab and Emerson's Napoleon, however (one not found between Ahab and his other prototypes), is a technical knowledge of the workaday world. As Ahab pores over his charts and calculates, from his knowledge of tides and currents, where to find Moby Dick, as he stands at the forge welding the shank of his own harpoon, as he smites the iron rod and uses it to magnetize the compass needle, he becomes, indeed, a representative of "the class of industry and skill," and thus, like Napoleon, and unlike figures such as King Lear, Manfred, and Job (or Daniel Webster, John Calhoun, and Lewis Cass, if you will), a laboring participant in the modern democratic, and pragmatic, age.

Ultimately though, Ahab is a much more complex and heroic figure than Emerson's representative man of the world. Most of this is due to the many sources, unrelated to Napoleon, that enriched Melville's characterization of his shaggy old whale hunter. Some of it though resulted from another book Melville turned to in the summer of 1850, Carlyle's *Heroes and Hero-Worship*,[22] which contained a treatment of Napoleon and the French Revolution that supplemented Emerson's chapter and showed Melville an intriguing way of perceiving and presenting political revolt as ontological heroics.[23]

In a key passage, Carlyle rebuts the notion that "the French Revolution was a general act of insanity" (200–01), defining it and all revolutions as part of "the struggle of men intent on the real essence of things, against men intent on the semblances and forms of things" (204). "We will hail the [next] French Revolution," Carlyle writes in 1840, "as shipwrecked mariners might the sternest rock, in a world otherwise all of baseless sea and waves. A true Apocalypse, though a terrible one, to this false withered artificial time; testifying once more that Nature is *preter*natural; if not divine, then diabolic; that Semblance is not Reality; that it has to become Reality, or the world will take fire under it,—burn *it* into what it is, namely Nothing!" (201–02). When Ahab tells Starbuck, "All visible objects, man, are but as pasteboard masks. . . . If man will strike, strike through the mask!" (144), he is formulating the purpose of his quest in Carlyle's transcendental terms. Similarly, when Ishmael offers his meditation on the whiteness of the whale and ends with the question "Wonder ye then at the fiery hunt?" (170), he has explained Ahab's motives in the same terms that Carlyle's passage explains the French Revolution, that is, as a response to the maddening notion that what we see around us "are but subtile deceits, not actually inherent in substances, but only laid on from without."[24]

"The Hero as King" is the chapter in which Carlyle's passage appears, and the hero and king he discusses in the context of the French Revolution is Napoleon. Like Emerson, Carlyle sees Napoleon in his first period as "a true Democrat" (240). "There was an eye to see in this man, a soul to dare and do. He rose naturally to be the King" (240). By the end of his career, however, Napoleon, according to Carlyle, had become unjust and tyrannous. Not only did he begin to rely heavily upon his conviction of the useful "*Dupeability* of men" (241), but he began to mistake semblances, such as coronations and consecrations, for realities. By the end, Napoleon "had gone that way of his," writes Carlyle with pity, "and nature also had gone her way. Having once parted with Reality, he tumbles helpless in Vacuity; no rescue for him. He had to sink there, mournfully as man seldom did; and break his great heart, and die" (243). This last sentence, of course, could serve as a description of Ahab's death as well as Napoleon's.

Although Ahab never develops Napoleon's appreciation of grandeur, never sees the material world as of ultimate importance, he does, during the course of the voyage, become more and more contemptuous of his men, more and more willing to sacrifice human life to attain his own "topmost greatness." While he begins as an archdemocrat, a Promethean figure willing to defy all "the omniscient gods" who are "oblivious of suffering man" (428), by the end he too has become oblivious because of his fatal egotism. Perhaps his most despicable act is his refusal to help Captain Gardiner search for his son; but earlier, of course, his characterization of his men as tools makes this behavior unsurprising. "May I forgive myself," he says to Captain Gardiner, thus revealing how great his sense of godlike power has become. But, of course, in his last battle he rediscovers his fatal human limitations, as the hemp grips his neck and he's pulled beneath the waves.

In two discernible ways, Melville merges his treatment of Ahab as a Napoleonic figure with a treatment of contemporary international politics. First, he intimates, as he did in *Mardi,* that there is nothing new under the sun and the lesson time teaches is that all is vanity, including political struggle, for the cycle of republics and monarchies is endless. When Ishmael facetiously identifies Napoleon as a modern masthead stander (as a statue atop the column of Vendôme), he says, "There is Napoleon; who . . . stands with arms folded, some one hundred and fifty feet in the air; careless, now, who rules the decks below; whether Louis Philippe, Louis Blanc, or Louis the Devil" (136). Louis Philippe, of course, was the French king ousted by the French revolution of 1848; Louis Blanc was the radical French journalist and member of the provisional government who devised the ill-fated scheme of national workshops for the unemployed Parisian workers in the spring of 1848; and Louis the Devil is Melville's reference to Louis Napoleon, the emperor's nephew, whose movement toward absolutism Melville had glimpsed in Paris. Melville's idea here is that kings and revolutionaries alike are most notably part of the "wilful world" that "hath not got hold of unchristian Solomon's wisdom yet" (355).[25] And this is also the key idea he develops in his use of the Hotel de Cluny in Paris to hint at "Ahab's larger, darker, deeper part." Like a tour guide addressing political exiles such as Louis Philippe, Metternich, and Charles Albert, Ishmael says,

> Winding far down within the very heart of this spiked Hotel de Cluny where we here stand—however grand and wonderful, now quit it;—and take your way, ye nobler, sadder souls, to those vast Roman halls of Thermes; where far beneath the fantastic towers of man's upper earth, his root of grandeur, his whole awful essence sits in bearded state; an antique buried beneath antiquities, and throned on torsoes! So with a broken throne, the great gods mock that captive king . . . Wind ye down there, ye prouder, sadder souls! question that proud, sad king! A family likeness! aye, he did beget ye, ye young exiled royalties; and from your grim sire only will the old State-secret come. [161]

This secret, assuming the dead king could speak, would be on the order of " 'All is Vanity.' ALL" (355), and like Shelley in "Ozymandias," Melville relies upon irony to convey it.

A second way Melville uses his narrative to develop a theme about contemporary French politics is his association of the crew of the *Pequod* with workers engaged in a fated revolt. Admittedly, as many critics have pointed out, Melville throughout the novel emphasizes the importance of the liberty, equality, and brotherhood of man, especially in his treatment of the Ishmael-Queequeg relationship, in the impassioned paean to the great democratic God in the first "Knights and Squires" chapter, and in the closing paragraphs of the "Fast-Fish and Loose-Fish" chapter; nevertheless, the Ishmael that tells the tale of the *Pequod*'s voyage only appears to share the pure democratic sensibilities of his younger self.[26] In many ways, he, like Ahab, perceives that the "people" measure up to no ideal, and his narrative continually dramatizes the primeval savageness that lies beneath the surface character of the crew, a savageness that appears when Ahab in his role as revolutionary incites them to "make war on the horrors of the deep!" (443). "We are all killers, on land and on sea," Ishmael admits at one point, "Bonapartes and Sharks included" (125).

The murderous action of "Forecastle—Midnight," the unholy tableaux of "The Quarter-Deck," "The Try-Works," and "The Candles" all serve to verify Starbuck's estimate of the men as "a heathen crew that have small touch of human mothers in them!" And even when viewed apart from their wild participation in Ahab's hellish rites, they are, as Ishmael says, no more than "mongrel renegades, and castaways, and cannibals—morally enfeebled" by Starbuck's "mere unaided virtue," Stubb's "invulnerable jollity of indifference," and Flask's "pervading mediocrity" (162).

Singling out two representatives of the people, the carpenter and the blacksmith, for chapter-length study, Melville provides a damning appraisal of the workingman, at least as he exists on the *Pequod*. "A stript abstract; an unfractioned integral" (388), the carpenter is a pure manipulator of wood, nothing more. He is skilled at "repairing stove boats, sprung spars, reforming the shape of clumsy-bladed oars" (387), but he nevertheless cannot think. "His brain," Ishmael relates, "if he had ever had one, must have early oozed along into the muscles of his fingers" (388). The old blacksmith Perth, who has ruined his life by drinking, is a similarly sad representative of the working class. "Silent, slow, and solemn; bowing over still further his chronically broken back, he toiled away, as if toil were life itself, and the heavy beating of his hammer the heavy beating of his heart. And so it was.—Most miserable!" (409).

Both the carpenter and the blacksmith wield hammers, and this tool is a key image in the novel; it identifies the crew of the *Pequod* as workingmen, and it supports Melville's theme that mankind in the mass often become mere thoughtless tools during a revolt. When Ahab nails the doubloon to the mast, he assumes the role of a manipulative leader of the workers of the ship: "Receiving the top-maul from Starbuck, he advanced towards the main-mast with the hammer uplifted in one hand, exhibiting the gold with the other" (142). (As the props suggest, we also see here Ahab's belief that the forces which move the men are fear on the one hand and greed on the other.) Ishmael, excited and incited by Ahab like all the others, explains himself by saying, "My oath had been welded with theirs; and stronger I shouted, and more did I hammer and clinch my oath, because of the dread in my soul" (155). And when the chase for Moby Dick is under way, Melville again uses the image of the hammer in his description of the crew. During the night that follows the second-day chase, "the sound of hammers, and the hum of the grindstone was heard till nearly daylight, as the men toiled by lanterns in the complete and careful rigging of the spare boats" (460). And finally, on the third day, as Moby Dick bears down upon the *Pequod*, the crew form a workingman's tableau, as they await in static, emblematic poses their destruction. "From the ship's bows," Melville writes, "nearly all the seamen now hung inactive; hammers, bits of plank, lances, and harpoons, mechanically retained in their hands, just as they had darted from their various employments; all their enchanted eyes intent upon the whale" (468).

In the United States, the icon of an arm holding a hammer symbolized the workingman or a workingman's association during the eighteenth century and the first half of the nineteenth century. It appeared on membership certificates of mechanic societies, on campaign posters, and on allegorical representations of American progress and western expansion, and its associations were primarily social and fraternal.[27] During the mid and late 1840s, however, with the rise of labor unionism and labor radicalism, the symbol became politicized, appearing in newspapers such as *Working Man's Advocate* and *Champion of American Labor*.[28] The European revolutions, moreover, with their attendant spotlighting of workers revolting at the instigation of communist and socialist intellectuals, tied the image to the "Red Revolution." With the Bloody June Days, the symbol of the arm and hammer, along with those of the sickle, the red flag, and the liberty cap, became exceptionally potent and to conservative thinkers connoted popular violence. In *Mardi*, when Melville refers to the hammers and sickles of the mob, when he mentions the red banner they carry, his imagery is familiar to us because we have seen its proliferation in the twentieth century. We all recognize its link to communism, and when Melville wrote *Moby-Dick*, many of his readers did as well.

NOTES

[1] See John Gerlach, "Messianic Nationalism in the Early Works of Herman Melville: Against Perry Miller," *Arizona Quarterly* 28 (Spring 1972): 5–26, for an able discussion of these passages. Melville's spread-eagle nationalism has been repeatedly examined; that it formed part of the American response to the European revolutions, however, has gone unnoticed. In fact, the two foremost studies of literary Young America (John Stafford, *The Literary Criticism of 'Young America': A Study in the Relationship of Politics and Literature, 1837–1850* [1952; rpt. New York: Russell and Russell, 1967], and Perry Miller, *The Raven and the Whale: The War of Words and Wits in the Era of Poe and Melville* [1956; rpt. Westport, Conn.: Greenwood Press, 1973]) have given the impression that Melville's contributions to the movement were embarrassingly belated, that he was a naïve enthusiast beating the drum after the band had stopped playing. In actuality, though, the country as a whole, in response to the revolutions of 1848–49, had become one large Young America, and Melville was merely contributing to the din sounding around him.

For an example of the purple prose that came into fashion as a result of the revolutions, see Frederick Merk, *Manifest Destiny and Mission in American History, A Reinterpretation* (New York: Knopf, 1963), p. 199.

[2] See my "Antidemocratic Emphasis in *White-Jacket*," *American Literature* 48 (March 1976): 13–28.

[3] *The Letters of Herman Melville*, ed. Merrell R. Davis and William H. Gilman (New Haven: Yale Univ. Press, 1960), p. 91.

[4] See, for example, Willie T. Weathers, "*Moby Dick* and the Nineteenth-Century Scene," *Texas Studies in Literature and Language* 1 (Winter 1960): 477–501; Charles H. Foster, "Something in Emblems: A Reinterpretation of *Moby-Dick*," *New England Quarterly* 34 (March 1961): 3–35; and Alan Heimert, "*Moby-Dick* and American Political Symbolism," *American Quarterly* 15 (Winter 1963): 498–534.

[5] James Duban, *Melville's Major Fiction: Politics, Theology, and Imagination* (DeKalb, Ill.: Northern Illinois Univ. Press, 1983), p. 123; Michael Paul Rogin, *Subversive Genealogy: The Politics and Art of Herman Melville* (New York: Knopf, 1983), pp. 114, 130.

[6] Lewis Mumford, *Herman Melville: A Study of His Life and Vision* (1929; rev. ed. New York: Harbinger Books, 1962), p. 124; Henry A. Murray, "In Nomine Diaboli," *New England Quarterly* 24 (December 1951): 435–52; rpt. in *Melville: A Collection of Critical Essays*, ed. Richard Chase (Englewood Cliffs, N.J.: Prentice-Hall, 1962), p. 63.

[7] The *Eroica*, as students of music know, was originally dedicated to Napoleon, but when he crowned himself emperor in May 1804, Beethoven, outraged, changed the title of the work to "Heroic Symphony, composed to celebrate the memory of a great man."

[8] Thomas Carlyle, *On Heroes, Hero-Worship and the Heroic in History* (1841; rpt. New York: AMS Press, 1969), p. 204.

[9] Herman Melville, *Moby-Dick; or, The Whale*, ed. Harrison Hayford and Hershel Parker (New York: Norton, 1967), p. 160. Hereafter cited parenthetically.

[10] "A volume should be written on the image of Napoleon in democratic America," Perry Miller declared over thirty years ago (*The Raven and the Whale*, p. 189), and his statement is still true.

[11] For an extended discussion of the war and battle imagery of *Moby-Dick*, see Joyce Sparer Adler, *War in Melville's Imagination* (New York: New York Univ. Press, 1981), pp. 58–61.

[12] Leon Howard, *Herman Melville: A Biography* (Berkeley: Univ. of California Press, 1967), p. 110.

[13] Jay Leyda, *The Melville Log: A Documentary Life of Herman Melville, 1819–1891* (1951; rpt. with additional material, New York: Gordian Press, 1969), 1:xxvi.

[14] Augustus Kinsley Gardner, *Old Wine in New Bottles* (New York: Francis, 1848), pp. 180, 181.

[15] Leyda, *The Melville Log*, 1:xxvi.

[16] Letter of Alan Melvill to Maria Melvill, June 11, 1818. Melville Family papers, Gansevoort-Lansing Collection, New York Public Library. (I am indebted to Jay Leyda for helping me transcribe this quotation.)

[17] Herman Melville, "Sketch of Major Thomas Melvill, Jr. By a Nephew," Melville Family Papers, Gansevoort-Lansing Collection, New York Public Library.

[18] Letter of Thomas Melville to Helen Melville, May 3, 1846, Melville Family Papers (Additions); Gansevoort-Lansing Collection; New York Public Library. The spelling errors are Thomas's.

[19] Merton M. Sealts, Jr., "Melville and Emerson's Rainbow," ESQ 26 (1980): 67.

[20] Ralph Waldo Emerson, Complete Works of Ralph Waldo Emerson, ed. Edward Waldo Emerson, 12 vols. (1903–04); rpt. New York: AMS Press, 1968), vol. 4, Representative Men, pp. 224, 223.

[21] Luther S. Mansfield and Howard P. Vincent point out this latter echo in their "Explanatory Notes," Moby-Dick (New York: Hendricks House, 1952), p. 823. Sealts, "Melville and Emerson's Rainbow," p. 76n57, notes several other passages in Melville's writings that echo sentences in Representative Men.

[22] See Merton M. Sealts, Jr., Melville's Reading: A Check-List of Books Owned and Borrowed (Madison: Univ. of Wisconsin Press, 1966), p. 48.

[23] Although this specific indebtedness has not received critical attention, Carlyle's pervasive influence on Moby-Dick has not gone unnoticed. The influence of Carlyle's style, of his ideas about the emblematic nature of the visible world, of his characterization of Teufelsdröckh, of his dark view of industrialism and technology are treated, respectively, in F. O. Matthiessen, American Renaissance: Art and Expression in the Age of Emerson and Whitman (New York: Oxford, 1941), pp. 384–85; Tyrus Hillway, Herman Melville (New York: Twayne, 1963), pp. 83–86; Howard, Herman Melville: A Biography, pp. 171–72, 178; Leo Marx, The Machine in the Garden (New York: Oxford, 1967), pp. 286, 297–99. The fullest discussion of the influence of Heroes and Hero-Worship upon Melville's creation of the heroic character of Ahab is Jonathan Arac, Commissioned Spirits: The Shaping of Social Motion in Dickens, Carlyle, Melville, and Hawthorne (New Brunswick, N.J.: Rutgers Univ. Press, 1979), pp. 148–63. For Arac, "Cromwell is the Carlyean hero who most resembles Ahab" (149).

[24] The chapter "The Whiteness of the Whale" treats many more ideas than this one, of course; furthermore, there are a number of subtle differences between Ahab's perception of the visible and Ishmael's. For the most sustained and informative comparison of the Ahabian and Ishmaelian epistemologies, see Robert Zoellner, The Salt-Sea Mastodon: A Reading of Moby-Dick (Berkeley: Univ. of California Press, 1973).

[25] For a discussion of the importance of Solomon and Ecclesiastes to Melville's thought and art, see Nathalia Wright, Melville's Use of the Bible (Durham, N.C.: Duke Univ. Press, 1949), pp. 95–101.

[26] See my "Kings and Commoners in Moby-Dick," Studies in the Novel 12 (Summer 1980): 101–13.

[27] See Josef and Shizuko Muller-Brockmann, History of the Poster (Zurich: ABC Verlag Zurich, 1971), p. 28; Morris B. Schnapper, American Labor: A Pictorial Social History (Washington, D.C.: Public Affairs Press, 1972), pp. 18, 47.

[28] See Sean Wilentz, Chants Democratic: New York City and the Rise of the American Working Class (New York: Oxford, 1985), pp. 343–46.

Neal L. Tolchin

A THING WRIT IN WATER:
ALLAN MELVILL'S EPITAPH

Deep & Secret grief is a cannibal of its own heart.　　　　　—Bacon

Deep memories yield no epitaphs　　　—Herman Melville, *Moby-Dick*

Two gender-related findings of the Harvard Study of Bereavement illuminate the role of mourning in *Moby-Dick*. ⟨. . .⟩ the male subjects of this study tend to define their sense of loss in terms of dismemberment, whereas the women studied register a sense of abandonment. The preceding chapters of this book have demonstrated that the imagery of dismemberment pervades Melville's work. Ahab's dismasted state, however, most dramatically performs this social symbolization of male bereavement. The Harvard Study has also found that one-third of the women interviewed displayed "generalized hostility" three weeks after their loss, while none of the men showed this reaction. Nevertheless, the male subjects reported that it took them longer to feel that they had overcome their bereavement; a third of the men reported an inability to cry, claiming that they felt choked up.[1] And it is this finding that takes us deeply into the complexities of grief and gender in *Moby-Dick*.

In his shattered sense of corporeal and psychic wholeness, Ahab is Melville's most uninhibited male mourner. The rage that surfaces in Ahab's character contrasts starkly with the genteel denial of anger often exhibited by Melville's male characters—the important exception to this being Ahab's prototype, *Redburn's* Jackson. Contemporaries of Melville could simply not accept the extent to which Ahab melodramatically vents his morbidity: this was the object of sharp attacks on the novel. Twentieth-century critics turn Ahab into anything but what Melville portrayed him as: a bereaved monomaniac. Ahab still expresses dark feelings which Melville's readers feel more comfortable translating into less painful abstractions.[2]

Why does Melville allow Ahab a heightened bereavement? Elsewhere in his fiction he largely obeys the cultural codes that burden women with the public symbolization of grief. I contend that Ahab performs the social role ascribed to the female mourner—although he exceeds even that role in the intensity of his public expression of grief—because his character is shaped by Melville's sense of his

From *Mourning, Gender, and Creativity in the Art of Herman Melville* (New Haven: Yale University Press, 1988), pp. 117–37.

mother's conflicted grief for his father. Through Ahab's character, Melville portrays the power of his mother's bereaved rage and its crucial influence on his own grief for his father. Although Ahab's identification with Maria Melville's grief is kept on the novel's margins, it momentarily breaches the surface in "The Candles," where Ahab, while attempting to " 'read my sire,' " claims for himself a " 'queenly personality.' " Ishmael portrays Ahab as both the damned maniac and the embattled hero in quest of an ultimate showdown with all the Evil in the universe, but Ahab's divided delineation has a great deal to do with the contradictory images of Maria's husband, as damned deathbed maniac and as an idealized figure that she communicated to her son through her conflicted grief.[3]

Ahab represents Melville's attempt to exorcise from his inner world the complex image of his father he internalized from his mother's grief. For this reason, Ahab exhibits the symptoms of Allan Melvill's last weeks of life: deathbed mania. Through Crazy Ahab, Melville attempts to transform the mania into both penetrating insight into the tragic dimensions of existence and the heroic resistance to Fixed Fate. Ahab's characterization expresses a doubleness that goes to the heart of the energies of the novel. A morbid figure and one of tragic grandeur, his character opens itself both to Melville's fears of the paternal image of the deathbed maniac that threatened him from within and to Melville's sense of the overwhelming and dangerous rage of his own unresolved grief, compounded by the influence of the rage of a mother's grief on the anger of a child's sense of abandonment by his parent.[4]

Ahab exists as the object of perception and creation of Ishmael, a narrator marked especially by a mordant sense of humor and by occasional insights into the complexity and the fluidity of reality underlying social representations. However, Ishmael's narration also often participates in the Victorian American social codes that militate against the public expression of intense feeling, such as what his culture termed excessive grief.[5] And both Ahab and Ishmael share the stage with a "tremendous apparition," Moby Dick (448). While, on the one hand, Ishmael perceives that the whale "must remain unpainted to the last"—"I have ever found your plain things the knottiest of all," he observes slyly—on the other hand, Ishmael views Ahab's intense bereavement through the cultural codes that cause Ahab to harbor "the mad secret of his unabated rage bolted up and keyed in him" while he endeavors to appear "but naturally grieved" after his return from the voyage on which Moby Dick sheared off his leg (228, 312, 162, 161). By portraying Ahab's unnatural bereavement in terms of his culture's social construction of grief and madness, Ishmael dramatizes how he must view Ahab's excessive grief in terms of monomania.

As Ishmael oscillates between his mixed response to Ahab's grief—he both condemns Ahab for expressing intense bereavement and enviously idealizes him for doing so—and Moby Dick's resistance to representation, the novel generates much of the energy and excitement of its rich language. This narrative shifting, combined with Ishmael's penchant for shiftiness as a narrator, splits Melville's attempt to represent his unresolved grief into confrontation with an incarnation of his living linking object role and his respect for the complexity of feeling that eludes social representations. When Moby Dick finally appears, Ishmael's imagery intimates his sense of the whale as "a thing writ in water," an inscription of the natural world's fluid writing but also an echo of Keats's gravestone epitaph: "Here lies one whose name was writ in water" (453).[6]

Both grief and the white whale, the novel suggests, cannot finally be possessed in the terms of social representation available to Ishmael. The theme of possession comes to the fore when Ishmael angrily protests against the legal argument that assumes women are property. "Possession," in Ishmael's scathing analysis, has become "the whole of the law" (333). In his representation of Moby Dick, which obliquely critiques his own convention-bound portrayal of Ahab's intense bereavement, Ishmael attempts to subvert patriarchal social codes in his preference for a more fluid state of affairs, one in which his readers are "but a Loose-Fish and a Fast-Fish, too" (334). The " 'fluid consciousness' " Sophia Hawthorne perceived in Melville transforms Moby-Dick's readers into Fast-Fish, held by a Loose-Fish of complex narrative animation—one that seduces us into the powerful experience of morbid grief, which threatens to subvert from within the melodramatic generic languages in which Ahab comes to life.[7]

The Soothing Savage

> The bereaved's continuing sense of "containing" the person lost gives
> rise to an elated state of mind.   —John Bowlby, Loss

In the linking object theory, the surviving parents transfers grief to the child. That process is paralleled in Moby-Dick by Ahab's success in wedding the crew to his aggrieved guest.[8] When Ahab crosses the lances of his mates, "it seemed as though, by some nameless, interior volition, he would fain have shocked into them the same fiery emotion accumulated within the Leyden jar of his own magnetic life" (145–46). Ishmael confesses that "because of the dread in my soul" he shouts out Ahab's oath against the whale along with the rest of the crew: "A wild, mystical, sympathetical feeling was in me; Ahab's quenchless feud seemed mine" (155). The transference of emotion works so successfully on the crew that "at times his [Ahab's] hate seemed almost theirs" (162). Ishmael, as well, "gave myself up to the abandonment of the time and the place" and sees Moby Dick through Ahab's eyes: as the embodiment of "the deadliest ill" (163). In the final chase scenes, Ahab's grief has fully taken hold of the crew's emotions. His "purpose now fixedly gleamed down upon the constant midnight of the gloomy crew" (437). "Alike, joy and sorrow, hope and fear, seemed ground to finest dust, and powdered, for the time, in the clamped mortar of Ahab's iron soul. Like machines, they [the crew] dumbly moved about the deck" (438).

Before Ahab effects the transference of his grief, Ishmael, in his relationship with Queequeg, the soothing savage, offers a counterstory to what he presents as the monomaniac obsession and the powerful influence of Ahab's bereavement. From the outset of the narrative, Ishmael reveals his interest in the subject of death and mourning. He presents us with an Etymology supplied by a Late Consumptive Usher, who loved to dust his grammar books because "it somehow mildly reminded him of his mortality" (1). Ishmael next inserts Extracts of passages on the whale gathered from world literature by a Sub-Sub-Librarian, with whom he enjoys sitting and feeling "poor-devilish, too; and grow[s] convivial upon tears . . . and in not altogether unpleasant sadness"(2).

From this evocation of the fashionable melancholy of sentimental literature, Ishmael turns to his narration proper with an expression of morbid feelings that flirts with exceeding the bounds of the sentimental and Byronic poses from behind which he often teases us. He edges his introduction of himself with aggressive and angry instructions: "Call me Ishmael. Some years ago—never mind how long precisely" (12). Momentarily, though, he shifts into an Irvingesque pose of genteel melancholy: "having little or no money in my purse, and nothing particular to interest me on shore, I thought I would sail about a little and see the watery part of the world" (12). He then confesses to feelings that are darker than the melancholy of the sentimental novel but which are recited in the hyperboles of a joky tone that immediately undercuts authentic emotion:

> It is a way I have of driving off the spleen, and regulating the circulation. Whenever I find myself growing grim about the mouth; whenever it is a damp, drizzly November in my soul; whenever I find myself involuntarily pausing before coffin warehouses, and bringing up the rear of every funeral I meet; and especially whenever my hypos get such an upper hand of me, that it requires a strong moral principle to prevent me from deliberately stepping into the street, and methodically knocking people's hats off—then, I account it high time to get to sea as soon as I can. This is my substitute for pistol and ball. (12)

Ishmael, while confessing to angry and suicidal feelings, also indicates his partial allegiance to genteel codes of feeling: by shipping out he regulates his morbidity. The introductory paragraph closes with his argument that "almost all men in their degree, some time or other, cherish very nearly the same feelings towards the ocean with me," that is, although he has just revealed socially unacceptable feelings, most people feel similarly, and they too seek out the ocean for solace and as an escape from acting out dark impulses. Ishmael's tone is usually described by critics in terms of expansiveness and fluidity, but its final emphasis often falls—as it does here—on the social control of feeling.[9]

Ironically, in signing up on the *Pequod,* Ishmael will find himself on a coffin warehouse of sorts and bringing up the rear of a funeral, especially after the carpenter makes Queequeg a coffin-canoe, Ahab fulfills the Parsee's riddle with its imagery that finally turns both Moby Dick and the *Pequod* into hearses, and Ishmael falls off Ahab's whaleboat, thus bringing up the rear of the *Pequod*'s funeral. The opening chapters of the novel take us through a series of scenes in which death and grief are evoked; however, these morbid themes are struck by a wonderfully alive, exuberant, and joshing voice that is careful not to overtly exceed Victorian American codes of feeling.

Upon his entry to Nantucket at night, Ishmael observes that the candles in the town's windows are "like a candle moving about in a tomb" (18). After he stumbles into a black church, The Trap, he thinks he's descended into Tophet (19). A visit to the whaleman's chapel affords Ishmael an opportunity to muse expansively on grief and death: "Each silent worshiper seemed purposely sitting apart from the other, as if each silent grief were insular and incommunicable" (39). He notices that "so plainly did several women wear the countenance if not the trappings of some unceasing grief, that I feel sure that here before me were assembled those, in whose unhealing hearts the sight of those bleak tablets [marble epitaphs] sympathetically caused old wounds to bleed afresh" (40).[10] Ishmael puts the emphasis on the ceaseless side of female grief: the aspect of bereavement Ahab melodramatically and, as Ishmael's genteel side sees it, offensively develops. Ishmael speculates, "How it is we still refuse to be comforted for those who we nevertheless maintain are dwelling in unspeakable bliss; why all the living so strive to hush all the dead; wherefore but the rumor of a knocking in a tomb will terrify a whole city. All these things are not without their meanings" (41). With characteristic dark humor, however, Ishmael joshes us about his willingness to face the mortal threat of a sailor's life: "But somehow I grew merry again. Delightful inducements to embark, fine chance for promotion" (41).

Ishmael feels a sense of foreboding when he eyes the gallows-like pots suspended from the topmast on the doorway of the Try-Pots Inn. He then sums up the imagery of the opening of the novel: "It's ominous, thinks I. A Coffin my Inn-keeper upon landing in my first whaling port; tombstones staring at me in the whaleman's chapel; and here a gallows! and a pair of prodigious black pots too! Are these last throwing out oblique hints touching Tophet?" (64). Into this morbid pattern of imagery, Ishmael places his comical conversion experience with Queequeg, the fallen cannibal. Descended from a royal Kokovokoian family, Queequeg desires to visit the West "to learn among the Christians, the arts whereby to make his people still happier than they were" (57). Soon disillusioned by "the practices of whalemen," Queequeg becomes "fearful [that] Christianity, or rather Christians, had unfitted him for ascending the pure and undefiled throne" of his forefathers; "as soon as he felt himself baptized again," he will return to his island (57).

Through Queequeg's characterization, Melville offers a rewriting of his memory of his father that runs counter to his later attempt to exorcise the linking object role through Ahab.[11] Queequeg does not equal Allan Melvill in any simple allegorical equation. Rather there are details in the delineation of Queequeg that bear on Melville's grief work. In Ishmael's relationship with Queequeg, Melville fantasizes a resolution of his conflicted grief. This relationship is framed by two deathbed scenes: the first, in Peter Coffin's marriage bed, slyly hints at the deathbed connotation; the second is an overt deathbed scene, which inverts Allan Melvill's death and provides the stage prop that ultimately saves Ishmael: the coffin life-buoy.

Ishmael first hears about his prospective bedmate from his landlord, Peter Coffin, who "sky-larks" with Ishmael by telling him that the sailor he will be sleeping with is out selling heads. Ishmael concludes the sailor must be " 'stark mad, and I've no idea of sleeping with a madman' " (26). But, insofar as Allan Melvill peers through facets of Queequeg's characterization, this is precisely what Ishmael will do: climb into bed with a displaced and inverted version of a deathbed maniac. To place his protagonist in such a situation realizes Melville's deepest fear: the threat of the usurpation of his sense of self by the image of the damned deathbed maniac his mother's grief had deposited into his formative consciousness.

As Ishmael, "at the dead of night," peers out terror-stricken at the monstrous creature—"the devil himself"—in his bedroom, he first describes Queequeg as taking his "new beaver hat" out of his bag (29). The factory Allan left at his death as the only inheritance to his family manufactured beaver hats and bearskin coats.[12] Later, when Queequeg is locked in a trance during his Ramadan observance, Ishmael throws his own "heavy bearskin jacket" over his friend (80). Queequeg's oddest garment is the heavy mat he wears as a kind of poncho. When Queequeg enters the bedroom he tries on what seems to him this "door mat": it was "uncommonly shaggy and thick, and I thought it a little damp"; when he doffed it, he noted that it had "a hole or slit in the middle" (28, 27). This would seem to be sexual innuendo, preparing the scene for Ishmael's comical conversion into Queequeg's wife and their subsequent marriage. In his initial association with the mat/womb, Queequeg, as a kind of site on which Melville's grief for Allan is rewritten, evokes what the linking object theory posits: the maternal encompassment of the father's image. In name, "Quee/queg" hints at the presence of the queenly personality that later emerges in the margins of Ahab's characterization.

Like Allan Melvill, who took great pride in his noble Scottish ancestry, Queequeg, also descended from noble ancestry, possesses "a certain lofty bearing" (52). But unlike the deathbed maniac and bankrupt Melvill, Queequeg "looked like a man who had never cringed and never had a creditor" (52). Queequeg, like Melville's father, winds up on his deathbed after he "caught a terrible chill which lapsed into a fever" (395). But the fallen cannibal inverts the failed businessman's death. Rather than Melvill's deathbed shouts, Ishmael, applying the codes of the good Christian death, is exposed to the "higher and holier" thoughts that flit across Queequeg's face (396).[13] As Pip observes, " 'Queequeg dies game' " (398). Queequeg, though, suddenly recovers from his illness, and he explains that "at a critical moment, he had just recalled a little duty ashore, which he was leaving undone; and therefore had changed his mind about dying" (398). "In a word, it was Queequeg's conceit, that if a man made up his mind to live, mere sickness could not kill him" (398). The calmly dying, then dutiful Queequeg, in control of his mortality, rewrites Melville's memory of both his father's deathbed mania and Allan Melvill's seeming abandonment of his duties to his large family.

Ishmael's marriage night with Queequeg in the Spouter Inn complexly rewrites this memory. Ishmael recalls a childhood experience after awakening to find Queequeg's arm "thrown over me in the most loving and affectionate manner. You had almost thought I had been his wife" (32). In it his cruel stepmother, who was "all the time whipping me, or sending me to bed supperless," orders him to spend the day in bed after he tries to climb up the chimney (32). While in bed, Ishmael suddenly feels a "supernatural hand...placed in mine" (33). The feeling of Queequeg hugging him evokes the memory of the sensations Ishmael felt while holding the hand of the "unimaginable, silent form or phantom" (33). In the comparison between the two experiences Ishmael sets up, the details related to Melville's grief work that play through Queequeg's characterization would seem to identify the phantom with a figure equivalent in Ishmael's life to the role Allan Melvill played in Melville's. In Queequeg the alternately terrifying and loving unimaginable form comes to life.[14]

In a moment parallel to the supernatural hand episode, Ishmael undergoes his conversion experience with Queequeg. A storm howls outside their window and "the evening shades and phantoms [were] gathering around the casements" (53). Ishmael's feelings while in Queequeg's "bridegroom clasp" now resurface: "I began to be sensible of strange feelings" (53). His intimacy with Queequeg acts cathartically on his former anger and morbidity:

> I felt a melting in me. No more my splintered heart and maddened hand were turned against the wolfish world. This soothing savage had redeemed it. There he sat, his very indifference speaking a nature in which there lurked no civilized hypocrisies and bland deceits. Wild he was; a very sight of sights to see; yet I began to feel myself mysteriously drawn towards him . . . I'll try a pagan friend, thought I, since Christian kindness has proved but hollow courtesy. (53)

After they enjoy a "social smoke" of the tomahawk, Queequeg "pressed his forehead against mine, clasped me round the waist, and said that henceforth we were married; meaning, in his country's phrase, that we were bosom friends; he would gladly die for me, if need should be" (53). Presenting Ishmael with his "embalmed head," dividing his money with him, and sharing his worship of Yojo, the too-good-to-be-true Queequeg lies in bed with Ishmael in their "hearts' honeymoon...a cosy, loving pair" (54).

In the fantasy of emotional closeness he provides Ishmael, Queequeg heals his friend's "splintered heart and maddened hand" and reopens him to fraternal feeling. Queequeg offers a momentary resolution of the grief work Melville performs in the other dimensions of his text. Nevertheless, Ishmael's affection for Queequeg covertly performs an angry gesture: it must have been intended by Melville to outrage and tweak his more conventional contemporary readers. As one critic has noted, it was sleeping with a man of dark skin, not the honeymoon burlesque, that would have offended some of Melville's contemporaries.[15] While Ishmael is melting in Queequeg's arms, Melville was turning his own maddened hand against the civilized hypocrisies of his more straitlaced readers.

In Queequeg's soothing savage influence on him, Ishmael fantasizes the control of the wildness that must have terrified Melville in his father's deathbed mania. But Queequeg has not extinguished Ishmael's morbidity. After Queequeg remains locked in his room all day and into the evening, Ishmael panics and attempts to break down the door. The landlady, Mrs. Hussey, is convinced Queequeg has killed himself because he has retrieved the harpoon she forbade him to take to his room. Upon gaining entry into the room, Ishmael finds Queequeg "cool and self-collected," with Yojo perched atop his head, deep in his Ramadan meditation (80). Claiming tolerance for any religion that does not cause its practioners to "kill or insult any other person," Ishmael confesses that "when a man's religion becomes really frantic"—as it seems to him it has with Queequeg—"when it is a positive torment to him," then he takes that individual aside and remonstrates with him (81). This incident persuades practical-minded Mrs. Hussey to order a sign announcing: " 'no suicides permitted here, and no smoking in the parlor' " (79).[16]

Queequeg's dark side scarily emerges from behind Ishmael's fantasies only once. After making himself comfortable on a sleeping sailor's behind, Queequeg flourishes his tomahawk above the sailor's head: " 'Perry easy, kill-e; oh! perry easy!' " (92). Aside from this revelation of cultural difference (his cannibalism), Queequeg appears before us very much as Ishmael wishes us to see him. He is the noble savage, saving the impertinent sailor knocked overboard on the trip out to New Bedford, displaying his skills in obstetrics by rescuing Tashtego from the whale's "tun," and finally saving Ishmael through his mystically inscribed coffin life-buoy.

It is Queequeg who suggests transforming his coffin into a life-buoy (430). While fashioning the life-buoy, the carpenter observes, " 'It's like turning an old coat; going to bring the flesh on the other side now' "—another evocation of Allan's coat factory (430). If Queequeg's characterization in part seems to rewrite and attempts to resolve Melville's conflicted grief, then his legacy to Ishmael, the coffin life-buoy, suggests that through Queequeg, Ishmael transforms his own morbidity into something life-giving. Queequeg's coffin refigures Allan Melvill's death and is the image of the durability of grief, now providing a source of sustenance and creativity (the coffin surfaces from a "vital centre") to which Ishmael clings in the "closing vortex" 470).[17]

The Parlor-Theater of Mourning

> But ere we start, we must dig a deep hole, and bury all Blue Devils,
> there to abide til the Last Day.
> >—Melville to Hawthorne, July 22, 1851, *Melville's Letters*

> Neither hearse nor coffin can be thine.
> >—Parsee to Ahab in Melville's *Moby-Dick*

In her discussion of antebellum mourning practices, social historian Karen Halttunen notes that in the 1850s "the genteel performance enacted by . . . middle-class men and women were becoming more openly and self-consciously theatrical."[18] Halttunen also discusses a social practice popular in the 1850s: the parlor-theater. In this middle-class entertainment, a stage was created in genteel parlors, and productions were mounted in which the line between audience and player was often blurred, as members of the audience were drawn into the performance. Within his narrative, Ishmael sets before us a version of the parlor theatrical in the chapters, prefaced by stage directions, in which Ahab seems to take over the novel. As audience to Ahab's "self-consciously theatrical" grief, Ishmael also finds himself swept across the narrative proscenium and, alternately, drawn into an identification with, resistance to, and an attempt to transform Ahab's "deep helpless sadness" (203).

When Ishmael first queries one of the owners of the *Pequod* about Ahab, Peleg responds: " 'I don't know exactly what's the matter with him; but he keeps close inside the house; a sort of sick, and yet he don't look so. In fact, he ain't sick; but no, he isn't well either' " (76). After losing his leg to Moby Dick on his last voyage, Ahab has been " 'a kind of moody—desperate moody, and savage some-times' " (77). While on the homeward voyage, Ahab " 'was a little out of his mind for a spell; but it was the sharp shooting pains in his bleeding stump that brought that about' " (77). Instinctively emphathizing with him, Ishmael feels "a certain wild vagueness of painfulness concerning him [Ahab]": "a sympathy and a sorrow for him, but for I don't know what, unless it was the cruel loss of his leg" (77). But he also feels something he cannot put into words: "a strange awe of him," but "not exactly awe; I do not know what it was. But I felt it" (77). In his narrative of Ahab's mad quest, Ishmael never does quite decide how he feels about the sometimes Satanic, sometimes nobly grand, bereaved whale hunter.

Ishmael's equivocal response to Ahab echoes Melville's unresolved grief for the father who had also been "a little out of his mind for a spell." But in Ahab, Melville also displaces the rage of his own grief. Ahab's doubleness thus inheres in his reenactment of Allan's deathbed mania and his expression of the anger of Melville's conflicted grief, which has blurred its conflicts with those of his mother's grief. " 'They think me mad,' " Ahab muses, " 'but I'm demoniac, I am madness maddened!' " (147). Ahab, however, plays a larger role: "in his frantic morbidness he at last came to identify with him [Moby Dick] . . . all his intellectual and spiritual exasperations" (160). To Crazy Ahab, Moby Dick personifies all evil. Ahab "piled upon the whale's white hump the sum of all the general rage and hate felt by his whole race from Adam down" (160).

"The truest of all men was the Man of Sorrows," Ishmael speculates, "and Ecclesiastes is the fine hammered steel of woe": "But even Solomon, he says, 'the man that wandereth out of the way of understanding shall remain' (i.e. even while living) 'in the congregation of the dead' " (355). "There is a wisdom that is woe," Ishmael sermonizes, "but there is a woe that is madness" (355). And from this pietistic perspective, Ahab, in his woe, has simply gone too far: he has exceeded the bounds of genteel bereavement.

But in his heightened, transgressive sense of bereavement, Ahab provides deep insight into the experience of mourning. After his ivory leg "all but pierced his groin" in a fall, Ahab connects the pain of his wound to Moby Dick. "All miserable events do naturally beget their like," he muses, "since both the ancestry and posterity of Grief go further than the ancestry and posterity of Joy"; "some guilty mortal miseries shall still fertilely beget to themselves an eternally progressive progeny of griefs beyond the grave" (385). To the degree he represents his biblical namesake, Ahab brings with him into Melville's fictive world the Old Testament's sense of the wisdom in woe, undiluted by the Victorian American fear of intense feeling Ishmael at times adopts. In the Elizabethan rhetoric he inhabits, Ahab finds that "all heart-woes [have] a mystic significance, and, in some men, an arch-angelic grandeur" (386). As Richard Brodhead points out, Melville imagines each of his characters in the fictional mode or genre most appropriate to them. Ahab himself admits as much: " 'Cursed be that mortal inter-indebtedness which will not do away with ledgers. I would be free as air; and I'm down in the whole world's books [in a double sense]' " (392).[19]

Ahab would seem himself the offspring of a bereavement that has led to madness: he is the son of a " 'crazy, widowed mother, who died when he was only a twelvemonth old' " (77).[20] Voicing the conventional view of Melville's culture toward excessive grief, Ishmael identifies Ahab as a monomaniac. According to the ideological codes that forbid a public expression of intense bereavement, Ahab must be defined as crazy. Ahab endeavors to appear "but naturally grieved" after he returns from the voyage on which Moby Dick dismembered him, but to do so means that he must conceal "the mad secret of his unabated rage bolted up and keyed in him" (161, 162). Ashore, Ahab must pose as the genteel mourner.

Through Ishmael's characterization of Ahab, Melville puts into question his culture's definitions of madness and natural grief. In his notes on the flyleaf of a volume of Shakespeare, Melville jotted down, "madness is undefinable."[21] Ahab's madness could be the required cultural labeling for the mourner who attempts to express the full depth of his bereavement, especially the anger, which Victorian Americans attempted both to regulate and to deny healthful public symbolization. Ahab is subversive in that he would openly and fully grieve. Melville angrily attacks his culture's rules for feeling by staging within literary stereotypes, and so deliberately distorting into melodramatic expression, Ahab's attempt at unabashed grief. These range from the biblical Ahab to the Elizabethan, romantic, and gothic heroes and villains Ahab plays off of. Popular culture genres as well give shape to his presentation. "With slouched hat," like a figure out of a dime novel or a Brockden Brown romance, "Ahab lurchingly paced the planks" (114). Ahab is so gloomy, melancholy, and dark that he could only be a composite—assembled from the cultural forms whose implicit ideological encodings relegate intense expression of negative feelings to unbelievably melodramatic figures.

Melville distorts Ahab's expression of bereavement to implicitly critique the cultural codes that prohibit cathartic expression of conflicted grief. In "The Candles," Ahab voices his grief in Elizabethan and gothic rhetoric that turns it into something ornately unreal. Standing before the corpusants that flame in the yard-arms "like gigantic wax tapers before an altar"—a kind of Gothic stage prop—Ahab seems to be speaking in front of the tapers that sometimes surrounded a corpse in Melville's time. The tapers, though, are the corpse in this case, as Ahab takes as his own the Parsee's worship of fire. Speaking as a tragic Elizabethan on the stage, Ahab claims, " 'In the midst of the personified impersonal [i.e., the fire], a personality stands here. Though but a point at best; . . . yet while I earthly live, the queenly personality lives in me, and feels her royal rights. . . . Oh, thou foundling fire . . . thou too hast thy incommunicable riddle, thy unparticipated grief. Here again with haughty agony, I read my sire' " (417). The importation of an alien diction not only threatens to empty his speech of feeling, but it nearly parodies the palpable unparticipated grief that underlies his mad quest. On the margins of this inauthentic language, Melville hints at the queenly personality of his mother that speaks through the social text of Ahab's enraged bereavement.[22]

Queen Nature, " 'thou dark Hindoo half of nature . . . thou art an infidel, thou queen,' " Ahab elsewhere says of her, appears in more homely guise as the "the step-mother world" that seems to "joyously sob" over Ahab in "The Symphony" (409, 426–27, 443).[23] With violins at full pitch, Melville stages Ahab's grief here in the genre of the sentimental novel. This chapter opens with the air and the sea playing conventional gender roles in a performance that parodies sentimental diction. "The pensive air was transparently pure and soft, with a woman's look" and the sea appears "robust and man-like" (442). The "feminine air" has "gentle thoughts," while the "masculine sea" possesses "strong, troubled, murderous thinkings" (442). With "the sun . . . giving this gentle air to this bold and rolling sea; even as bride to groom," "the poor bride gave her bosom away" with "fond, throbbing trust" and "loving alarms" (442).

Into this saccharine scene, Melville inserts Ahab, who "dropped a tear into the sea" (443). Observing Ahab's betrayal of emotion, the son-like chief mate, Starbuck, "seemed to hear in his own true heart the measureless sobbing that stole out of the centre of the serenity around" (443). Overcome by his own narration of his melancholy history to Starbuck, Ahab pauses to ask him to " 'brush this old hair aside; it blinds me, that I seem to weep' " (444). In his appeal to Ahab's domestic side to turn him away from his quest, Starbuck delivers a speech straight out of sentimental fiction: " ''Tis my Mary, my Mary herself! She promised that my boy, every morning, should be carried to the hill to catch the first glimpse of his father's sail! . . . See! see! the boy's face from the window! the boy's hand on the hill!' " (444). Like the representations of mourners in the popular culture, Ahab's glance was "averted" (444).[24] Ahab concludes this chapter by retreating into the diction of melodrama. In the voice of the Byronic hero he muses: " 'Is it I, God, or who, that lifts this arm? . . . Where do murderers go, man! Who's to doom, when the judge himself is dragged to the bar?'" (445). Like a lurid gothic character, Ahab finally "blanched to a corpse's hue with despair" (445).

Ultimately, Ishmael fails in his efforts to control Ahab's excessive grief by keeping it within the bounds of the melodramatic generic languages through which he imagines Ahab. Ahab's terrifying impact on Ishmael and on the other principals of the narrative disrupts and unsettles the novel and overrides Ishmael's gamesome manipulation of literary genres. Ishmael feels "foreboding shivers" when he catches his first glimpse of Ahab's "overbearing grimness" (109, 110). The pugnacious mate Stubb flees from the "overbearing terrors" in Ahab's "aspect" (113). When Starbuck fantasizes making Ahab his prisoner, he cannot act against him because "'he would be more hideous than a caged tiger, then. I could not endure the sight; could not possibly fly his howlings'" (422).

In his first speech Ahab observes that going to his cabin "'feels like going down into one's tomb'": "'my grave-dug berth'" (112). Ahab terrifies, on the one hand, because he brings out into the open Melville's fear of his internalization of the image of his father as deathbed maniac and as possibly damned according to his mother's Calvinism. But just as frightening is the uninhibited rage Ahab vents—an overwhelming anger that evokes a child's distorted perception of the rage and conflicts of Maria Melville's grief, as it influenced Melville's own adolescent grieving. What makes this all the more difficult for Melville to come to terms with is the other side of his mother's image of his father: that of the beloved, idealized figure. Ahab first stands before the crew as a "moody stricken" figure "with a crucifixion in his face; in all the nameless regal overbearing dignity of some mighty woe" (111). To her grandchildren Melville's mother seemed "stern" and of a "dignified stateliness." It would seem that Ahab's portrayal blurs Melville's recollection of the regal overbearing dignity of his moody stricken mother's grief with his fears of his father's deathbed mania and his need to keep alive the noble image of his father.[25]

The fears Ahab elicits seem directly related to Melville's disturbing memory of his father's deathbed mania. "Of all mortals," Ishmael says of Queequeg on his deathbed, "some dying men are the most tyrannical" (397). Starbuck directly and intimately interacts with Ahab. Of the impact Ahab makes on Starbuck, Ishmael observes: "That immaculate manliness we feel within ourselves . . . bleeds with keenest anguish at the undraped spectacle of a valor-ruined man" (104). Starbuck's bravery "cannot withstand those more terrific, because more spiritual terrors, which sometimes menace you from the concentrating brow of an enraged and mighty man" (104). By the end of the quest, "there lurked a something in the old man's eyes, which it was hardly sufferable for feeble souls to see" (437).[26]

The Endless End: A Fluid Epitaph

Death is only a launching into the region of the strange Untried; it is but the first salutation to the possibilities of the immense Remote, the Wild, the Watery, the Unshored.   —Herman Melville, *Moby-Dick*

The final chapters of the novel present several perspectives on bereavement. In the "shameful story" of the blacksmith Perth's "wretched fate," Ishmael offers a little moral tale—the kind that might have been found in a pietistic antebellum magazine—about the "fifth act of the grief" of an alcoholic's "life's drama" (401).[27] Our first image of Perth evokes Melville's memory of his father's fatal winter exposure. On "one bitter winter's midnight," Perth, fearing that he may lose his feet to frostbite, seeks shelter in a barn (401). Once a prosperous blacksmith with a wife and children, Perth drinks his way into the loss of his home and family and becomes "a vagabond in crape; his every woe unreverenced" (402). Had Perth died immediately after his ruin, Ishmael points out, his wife might have had a fashionable "delicious grief" (401). Instead, the sea beckons "alluringly" to Perth's "death-longing eyes": " 'Here is another life without the guilt of intermediate death . . . Come hither! put up *thy* gravestone, too, within the churchyard' " (402).

Ahab measures his own condition against Perth's: " 'I am impatient of all misery in others that is not mad . . . How can'st thou endure without being mad?' " (403) More to Ahab's liking is Pip's bereaved lunacy, with its evocation of "heaven's sense" (347). Pip falls out of Stubb's whaleboat during the hunt and the latter by abandoning Pip "indirectly hinted, that though man loves his fellow, yet man is a money-making animal" (346). Seeing in Pip's madness a kind of " 'holiness,' " Ahab adopts him and takes him to live in his cabin (427). Railing at the " 'frozen heavens' "—" 'Ye did beget this luckless child, and have abandoned him' "—Ahab sentimentally confesses the impact of Pip's suffering on him, " 'Thou touchest my inmost centre, boy; thou art tied to me by cords woven of heart-strings' " (428). With his hand in Ahab's, Pip observes, " 'had Pip but felt so kind a thing as this, perhaps he had ne'er been lost!' " (428).

In Ahab's relationship with Pip, Melville toys with the anger of his own memory of being abandoned by his father. Finally, Ahab also abandons Pip because he finds him " 'too curing to my malady' " (436). Pip, though, offers himself to Ahab as a surrogate limb: " 'do ye but use poor me for your one lost leg; . . . I ask no more, so I remain a part of ye' " (436). Insofar as Ahab's dismemberment symbolizes his bereavement, Pip, evoking here Melville's childhood self abandoned by his father, attempts to undo the loss by making Ahab whole again. But Pip merged with Ahab would too explosively reconnect Melville's unresolved feeling of abandonment (Pip) to his displaced bereaved rage (Ahab).[28]

Moby Dick himself provides another version of bereavement. As "a long sleek on the sea," the whale seems to "shed off enticings" (445, 447). "Soft metallic-like marks as of some swift tide-rip, at the mouth of a deep and rapid stream" cover him (445). When Moby Dick breaches the surface, Ishmael notices his "scrolled jaw" (448). Ishmael explains that a whale's submerged course can be discerned by the canny whale hunter who can decipher "the proverbial evanescence of a thing writ in water, a wake" (453). Moby Dick thus seems characterized as a kind of fluid writing, but the imagery of the novel's conclusion also associates him with bereavement—the play on wake of the preceding quote. The whale's pyramidical white hump alludes to the Egyptian burial site, and, as noted earlier, a thing writ in water alludes to Keats's gravestone epitaph (159). When "this tremendous apparition" menaces a whale boat his "glittering mouth yawned beneath the boat like an open-doored marble tomb" (448). After the Parsee becomes entangled in his whale line and pinned to Moby Dick, the whale becomes the first hearse of the Parsee's prophecy (464).

For Ishmael, Moby Dick's whiteness conjures up elusive ambiguity; "the most meaningful symbol of spiritual things" but also "the intensifying agent in things the most appalling to mankind" (169). And the whale, as an object of perception, resists our attempts at representation. Confessing his inability to read the whale's brow, Ishmael exclaims, "I put that brow before you. Read it if you can" (293). However, our attempts to do so are undercut by Ishmael's claim that "in gazing at such scenes, it is all and all what mood you are in" (317). The whale, according to Ishmael, "must remain unpainted to the last" (228).

Moby Dick's association with bereavement, then, can only be a result of Ahab's obvious projections onto him, of the covert need to grieve Melville expresses through Ishmael—or, in a larger sense, of the work of mourning Melville performs in the novel. When the *Rachel,* searching for Captain Gardiner's lost twelve-year-old son, enters the novel's last chapters, Melville's grief for the father he lost at twelve rises closer to the surface (435). Earlier, the *Pequod*'s crew had heard in the night "a cry so plaintively wild and unearthly—like half-articulated wailings of the ghosts of all Herod's murdered Innocents" (428). Ahab, perhaps realizing these were men lost at sea, claimed they were the cries of bereaved seals; the old Manx sailor later says it was indeed the men on Gardiner's lost boat whose cries were heard (429). Gardiner pleads with Ahab, a fellow Nantucketeer, to help in the search for the boy, but the *Rachel* has also brought news of having done combat with Moby Dick only " 'yesterday,' " and Ahab obsessively flies off after his prey (434).[29]

As if in contrast to a father's bereaved search for his lost twelve-year-old—an inverted version of twelve-year-old Melville's grief—Ishmael portrays Ahab as acting out his bereaved rage destructively. After Moby Dick wrecks the *Pequod,* Ahab exclaims as he flings his harpoon, " 'Oh, now I feel my topmost greatness lies in my topmost grief' " (468). In his very attempt to fully possess and feel his grief, Ahab strangles himself on the whale-line that "ran foul" (468). And as researchers of mourning have observed, the separation pain of grief is often experienced as a choking sensation. In what looks like a fatal expression of grief, the conventional side of Ishmael symbolizes the consequences—in terms of the dominant social codes of Melville's culture—of allowing one's bereavement a full expression.[30]

The alternative to cathartic grief can be glimpsed in Ishmael's rescue by that stock biblical figure of bereavement, Rachel, genteelly "weeping for her children" (436).[31] The "devious cruising" *Rachel* discovers Ishmael—now viewed as a standard character in the sentimental novel, "another orphan"—in "her retracing search after her missing children" (470). The novel's conclusion thus displaces the marginalized appearance of Maria Melville's powerful grief in Ahab's monomania with a conventional figure used by Melville's culture to burden women with the public, but restrained, symbolization of grief. However, the bereaved rage that Ishmael refuses to allow Ahab to authenticate in public discourse does not remain buried beneath "the great shroud of the sea" for long (469). In *Pierre*, the ambiguities of Melville's unresolved grief more powerfully and disruptively breach the surface of his imagination.

NOTES

[1] Melville cites the "Deep and Secret grief" quote from Bacon in notes, probably made in the summer of 1849, on the flyleaf of vol. 7 of his edition of Shakespeare, which contained *Lear, Othello,* and *Hamlet.* Charles Olson reproduces only part of these notes (*Call Me Ishmael* [San Francisco: City Lights Books, 1947], 39, 52). For the Bacon quote see Luther Mansfield and Howard P. Vincent, eds., *Moby-Dick,* (New York: Hendricks House, 1952), 643–44. In their invaluable notes, they also cite De Quincey, whom Melville read shortly before he began *Moby-Dick,* on the "mysterious handwritings of grief" in the brain, which "are not dead, but sleeping. . . . In some potent convulsion of the system, all wheels back into its earliest elemental stage" (704). On the Harvard study, see Ira Glick et al., *The First Year of Bereavement* (New York: John Wiley and Sons, 1974), chap. 13, 261–82, esp. 263–65, 271.

[2] On antebellum reviewers' detestation of what they called "morbidity," see Nina Baym, *Novels, Readers, and Reviewers: Responses to Fiction in Antebellum America* (Ithaca: Cornell University Press, 1984), 142. For instance, *House of Seven Gables* was found "morbid" by one reviewer (Baym, *Novels, Readers, and Reviewers,* 177). Melville seems to be playing on this popular prejudice when he identifies Ahab as poisoned by "'a half-wilful overruling morbidness at the bottom of his nature'" (*Moby-Dick,* eds. Harrison Hayford and Hershel Parker [New York: Norton, 1967], 111; hereafter cited in the text). Melville's crony, Evert Duyckinck, mockingly objects to *Moby-Dick*'s "association of whaling and lamentation," which seemed to him "why blubber is popularly associated with tears." *Southern Quarterly Review* (Jan. 1852) calls Ahab "a monstrous bore"; and the *London Morning Advertiser* (Oct. 24, 1851) complains of Ahab's madness: "'Somewhat too much of this!'" (in Mansfield and Vincent, eds., *Moby-Dick,* xvii, xx; and Watson G. Branch, *Melville: The Critical Heritage* [London: Routledge and Kegan Paul, 1974], 252).

For an exploration of monomania in Melville's culture, see Henry Nash Smith, *Democracy and the Novel* (New York: Oxford University Press, 1978), chap. 3, 35–55; and Vieda Skultans, *Madness and Morals: Ideas on Insanity in the Nineteenth Century* (London: Routledge and Kegan, Paul, 1975).

See Mansfield and Vincent's introduction for a good survey of attitudes of early twentieth-century critics to Ahab. After the 1920s, when critics identified Ahab with Melville, the tendency was to identify Ahab with the various bogeymen of the critic's political moment. However, such critics as William Ellery Sedgwick (1944) could speak of "Ahab's noble madness that sprang from an excess of humanity" (Mansfield and Vincent, eds., *Moby-Dick,* xxvii).

[3] Mansfield and Vincent note that the aspect of the biblical Ahab's story which most interested Melville's contemporaries was Ahab's usurpation of Naboth's paternal inheritance, his vineyard (*Moby-Dick,* n. to 637). Melville might have been unconsciously drawn to Ahab in part by the way this appropriation mirrored how his mother's bereaved image of his father displaced his own sense of paternal identification and inheritance. For the way Ahab's story was used in antebellum political rhetoric, see Michael Paul Rogin, *Subversive Genealogy: The Politics and Art of Herman Melville* (New York: Knopf, 1983), chap. 4, 102–54. Rogin gives a fine precis of the earlier political readings and he goes beyond them by transforming the political allegories of these critics into a sense for how *Moby-Dick*'s language is "deeply enmeshed in the crisis of 1850," i.e., the slavery issue in the U.S. and the failed revolutions abroad (*Subversive Genealogy,* 107). Rogin draws attention especially to how "Melville's family connections to Indian dispossession and slavery" left their mark on his art (*Subversive Genealogy,* 107, 143). The scholarship Rogin summarizes includes William T. Weathers, "*Moby-Dick* and the Nineteenth-Century Scene," *Texas Studies in Literature and Language* 1 (Winter 1960): 477–501; Charles H. Foster, "Something in Emblems: A Reinterpretation of *Moby-Dick,*" *The New England Quarterly* 34 (Mar.

1961): 3–35; and Alan Heimert, "*Moby-Dick* and American Political Symbolism," *American Quarterly* 16 (Apr. 1963): 498–534.

In the source that Mansfield and Vincent suggest for Fedallah—*1001 Days, Persian Tales*—a dervish, who possesses the power of "'reanimating a dead body, by flinging my own Soul into it,'" revives a dead nightingale to assuage a queen's grief (*Moby-Dick*, 732). For a different view of Ahab's claim to a "queenly personality," see Robert Zoellner: "This is superb rhetoric, but it is false fact. Ahab has willfully destroyed his 'personality,' and obliterated its 'queenly' freedom" (*The Salt-Sea Mastodon: A Reading of* Moby-Dick [Berkeley: University of California Press, 1973], 100).

T. Walker Herbert argues that in his grief for his father Melville simultaneously absolved him and identified with his mother's probable damnation of him from her Dutch Reformed perspective. Allan's death shattered a tenuous balance in which Melville had been able to harmonize his parents' respective Unitarian and Dutch Reformed views. See Chap. 1 for my reading of Maria's idiosyncratic Calvinism, one more mixed with genteel codes than Herbert implies (Moby-Dick *and Calvinism: A World Dismantled* [New Brunswick, N.J.: Rutgers University Press, 1977], chap. 3, 57–68, esp. 60–61).

As noted in Chapter 1, given that Allan Melvill appeared in her life shortly after her heroic father, General Peter Gansevoort, died, Maria may have turned Allan into a living linking object to her father. If so, this may illuminate Ishmael's need to imbue Ahab with excessive heroic qualities, at the same time that Ahab's damnation suggests that he is being viewed from Maria's Dutch Reformed perspective.

Nathalia Wright points out that the biblical Ahab is already a figure of doubleness: he is a composite of two sources, one of which found him able and the other viewed him as a dangerous innovator (*Melville's Use of the Bible* [Durham, N.C.: Duke University Press, 1949], 62).

[4] Putting the stress on the cultural context of what he finds to be Melville's religious crisis, Herbert argues that by allowing "spiritual dislocations" and their attendant "feverish excitement" to surface, Melville "became convinced that his true creativeness lay in braving this tumult, winning the articulation of a 'vital truth,' in contention with apparent madness." Herbert links Ahab to Allan insofar as both could be described as liberal heretics as depicted by Calvinist rhetoric (Moby-Dick *and Calvinism*, 18, 40).

Richard Chase reads Ahab as "both father and son" (cited in Mansfield and Vincent, eds., *Moby-Dick*, xxix). Newton Arvin characterizes Moby Dick as an "archetypal Parent . . . the mother also, so far as she becomes a substitute for the father." Moby Dick also evokes "the violently contradictory emotions that prevail between parent and child" (*Herman Melville* [New York: William Sloane, 1950], 173). Edwin Haviland Miller calls *Moby-Dick* "a study of the rivalry of the 'son' (Ishmael) with the father (Ahab)"; and he finds that "Ahab fathers Ishmael," in as much as the latter writes the former's story (*Herman Melville: A Biography* [New York: Braziller, 1975], 182, 210).

[5] See Francis Parkman, "Occasions and Remedy of Excessive Grief," in *An Offering of Sympathy to the Afflicted . . .*, 3d ed. (Boston: James Monroe & Co., 1842), 109–17. Baym argues that antebellum reviewers viewed the novel as "an agent of social control" (*Novels, Readers, and Reviewers*, 170). One contemporary reviewer, conflating Ishmael and Melville, describes the novel's narrator as performing with "the ease and polish of a finished gentleman" (*Philadelphia American Saturday Courier* [Nov. 22, 1851], cited in Hershel Parker and Harrison Hayford, eds., *Moby-Dick as Doubloon: Essays and Extracts 1851–1970* [New York: Norton, 1970], 52).

Critics rarely review Ishmael negatively. Zoellner, though, notes that the verbal resolutions which satisfy Ishmael do not satisfy Melville (*Salt-Sea Mastodon*, 216). Deploying Sacvan Bercovitch on the jeremiad, James Duban subtly argues that "the exclusive tendencies of the covenant psychology undergirding all jeremiads lead Ishmael to betray the abolitionist egalitarianisms he purports to champion." "Ishmael . . . is the American child who trips over his own conceptual shoestrings while seeking to flee the brutality of his nation's past" (*Melville's Major Fiction: Politics, Theology, and Imagination* [DeKalb: Northern Illinois University Press, 1983], 108, 137).

[6] Cited in David Perkins, ed., *English Romantic Writers* (New York: Harcourt Brace Jovanovich, 1967), 1115. See Mansfield and Vincent, eds., *Moby-Dick*, 827. They also suggest that the biblical Moab, a possible source for *Moby*, in Hebrew means "seed of the father," while *Ahab* in Hebrew means "the brother of the father," or "uncle or father of the brother" (*Moby-Dick*, 695, 637). This last etymology bears on Edward Edinger's suggestion that Maria did not commit herself emotionally to her husband but remained attached to her family, esp. her brother: "making the psychic atmosphere of Melville's family that of a matriarchy in which the mother is the central figure and the masculine authority resides not with the father but with the maternal uncle" (*Melville's* Moby-Dick: *A Jungian Commentary: An American Nekyia* [New York: New Directions, 1975], 7–8). In his letters, Allan addresses Peter Gansevoort as brother.

[7] Sophia Hawthorne cited in Eleanor Melville Metcalf, *Herman Melville: Cycle and Epicycle* (Cambridge: Harvard University Press, 1953), 106.

[8] The important difference between Ahab and the bereaved parent is that Ahab is acting consciously and willfully. My point is that the effect is the same: the transference of emotion.

[9] A desire to reunite with the deceased underlies the suicidal urges of some victims of pathological mourning (see John Bowlby, *Loss: Sadness and Depression* [New York: Basic Books, 1980], 301–06). Significantly, Ishmael next describes the Manhattanite water-gazers: the harbor they gravitate toward must have been strongly associated in Melville's memory with his father's fall, because Allan Melvill's import firm was in lower Manhattan. Zoellner observes that "Ishmael's off-hand tone is a screen deliberately thrown up to distract us from certain terrible urgencies of his being" (*Salt-Sea Mastodon*, 119).

[10] Ann Douglas notes that in *Moby-Dick* women are "the mourners and losers: they have no other role" (*The Feminization of American Culture* [New York: Knopf, 1977], 367).

[11] Zoellner calls Queequeg "the very figure and image of death." In befriending Queequeg, Ishmael gets on friendly terms with death. But, "as a figure of death, he is a source of life" because the coffin which saves Ishmael "is really Queequeg transmogrified" (*Salt-Sea Mastodon*, 217, 220, 234).

[12] The scary night spent alone with Queequeg may gesture towards Melville's memory of spending a night alone with his father at the Courtland Street dock after the rest of the family removed to Albany in the wake of Allan's bankruptcy (William H. Gilman, *Melville's Early Life and* Redburn [New York: New York University Press, 1951], 42). Rogin also argues that Melville's coast imagery evokes Allan Melvill (*Subversive Genealogy*, passim).

[13] Of Queequeg's deathbed scene, James Grove argues: "Queequeg facing death seems to mock the sentimental literature's depictions of death," because it is a cannibal, not a Christian, who serenely faces death. While noting that Ishmael narrates sentimentally here, Grove maintains that Queequeg's failure to die "trivializes" the sentimental conventions of the deathbed scene. However, Grove admits that Melville "might have wanted the scene to be read straight" ("Melville's Vision of Death in *Moby-Dick*: Stepping Away from the 'Snug Sofa,' " *New England Quarterly* 52 (June 1979): 185, 186, 187).

[14] If Queequeg's characterization gestures towards Allan Melvill, then Ishmael, as partially shaped by Maria Melville's bereavement, is his wife. John Seelye suggests that the "supernatural hand" belongs to Ishmael's dead mother (*Melville: The Ironic Diagram* [Evanston, Ill.: Northwestern University Press, 1970], 61). Melville may here register his sense of losing Maria to her grief for Allan. Further, after Allan's death she may have seemed changed to him, like a stepmother.

[15] See Priscilla Zirker, "Evidence of the Slavery Dilemma in *White-Jacket*," *American Quarterly* 18 (Fall 1966): 480.

[16] The survival of Ishmael's morbidity may perhaps best be seen in chap. 94, "A Squeeze of the Hand," in which Ishmael needs to squeeze the sperm to feel "divinely free from all ill-will, or petulance, or malice" (348). In chap. 69, "The Funeral," Ishmael's anger surfaces as he sardonically observes of the whale carcass set adrift: "There's a most doleful and most mocking funeral! The sea-vultures all in pious mourning . . . In life but few of them would have helped the whale, I ween, if peradventure he had needed it" (262). Yojo's Ramadan trance seems to invert the circumstances of Allan Melvill's death, in which sleeplessness led to mania, not to Queequeg's Ramadan meditation.

[17] Grove argues that the sinking of the *Pequod* inverts the deathbed scene of "consolation-graveyard" literature ("Melville's Vision of Death," 185).

[18] Karen Halttunen, *Confidence Men and Painted Women: A Study of Middle-Class Culture in America, 1830–1870* (New Haven: Yale University Press, 1982), 172.

[19] Mansfield and Vincent cite Byron and Carlyle as Melville's sources for the notion of grief as a conduit to wisdom (*Moby-Dick*, 800). Given that Hawthorne was writing *The House of the Seven Gables*, with its morbid interest in questions of social inheritance, while Melville was writing *Moby-Dick*, one imagines that Ahab's ideas about the inheritance of grief could have formed part of the two authors' discussions. Richard Brodhead, *Hawthorne, Melville, and the Novel* (Chicago: University of Chicago Press, 1973), 17.

[20] This may be another allusion to Melville's sense of his mother's transformation by the loss of Allan.

[21] Olson, *Call Me Ishmael*, 54. Also see Melville on Charles Fenno Hoffman's madness: "in all of us lodges the same fuel to light the same fire. And he who has never felt, momentarily, what madness is has but a mouthful of brains" (letter to Evert A. Duyckinck, April 5, 1849, *Melville's Letters*, eds. Merrell Davis and William H. Gilman [New York: Yale University Press, 1960], 83).

[22] Because it was Fanny Kemble's Shakespearean readings, especially of Lady Macbeth, in Boston on Feb. 1849 that re-ignited Melville's interest in Shakespeare, while writing *Moby-Dick* he may have associated the bard with a female presence (Leon Howard, *Herman Melville: A Biography* [Berkeley: University of

California Press, 1951], 165; and his "Melville's Struggle with the Angel," *Modern Language Quarterly* 1 [June 1940]: 201).

[23] Thomas Vargish believes that this imagery derives from the Gnostic myth of the fallen mother ("Gnostic Mythos in *Moby-Dick*," *PMLA* 81 [1966]: 272–77).

[24] Halttunen, *Confidence Men and Painted Women*, 132.

[25] An important link between Ahab's mania and Allan's is that while Allan's was brought on by overwork and sleeplessness, Ahab, in the last part of the novel, becomes a sleepless figure, obsessively driven in his quest for revenge. Even early in the novel Ishmael speaks of "the sleeplessness of his [Ahab's] vow" (173).

The characterization of Maria Melville is from Amy Puett, "Melville's Wife: A Study of Elizabeth Shaw Melville," Ph.D. diss., Northwestern University, 1969, 101. Mrs. Glendinning in *Pierre*, believed to be in part modeled on Maria Melville, is also described as "queenly" ("Introduction," in Henry Murray, ed., *Pierre* [New York: Hendricks House, 1949], xli–xlii).

[26] Ishmael evinces one way of managing the anxieties Ahab provokes when he genially observes, "we are all somehow dreadfully cracked about the head, and sadly need mending" (78). "Here goes for a cool, collected dive at death and destruction," he elsewhere blithely suggests (197).

Ishmael also presents two other maniacs: Elijah and Gabriel. Elijah is a "crazy man" who accosts Ishmael in New Bedford and offers him cryptic warnings against shipping out with Ahab (88). Ishmael is "riveted with the insane earnestness of his manner"; later, "the ragged Elijah's diabolical incoherence uninvitedly [were] recurring to me, with a subtle energy I could not have before conceived of" (86, 109). Of Gabriel, Ishmael observes that in his "sleepless, excited imagination [were] all the preternatural terrors of real delirium" (266). Starbuck and Melville share at least one thing in common: both had lost a father and a brother (104).

[27] For evidence that Melville read a pietistic children's magazine, see Robert Sattlemeyer and James Barbour, "A Possible Source and Model for the Story of China Aster in Melville's *The Confidence-Man*," *American Literature* 48 (January 1977): 577–83. The reviewer for the *Spectator* (Oct. 1851) commented on the "magazine article writing" in *Moby-Dick*. Perth's story may also parody Longfellow's "The Village Blacksmith"; and Perth's "virtuous elder brother" possibly alludes to Gansevoort (Mansfield and Vincent, eds., *Moby-Dick*, xx, 815, 816).

[28] Sharon Cameron observes that when Ahab orders Pip below this indicates a "refusal to allow grief and rage to face each other when they will not reduce to an identity" (*The Corporeal Self: Allegories of the Body in Melville and Hawthorne* [Baltimore: Johns Hopkins University Press, 1981], 19).

[29] The coat factory imagery once more appears when Stubb says of the bereaved Gardiner that he looks as though " 'some one in that missing boat wore off . . . [his] best coat" (434). In a possible source for the seals—Captain James Colnett's *A Voyage to the South Atlantic*—their cries are compared to the "shrieks and lamentations so like those produced by the female voice" (Mansfield and Vincent, eds., *Moby-Dick*, 824).

[30] Mansfield and Vincent claim Ahab's "topmost grief" echoes Carlyle's "Man's Unhappiness . . . comes of his greatness" (*Moby-Dick*, 828). Beverly Raphael, *The Anatomy of Bereavement* (New York: Basic Books, 1983).

[31] Melville may also be parodying his culture's theatrical sense of grief by alluding to the actress Rachel, well-known for her emotional performances. While in Paris, Melville attempted to see "Madame Rachel" (Eleanor Melville Metcalf, ed., *Melville's Journal of a Visit to London and the Continent, 1849–1850* [Cambridge: Harvard University Press, 1948], 57).

For the biblical Rachel see Jer. 31:15. A contemporary poem, R. S. Chilton's "The Burial at Marshfield," contains the lines: "Ay, well may'st thou mourn, like a RACHEL, today, / Dear Goddess of Freedom, and weep by his grave" (*The Knickerbocker Gallery* [New York: Samuel Hueston, 1854], 373).

Edward J. Ahearn

A MUTUAL, JOINT-STOCK WORLD

Ｈow avoid this oppressive economic order, which, despite religious, philosophical, suprahistorical, and exotic impulses discussed earlier, intrudes throughout? Ishmael and Ahab attempt it by mobilizing what are essentially libidinal energies, though in different ways that are perhaps in keeping with the associations of their biblical names: sexual transgression, racial crossing, religious blasphemy, and infidelity. Nonetheless the two share some qualities, and we must keep them both in mind in considering the erotic as an attempted escape from enslavement to the economic.

The sexual dimension of Ishmael's moments of happiness with others is unmistakable, in the analogy of Queequeg sitting up "stiff as a pike-staff" (120)[1] , as in Ishmael's remarks about "how elastic our stiff prejudices grow when love once comes to bend them" when they are in bed again (149). It is indeed not only a question of sex but also of love, as in the "melting" with Queequeg already discussed and in the mutual masturbatory motif of "A Squeeze of the Hand" (526–27), where Ishmael says that his fingers "serpentize and spiralize" in the "inexpressible sperm," until he confuses the hands of others with his own. The blurring of the separate self inaugurated in "A Bosom Friend" and which leads to a warning in "The Mast-Head" here comes to fruition, reminding us of Deleuze and Guattari's argument about how the socioeconomic order inhibits the various "flows" of bodily and psychic elements. Indeed the melting and flowing lead to a sentimental version of Irigaray's utopian relations among humans. Sensing himself "divinely free" of anger, ill will, petulance, and malice, rejecting acerbities, ill humor, and envy, Ishmael experiences "a strange sort of insanity" and addresses his "dear fellow beings": "Come; let us squeeze hands all around; nay, let us all squeeze ourselves into each other; let us squeeze ourselves universally into the very milk and sperm of kindness." Here the sexual content of the experience allows the biblical motif's transformation but also realization, in the mingling of no longer atomized individuals.

From *Marx and Modern Fiction* (New Haven: University Press, 1989), pp. 180–90.

Ishmael immediately opposes this experience to the normal social world: love, family, home, work, pleasure, national identity—"the wife, the heart, the bed, the table, the saddle, the fire-side, the country." Wife and marriage are part of these "attainable" but "lower" felicities; hence, in keeping with the length of the voyage, the heterosexual and the familial are virtually invisible. Ishmael's praise of the women of New Bedford and Salem is exceptional and ends by implicitly criticizing the role of Puritan religion (127). Starbuck and the unfortunate Gardiner alone are devoted to wife and children (624, 640). Ishmael is an orphan who mentions only his stepmother, and that in a context of punishment and paralyzing fear (119–20). Ahab recognizes a divine father against whom he struggles but no mother (617); two brief references to his marriage stress the unhappiness of his "sweet, resigned girl" wife, whom he widowed in marrying, "leaving but one dent in [his] marriage pillow" (177, 651). In spite of some passages in which the whale is given bisexual qualities, the female body is rigorously excluded from the book, and sexual relations among men and women are few.

But the male body and homosexual acts are blazoned forth almost at every turn—in the language of crotch, yard, stiffness, squeezing hand, sperm, and bowels already encountered, as in the name of the whale, given as a chapter title (276) after the suggestive gap in the text that concludes the midnight orgy. (The second occurs, with equal significance, just after the passage on squeezing case [527].) Elsewhere we encounter references to colics and unnatural gases (523, 619): Ishmael offers to unbutton the whale for us and show us among other things his bowels (559, 566). "The Tail" includes a paean to massive male beauty and to the "elasticity" of that organ of the whale (482–87). Ishmael himself rejoices in his spine and in "the firm audacious staff of that flag," which he flings out to the world (456–57). The chapter on the whale's penis has been evoked, but we have not mentioned that the mincer clothes himself in it, in the context of puns on words like cock, ass, and prick (529–31). Nor have we yet noted that this "unaccountable cone" is preceded by the obtrusively phallic description of the ship's wigwam, a comical erection complete with limber bone, tufted apex, and loose hairy fibers (165). The male body, providing the pleasure that according to Irigaray society must hide, is on the contrary massively represented throughout the book, to the point that Ishmael's conceit about using his body for writing (563) becomes very nearly literalized.[2]

But all does not occur in the absence of anguish and guilt. The whale's penis has, after all, been cut off, and its sheath (or cassock) is worn by a mincer; the chapter also includes a reference to the biblical text condemning sodomy and ends on one to archbishops. Gomorrah for its part is mentioned from the second chapter, significantly it turns out in relation to a Negro church (100–101). We have seen that the biblical condemnation of sexual transgression appears almost in passing in Father Mapple's sermon. "A Squeeze of the Hand" ends incongruously with a vision of angels in heaven, "each with his hands in a jar of spermaceti" (527). Even more tellingly, Ishmael's first happiness with Queequeg is preceded by his childhood memory of punishment for "cutting up some caper," followed by the "troubled nightmare of a doze," the sense of a "supernatural hand" placed in his, a "horrid spell" that he has "shudderingly remembered . . . to this very hour" (119–20). "Take away the awful fear," he says, and the nightmare and the experience of awakening with Queequeg are "very similar"! The castration motif, the reiteration of the biblical condemnation, the paralyzing fear—these afflict even Ishmael, who to that extent has not escaped the sexual economy, enforced through psychological and religious terror, that he opposes.

As for Ahab, the aged phallic quality that we have noted in him is pictured as destructive by Ishmael—in Pip at the time of the orgy, and perhaps also at the end (641–42). The castration threat is there too. Boarding another ship, he slides "his solitary thigh into the curve of the hook (it was like sitting in the fluke of an anchor, or the crotch of an apple tree)" (548). Later we learn that he was once mysteriously injured in a fall by his artificial leg itself, which had "stake-wise smitten, and all but pierced his groin; nor was it without extreme difficulty that the agonizing wound was entirely cured" (575). Ahab, then, we may consider the inevitable negative image of the liberating homosexuality of Ishmael, imposed on Melville's book by all the psychic and social forces that *Moby-Dick* also reveals and attacks. This link between the two men is all the more compelling in that they share not only homosexuality but also demonism, madness, and resistance to the dominant economic order—all of which the book emphasizes and all of which we must grasp as interrelated.

Hence Ishmael thinks of the whale's breach as a spasmodic "snatching at the highest heaven," which he relates to his recurrent dream of a "majestic Satan thrusting forth his colossal claw from the flame Baltic of Hell" (although he grants that when in the mood of Isaiah he might instead think of archangels [486]). The grandiose satanism of the passage, the theme of rebellion, and the infernal imagery recall many of Ishmael's reflections on Ahab and suggest why he has so much sympathy for his heroic but monomaniacal protagonist. Ishmael has his own experiences of depression and deep sorrow, though characteristically he asserts his ability to rise above these moods (498, 535–36). And the strange "insanity" that he experiences when squeezing case is an expansive and positive rather than destructive state.

The moments when Ahab is touched by such sentiments are rare and fleeting; the last is in his relationship with Pip, also mad. Instead terrible suffering is reiterated, variously and sometimes contradictorily expressed in terms of tragedy, fate, the titanic, the demonic, and the satanic (with typical imagery of fire, magnetic power, fearsome eyes, and so on). This is related to the fact that Ahab is considered mad—only briefly according to Peleg (177), but in Ishmael's later version "a raving lunatic" who had to be tied to his hammock, in his delirium swinging "to the mad rockings of the gales" (284). Ahab considers himself "demoniac," "madness maddened" (266).

Many of the motifs associated with Ahab's madness are expressed in a passage where Ishmael describes it in terms that are hard not to call schizophrenic (302–3). The unbearable intensity of Ahab's "blazing brain" while he sleeps is pictured as a chasm containing flames, lightning, fiends, and hell, causing him to burst from his stateroom with a wild cry and glaring eyes as if his bed were on fire. This expresses his unbalanced state in traditional infernal imagery. But a titanic motif, the generation of a vulture feeding on Prometheus, refers to the development in Ahab of an "agent" separate from him, which Ishmael sees as his soul, "dissociated" from his mind, from which it seeks escape, being no longer "integral" with it. Finally, in Ishmael's analysis, Ahab's monomaniacal "purpose" becomes, against both gods and angels, a "vacated thing, a formless somnambulistic being," "a blankness in itself."

Despite the infernal and titanic imagery, Ahab's dissociated "purpose" transcends the mystified ethical opposition in the angel-devil dichotomy. Rather the issue is schizophrenia, with Ahab, divided within his being and raving in his bound state, recalling the experience of the mad narrator of Nerval's *Aurélia*. It is useful to recall Deleuze and Guattari's view of schizophrenia as characteristic of the modern socioeconomic order, their insistence on the contrast between the catatonic body and the demonically intense psychic life of the patient, as well as their argument that the schizoid's delirium, like that in *Aurélia* and like much in *Moby-Dick*, typically involves an experience of the entire history of the world, communicating among all periods and regions, all societies and races: schizophrenic delirium, according to them, is inherently racial, though not necessarily racist. The focus on race, the exoticism, the expansion to virtually all ages and regions of human experience, are related features of *Moby-Dick*. In the figure of Ahab the schizoid state appears as horrible suffering and madness; in Ishmael's survival, the work perhaps shadows forth more positive versions of psychic experience.

We have seen that, although happy to be paid, Ishmael systematically attacks the economic order, that his "insanity" in squeezing case is set in opposition to the structures and experiences of family, work, and society. Ahab's more destructive madness is also set in extremely interesting relationship with the world of money and commerce, suggesting an opposition but also at points a strange collusion between the economic and demonic.

For one thing, in "The Ship" (163–78), amid the description of the vessel, the owners as "Quakers with a vengeance," and the barbaric "erection" of the wigwam, we come upon the prototypical evocation of Ahab before he is even named. The ingredients include biblical names, Scandinavian and Roman allusions, qualities of "superior natural force," "globular brain," "ponderous heart," independent thinking under the impact of unharnessed nature, and "nervous lofty language," and therefore a destiny formed for "noble tragedies," including an indispensable "morbidness." Ahab in his essential aspects emerges without warning from the setting of the ship. Hypocritical religion, unavowed but unmistakable phallic sexuality, the driving economic motif, and the morbidly tragic hero all cohabit, from the beginning, though the relationships among them are unexplained.

Near the end of "The Ship," we learn for the first time of Ahab's madness in

Peleg's statement that Ahab was "out of his mind for a spell" (177). As Ishmael later explains (285–86), Ahab dissembled his madness sufficiently for the owners to take advantage of it without realizing its full extent—a curious instance of complicity and contradiction between economic motives and deformed emotional needs. Ishmael's scorn for the pious Nantucket owners emerges again as he suggests that "the calculating people of that prudent isle" found that Ahab's "dark symptoms" made him "all the better qualified" for the whale hunt. Had the "aghast and righteous souls" realized Ahab's "all-engrossing object," however, they would have "wrenched the ship from such a fiendish man." From the perspective of (religiously mystified) profit, emotional frenzy may be useful; profit once threatened, however, frenzy becomes diabolical—"fiendish": "They were bent on profitable cruises, the profit to be counted down in dollars from the mint. He was intent on an audacious, immitigable, supernatural revenge."

Ahab's refusal to submit to the requirements of the commercial emerges during the voyage in his conflicts with Starbuck (whose name suggests an ultimately futile struggle against fate). Starbuck exemplifies in humane form the values that the book so thoroughly questions—religion, duty, profit, family. He alone thinks lovingly of wife and child (624); he alone defends the interests of the owners, in persuading Ahab to stop the oil leak (584–87). His exhortation to his boat crew, "(Pull, my boys!) Sperm, sperm's the play! This at least is duty; duty and profit hand in hand!" (321), contrasts appropriately with the uses of pulling, sperm, play, and hands in Ishmael's libidinal counterexperience.

Ahab and Starbuck have their first confrontation (257–65) when Ahab uses the doubloon, in a context of satanic, magnetic, and magical motifs, to incite the crew to the hunt for *Moby-Dick,* leading to the "infernal orgies" that Starbuck condemns (267). Starbuck argues for "business," barrels for the Nantucket market. Ahab's response rejects the commercial in favor of a magnification of emotional experience: "Nantucket market! Hoot! . . . If money's to be the measurer, man, and the accountants have computed their great counting-house the globe, by girdling it with guineas, one to every three parts of an inch; then, let me tell thee, that my vengeance will fetch a great premium *here!*" When Ahab thus smites his chest, he asserts the value of the personal against a money impulse that he sees as imprisoning the entirety of the world—as forceful an expression as anything in Marx of the destruction of the human by the international money system. But Ahab's explanation of his stance immediately veers off into the metaphysical and religious. He is willing to risk blasphemy in order to strike at the inscrutable force behind the "pasteboard masks" of all things, and Ishmael adds a note about the fatality involved in "the innermost necessities in our being," which "still drive us on." Metaphysical quests, the existence of inner fatalities, do not eliminate the central conflict between Ahab and the commercial order. In some sense nurtured by that order, Ahab's madness and demonism now take on an essential meaning of opposition to it.

Nonetheless, the complexity between the two "systems" that I have mentioned works also in the other direction, in that Ahab first interests and then continues to motivate his crew with money. In Ahab's mind, his motive and object are mad, his means sane (285). According to Ishmael's surmises, he mobilizes his tools, the crew, with money (313–14). Ishmael imagines Ahab comparing himself to crusaders, who committed burglaries on the way to their final "romantic object." Again the cynicism about the purity of religious motives surfaces. In his "romantic" quest, though, Ahab must take into account what he calls the sordidness of the "manufactured man," whom he will therefore not deprive of "all hopes of cash— aye, cash." The reference to manufacture is exceptional, in a book devoted to whaling, in its origins a preindustrial mode of producing profit. But it conveys well the notion of human beings as created by a societal and cultural system—as well as Ahab's pretension not to be so "manufactured."[3]

Melville postpones till near the end close attention to the "Spanish ounce of gold," the sixteen-dollar piece (259) that is to reward the man who first raises Moby Dick. (This turns out to be Ahab himself, perhaps another indication of the link between him and the realm of the economic.) It is only in "The Doubloon" (540–46) that the coin and its significance are examined; in a world overshadowed by the money system, Marx would say, it is only late in the game that the impulse to consider and display the fantastic money form emerges.

The coin indeed has the fascination and prestige of the precious metal-money fetish. Of "purest, virgin gold," raked "out of the heart of gorgeous hills," near the "golden sands" of "many a Pactolus," it seems to embody the primal beauty of nature, with qualities of purity, utter newness, innocence. It has a paradisal quality, therefore, which is enhanced by the fact that among the nonprecious metals sur-rounding it the coin has remained "untouchable and immaculate to any foulness." King Midas, however, lurks in the background, and the evils with which money can be associated are suggested in the chapter's sequence of interpretations of the doubloon's meaning.

Ahab has not until now inspected the "strange figures and inscriptions" stamped on the coin, which beyond its monetary worth is "sanctified" and "re-vered" as Moby Dick's "talisman." This added significance of the doubloon accords with the search for meanings in the book and with Ishmael's comment in regard to Ahab's contemplation of the gold piece: "Some certain significance lurks in all things, else all things are little worth, and the round world itself but an empty cipher, except to sell by the cartload, as they do hills about Boston, to fill up some morass in the Milky Way." Here Ishmael shares Ahab's disdain for the financial, which amounts to selling dirt to fill up a void; "worth" in his view is identified with "significance." In this sense Ahab has unknowingly chosen his coin well, since the "noble golden coins" of South America are "as medals of the sun and tropic token-pieces," filled with a "profusion" and a "preciousness" of natural, cosmic, and human imagery, "so Spanishly poetic." The doubloon is "a most wealthy example of these things" ("wealth" again referring to meaning rather than money), cast in a country in the "middle of the world," "midway up the Andes," in an "unwaning clime that knows no autumn." Amid representations of mountains, flowers, towers, and cocks, the reader perceives ("you saw") the "cabalistics" of the zodiac.

The coin thus succeeds those other examples of symbolic systems—obscure

paintings, sermons, hieroglyphics, the whale. In this chapter it becomes the reference for the establishment of significance; in this sense, too, as Marx argued, money
dominates human existence, by becoming, as here, the master code. Only Flask
refuses this extension of the coin's importance: "I see nothing here, but a round
thing made of gold, and whoever raises a certain whale, this round thing belongs to
him." But he makes a miscalculation in the number of cigars the coin would buy for
him. Pip's declension of the verb "to look" instead indicates how the others, in this
unprecedentedly systematic attempt at interpretation, look at the coin as a source
of meaning. Thus, Ahab's interpretation is egotistical and satanic; Starbuck's, with
equal predictability, sadly Christian. The Manxman, who learned signs from a witch
in Copenhagen, presages an evil outcome for the ship and interprets Fedallah's
reverence before the coin as showing that he is a fire worshipper. More interesting,
though, are the responses of Stubb, Queequeg, and Pip.

Queequeg's tattooed body looks like the zodiac itself, according to the Manxman, who describes the harpooner's unsuccessful search for relationships between
the signs on the coin and parts of his body—thigh, calf, bowels, and the archer—
"Something there in the vicinity of his thigh." The bodily thematic of the book is
recalled here, as Queequeg in effect attempts to establish links between the money
code and the cosmic theory and mystical treatise on truth that we later learn are
inscribed on his body (593). An immemorial, perhaps utterly mythic and now
certainly abolished, state of human life, in which the earth and heavens were
experienced directly in the unified and unrepressed body, thus in "The Doubloon"
confronts the modern system, characterized by bodily repression and sexual guilt
as well as by the dominance of the economic and of the money code.

Stubb's and Pip's reactions return us to other oppressive features of
nineteenth-century society linked to money. Stubb sensibly uses an almanac to
interpret the zodiac, which he reads as a depressing allegory of the cycle of human
life, something like Ishmael's views when he is in a negative mood. Stubb also recalls
seeing numerous doubloons and other coins from many countries, and his reference to the diamond-cutting center Golconda reemphasizes the theme of wealth.
His own imagined use of the coin, in a slave market or on Manhattan's East River,
corresponds with his sailing activities and with his awareness of the monetary value
of slaves. He it was who warned Pip that he would not retrieve him for jumping out
of the boat a second time because whales are thirty times more valuable than
slaves. Ishmael told us then not to blame Stubb too harshly for Pip's madness (526);
Stubb is merely reflecting the inhuman money system.

Pip, preeminent victim in the work, appropriately gets the last word in the
chapter. As noted, his declension of "to see" emphasizes the problem of interpretation. His reference to crows and minstrel songs evokes racial issues, as does his
memory of his father's discovery of an "old darkey's wedding ring" overgrown
inside a cut down pine tree: "How did it get there?" This is one of the rare
references to wedding in *Moby-Dick;* Pip's own sexual experiences may instead be
suggested by his view of the coin as the ship's navel and his idea of unscrewing it.

But together with race, he ends on religion and money: "Oh, the gold! the precious, precious gold!—the green miser 'll hoard ye soon! Hish! Hish! God goes 'mong the worlds blackberrying." Whatever God sponsors human life of this kind is mischievous, to say the least. At the end, moreover, all comes down to the fascination of wealth—"the precious, precious gold!" The sea will swallow all in the end, though—the "green miser," like wisdom, "the miser-merman," who supposedly revealed "his hoarded heaps" to Pip in his madness (525). Major themes of the work—religion and God, the search for wisdom, race and sex—all are here reduced to the impulse to acquire and retain gold. Ahab, rebelling against the commercial system, in "The Quarter-Deck" and "The Doubloon" nonetheless presides over a ritual and a system of meaning in which the money drive dominates and destroys all.

NOTES

[1] I cite *Moby-Dick; or, The Whale,* ed. Harold Beaver (Harmondsworth, Middlesex: Penguin, 1972). This edition contains extensive bibliography and commentary. The introduction and bibliography in *New Essays on* Moby-Dick, ed. Richard H. Brodhead (Cambridge: Cambridge University Press, 1986) survey significant recent approaches and present several useful new essays.

[2] For the above, see the notes to the Penguin edition; also: Sharon Cameron, *The Corporeal Self: Allegories of the Body in Melville and Hawthorne* (Baltimore: Johns Hopkins University Press, 1981); Ann Douglas, *The Feminization of American Culture* (New York: Alfred A. Knopf, 1977); Leslie Fiedler, *"Moby-Dick:* The Baptism of Fire and the Baptism of Sperm," in *Love and Death in the American Novel,* 520–52; and Robert Shulman, "The Serious Functions of Melville's Phallic Jokes," *American Literature* 33 (1961): 179–94. For the psychoanalytic dimension, below, see (for Freud and Lacan) Régis Durand, " 'The Captive King': The Absent Father in Melville's Text," in *The Fictional Father: Lacanian Readings of the Text,* ed. Robert Con Davis (Amherst: University of Massachusetts Press, 1981), 48–72, and Edward F. Edinger, *Melville's* Moby-Dick: *A Jungian Commentary, an American Nekyia* (New York: New Directions, 1978).

[3] Natural and agricultural motifs abound in the book, whereas allusions to manufacturing are rare (e.g., 561). But see Charles Olson's argument that whaling was the forerunner of the petroleum industry (*Call Me Ishmael* [San Francisco: City Lights, 1947], 16–25) and arguments by Brodhead, "Trying All Things: An Introduction to *Moby-Dick,*" in his *New Essays,* 1–21; also Leo Marx, *The Machine in the Garden: Technology and the Pastoral Ideal in America* (New York: Oxford University Press, 1964). For what follows, see Scott Donaldson, "Damned Dollars and a Blessed Company: Financial Imagery in *Moby-Dick,*" *New England Quarterly* 46 (1973): 279–83; Russell and Clare Goldfarb, "The Doubloon in *Moby-Dick,*" *Modern Language Quarterly* 2 (1961): 251–58; and Richard D. Rust, " 'Dollars Damn Me': Money in *Moby-Dick,*" in *Geschichte und Gesellschaft in der amerikanischen Literatur,* ed. Karl Schubert and Ursula Muller-Richter (Heidelberg: Quelle & Meyer, 1975), 49–54.

Leo Bersani

INCOMPARABLE AMERICA

Should America be orphaned? Can you become an orphan if you already know who your parents are? Put in these terms, the problems inherent in the resolve of nineteenth-century American writers to forge a great national literature freed from parental European influence may begin to seem not merely grave but unsolvable. One of the most stirring and militant versions of this call for an independent American literature can be found in Herman Melville's "Hawthorne and His Mosses," an essay written for the *Literary World* in the summer of 1850, during the composition of *Moby-Dick*. The fact that Hawthorne is extravagantly praised in the first part of the essay, even though Melville—"to be frank (though, perhaps, rather foolish)"—admits in the second part (written a day later) that he hadn't yet read all the stories in *Mosses from an Old Manse,* suggests that Hawthorne himself may not be exactly central to the argument he inspires. If Hawthorne is compared to Shakespeare in this essay, and if Melville defiantly defends the comparison against those who may be shocked "to read of Shakespeare and Hawthorne on the same page," it is in order to move beyond Hawthorne, to suggest that while Hawthorne himself is not as great as Shakespeare, someone else will soon appear to rival the greatest English writer. "If Shakespeare has not been equalled, give the world time, and he is sure to be surpassed, in one hemisphere or the other." Actually Melville has already been much more precise geographically. "Believe me, my friends, that men not very much inferior to Shakespeare, are this day being born on the banks of the Ohio." Shakespeare will be surpassed, that is, by an American. But if America is to produce writers at least equal to the greatest European writers, it will not be by imitating European models. American literary greatness requires an originality that carries within it the danger of failure, a danger that, in the most remarkable passage of the essay, Melville happily embraces:

> But it is better to fail in originality, than to succeed in imitation. He who has never failed somewhere, that man can not be great. Failure is the true test of

From *The Culture of Redemption* (Cambridge, MA: Harvard University Press, 1990), pp. 136–54.

greatness. And if it be said, that continual success is a proof that a man wisely knows his powers,—it is only to be added, that, in that case, he knows them to be small. Let us believe it, then, once for all, that there is no hope for us in these smooth pleasing writers that know their powers. Without malice, but to speak the plain fact, they but furnish an appendix to Goldsmith, and other English authors. And we want no American Goldsmiths; nay, we want no American Miltons. It were the vilest thing you could say of a true American author, that he were an American Tompkins. Call him an American, and have done; for you can not say a nobler thing of him.—But it is not meant that all American writers should studiously cleave to nationality in their writings; only this, no American writer should write like an Englishman, or a Frenchman; let him write like a man, for then he will be sure to write like an American. Let us away with this leaven of literary flunkyism towards England. If either must play the flunky in this thing, let England do it, not us. While we are rapidly preparing for that political supremacy among the nations, which prophetically awaits us at the close of the present century; in a literary point of view, we are deplorably unprepared for it; and we seem studious to remain so. Hitherto, reasons might have existed why this should be; but no good reason exists now. And all that is requisite to amendment in this matter, is simply this: that, while freely acknowledging all excellence, everywhere, we should refrain from unduly lauding foreign writers, and, at the same time, duly recognize the meritorious writers that are our own;—those writers, who breathe that un-shackled, democratic spirit of Christianity in all things, which now takes the practical lead in this world, though at the same time led by ourselves—us Americans. Let us boldly contemn all imitation, though it comes to us graceful and fragrant as the morning; and foster all originality, though, at first, it be crabbed and ugly as our own pine knots.[1]

This unashamed expression of an intense national pride at once creates and obscures considerable problems. America is preparing to assert its "political supremacy among the nations." Only "in a literary point of view" are we lagging behind; the great American writer will, then, give to his country a cultural authority equal to its political authority. This authority rests, however, on a form of government that subverts its very basis: the democratic idea of equality makes somewhat problematic Melville's comfortable, indeed emphatic promotion of nondemocratic cultural and political relations between America and the rest of the world. A society that asserts both the limits and the provisional nature of authority is about to dominate other societies, and Melville is so excited by that idea that he wants no form of domination to be left out. The American spirit of equality has to be first everywhere in both letters and politics.

Moby-Dick both represents and seeks to evade the difficulties raised by the imperialist militancy of the democratic spirit. We can already see Melville's predilection—also confirmed by the rhetoric of *Moby-Dick*—for concepts whose terms appear to cancel each other out. The proven value of the democratic ideal justifies America's accession to supreme power in the nondemocratic relations among countries (relations consonant, in the case of other states, with their internal hierarchies of power). This entire section of "Hawthorne and His Mosses" is characterized by its conceptual incompatibilities. Not content to say that an original failure is better than a successful imitation, or even that a man must have risked failure to attain greatness, Melville asserts, in a significant logical jump from the two previous propositions: "Failure is the true test of greatness." Most important, this habit of thought makes it nearly impossible to imagine how the great American work might be produced. Melville's invocation of American greatness is almost obsessively comparative. Hawthorne is not "greater than William of Avon, or as great. But the difference between them is by no means immeasurable. Not a very great deal more, and Nathaniel were verily William." This fidelity to, and meticulous quantifying of, the notion of greatness continues in the comparison between Shakespeare and all other writers, both past and present. "This, too, I mean, that if Shakespeare has not been equalled, give the world time, and he is sure to be surpassed, in one hemisphere or the other." But the condition of such surpassing seems to be the erasure of the continuities allowing us to recognize, for example, that Shakespeare has been surpassed. The passage is most remarkable for its extravagant—and perhaps peculiarly American—expression of an impossible dream: that of a literature without debts, which would owe nothing to the past.[2] How is original American greatness to be measured (since it is apparently to be measured) or even identified? The answer is defiant, but scarcely illuminating: "no American writer should write like an Englishman, or a Frenchman; let him write like a man, for then he will be sure to write like an American." The question should probably be reformulated as: Is it possible to write *like* nobody—without, however, eliminating the possibility of writing *better* than anyone else or being favorably compared with those to whom one owes nothing? American originality will write a glorious new chapter in the history of world literature only if it rejects its place in that history.

Moby-Dick, in extraordinary ways, accepts and struggles with the pressure of these contradictions. It is clear that Melville has no intention of waiting for those men just being born on the banks of the Ohio to prove their genius. *Moby-Dick is* the great original American book invoked in "Hawthorne and His Mosses"; or, at the very least, it squarely meets the challenge of that essay. Melville will take an American subject—even a provincial American subject: the industry of whaling— and show that the greatest literature can be made from that subject. It is not a question of proving that a lot can be made out of a little, but rather of showing that what may seem to be a little is already a lot. "To produce a mighty book," Ishmael declares, "you must choose a mighty theme. No great and enduring volume can ever be written on the flea, though many there be who have tried it" (379). Whaling is inherently a mighty subject, and to embrace it is to try to hold something that itself reaches out and connects to everything else in human time and cosmic space. Ahab may be crazy to assign evil intentions to a dumb brute, but the pursuit of Moby Dick can't help being a hunt for sense. A whaling expedition is inevitably an adventure in reading; the whale is a primary text of nature itself. Not only that: even as Melville's novel goes along, it is constantly being submitted to a vigilant comparison to other cultural models. There is a cultural encyclopedism in *Moby-Dick* as well as a cetological encyclopedism. It is not that the entries exhaustively treat any subject, but the encyclopedic intention—which is perhaps all the encyclopedic novel ever gives us in any case—is obvious with respect to foreign cultures as well as to whaling. It is as if the great American novel had constantly to be measuring itself against the highest achievements of other cultures, and in *Moby-Dick* this means testing the American book's capacity to appropriate a vast field of cultural reference. Melville's splendidly arrogant claim is that almost everything in world culture might be made to serve his subject. The "comprehensiveness of sweep" of Ishmael's thoughts of Leviathan reaches out, most notably, to the Bible, to Shakespeare, and to Greek tragedy, and these illustrious references lose some of their autonomous worth in order to serve *Moby-Dick*, to become mere aids to intelligibility—analogical satellites—in an American drama. It is not merely that *Moby-Dick* is worthy of being compared to either *King Lear* or *Oedipus Rex*. Instead it must be compared to both at the same time; only an encyclopedic range of cultural reference can do justice to Melville's mighty theme. His book reenacts several biblical dramas (Ahab, Ishmael, Ezekiel, Rachel, and others), the Greek tragedies of fatality, and Lear's tragic intimacy with nature and madness. *Moby-Dick* is therefore not only as great as any one of these references; in needing them all to explain itself, it also proposes to surpass them all. Cetological erudition in *Moby-Dick* is only the first step in an enterprise of cannibalistic encyclopedism. Like its monster-hero, Melville's novel opens its jaw to devour all other representations from Lear's Fool to Vishnoo the Hindu god.

And yet all this is something of a joke (although one that can also turn on itself and make another kind of joke of joking):

> Friends, hold my arms! For in the mere act of penning my thoughts of this Leviathan, they weary me, and make me faint with their outreaching comprehensiveness of sweep, as if to include the whole circle of the sciences, and all the generations of whales, and men, and mastodons, past, present, and to come, with all the revolving panoramas of empire on earth, and throughout the whole universe, not excluding its suburbs. (379)

"Not excluding its suburbs"? Something, obviously, has gone awry. The hyperbole of the first part of this passage may already have made us somewhat suspicious, but how are we to place that phrase about the universe's suburbs in a serious claim about *Moby-Dick*'s mighty theme? Much has been written about the humor in Melville's novel, especially as a counterpoint to Ahab's monomaniacal pursuit of the whale. The possibility of sinister and far-reaching significance in the whale is often dissipated by all the mocking allusions to the philosophical profundity necessary to uncover that significance. Besides, the last thing a whaling ship needs is a serious philosophical mind. Indeed, this is the explicit lesson of "The Mast-head" chapter, where Ishmael warns Nantucket shipowners to beware that "sunken-eyed young Platonist [who] will tow you ten wakes round the world, and never make you one pint of sperm the richer" (139). The cultural appropriations meant to authenticate *Moby-Dick*'s claim to greatness are exposed as both laughingly inappropriate to the book's subject and even somewhat ridiculous in themselves. Not only that: in spite of what might seem like a heavy dose of cetology for a work of fiction, Ishmael actually encourages us to be distrustful of his research and presumed knowledge about the whale. The book's cetological erudition—based on remarkably partial sources—is often nothing more than a parody of the erudition of others, and the "proofs" offered of the whale's extraordinary powers most frequently consist (as in "The Affidavit" chapter) of hearsay and assertion.[3] More is at stake here than Ishmael's resistance to Ahab's monomania, more than a presumably viable human- istic alternative to interpretive madness. It is as if the writing of *Moby-Dick* became for Melville the eerie process of dismissing the very ambitions that the novel also seeks so strenuously to realize, as if a kind of leveling indifference had taken over or—most interestingly—as if the notion of American literary greatness were dropped in order to be reinvented, but reinvented *as* something lost, indefensible, abandoned.

What is it, in *Moby-Dick*'s primary project, that might explain Melville's ap- parent indifference toward it, even his subversion of it? In *Moby-Dick* the political implication of the contradictions hinted at in "Hawthorne and His Mosses" becomes inescapable. More exactly, the notion of American literary greatness is politically represented in *Moby-Dick*, and this means trying to give some coherence or plausibility to the idea of a democratic greatness.[4] The "august dignity I treat of," Ishmael writes in the early section introducing Ahab and his mates,

> is not the dignity of kings and robes, but that abounding dignity which has no robed investiture. Thou shalt see it shining in the arm that wields a pick or drives a spike; that democratic dignity which, on all hands, radiates without end from God; Himself! The great God absolute! The centre and circumference of all democracy! His omnipresence, our divine equality!
> If, then, to meanest mariners, and renegades and castaways, I shall here- after ascribe high qualities, though dark; weave round them tragic graces; if even the most mournful, perchance the most abased, among them all, shall at times lift himself to the exalted mounts; if I shall touch that workman's arm with some ethereal light; if I shall spread a rainbow over his disastrous set of sun; then against all mortal critics bear me out in it; thou just Spirit of Equality, which hast spread one royal mantle of humanity over all my kind! (104–105)

Nothing in this passage suggests a rejection of the principle of aristocratic privilege. On the contrary: Ishmael promises a multiplication of the signs and accoutrements of a society based on privilege. He will ascribe "high qualities" to the heroes of his narrative, "weave around them tragic graces," touch them with "ethereal light" and lift them to "exalted mounts"; "pearl" and "finest gold" translate the genius of Bunyan and Cervantes, and Andrew Jackson is imagined as having been "thundered" higher than a throne. "Democracy" here consists in the fact that none of this preeminence is predetermined: in a democratic society, anybody can be lifted to royalty. The principles that determine places within a hierarchy have been changed, but the hierarchical structure has remained intact. It is simply that now the "champions" will come from "the kingly commons." In *Moby-Dick* the rhetoric of democracy has become oxymoronic: in a democracy, equality founds and legitimates inequality.

Ahab's "irresistible dictatorship" perfectly represents this conversion of democracy into royalism. His absolute domination of the crew provides a democratic sanction of despotism. It is true that to a certain extent "the paramount forms and usages of the sea" reinforce a captain's authority independently of his intrinsic merit. In this sense a ship is less like a democracy than a monarchy, and can even call to mind those "royal instances" when "external arts and embellishments" have "imparted potency" to "idiot imbecility." But having granted this, Ishmael insists that the greatness of Ahab owes nothing to the prestige of inherited forms, that—and we can add: like the greatness of America itself or that of the American literary works invoked in "Hawthorne and His Mosses"—it is a wholly original greatness, one without history or traditions. Unlike the "tragic dramatists" who, wishing to "depict mortal indomitableness in its fullest sweep and direct swing," never forget to lend their heroes the persuasive power of "external arts and embellishments," Ishmael sees his captain Ahab as moving before him

> in all his Nantucket grimness and shagginess; and in this episode touching Emperors and kings, I must not conceal that I have only to do with a poor old whale-hunter like him; and, therefore, all outward majestical trappings and housings are denied me. Oh, Ahab! What shall be grand in thee, it must needs be plucked at from the skies, and dived for in the deep, and featured in the unbodied air! (129–130)

Far from being a democratic rejection of emperors and kings, *Moby-Dick* proposes a unique expansion of the monarchic principle. Ahab will earn his right to be called King Ahab, to have his meals with his three mates compared to "the Coronation banquet at Frankfort, where the German Emperor profoundly dines with the seven Imperial Electors." Ahab embodies and realizes the ambition of the novel itself: to have a royal preeminence over European literature without borrowing anything from European models of literary greatness.

And yet the very condition of this success is of course a massive borrowing from those models. The justification of Ahab's kingship is perhaps original and democratic; but the implicit argument for kingship itself comes from abroad, and this condemns Ishmael to analogical proofs of Ahab's greatness. That is, his royal nature will be confirmed by both passing (the German emperor) and sustained (Lear) comparisons between him and other royal natures, by continuous assertions that no royal example is too high to describe him. Melville defines the idea of greatness itself—both for his book and his tragic hero—by constant appeals to our cultural recognitions, thus destroying the argument for originality with its proofs. Or, to put this another way, originality turns out to be nothing more than multiplication of the same. *Moby-Dick*'s greatness is unlike that of any other book, and Ahab's royal nature is not to be thought of as comparable to that of other kings and emperors precisely because they can be compared to so many other books and kings. Originality occurs, as it were, after a certain threshold of absorption has been passed, and *Moby-Dick*'s cultural encyclopedism is a peculiarly American attempt to quantify quality, to produce originality through mass. Once again we are forced to recognize the novel's oxymoronic argument: democracy produces the greatest kings, and analogy authenticates originality. Thus Melville wins his argument for Ahab by destroying the very reason for making the argument in the first place: the unassimilable, unrecuperable uniqueness of the democratic personality.

If the democratic ideas of intrinsic worth, and of equal opportunity to assert that worth, are shown to have oligarchic consequences, these consequences are also vindicated in the novel's metaphysical terms. Although Ahab's monomania is most explicitly defined as his transferring the idea of (and, in an even madder way, the responsibility for) "all evil" to Moby Dick, there are hints in the novel that he may also see the whale in terms closer to those used by Ishmael in the central chapter on "The Whiteness of the Whale." Then Moby Dick would not only embody "that intangible malignity which has been from the beginning" (160); more subtly, and more terrifyingly, he would figure the absence of any intentionality whatsoever outside the human mind. This, as we shall shortly see, is the basis for what I will call the crisis of interpretation in *Moby-Dick*. Ahab's defiant invocation to fire in "The Candles" best indicates this shift of metaphysical emphasis: "In the midst of the personified impersonal, a personality stands here. Though but a point at best; whencesoe'er I came; wheresoe'er I go; yet while I earthly live, the queenly personality lives in me, and feels her royal rights" (417). From this perspective, the pursuit of Moby Dick is perhaps less mad; it is precisely because the whale *is*, as Starbuck says, merely a dumb brute that its power to do so much harm is intolerable. It may *unintentionally destroy*. To be attacked by the whale is not to encounter an enemy; rather, as Ahab at least suggests, it is to have the catastrophic experience of personality's contingency in the universe. Even more intolerable than Moby Dick's intelligent malignity would be its lack of any design at all, for then Ahab's pursuit would be a madly (and comically) incongruous motivation in a universe where purely physical laws govern the movements and meetings of objects. Ahab's assertion of personality—even more, his assertion of royal prerogatives for his "queenly personality"—would then be at once senseless and heroic, a necessarily unheard protest against his having been thrown into the wrong universe, against *this* universe's metaphysical uncongeniality.

Self-assertion is, then, vindicated in *Moby-Dick* as the most profound manifestation of a metaphysical pathos. The value given to personality in a democratic society might be thought of as the political corollary of the novel's philosophical bias in favor of political and metaphysical and literary self-assertions. Against those aristocratic societies where individual personality is largely irrelevant to a hierarchy of power determined by inherited privileges and reinforced by external arts and embellishments, Melville argues for a society (if not a universe) where the individual personality counts, indeed is determinant, in the distribution of power. But it is the very assertion of the rights of self which risks destroying those conditions allowing for it in the first place. In the terms of an unrelenting logic enacted by *Moby-Dick,* democracy ultimately promises the unintended and politically tragic consequence of its own extinction. Melville persuasively expresses the thrill of the democratic promise, both for the individual and for literature, but that thrill is perhaps inseparable from the prospect of unlimited power. The excitement *about* Ahab in *Moby-Dick* is provoked by the spectacle of what might be called an earned despotism. The *Pequod* is the social realization of a fantasy of intrinsic kingship. The opportunity for self-expression and self-assertion in a democratic society is, Melville's novel suggests, existentially translated as a will to power, despotism is the social logic within an argument for the rights of personality.

But we also have Ishmael and the *Pequod*'s crew. Another type of society is—or so it appears—constituted in the margins of Ahab's rule. There seems to be a social space in *Moby-Dick* outside the circle of fascinated subjugation to Ahab's monomania. And this space would be defined by a kind of democratic camaraderie in shared work.[5] There is, for example, the convivial atmosphere during the hoisting, cutting, and lowering of the whale's blubber, a task accompanied by fraternal swearing and the transformation of part of the crew into a "wild" operatic chorus. See especially the famous description of the men squeezing lumps of sperm back into fluid, an activity that frees Ishmael "from all ill-will, or petulance, or malice of any sort whatsoever":

> Squeeze! squeeze! squeeze! all the morning long; I squeezed that sperm till I myself almost melted into it; I squeezed that sperm till a strange sort of insanity came over me; and I found myself unwittingly squeezing my co-laborers' hands in it, mistaking their hands for the gentle globules. Such an abounding, affectionate, friendly, loving feeling did this avocation beget; that at last I was continually squeezing their hands, and looking up into their eyes sentimentally; as much as to say,—Oh! my dear fellow beings, why should we longer cherish any social acerbities, or know the slightest ill-humor or envy! Come; let us squeeze hands all round; nay, let us all squeeze ourselves into each other; let us squeeze ourselves universally into the very milk and sperm of kindness. (348–349)

The fraternal warmth engendered by this communal activity seems to be the best antidote to Ahab's mad isolation. It is, in terms of the book's major metaphorical opposition, a return from the dangers of sea to the security of land. Ishmael goes on to interpret what he has just described in precisely such terms. Having learned that "man must eventually lower, or at least shift, his concert of attainable felicity; not placing it anywhere in the intellect or the fancy; but in the wife, the heart, the bed, the table, the saddle, the fire-side, the country," he is "ready to squeeze case eternally" (349). But this is a tame and pious conclusion to what we have just read, and it is difficult to see what wife, fireside, and country have to do with the "strange sort of insanity" that leads Ishmael—made drunk by the touch of "those soft, gentle globules of infiltrated tissues" and the "uncontaminated aroma" of "that inexpressible sperm"—to begin squeezing his comrades' hands and gazing "sentimentally" into their eyes, dreaming of an ecstatic loss of self in a universal melting squeeze. I don't mean simply that the need to place happiness in wife and fireside seems a strangely inappropriate lesson to be drawn from such an obviously homoerotic experience, but rather that the homoeroticism itself is merely the secondary expression of a comically anarchic sensuality. Ishmael's coworkers allow for the momentary focusing and socializing of a sensuality that is so idiosyncratic, so frankly irreducible to any viable social bond—in Ishmael's own words, so insane—that it can only be *described*—accommodated by language—as a joke. The joke is emphasized by the corny, decidedly nonpious vision at the end of the passage: "In visions of the night, I saw long rows of angels in paradise, each with his hands in a jar of spermaceti."

Much has been made of homoeroticism in *Moby-Dick*, and this is not astonishing in view of the novel's hints in this direction.[6] The major piece of presumed evidence is of course the Ishmael-Queequeg relation, in which Ishmael seems not at all reluctant to portray himself as the huge savage's contented wife. On the one hand, as a couple Ishmael and Queequeg both prefigure and personalize the fraternal feelings in such tasks as cutting into the whale's blubber and reconverting its sperm into liquid. On the other hand, Ishmael gives a highly eroticized account of the friendship. After their first night together in the same bed at the Spouter Inn in New Bedford, Ishmael awakes to find Queequeg's arm thrown over him "in the most loving and affectionate manner," as if he "had been his wife" and were being held in a "bridegroom clasp" (32–33). The next night they seal their friendship, once again in bed, with "confidential disclosures," just as man and wife often choose their bed to "open the very bottom of their souls to each other." "Thus, then," this passage ends, "in our hearts' honeymoon, lay I and Queequeg—a cosy, loving pair" (54). During the voyage, when they are both tied to the same monkey rope (in the "humorously perilous business" of Queequeg's going over the side of the ship to insert a blubber hook into the whale's back, where he must remain during the whole stripping operation), they are not simply "inseparable twin brother[s]" but are "for the time . . . wedded" (271).

There is no ambiguity whatsoever in all these eroticizing allusions. They clearly instruct us to think of the bond between Ishmael and Queequeg as not unlike marital bonds, and it can be argued that they do this with no suggestion of homosexual desire. I say this somewhat tentatively because we might also say that homosexual desire is precisely what is signified by those conjugal signifiers. But where exactly is the signified? Is there a *subject* of homosexual desire in *Moby-Dick?* Far from representing either unequivocal homosexuality or surfaces of heterosexual desire troubled by repressed homosexual impulses, Melville's characters have no sexual subjectivity at all. Critics readily admit how little the wholly improbable soliloquies of Melville's characters conform to the discursive parameters of realistic fiction; they have more difficulty recognizing that those soliloquies adequately represent the essence of the characters. Interiority in *Moby-Dick* is almost entirely philosophical; each character is a certain confluence of metaphysical, epistemological, and social-ethical positions. Homoeroticism can enter the novel so easily because, psychologically, there is nothing at stake. In Balzac, Gide, and Proust, homosexual desire is a fact of great psychological significance, whereas it may be a peculiarity of American literature—Cooper, Twain, and Hemingway come to mind—that it frequently presents homosexual situations that are psychologically inconsequential, unconnected to characterization. Ishmael's marital metaphors reveal nothing about him because there is nowhere in the novel an Ishmael about whom such metaphors can be revealing.

This does not mean that they are unimportant: their very significance depends on *not* providing an intelligible alternative to Ahab's despotism. Each time the novel spells out any such alternative, it is in terms that do little more than negatively repeat what they oppose. Thus the land is opposed to the sea, and Ahab's unhappy solitude is set against the quiet joy of domestic ties. Starbuck is the principal advocate of intelligible alternatives to Ahab, such as wife and family, the land, fraternal compassion, and a democratic respect for the rights of others. But if Ahab's tyrannical rule enacts the ultimate logic of the privileges that democracy would accord personality, then perhaps the very principle of oppositional couplings cannot be trusted. Only something that does not enter into logical opposition can be "opposed" to Ahab. Politically this means that in order to escape the antidemocratic consequences inherent in the democratic ideal, a type of social relation must be imagined that is neither autocratic nor democratic.

Ishmael's response to Queequeg and the crew is the testing of this other relation, although each time he tries to analyze it he also banalizes it, as in the Starbuck-like contrast between the intellect and the fireside. But, just as Ishmael's insane ecstasy while squeezing blobs of sperm is irreducible to any of these terms, so the introduction of homoeroticism into the novel prevents his representation of Queequeg and the crew from being one of a society united in the bonds of friendship created by communal work. This homoeroticism, however, never settles into what would be merely another type of oppositional grouping. By figuring what I have called a nonpsychological homosexuality, Melville proposes a social bond based not on subordination to the great personality embodied by Ahab, not on the democratic ideal of power distributed according to intrinsic worth, not on those feelings binding either two friends or the partners in a marriage, not, finally, on the transgressed homage to all such legitimated social bonds in conventional images of

homosexual desire. (Proust serves as a good example of the homosexual writer
unable, for the most part, to account for his own desires except as transgressive
replications of the socially accepted bonds they only superficially exclude.)

The casual humor of both the early section on Ishmael's "marriage" to
Queequeg and the description of sperm squeezing helps to transform the representation of both friendship and homoeroticism into an inconceivable social
bond. In so doing it evokes, in an unexpected way, the originality of American
society, which Melville is both attached to and unable to describe. Ishmael's humor
is a way of simultaneously proposing and withdrawing definitions and identifications,
of using what are, after all, the only available categories, social and linguistic, to coax
into existence as yet unavailable terms. Even the most inappropriate descriptions
can serve this dislocating function. Thus, though I may have been right to argue that
the reference to wife, heart, and fireside is a taming irrelevance in the squeezing-
sperm chapter, the terms also disturbingly suggest an unformulated relation between a kind of anarchic sensuality and a socially viable domesticity. Similarly, far
from being a parodistic version of normal marriage or a domesticating of homosexual bonds, the Ishmael-Queequeg marriage enacts a sensuality that cannot be
reduced to the psychology of either heterosexual or homosexual desire, a sensuality at once nontransgressive and authorized by nothing beyond Ishmael's mode of
addressing it.

Lest this begin to sound like an argument for the socially unthreatening nature
of homoeroticism, I want to insist on the absence of authorization. Melville makes
it clear that the society in which these new relations are being tested is a society
wholly outside society. From the very first pages, going to sea is presented as a
letting go of all social, conceptual, and sexual familiarity. The first chapter of *Moby-
Dick* is an extraordinarily haunting invocation of seagoing as a "substitute for pistol
and ball," a deliberate removal from life itself. A whole city is transformed into a
collective suicidal longing when Ishmael evokes thousands of men "posted like silent
sentinels all around the town" and "fixed in ocean reveries." We should keep in
mind this powerfully oneiric image of a humanity thronging "just as nigh the water
as they possibly can without falling in," anxious to abandon the ship of society for
the magnetizing and original death promised by the sea. The first chapter clearly
warns us not to consider any bonds or fellowship that may develop or, in the case
of Ishmael or Queequeg, be confirmed on board the *Pequod* as compatible with
the society of the land.

Is the *Pequod,* to the extent that it functions outside Ahab's domination, the
image of an authentically democratic work society? Perhaps—but the workforce is
constituted by a hybrid collection of exiles and outcasts. Not only does the biblical
name by which the narrator invites the reader to address him in the novel's first line
resonate with such connotations; the latter aptly describe the crew of the *Pequod.*
Ishmael's emphasis on all the countries and races represented on the ship invites us
to see the crew as a kind of international fraternity of men united in harmonious
and useful work. But there is an equally strong emphasis on the wild, untutored,

asocial nature of the men in that fraternity. "They were nearly all Islanders in the Pequod, *Isolatoes* too, I call such, not acknowledging the common continent of men, but each *Isolato* living on a separate continent of his own" (108). It is, as Starbuck says, "a heathen crew ... whelped somewhere by the sharkish sea" (148), a crew, as Ishmael puts it, "chiefly made up of mongrel renegades, and castaways, and cannibals" (162). Indeed whalers in general are "floating outlaws," manned by "unaccountable odds and ends of strange nations come up from the unknown nooks and ash-holes of the earth" (198).

Ishmael himself must be thought of as belonging to that group; he is its expression.[7] He is so casual in his dismissals of ordinary assumptions about social bonds that we may easily miss his readiness to reject the values of the land. "For my part," he announces in chapter one, "I abominate all honorable respectable toils, trials, and tribulations of every kind whatsoever." In context, this is playfully perverse hyperbole; but it also belongs to what amounts to a systematic rejection of the civilized ethics of a democratic and Christian land society. Honorable respectable toils are abominated; the chapter on Fast-Fish and Loose-Fish is a Swiftean mockery of legal systems in which rights to ownership are often identical to the brute force necessary to claim possession; and Christianity itself is implicitly dismissed in the comparison of images of physical "robustness" in art ("in everything imposingly beautiful, strength has much to do with the magic") to "the soft, curled, hermaphroditical Italian pictures" of Christ, which "hint nothing of any power, but the mere negative, feminine one of submission and endurance, which on all hands it is conceded, form the peculiar practical virtues of his teachings" (315). The *Pequod* is not, however, a reconstitution of politics, morality, or religious beliefs on some presumably more natural basis. Queequeg's religion is as unsatisfactory as Christianity, and Ishmael's infinite tolerance, far from being grounded in a faith where tolerance is preached as a virtue, merely expresses his unwillingness to be intolerant in the name of any faith whatsoever. Nor is Ishmael willing to swear allegiance to the *Pequod*'s society of savages as a type of social organization. "I myself am a savage, owning to no allegiance but to the King of the Cannibals; and ready at any moment to rebel against him" (232).

Is the *Pequod* an image of America?[8] It is the settlement of America reenacted, but uncompromisingly radicalized. The "unaccountable odds and ends" from all over the world who ended up in America were of course not only castaways and cannibals; nor were they all, for that matter, unaccountable. But by insisting on the *Pequod*'s nearly total break with the land and the past, Melville simultaneously evokes the origins of America as a house for exiles from everywhere and makes those origins absolute. That is, he evokes the possibility of exile as a wholly new beginning and brutally deprives it of the comforting notion of loss. There is no dream that has been frustrated, no second chance for forms of life imagined, but then blocked in their realization, somewhere else. The sea is wildness and anarchy; it opposes to both Ahab's despotism and the democratic vision a kind of social suicide. Thus Melville's novel dreams metaphorically of that absolute break with

Europe which of course never took place, of a risky willingness to "come to America" with no social vision at all, with nothing but an anxious need to die to society and to history. Far from fulfilling a European dream, America would therefore have to be invented by those "thousands upon thousands of mortal men" who at first wanted nothing more than to flee from the land but who, having joined the crew of exiles and renegades from all over the hated world, now find themselves suspended in their dying and are obliged to redefine the social itself.

I have argued that, principally through Ahab, *Moby-Dick* dramatizes the oxymoronic impasse of democracy: the great man's despotism realizes the democratic dream of equality. But *Moby-Dick* also reinvents that politically infernal rhetoric as a political promise: it dreams a society owing nothing whatsoever to known social ideas. What this society after social death might actually be, we can say no more than Melville (or Ishmael) himself can. What can be said is only what has already been said, and Ishmael's way of coercing all that used speech into unimagined significances is to withdraw humorously from nearly all his propositions. He can say what he means only by refusing to mean what he says. America's history will take place in the space at once cluttered and blank where all imaginable social bonds have been simultaneously figured and dissolved. Melville's America is a historical meta-oxymoron: it defeats the defeating oxymoron of a democracy ruined by the fulfillment of its own promise by erasing all promises in order to make the wholly unauthorized promise of an absolutely new society.

The representation of Melville's America is thus inseparable from a crisis of meaning. On the one hand, the interpretive faculty is associated with madness. It is not only that "all evil" is personified in Moby Dick, but also that Ahab sees evil omens and portents everywhere. The mass of information given to us about whales and whaling is obviously designed to counteract this madness; here the encyclopedia functions as an antidote to overreading, as a source of reliable facts, as a comfortable and necessary myth of a collection of knowledge unaffected by the collector's passions. "So ignorant are most landsmen of some of the plainest and most palpable wonders of the world, that without some hints touching the plain facts, historical and otherwise, of the fishery, they might scout at Moby Dick as a monstrous fable, or still worse and more detestable, a hideous and intolerable allegory" (177).

But this is somewhat disingenuous. The most persistent and extravagant sign reader in the novel is Ishmael. His allegorical wisdom, it is true, is of fairly modest quality; nor does he hesitate to mock it himself. What is interesting, as others have noted, is the interpretive habit itself or, more strangely, the inability to stop reading, even though the object to be read may be unreadable. *Moby-Dick* is full of enigmatic texts. First and foremost, there is the whale, both as a species and in its individual features and behavior. There is also the doubloon, with its "strange figures and inscriptions"; in chapter 99, Ahab, Starbuck, Stubb, Flask, the Manxman, Queequeg, Fedallah, and Pip all perform interpretively—producing little more than self-characterizations—in front of the gold coin. If Ahab interprets "in some mono-maniac way whatever significance might lurk" in the doubloon's markings, "some certain significance," Ishmael nonetheless adds, "lurks in all things, else all things are little worth, and the round world itself but an empty cipher, except to sell by the cartload, as they do hills about Boston, to fill up some morass in the Milky Way" (358). Even Queequeg's tattoos are described as hieroglyphics containing "a complete theory of the heavens and the earth, and a mystical treatise on the art of attaining truth"; and looking at that unsolvable riddle, Ahab wildly exclaims: " 'Oh, devilish tantalization of the gods!' " (399). Most remarkably, however tragically frustrated or humorously tentative all such readings may be, the very course of events in the novel spectacularly confirms the power of reading. Not only do all the omens and portents turn out to be omens and portents of what actually happens to the *Pequod* and its crew; Elijah's dire prophecy also accurately prefigures the voyage's tragic end (" 'Good bye to ye! Shan't see ye again very soon, I guess; unless it's before the Grand Jury' " [91]); and the demonic Fedallah's prediction—one doesn't even know what text he reads—of how he and Ahab will die is fulfilled with uncanny precision.

    Moby-Dick is a chaos of interpretive modes. As a drama of interpretation, Melville's novel appears to center on Ahab. But Ahab represents only one type of interpretive activity, and in a sense it is the crudest and the easiest to discredit. For him, Moby Dick is a symbol of evil that, in its vicious attacks, fittingly partakes of the nature of what it symbolizes. Ahab is guilty of a double mistake of logic: he unjustifiably infers an agent or course of evil from the observable phenomenon of human "sufferings and exasperations," and then he identifies a possible manifestation of that evil with its essence. Having done that, he—and with him now the crew—begins to see all things as signs. Although the symbolic reading is particular to Ahab (nothing indicates that the crew shares Ahab's philosophically sophisticated madness of attributing the sum of human woes to the whale they are chasing), a degraded form of symbolic interpretation manifests itself as the superstition of signs. Instead of symbols, we have portents: the darting away of "shoals of small harmless fish . . . with what seemed shuddering fins," the "tri-painted trinity of flames" when the ship's three masts are set on fire by lightning during the typhoon, and the seizing of Ahab's hat from his head by a savage sea hawk. Symbolism is a vertical mode of interpretation (Moby Dick is transcended by the metaphysical reality he points to), but the ominous sign can be thought of as a metonymic slip. It is as if part of a pattern of catastrophe had been detached from the pattern and moved ahead of its realization in time. The omen announces the events to which it belongs; it is the beginning of a catastrophe that has not yet begun.

    There is, more generally, the interpretation of the entire novel as a philo-sophical parable in which going to sea figures the risky movement of speculative thought, of thought unanchored, set loose from all evidential "land" securities. I also spoke earlier of the interpretive analogies meant to authenticate Melville's "mighty theme." The very syntax of analogy ("just as . . . so . . .") suggests the equal status of this strange and isolated incident in the annals of whaling and the most memorable moments of human history and culture. Finally, the local descriptive metaphor in *Moby-Dick* can even work in the opposite direction, to normalize and domesticate the drama aboard the *Pequod*. In describing the crew's transfixed horror when, during a lightning storm, the ends of the three tall masts catch fire and silently burn "like three gigantic wax tapers before an altar," Ishmael writes: "From the arched and overhanging rigging, where they had just been engaged securing a spar, a number of the seamen, arrested by the glare, now cohered together, and hung pendulous, like a knot of numbed wasps from a drooping, orchard twig" (415–416). This astonishing comparison assimilates a moment of crazy panic on the *Pequod* to an ordinary rural scene, and in so doing it casually naturalizes melodrama, making the sailor's terror into—asking us to read their terror as—something as unexceptional as immobile wasps on a twig. Thus the most melodramatic of scenes is domesticated, and the exceptional scenes of human tragedy are reintegrated into the vast tableau of nature, where relations may be constituted by nothing more meaningful than the visual resemblance between two distant points in space.

Ishmael's principal function is, however, less to add to interpretive modes than to be the hermeneutical ground of *all* modes of interpretation. That is, he defines the conditions of possibility for all interpretive activity in *Moby-Dick*, and we can define that condition as Ishmael's invalidating tolerance of the search for meanings. If the interpretive process cannot be stopped, if the novel is a relentless, nearly grotesque compulsion to read significance into all objects and events (a compulsion ranging from Ahab's mad symbolism to Ishmael's allegorizing speculations on the thickness of the whale's blubber), Ishmael's humor simultaneously withdraws all credibility from the sense he ceaselessly proposes. Thus the principal question we face in reading this encyclopedic demonstration of interpretive processes is how to read the deployment of those processes. Next to that problem, Ahab is comparatively simple to understand; indeed, his immediately recognizable tragic stance, and his monomaniacal madness, may delay our recognition of the far greater radicality of Ishmael. For the reader, the primary enigmatic text is not Moby Dick, but Ishmael's relation to the possible readings of Moby Dick. Is there any view of the story, or any interpretive mode, that escapes Ishmael's repeated retreat from all points of view? We might think of this retreating move as one of irony; Ishmael's ironic humor interprets interpretation by a noncritical but no less effectively destructive step back from all interpretations. Humor is the tonal sign of this step; it gives a voice to that suspensive move of consciousness which invalidates its objects without erasing them, merely by reflecting them at a certain distance. This move can, finally, consist in the erasure of the tonal sign of humor itself—as in "The Fountain" chapter, which Ishmael ends on a serious note, stepping back from the humor just preceding the end and making of his very seriousness the lightest mode of thought, merely another sign of consciousness in retreat.

The consequence of all this is that *Moby-Dick* becomes a novel unavailable to the culture it still manages to define (while making the generous, even utopian assumption that such readings as the one I am proposing *are* available to that culture). Melville's novel is the literary equivalent of that "dumb blankness full of meaning" which is what Ishmael finds so awesome in the whale's whiteness. We may continue to speak of *Moby-Dick* (as the novel itself demonstrates, criticism is unstoppable), but we can at least hope for an appropriately impoverished reading, one that principally describes how the narrative anticipates, entertains, and withdraws its assent from all our interpretive moves. The chapter on "The Whiteness of the Whale" analyzes the symptoms of a mind afflicted with an oxymoronic perception of the universe. Reality is an infinitely meaningful absence of meaning, and *Moby-Dick*—a novel of metaphysical realism—repeats that textuality in its own apparently unlimited capacity to entertain unauthorized interpretations. But this type of textuality—in which unreadability is identical to a limitless availability to interpretation—may be the condition of the novel's originality. American literature can be great not by being as good as or even better than European literature; it must be, in the full force of the term, incomparable. Thus Ishmael will not only destroy the terms of comparison; he will also invalidate the very process of comparison—the unrelenting analogical habit—to which he appeals in order to validate his project of writing a "mighty book." *Moby-Dick* outdoes the cultural references it appropriates by dismissing itself; the simultaneous proposal and erasure of sense produces a book bloated with unaccepted sense. The extraordinary originality of Melville's work is that it somehow subsists—materially—as a book orphaned by its content.

The only surviving analogy of this shipwreck of sense is the analogy with America itself. Not only does the *Pequod*'s crew reenact the origin of American society as a break with the very idea of the social; the hermeneutic suspension of every interpretive move in the novel gives a kind of plausibility to the difficult idea of an historical originality.[9] It suggests that the originality of America cannot consist in a chimerical absolute break with its European past, but rather in what might be called an encyclopedic nonendorsement of that past. In America, as in Melville's novel, the massive borrowing from other cultures is identical to a self-distancing from other cultures. Sense is borrowed without being subscribed to, and the very indiscriminacy of the borrowing should produce a society without debts, one that never holds what it nonetheless greedily takes. *Moby-Dick* is at once politically, aesthetically, and economically utopian in that it invites America to *dissipate its capital.* This is not, I believe, merely another capitalistic or liberal mystification: far from merely offering the illusion of a break with established orders (an illusion so comforting that it would actually weaken our resistance to those same orders), *Moby-Dick* proposes no object of loyalty or of desire except the continuously repeated gesture of not receiving the wealth it appropriates.

The encyclopedism of *Moby-Dick* is, then, in no way redemptive. Never using either its cetological erudition or its cultural borrowings to monumentalize the truly raw materials of the American life, Melville's novel takes the same risks as the country it finally honors, not by taking the lead in world literature but by repeating its impoverished beginning, its utopian negations. *Moby-Dick* is indeed our mighty book, not because it makes a whole of the fragments of America but rather because, in its sheer massiveness, it never stops demonstrating (as if to inspire courage) the sustaining, self-renewing powers of historical and cultural orphanhood.

NOTES

[1] Herman Melville, *Moby-Dick*, ed. Harrison Hayford and Hershel Parker (New York: Norton, 1967), pp. 545–546. Further page references to this edition are given in text.

[2] Richard Poirier discusses the complications—the often conflicting energies—in American writers' perception of their relation to a cultural past in *The Renewal of Literature: Emersonian Reflections* (New York: Random House, 1987).

[3] Nearly half the cetological passages in *Moby-Dick* come from books *on* whaling, in which references to whales can hardly be taken as proof of the hold exercised by the whale, everywhere and at all times, on human attention. We also know, thanks to the work of Luther S. Mansfield and Howard P. Vincent for the 1952 Hendricks House edition of *Moby-Dick*, that while implying that he had read all the authorities he mentions, Melville's research often "went no further than his much-used copy of Beale's *Natural History of the Sperm Whale*" (editors' note, *Moby-Dick*, p. 117). Ishmael's research also parodies the research of other cetology efforts: the "long detailed list of the outfits for the larders and cellars of 180 sail of Dutch whalemen" (371) is a takeoff on a pedantically statistical passage in William Scoresby's *History and Description of the Northern Whale Fishery*. Finally, the proofs offered in "The Affidavit" chapter of the sperm whale's acting "with wilful, deliberate designs of destruction to his pursuers" consist of little more than examples of ships attacked by a whale, and the chapter ends with the contention that the sea monster whose capture in the Sea of Marmora is related by Procopius was a sperm whale, a contention supported by an astonishingly vague evidential chain:

> "*Further investigations* [what are they?] have recently proved to me, that in modern times there have been isolate instances of the presence of the sperm whale·in the Mediterranean. *I am told, on good authority,* that on the Barbary coast, a Commodore Davis of the British navy found the skeleton of a sperm whale. Now, as a vessel of war readily passes through the Dardanelles, hence a sperm whale could, by the same route, pass out of the Mediterranean into the Propontis.
>
> "In the Propontis, *as far as I can learn,* none of that peculiar substance called *brit* is to be found, the ailment of the right whale. *But I have every reason to believe* that the food of the sperm whale—squid or cuttlefish—lurks at the bottom of that sea, because large creatures, but by no means the largest of that sort, have been found at its surface. *If, then, you properly put these statements together, and reason upon them a bit,* you will clearly perceive that, according to all human reasoning, Procopius's sea-monster, that for half a century stove the ships of a Roman Emperor, must in all probability have been a sperm whale." (181–182; emphasis mine).

[4] Much of the recent criticism of *Moby-Dick* has been concerned with the novel's political significance. These readings have generally been of a referential nature, pinpointing moments and events in mid-nineteenth-century America to which Melville's work would be addressing itself. Alan Heimert's article "*Moby-Dick* and American Political Symbolism" is seminal in this respect. Among Heimert's major claims are that "Melville associated the quest of the 'sublime' White Whale with imperial aspirations" and that behind Moby Dick and Ahab stand, respectively, Daniel Webster and John C. Calhoun; in *American Quarterly*, 15 (Winter 1963), 498–534. More recently, Michael Paul Rogin has argued that "Melville is a recorder and interpreter of America's society whose work is comparable to that of the great nineteenth-century European realists" and, more specifically, that "*Moby-Dick* registers the dependence of America's freedom on America's slavery, and the threat of American slavery to destroy America's freedom"; *Subversive Genealogy: The Politics and Art of Herman Melville* (New York: Knopf, 1983), pp. ix, 121.

[5] This argument is made in C.L.R. James's stirringly personal book, *Mariners, Renegades and Castaways: The Story of Herman Melville and the World We Live In* (New York: C.L.R. James, 1953). The *Pequod*'s crew, James writes, "owe no allegiance to any body or anything except the work they have to do and the relations with one another on which that work depends" (p. 20). "The contrast is between Ahab and

the crew"; Melville endowed the crew with "the graces of men associated for common labor" (p. 30).

I will soon be raising objections to the widespread tendency to see Ishmael as a viable alternative to Ahab. From a different perspective, Donald E. Pease has also argued against such a reading. Criticizing the tendency of F. O. Matthiessen and "forty years of Cold War critics" to turn to Ishmael as, in contrast to Ahab, "the principle of America's freedom," Pease makes a persuasive case for the structural interdependence of Ahab and Ishmael. "Ahab's compulsion to decide *compels* Ishmael *not* to decide." And: "The fate befalling Ahab's decisive conversion of work into deed determines Ishmael's need of a realm in which the indeterminate play of endless possible actions overdetermines his *in*decision." Pease, "*Moby Dick* and the Cold War," in *The American Renaissance Reconsidered: Selected Papers from the English Institute, 1982–83,* ed. Walter Benn Michaels and Donald E. Pease (Baltimore: Johns Hopkins University Press, 1983), p. 147.

[6] To mention two ends of a kind of moral spectrum of perspectives on homosexuality in *Moby-Dick:* Leslie Fiedler, in *Love and Death in the American Novel* (New York: Stein and Day, 1966), finds Melville (and other American writers) unable to deal with adult heterosexual love. Robert K. Martin, in *Hero, Captain, and Stranger: Male Friendship, Social Critique, and Literary Form in the Sea Novels of Herman Melville* (Chapel Hill: University of North Carolina Press, 1986), reinterprets this failure as an accomplishment of the highest order. "The homosexual relationship," he writes, "is invested by Melville with radical social potential; it is through the affirmation of the values of nonaggressive male-bonded couples that the power of the patriarch can be contested and even defeated" (p. 70). Martin's argument has an engaging specificity. The patriarchal structure might be broken down by a kind of communal masturbatory narcissism: "Men coming together [in group masturbation] are not men fighting each other, or even men hurting whales" (p. 82). The pacification of the phallus through masturbation remains, however, a problematic notion.

[7] I say this fully aware of what might be called the narratological problem of Ishmael. Melville doesn't take much trouble to maintain his presence throughout the novel; for several chapters in a row, Ishmael the character disappears, and a fairly conventional omniscient narrator takes over. It could also be said that Ishmael is very unlike the other members of the crew—in his understanding of Ahab, his humor, his intellectuality. If I use "Ishmael" to refer consistently to *Moby-Dick*'s narrator, it is because I think the very inconsistencies, and the apparent irreducibility of the narrative voice to a psychologically reliable narrative persona, themselves define a nearly undefinable, nearly unrecognizable persona that, mainly for the sake of convenience, we can call "Ishmael." But to use this name consistently, as I have done, does not obviously mean that a conventional psychological or moral identity corresponds to the name. Ishmael must be as elusive, even as absent, as that incomparable America he nonetheless strives to express. And if, as a character, he is different from the rest of the crew, he is, more significantly, also a philosophical articulation of their estrangement, of the *isolato* condition.

[8] The distance between this America and historical America is also suggested, from another perspective, by the ship's name. The Pequod Indians, a reputedly bloodthirsty Connecticut tribe, were massacred by militia from Hartford in 1637. If Melville's *Pequod* is an image of America, it is an America expelled from America and eliminated by America. Rogin writes that in naming Ahab's ship *Pequod,* Melville paid ironic homage to a process in which "the conquest of savages and the acquisition of their power" is implicitly seen as "regeneration through violence" (*Subversive Genealogy,* p. 124). For a study of this process, see Richard Slotkin, *Regeneration through Violence* (Middletown: Wesleyan University Press, 1973).

[9] In *Pierre* Melville himself will satirize the illusion of literary originality. A critique of the possibility of originality from the perspective of a poststructuralist ideology of textuality can be found in Edgar Dryden, "The Entangled Text: Melville's *Pierre* and the Problem of Reading," *boundary 2,* 8 (July 1979). Joseph Riddel addresses the same question in "Decentering the Image: The 'Project' of 'American' Poetics?" in *Textual Strategies: Perspectives in Post-Structuralist Criticism,* ed. Josué V. Harari (Ithaca: Cornell University Press, 1979), pp. 322–358.

CONTRIBUTORS

HAROLD BLOOM is Sterling Professor of the Humanities at Yale University and Henry W. and Albert A. Berg Professor of English at the New York University Graduate School. He is a 1985 MacArthur Foundation Award recipient, served as the Charles Eliot Norton Professor of Poetry at Harvard University (1987–88), and is the author of nineteen books, the most recent being *The Book of J* (1990). Currently he is editing the Chelsea House series Modern Critical Views and The Critical Cosmos, and other Chelsea House series in literary criticism.

F. O. MATTHIESSEN was Professor of English at Harvard University until his suicide in 1950. A member of the National Institute of Arts and Letters, he also wrote numerous works; among them are *Translation: An Elizabethan Art* (1931), *The Achievement of T. S. Eliot: An Essay on the Nature of Poetry* (1935), and critical studies on Poe, Henry James, and Dreiser. He also edited Melville's *Selected Poems* (1944).

MAURICE FRIEDMAN is Professor of Religious Studies at San Diego State University. He has written *Contemporary Psychology: Revealing and Obscuring the Human* (1984) and has edited and written on the writings of Martin Buber.

ROBERT H. ZOELLNER is Professor of English at Colorado State University–Fort Collins.

BAINARD COWAN is Associate Professor of English at Louisiana State University, and has written articles on Dante and Walter Benjamin.

MICHAEL PAUL ROGIN is Professor of Political Science at the University of California–Berkeley. He is the author of *The Intellectuals and McCarthy: The Radical Specter* (1967), *Fathers and Children: Andrew Jackson and the Subjugation of the American Indian* (1975), and *Ronald Reagan, the Movie and Other Episodes in Political Demonology* (1987).

WILLIAM B. DILLINGHAM is Professor of English at Emory University. He is the author of *An Artist in the Rigging: The Early Work of Herman Melville* (1972) and is also coauthor of *Humor of the Great Southwest* (1964).

LARRY J. REYNOLDS is Professor of English at Texas A & M University. Among his works are a critical biography of James Kirke Paulding, an American writer who also served as Van Buren's secretary of the navy, and articles in *American Transcendental Quarterly* and *Melville Society Extracts*.

NEAL L. TOLCHIN is a professor in the English department at Hunter College and has taught American literature at the State University of New York–Stony Brook. He has also written articles on Melville's *Redburn* and the conception of bereavement in literature.

EDWARD J. AHEARN is Francis Wayland Professor and Professor of Comparative Literature and French Studies at Brown University. He is the author of *Rimbaud: Visions and Habitations* (1983) and has written frequently on Flaubert and Mallarmé.

LEO BERSANI is Professor of French at the University of California–Berkeley. Among his writings are *Marcel Proust: The Fictions of Life and of Art* (1965), *A Future for Astyanax: Character and Desire in Literature* (1976), *The Freudian Body: Psychoanalysis and Art* (1986), as well as works on Baudelaire, Mallarmé, and AIDS.

BIBLIOGRAPHY

Adams, Robert Martin. "Masks, Screens, Guises: Melville and Others." In *Nil: Episodes in the Literary Conquest of Void during the Nineteenth Century.* New York: Oxford University Press, 1966, pp. 131–48.

Adams, Michael Vannoy. "Getting a Kick Out of Captain Ahab: The Merman Dream in *Moby-Dick.*" *Dreamworks* 4 (1984–85): 279–87.

Adler, Joyce Sparer. "*Moby-Dick* as Symbolic Poem of War and Peace." In *War in Melville's Imagination.* New York: New York University Press, 1981, pp. 55–78.

Allen, Mary. "The Incredible Whale: Herman Melville." In *Animals in American Literature.* Urbana: University of Illinois Press, 1983, pp. 18–35.

Arvin, Newton. *Herman Melville.* New York: William Sloane Associates, 1950.

Baritz, Loren. "The Demonic: Herman Melville." In *City on a Hill: A History of Ideas and Myths in America.* New York: John Wiley & Sons, 1964, pp. 271–332.

Baurecht, William. "To Reign Is Worth Ambition: The Masculine Mystique in *Moby-Dick.*" *Journal of American Culture* 9 (1986): 53–62.

Bender, Bert. "Meditation and the Life-Waters." In *Sea-Brothers: The Tradition of American Sea Fiction from* Moby-Dick *to the Present.* Philadelphia: University of Pennsylvania Press, 1988, pp. 19–39.

Berthoff, Warner. *The Example of Melville.* Princeton: Princeton University Press, 1962.

Bluestein, Gene. "Ahab's Sin." *Arizona Quarterly* 41 (1985): 101–16.

Boughn, Michael. "Eros and Identity in *Moby-Dick.*" *American Transcendental Quarterly* 1 (1987): 179–96.

Bowen, Merlin. *The Long Encounter: Self and Experience in the Writings of Herman Melville.* Chicago: University of Chicago Press, 1960.

Brodtkorb, Paul, Jr. "Ahab as the Problematic Other." In *Ishmael's White World: A Phenomemological Reading of* Moby Dick. New Haven: Yale University Press, 1965, pp. 62–82.

Cameron, Sharon. *"Moby-Dick; or, The Whale."* In *The Corporeal Self: Allegories of the Body in Melville and Hawthorne.* Baltimore: Johns Hopkins University Press, 1981, pp. 35–58.

Camus, Albert. "American Classics through French Eyes: Melville." In *Transatlantic Mirrors: Essays in Franco-American Literary Relations,* edited by Sidney D. Braun and Seymour Lainoff. Boston: Twayne, 1978, pp. 80–83.

Canaday, Nicholas, Jr. "Ahab and the Authority of God." In *Melville and Authority.* Gainesville: University of Florida Press, 1968, pp. 37–61.

Chai, Leon. "Ishmael and Epistemic Authority." In *Romantic Foundations of the American Renaissance.* Ithaca: Cornell University Press, 1987, pp. 211–23.

Chandrasekharan, K. R. "Melville and the 'Dark Hindoo Half of Nature.'" In *Asian Response to American Literature,* edited by C. D. Narasimharah. Delhi: Vikas Publishers, 1972, pp. 192–98.

Chase, Richard. *Herman Melville: A Critical Study.* New York: Macmillan, 1949.

Clark, Robert. "Herman Melville." In *History and Myth in American Fiction 1823–52.* New York: St. Martin's Press, 1984, pp. 132–51.

Coale, Samuel Chase. "Melville to Mailer: Manichean Manacles." In *In Hawthorne's Shadow: American Romance from Melville to Mailer.* Lexington: University Press of Kentucky, 1985, pp. 22–45.

Coates, Paul. "In the Realm of Transportation: The Masquerade of Herman Melville." In *The Double and the Other: Identity as Ideology in Post-Romantic Fiction.* New York: St. Martin's Press, 1988, pp. 111–16.

Cook, Reginald L. "Big Medicine in *Moby Dick.*" *Accent* 8 (1948): 102–9.

Dryden, Edgar A. *Melville's Thematics of Form: The Great Art of Telling the Truth.* Baltimore: Johns Hopkins University Press, 1968.

Durand, Régis. "'The Captive King': The Absent Father in Melville's Text." In *The Fictional Father: Lacanian Readings of the Text,* edited by Robert Con Davis. Amherst: University of Massachusetts Press, 1981, pp. 48–72.

Edinger, Edward A. *Melville's* Moby-Dick: *A Jungian Commentary.* New York: New Directions, 1978.

Feidelson, Charles, Jr. "Four American Symbolists." In *Symbolism and American Literature.* Chicago: University of Chicago Press, 1953, pp. 6–43.

Fiedler, Leslie. "Achievement and Frustration: The Failure of Sentiment and the Evasion of Love." In *Love and Death in the American Novel.* Rev. ed. New York: Stein and Day, 1966, pp. 337–90.

Finholt, Richard. "Melville's Mad Messiah." In *American Visionary Fiction: Mad Metaphysics and Salvation Psychology.* Port Washington, NY: Kennikat Press, 1978, pp. 61–82.

Finkelstein, Dorothee Metlitsky. *Melville's Orienda.* New Haven: Yale University Press, 1961.

Forrer, Richard. "*Moby-Dick*: The Problem of Theodicy." In *Theodicies in Conflict: A Dilemma in Puritan Ethics and Nineteenth-Century American Literature.* Westport, CT: Greenwood Press, 1986, pp. 194–212.

Franklin, H. Bruce. *The Wake of the Gods: Melville's Mythology.* Stanford: Stanford University Press, 1963.

Gilman, William H. "The Hero and the Heroic in American Literature: An Essay in Definition." In *Patterns of Commitment in American Literature,* edited by Marston LaFrance. Toronto: Carleton University/University of Toronto Press, 1967, pp. 3–17.

Glenn, Barbara. "Melville and the Sublime in *Moby-Dick.*" *American Literature* 47 (1976): 165–81.

Gross, Theodore L. "Herman Melville: The Nature of Authority." In *The Heroic Ideal in American Literature.* New York: Free Press, 1971, pp. 34–50.

Gunn, Giles. "The American Writer and the Formation of an American Mind: Literature, Culture, and Their Relation to Intimate Values." In *The Interpretation of Otherness: Literature, Religion, and the American Imagination.* New York: Oxford University Press, 1979, pp. 159–74.

Haberstroh, Charles J., Jr. "*Redburn, White-Jacket, Moby-Dick:* Full Circle." In *Melville and Male Identity.* Rutherford, NJ: Fairleigh Dickinson University Press, 1980, pp. 73–102.

Halverson, John. "The Shadow of *Moby-Dick.*" *American Quarterly* 15 (1963): 436–46.

Hauck, Richard Boyd. "The Descent to Faith: Herman Melville: Queequeg's Coffin." In *A Cheerful Nihilism: Confidence and "The Absurd" in American Humorous Fiction.* Bloomington: Indiana University Press, 1971, pp. 93–111.

Hayford, Harrison. "'Loomings': Yarns and Figures in the Fabric." In *Artful Thunder: Versions of the Romantic Tradition in American Literature in Honor of Howard P. Vincent,* edited by Robert J. DeMott and Sanford E. Marovitz. Kent, OH: Kent State University Press, 1975, pp. 119–37.

Heimert, Alan. "Empiricism and the American Novel." In *Reality and Idea in the Early American Novel.* The Hague: Mouton, 1971, pp. 33–48.

————. "*Moby-Dick* and American Political Symbolism." *American Quarterly* 15 (1963): 498–534.

Hirsch, David H. "Verbal Reverberations and the Problem of Reality in *Moby Dick*." *Books at Brown* 24 (1971): 45–67.

Horsford, Howard C. "The Design of the Argument in *Moby-Dick*." *Modern Fiction Studies* 8 (1962): 233–51.

Howard, Leon. "Herman Melville: *Moby Dick*." In *The American Novel: From James Fenimore Cooper to William Faulkner,* edited by Wallace Stegner. New York: Basic Books, 1965, pp. 25–34.

Irwin, John T. "Hawthorne & Melville." In *American Hieroglyphics: The Symbol of the Egyptian Hieroglyphics in the American Renaissance.* New Haven: Yale University Press, 1980, pp. 239–349.

Kaul, A. N. "Herman Melville: The New-World Voyageur." In *The American Vision: Actual and Ideal Society in Nineteenth-Century Fiction.* Westport, CT: Greenwood Press, 1963, pp. 214–79.

Knox-Shaw, Peter, "Captain Ahab and the Albatross: *Moby Dick* in a Period Context." In *The Explorer in English Fiction.* New York: St. Martin's Press, 1986, pp. 91–112.

Lebowitz, Alan. *Progress into Silence: A Study of Melville's Heroes.* Bloomington: Indiana University Press, 1970.

Levene, Robert S. "Follow Your Leader: Captains and Mutineers in Herman Melville's *Benito Cereno*." In *Conspiracy and Romance: Studies in Brockden Brown, Cooper, Hawthorne, and Melville.* New York: Cambridge University Press, 1989, pp. 165–230.

Lewicki, Zbigniew. "*Moby Dick*: Apocalypse as Regeneration." In *The Bang and the Whimper: Apocalypse and Entropy in American Literature.* Westport, CT: Greenwood Press, 1984, pp. 21–32.

Leyda, Jay. *The Melville Log: A Documentary Life of Herman Melville 1819–1891.* New York: Harcourt, Brace, 1951.

Lord, George deForest. "The Ivory *Pequod* and the Epic of Illusion." In *Trials of the Self: Heroic Ordeals in the Epic Tradition.* Hamden, CT: Archon Books, 1983, pp. 157–91.

MacLean, Robert M. "Locked Out: *Moby-Dick* and the Flotsam of Narrative Continuity." In *Narcissus and the Voyeur: Three Books and Two Films.* The Hague: Mouton, 1979, pp. 93–137.

McWilliams, John P., Jr. "Mirror Men." In *Hawthorne, Melville, and the American Character: A Looking-Glass Business.* New York: Cambridge University Press, 1984, pp. 155–74.

Marovitz, Sanford E. "Old Man Ahab." In *Artful Thunder: Versions of the Romantic Tradition in American Literature in Honor of Howard P. Vincent,* edited by Robert J. DeMott and Sanford E. Marovitz. Kent, OH: Kent State University Press, 1975, pp. 139–61.

Martin, Robert K. *Hero, Captain, Stranger: Male Friendship, Social Critique, and Literary Form in the Sea Novels of Herman Melville.* Chapel Hill: University of North Carolina Press, 1986.

Marx, Leo. "Melville's Parable of the Walls." In *The Pilot and the Passenger: Essays on Literature, Technology, and Culture in the United States.* New York: Oxford University Press, 1988, pp.

————. "Two Kingdoms of Force." In *The Machine in the Garden: Technology and the Pastoral Ideal in America.* New York: Oxford University Press, 1964, pp. 227–353.

Messinger, Christian K. "Organized Sport and Its Reporters: Transformation of Sport in

Industrial America." In *Sport and the Spirit of Play in American Fiction: Hawthorne to Faulkner.* New York: Columbia University Press, 1981, pp. 83–92.

Miller, James E., Jr. "Hawthorne and Melville: The Unpardonable Sin." In *Quests Surd and ABsurd: Essays in American Literature.* Chicago: University of Chicago Press, 1967, pp. 209–38.

Morse, David. "Herman Melville: 'Scaffoldings Scaling Heaven.'" In *American Romanticism: From Melville to James.* Volume 2. Totowa, NJ: Barnes & Noble, 1987, pp. 11–79.

Murray, Henry A. "In Nomine Diaboli." *New England Quarterly* 25 (1951): 435–52.

Mushabac, Jane. "Whales and Confidence." In *Melville's Humor: A Critical Study.* Hamden, CT: Archon Books, 1981, pp. 79–147.

Noble, David W. "Cooper, Hawthorne, Melville." In *The Eternal Adam and Its New World Garden: The Central Myth in the American Novel since 1830.* New York: George Braziller, 1968, pp. 34–47.

Oglesby, Carl. "Melville, or Water Consciousness & Its Madness: Fragment from a Work-in-Progress." *TriQuarterly* 23/24 (1972): 123–41.

Parker, Hershel, and Harrison Hayford, ed. *Moby-Dick as Doubloon: Essays and Extracts 1851–1970.* New York: Norton, 1970.

Patterson, Mark R. "Melville: Authority of Confidence." In *Authority, Autonomy, and Representation in American Literature 1776–1865.* Princeton: Princeton University Press, 1988, pp. 189–239.

———. "Democratic Leadership and Narrative Authority in *Moby-Dick.*" *Studies in the Novel* 16 (1984): 288–303.

Pavese, Cesare. "Preface to *Moby-Dick.*" In *American Literature: Essays and Opinions.* Translated by Edwin Fussell. Berkeley: University of California Press, 1970, pp. 69–74.

Peach, Linden. "Man-out-of-Clothes: Melville's Debt to Carlyle." In *British Influence on the Birth of American Literature.* New York: St. Martin's Press, 1982, pp. 138–61.

Pease, Donald E. "*Moby Dick* and the Cold War." In *The American Renaissance Reconsidered,* edited by Walter Benn and Donald E. Pease. Baltimore: Johns Hopkins University Press, 1985, pp. 113–31.

Percival, M. O. *A Reading of* Moby-Dick. Chicago: University of Chicago Press, 1950.

Pommer, Henry. *Milton and Melville.* Pittsburgh: University of Pittsburgh Press, 1950.

Pryse, Marjorie. "*Moby-Dick:* Social Physics and Metaphysics." In *The Mark and the Knowledge: Social Stigma in Classic American Fiction.* Columbus: Ohio State University Press/ Miami University, 1979, pp. 49–91.

Robinson, Douglas. "Call Me Jonah." In *American Apocalypses: The Image of the End of the World in American Literature.* Baltimore: Johns Hopkins University Press, 1985, pp. 125–62.

Rose, E. J. "Melville, Emerson, and the Sphinx." *New England Quarterly* 36 (1963): 249–84.

Rosenbery, Edward. H. *Melville.* London: Routledge & Kegan Paul, 1979.

Roth, Marty. "Melville and Madness." *Arizona Quarterly* 41 (1985): 119–30.

Rowe, Joyce A. "Conclusion: *Moby-Dick* and Our Problem with History." In *Equivocal Endings in Classic American Novels.* Cambridge: Cambridge University Press, 1988, pp. 127–37.

Sarbu, Aladar. "Melville, Our Contemporary." *Acta Litteraria* 27 (1985): 295–306.

Sedgwick, William Ellery. *Herman Melville: The Tragedy of Mind.* Cambridge, MA: Harvard University Press, 1945.

Seelye, John D. "The Golden Navel: The Cabalism of Ahab's Doubloon." *Nineteenth-Century Fiction* 14 (1960): 350–55.

Sewall, Richard B. "*Moby-Dick*." In *The Vision of Tragedy*. New Haven: Yale University Press, 1959, pp. 92–105.

Shulman, Robert. "The Serious Functions of Melville's Phallic Jokes." *American Literature* 33 (1961): 179–94.

Simpson, David. "Herman Melville: Chasing the Whale." In *Fetishism and Imagination: Dickens, Melville, Conrad.* Baltimore: Johns Hopkins University Press, 1980, pp. 70–90.

Slochower, Harry. "*Moby-Dick;* The Myth of Democratic Expectancy." *American Quarterly* 2 (1950): 259–69.

Spanos, William V. "The 'Nameless Horror': The Errant Art of Herman Melville and Charles Hewitt." *boundary 2* 9, No. 1 (Fall 1980): 127–39.

Stern, Milton R. *The Fine Hammered Steel of Herman Melville.* Urbana: University of Illinois Press, 1968.

———. "Melville's Tragic Imagination: The Hero without a Home." In *Patterns of Commitment in American Literature,* edited by Marston LaFrance. Toronto: Carleton University/University of Toronto Press, 1967, pp. 39–52.

Vincent, Howard P. *The Trying-Out of* Moby-Dick. Boston: Houghton Mifflin, 1949.

Watts, Emily Stipes. "The Yankee Peddlar and the Con Man." In *The Businessman in American Literature.* Athens: University of Georgia Press, 1982, pp. 34–44.

Wright, Nathalia. *Melville's Use of the Bible.* Durham, NC: Duke University Press, 1949.

Yeager, Freda E. "The Dark Ishmael and the First Weaver in *Moby-Dick.*" *Arizona Quarterly* 41 (1985): 152–68.

Zuckert, Catherine H. "Melville's Meditations: *Moby Dick.*" In *Natural Right and the American Imagination.* Savage, MD: Rowman & Littlefield, 1990, pp. 101–12.

ACKNOWLEDGMENTS

"Moby-Dick" by Lewis Mumford from *Herman Melville* by Lewis Mumford, © 1929 by Harcourt, Brace & Co., Inc. Reprinted by permission of Harcourt Brace Jovanovich.

"The Craft of Herman Melville" by R. P. Blackmur from *The Lion and the Honeycomb: Essays in Solicitude and Critique* by R. P. Blackmur, © 1938, 1955 by Richard P. Blackmur. Reprinted by permission of Harcourt Brace Jovanovich.

"Ahab" by W. H. Auden from *The Enchafèd Flood; or, The Romantic Iconography of the Sea* by W. H. Auden, © 1950 by the Rector and Visitors of the University of Virginia. Reprinted by permission of The University Press of Virginia.

"Wicked Book" by Lawrance Thompson from *Melville's Quarrel with God* by Lawrance Thompson, © 1952 by Princeton University Press, renewed 1980 by Princeton University Press. Reprinted by permission.

"Melville" by Marius Bewley from *The Eccentric Design: Form in the Classic American Novel* by Marius Bewley, © 1953, 1959 by Marius Bewley. Reprinted by permission of Columbia University Press.

"Ishmael and Ahab" by Alfred Kazin from *Atlantic Monthly* 198, No. 5 (November 1956), © 1956 by The Atlantic Monthly Company. Reprinted by permission.

"In the Scene of Being" by Denis Donoghue from *Hudson Review* 14, no. 2 (Summer 1961), © 1961 by The Hudson Review, Inc. Reprinted by permission.

"Moby Dick" by A. R. Humphreys from *Melville* by A. R. Humphreys, © 1962 by A. R. Humphreys. Reprinted by permission of Mrs. A. R. Humphreys.

"Melville and the Tragedy of Nihilism" by Joyce Carol Oates from *The Edge of Impossibility: Tragic Forms in Literature* by Joyce Carol Oates, © 1972 by Joyce Carol Oates. Reprinted by permission.

"The Romantic Hero and That Fatal Selfhood" by Raney Stanford from *Centennial Review* 12, No.4 (Fall 1968), © 1968 by The Centennial Review. Reprinted by permission.

"In the Splendid Labyrinth: *Moby-Dick"* by Martin Leonard Pops from *The Melville Archetype* by Martin Leonard Pops, © 1970 by Martin Leonard Pops. Reprinted by permission of the author.

"Moby-Dick and *Pierre:* The Struggle for Possession" by Ann Douglas from *The Feminization of American Culture* by Ann Douglas, © 1977 by Ann Douglas. Reprinted by permission of Alfred A. Knopf Inc.

"A Jonah's Warning to America in *Moby-Dick"* by Carolyn L. Karcher from *Shadow over the Promised Land: Slavery, Race, and Violence and Melville's America* by Carolyn L. Karcher, © 1980 by Louisiana State University Press. Reprinted by permission.

"Herman Melville" by David Simpson from *Fetishism and Imagination: Dickens, Melville, Conrad* by David Simpson, © 1982 by David Simpson. Reprinted by permission of Johns Hopkins University Press.

" 'More Demon Than Man': Melville's Ahab as Gothic Villain" by Tony Magistrale from *Extrapolation* 27, No. 3 (Fall 1986), © 1986 by The Kent State University Press. Reprinted by permission.

"*Moby-Dick:* The Great American Love Story" by Joseph Allen Boone from *Tradition Counter Tradition: Love and the Form of Fiction* by Joseph Allen Boone, © 1987 by The University Press of Chicago. Reprinted by permission of The University of Chicago Press.

"Melville's Whited Sepulchres" by David S. Reynolds from *Beneath the American Renaissance: The Subversive Imagination in the Age of Emerson and Melville* by David S. Reynolds, © 1988 by David S. Reynolds. Reprinted by permission of Alfred A. Knopf Inc.

"Blaming the Victim" by Wai-Chee Dimock from *Empire for Liberty: Melville and the Poets of Individualism* by Wai-Chee Dimock, © 1989 by Princeton University Press. Reprinted by permission.

"*Moby-Dick:* An Utter Wreck" by Bruce L. Grenberg from *Some Other World to Find: Quest and Negation in the Works of Herman Melville* by Bruce L. Grenberg, © 1989 by the Board of Trustees of the University of Illinois. Reprinted by permission of the University of Illinois Press and the author.

"Ahab and the Carpenter" by Pamela Schirmeister from *The Consolations of Space: The Place of Romance in Hawthorne, Melville, and James* by Pamela Schirmeister, © 1990 by the Board of Trustees of the Leland Stanford Junior University. Reprinted by permission of Stanford University Press.

"The Fate of the Ungodly God-like Man" by F. O. Matthiessen from *American Renaissance: Art and Expression in the Age of Emerson and Whitman* by F. O. Matthiessen, © 1941 by Oxford University Press, Inc. Reprinted by permission.

"Captain Ahab: Modern Promethean" (originally titled "Nietzsche's Zarathustra and Melville's Captain Ahab") by Maurice Friedman from *Problematic Rebel: An Image of Modern Man* by Maurice Friedman, © 1963 by Maurice Friedman. Reprinted by permission.

"Ahab's Entropism and Ishmael's Cyclicism" (originally titled "Green Skulls: Ahab's Entropism and Ishmael's Cyclicism") by Robert Zoellner from *The Salt-Sea Mastodon: A Reading of* Moby-Dick by Robert Zoellner, © 1973 by The Regents of the University of California. Reprinted by permission of The University of California Press.

"*Moby-Dick* and the American 1848" by Michael Paul Rogin from *Subversive Genealogy: The Politics and Art of Herman Melville* by Michael Paul Rogin, © 1979, 1980, 1983 by Michael Paul Rogin. Reprinted by permission of Alfred A. Knopf Inc.

"Reading Ahab" by Bainard Cowan from *Exiled Waters:* Moby-Dick *and the Crisis of Allegory* by Bainard Cowan, © 1982 by Louisiana State University Press. Reprinted by permission.

"Ahab's Heresy" by William B. Dillingham from *Melville's Later Novels* by William B. Dillingham, © 1986 by the University of Georgia Press. Reprinted by permission.

"Moby-Dick, Napoleon, and the Workers of the World" by Larry J. Reynolds from *European Revolutions and the American Literary Renaissance* by Larry J. Reynolds, © 1988 by Yale University. Reprinted by permission of Yale University Press.

"A Thing Writ in Water: Allan Melvill's Epitaph" by Neal L. Tolchin from *Mourning, Gender, and Creativity in the Art of Herman Melville* by Neal L. Tolchin, © 1988 by Yale University. Reprinted by permission of Yale University Press.

"A Mutual, Joint-Stock World" by Edward J. Ahearn from *Marx and Modern Fiction* by Edward J. Ahearn, © 1989 by Yale University. Reprinted by permission of Yale University Press.

"Incomparable America" by Leo Bersani from *The Culture of Redemption* by Leo Bersani, © 1990 by the President and Fellows of Harvard College. Reprinted by permission of Harvard University Press.

INDEX